Women's
Re-Visions
of
Shakespeare

❦

Women's Re-Visions of Shakespeare

*On the Responses of Dickinson, Woolf, Rich,
H.D., George Eliot, and Others*

Edited by

MARIANNE NOVY

UNIVERSITY OF ILLINOIS PRESS
Urbana and Chicago

Library of Congress Cataloging-in-Publication Data

Women's re-visions of Shakespeare / edited by Marianne Novy.
    p. cm.
Early versions of some of these essays were presented at a Modern
Language Association Convention Special Session in 1983; others were
prepared for a Special Session in 1987, or for the seminar on Women's
Responses to Shakespeare at the Shakespeare Association of America
Annual Meeting in 1988.
    ISBN 0-252-01698-X (cloth : alk. paper). —ISBN 0-252-06114-4
(paper : alk. paper)
    1. Shakespeare, William, 1564–1616—Characters—Women.
2. Shakespeare, William, 1564–1616—Criticism and interpretation.
3. Women in literature.   4. Sex role in literature.   5. Feminist
literary criticism.   6. Women—Books and reading.   I. Novy,
Marianne, 1945–   .
PR2991.W65   1990   *AAX3825*
822.3'3—dc20   89– 39088
                                                         CIP

For our mothers, our daughters,
and all women readers

Contents

Acknowledgments   ix

MARIANNE NOVY
Women's Re-Visions of Shakespeare 1664–1988   1

SUSAN J. WOLFSON
Explaining to Her Sisters: Mary Lamb's *Tales from Shakespear*   16

CHRISTY DESMET
"Intercepting the Dew-Drop": Female Readers and
Readings in Anna Jameson's Shakespearean Criticism   41

MARY LOEFFELHOLZ
Miranda in the New World: *The Tempest* and
Charlotte Barnes's *The Forest Princess*   58

MARGARET J. ARNOLD
Coriolanus Transformed: Charlotte Brontë's
Use of Shakespeare in *Shirley*   76

MARIANNE NOVY
Daniel Deronda and George Eliot's Female
Re-Vision of Shakespeare   89

PAULA BENNETT
"The Orient is in the West": Emily Dickinson's
Reading of *Antony and Cleopatra*   108

CHRISTINE FROULA
Virginia Woolf as Shakespeare's Sister: Chapters in a
Woman Writer's Autobiography   123

SUSAN STANFORD FRIEDMAN
Remembering Shakespeare Differently: H. D.'s *By Avon River*   143

GAYLE GREENE
Margaret Laurence's *Diviners* and Shakespeare's
Tempest: The Uses of the Past   165

PETER ERICKSON
Adrienne Rich's Re-Vision of Shakespeare   183

JOAN HUTTON LANDIS
"Another Penelope": Margaret Hutton
Reading William Shakespeare   196

NATALIE B. STRONG AND CAROLYN R. SWIFT
Toward a Feminist Renaissance: Woman-Centering
Shakespeare's Tragedies   212

MADELON SPRENGNETHER
Reading as Lady Macbeth   227

CAROL THOMAS NEELY
Epilogue: Remembering Shakespeare, Revising Ourselves   242

Notes on Contributors   253

Index   255

Acknowledgments

Early versions of several of these essays were presented at a Modern Language Association Convention Special Session in 1983; most of the others were prepared for another Special Session in 1987 or for the seminar on Women's Responses to Shakespeare at the Shakespeare Association of America Annual Meeting of 1988. Members of the seminar all commented helpfully on one another's essays and on the general topic. Although their papers for these events could not be included here, Shirley Nelson Garner, Judith Lee, Naomi Miller, Constance Relihan, and William J. Sullivan, other participants, contributed importantly to our collective project by their writing and discussion, as did Alice Fox, whose terminal illness prevented her from expanding her paper for publication. In the transition from conference to book, I frequently called on Carol Neely's judgment, and she responded with characteristic painstaking attention. I would also like to thank Mary Loeffelholz and Peter Erickson for suggestions at this stage, and Judith Kegan Gardiner for her reading of the entire manuscript. Other help came from graduate assistants Monette Tiernan, Therese Walsh, and Matthew Coyne, and from Elizabeth Ermarth, Marcia Landy, Edwin Marrs, Jo O'Brien Schaefer, and Richard Tobias. Dennis Kennedy gave suggestions I hope to take in this anthology's companion volume.

My own early thought about the project was helped by the American Association of University Women Educational Foundation, with the fellowship awarded me for 1985–86. Thanks are due to the editors of *Sagetrieb* and *Studies in English Literature* for permission to reprint shortened versions of essays that first appeared in their journals.

More personally, I would like to record my gratitude for many years of encouragement by my mother, Dorothy Kern, who lived to hear of much of the progress of this book, though not its completion. My husband, David Carrier, has continually supplied me with books by women writers, and has helped in many other ways. My daughter, Elizabeth, has maturely used papers not from this manuscript to make airplanes and drawings.

Women's
Re-Visions
of
Shakespeare

MARIANNE NOVY

Introduction: Women's Re-Visions of Shakespeare 1664–1988

"I charge you, O women, for the love you bear to men, to like as much
of this play as please you."

Rosalind, *As You Like It*

"Re-vision—the act of looking back, of seeing with fresh eyes, of entering an old text from a new critical direction."

Adrienne Rich, "When We Dead
Awaken: Writing as Re-Vision"

This anthology brings two usually discrete concerns—feminist criticism of Shakespeare and feminist criticism of women readers and writers—together for a conversation. The essays assembled recover a long
tradition of female readings of Shakespeare and show inflections of gender in the history of Shakespeare's reception; their analyses also provide
new directions for feminist theories of literary history and reader response. Contemporary critics argue whether Shakespeare's plays subordinate or empower women;[1] these essays show a history in which many
women have used Shakespeare to empower themselves.

For centuries women have been reading Shakespeare with a point of
view related to their social position as women and thereby offering a critical direction new in their own time and culture. In letters, prefaces, and
essays, poems, novels, and plays from the seventeenth century on and in
journals, classrooms, and discussion groups, women have contributed to
constructing a cultural image of Shakespeare they could find congenial,
and have re-constructed previous images by analyzing and rewriting the
gender relations in his plays.

Like many aspects of women's history, women's record of creating
and transforming readings of Shakespeare has been neglected. Brian Vickers's six-volume anthology, *Shakespeare: The Critical Heritage, 1623–1801*,
includes only six entries by women. G. B. Evans's anthology, *Shakespeare:
Aspects of Influence*, refers to no woman writer. Ruby Cohn's *Modern
Shakespeare Offshoots* discusses two works by women and eighty-three by

men.[2] On the other hand, the works discussed in the current anthology would not be well served by the category of "influence studies" or "offshoots." The essays show that these are not readings passively receiving Shakespeare or writings dutifully imitating him but enterprises of both creativity and criticism. Furthermore they show that women's responses to Shakespeare often challenge the most influential feminist analyses of how women respond to a male author.

In *The Madwoman in the Attic,* Sandra Gilbert and Susan Gubar declare that the woman writer finds that male authors' images of women, "by reducing her to extreme stereotypes (angel, monster), drastically conflict with her own sense of her self—that is, of her subjectivity, her autonomy, her creativity."[3] Without evidence, they assume that women writers have been most affected by Shakespeare's characterizations of Goneril, Regan, and Lady Macbeth—negative images of women's self-assertion— and model responses to Shakespeare to parallel their documented history of women's anxious or enraged responses to Milton.

Contrary to such generalizations, however, these essays show a long historical record of women's identifications with a range of Shakespearean characters and, more surprisingly, with Shakespeare himself. Explicit feminist protest against Shakespeare emerged fairly recently out of a tradition that more often appropriated Shakespeare for women. Earlier rewritings of his plots made woman-centered points subtly while some contemporary rewritings make them more boldly.

Let me put these essays in the context of the responses of other women, from the seventeenth century on, discussing first women's visions of Shakespeare himself and then their visions and re-visions of his female characters. Why have so many women written about Shakespeare? An older criticism would say that this proves Shakespeare's universality. Here, however, I historicize, by showing affinities between different centuries' cultural constructions of Shakespeare and cultural constructions of women. Three images of Shakespeare have particular resonance for women's history: the outsider, the artist of wide-ranging identification, and the actor.

In the seventeenth and much of the eighteenth century, before Shakespeare was enshrined in the literary canon, he had a cultural image as an outsider to many established institutions. He lacked university education; he wrote in the popular form of the drama, rather than the most prestigious form of the epic; and he broke many of the rules of dramatic construction favored by literary critics.[4] If he wrote well—a debatable question—it was because of gifts of Nature, not of Art. There are good historical reasons why women writers, and even women readers, might feel analogously outside literary institutions and might take this Shake-speare as a model who showed that they could succeed anyway.

In her preface to *The Dutch Lover* (1673), Aphra Behn used Shakespeare's supposed lack of learning to her own advantage: "Plays have no great room for that which is men's great advantage over women, that is Learning; We all well know that the immortal Shakespeare's Plays (who was not guilty of much more of this than often falls to women's share) have better pleas'd the world than Johnson's works."[5] Other early women writers, if less explicit about linking Shakespeare's achievements to their own, showed a similar interest in the image of the nonacademic Shakespeare. Margaret Cavendish, in "A General Prologue to all my Playes" (1662), wrote:

> Although less learning, yet full well he writ;
> For all his Playes were writ by Natures light
> Which gives his Readers, and Spectators Sight.[6]

A few lines later, she would present her own plays as "the buildings of my natural wit." In the next century (1769) the critic Elizabeth Montagu, also an outsider to educational institutions, defended Shakespeare—and by implication her own writing on him—against the neo-Aristotelians of her day: "these connoisseurs, whose acquaintance with the characters of men is formed in the library, not in the street, the camp, or village."[7]

Cavendish, Behn, and Montagu, like many women who wrote in the seventeenth and eighteenth centuries, had a sense of themselves as outsid-ers which, their biographies show, was justified.[8] In their time, the image of Shakespeare as an outsider was prevalent enough to make this glover's son, this rule-breaking child of nature, an indication that they too could achieve by following their own perceptions.

Debate about Shakespeare's deviations from the learned practice of art was in part a function of the movement from neoclassicism to roman-ticism; criticism valued academic rules less in the nineteenth century, and the outsider was a more common image of the writer, whether male or fe-male. In this volume Paula Bennett argues that Emily Dickinson linked herself and Shakespeare as outsiders, not because of rule-breaking or lack of education but because of their poetic imagination.

In the twentieth century, women's greater feminist self-consciousness about exclusion from culture could lead to an interest, in such writers as Virginia Woolf and H.D., in Shakespeare's role in showing cultural boundaries as permeable, permitting an outsider to be an insider at the same time. Sylvia Townsend Warner's use of Shakespeare for this purpose is explicit: "Women, entering literature, entered it on the same footing as

William Shakespeare."[9] As Montagu had argued that Shakespeare's characters came not from the library but from "the street, the camp, the village," Townsend Warner declared that lack of academic training gave him a "kind of workaday democracy, an ease and appreciativeness in low company," and unlike Montagu she explicitly claimed this as an advantage for women writers as well.[10]

Both Montagu and Townsend Warner explicitly link the image of Shakespeare the outsider with another image also important to women writers—Shakespeare the artist of wide-ranging characterization. Women were pioneers in writing about character in Shakespeare and developing the image of his protean flexibility of identity long before interest in his characterization ruled criticism. In 1664 Margaret Cavendish was the first to write at length about his skill in characterization: "So well he hath Express'd in his Playes all Sorts of Persons, as one would think he had been Transformed into every one of those Persons he hath Described," she began, and enumerated many examples."[11]

About one hundred years later (1760) Montagu praised Shakespeare's characterization with a similar image of metamorphosis: "he alone, like the dervise in the Arabian tales, can throw his soul into the body of another man, feel all his sentiments, perform his functions, and fill his place."[12] The new eighteenth-century emphasis on sympathy in esthetics and ethics promoted further development and influence for Montagu's pioneering views.[13] Her *Essay on the writings and Genius of Shakespeare* (1769) was reprinted half a dozen times by the turn of the century and helped to construct soon-widely-accepted emphases on his exceptional capacity for identification and ability to create sympathy for his characters.[14]

The romantic view of Shakespeare which dominated in the nineteenth century developed, at least in part, out of Montagu's. Using an image of self-transformation much like hers and Cavendish's, Coleridge wrote that Shakespeare "passes into all the forms of human character and passion, the one Proteus of the fire and the flood."[15] Hazlitt agreed, and his language closely connected Shakespeare with the nineteenth-century female ideal: "His talent consisted in sympathy with human nature, in all its shapes, degrees, depressions, and elevations. . . . He was the least of an egoist that it was possible to be."[16] For a nineteenth-century woman writer, as I argue in my essay on George Eliot, Shakespeare proved that writing need not be selfish and self-abnegation need not preclude achievement. Charlotte Brontë similarly links Shakespeare's characterization to ethics in *Shirley;* as Margaret Arnold discusses, Caroline uses a reading of *Coriolanus* to teach Robert sympathy and temporarily moves him from "the narrow line of private prejudices" to "the large picture of human nature."[17]

A transmuted version of this sympathetic Shakespeare is crucial to both H.D. and Virginia Woolf, as we see in this volume's essays by Susan Stanford Friedman and Christine Froula; Sharon O'Brien has made a similar argument about his role for Willa Cather.[18] As Hazlitt and Coleridge had contrasted Shakespeare and Milton, these writers often oppose Shakespeare's sensibility to that of other writers seen as more egoistic or more masculine. For Cather, the contrast was with Kipling. For H.D., it was with Marlowe and Raleigh. Woolf repeats the contrast with Milton, writing that *Paradise Lost* contains "nothing like Lady Macbeth's terror or Hamlet's cry, no pity or sympathy or intuition."[19] Shakespeare is her prime example of the great artist's androgynous mind, contrasting with the excessive masculinity of Kipling, Milton, Jonson, and Wordsworth.[20] Woolf, H.D., and Cather, like Brontë and Eliot, all associate Shakespeare, explicitly or implicitly, with qualities that they see as feminine. In spite of the feminist critique of androgyny as a model for female development, perhaps it is a useful term for this aspect of Shakespeare's image—its inclusion of qualities contrasted with a cultural construction of masculinity.[21]

In *The Madwoman in the Attic,* Gilbert and Gubar give much evidence that Western culture has often seen literary authority as masculine. Nevertheless, this collection shows that one survival strategy for many women writers may have been to construct an image of one male author whose metaphorical gender, at least, was somehow not only masculine.[22] This version of Shakespeare could be a model with whom they could feel some affinity—one great counter-example to the image of the writer as stereotypically male. They did not need to define their creativity exclusively as rebellion, in the agonistic model of literary influence Gilbert and Gubar borrow from Harold Bloom; in relation to Shakespeare, they could also see creativity as appropriation.[23]

Perhaps this image of creativity might be particularly congenial because of the flexibility of ego boundaries and ease of identification with others shared by many women in our culture. These traits, attributed by the psychologist Nancy Chodorow to the gendering of child-rearing patterns, provide a reason why women might find it appealing to develop their creativity in part by identification with another writer, and might be especially likely to construct their image of the ideal writer as one who also has flexible ego boundaries and ease of identification.[24]

A closely related reason why women might identify with Shakespeare is the biographical base of Shakespeare's metamorphic power—his career as an actor, unparalleled among the more stereotypically masculine writers with whom he might be contrasted.[25] The descriptions of his power of self-transformation quoted from Cavendish and later critics echo language used from the seventeenth through the nineteenth century to describe successful actors.[26] Elizabeth Montagu makes this link explicit: "he makes his person say what one would imagine could not occur to any one who was not in their very circumstances. I imagine that being an actor might a little assist him in this respect; the writer puts down what he imagines, the actor what he feels, the characters and the situations are in some degree realised in the acting." Montagu makes this observation in a private letter;[27] I have found few other comments on Shakespeare as an actor until very recent criticism. Further research may uncover more, but perhaps the social suspicion of the actor, and the related nineteenth-century tendency to read the plays as poetry or novels, meant that this image was too dangerous for most women writers to use, if they were taking Shakespeare as a model.

Many different contexts link actors and women. Twentieth-century psychologists' language about actors is rather close to Chodorow's language about women.[28] In Shakespeare's own time, actors and women both were frequently accused of being deceitful and changeable.[29] If women were outsiders by sex, actors were outsiders by profession: in addition to the other reasons mentioned earlier, Shakespeare was an outsider because he was an actor. One of the first extant references to him associates actors, women, trespassing, and deceit: Robert Greene called him "an upstart Crow, beautified with our feathers" (probably the words of other playwrights who were not actors) and attributed to him a *"Tygers hart wrapt in a Players hyde,"* a parody of Shakespeare's own line "tiger's heart wrapt in a woman's hide" (*3HVI* 1.4.137).[30] Many of his own characters and plots associate women and acting.[31]

Is one of the reasons some women have identified with Shakespeare the (hypothetical) fact that Shakespeare himself identified with women, partly because of the similar cultural prejudices against both? Possibly the identification was promoted by the Elizabethan employment of boy actors in women's parts, which could suggest that the two sexes were not altogether dichotomous.[32] Whatever the cultural and personal causes, many women readers and writers have found or constructed something unusually convincing in most of his female characters. To their visions and revisions of these characters I will now turn.

The record of discussions of these characters points up changing historical constructions of women. Margaret Cavendish's praise of the variety of persons into which Shakespeare seemed able to transform himself includes, along with many male examples, this comment: "one would think that he had been Metamorphosed from a Man to a Woman, for who could Describe *Cleopatra* Better than he hath done, and many other Females of his own Creating, as *Nan Page*, Mrs. *Page*, Mrs. *Ford*, the Doctors Maid, *Bettrice*, Mrs. *Quickly*, *Doll Tearsheet*, and others, too many to Relate."[33] Idiosyncratic though she was, Cavendish shows the influence of Restoration culture in her delight in female characters who are active, witty, and in several cases sexually free.

A century later, the qualities Elizabeth Montagu was interested in pointing out in female characters were maternal love in *King John*'s Constance and sentiment in Lady Macbeth.[34] In 1775, when Elizabeth Griffith claims "Shakespeare could not only assume all characters, but even their sexes too," she is discussing Imogen's outraged defense of her faithfulness to her husband.[35]

Griffith shows the marks not only of the sentimentalism but also of the protofeminism of her period. Her *Morality of Shakespeare's Drama Illustrated*, published, from the start, under her own name and therefore identified as a woman's work, provides the first example of explicit concern with Shakespeare's image of power relations in marriage. Discussing *The Taming of the Shrew*, she thinks that in Kate's last speech "the doctrine of *passive obedience and non-resistance* in the state of marriage" is "carried, perhaps, rather a little too far" but then, like some recent feminists, wonders about Kate's sincerity as she compares her to "too prompt reformees, who are apt to run into the very contrary extreme, at once; betraying more of the *time server,* than the *convert.*" Griffith may also begin the feminist tradition of analyzing the misogyny of a previous critic, when she remarks that Warburton's comments on women's love of clothes, in his discussion of the same play, are "being severe on our sex at a very cheap rate, indeed, foibles, passions and inconsiderable attachments are equally common to all mankind, without distinction of gender."[36]

In the nineteenth century, male and female critics diverge markedly in the way they read Shakespeare's female characters.[37] Male critics such as Coleridge and Hazlitt group them all together, emphasize their attachment to others and to social continuity, credit them with emotion rather than thought, and minimize the importance of their words (Hazlitt even complains that "we cannot tell whether they were black, brown, or fair").[38] By contrast, women such as Mary Lamb, Anna Jameson, and Mary Cowden Clarke emphasize the diversity and, often, the strength of the female characters. Mary Lamb, as Susan Wolfson shows, portrays Helena of *All's Well* as an example of how a woman could succeed through witty resourcefulness. Anna Jameson, as Christy Desmet discusses, sees complexity in Isabella, Constance, and Lady Macbeth through her identification with them. Nina Auerbach has shown how, by writing character studies and inventing biographies, Jameson and Cowden Clarke and the actress Ellen Terry liberate Shakespeare's women from the confines of their plots.[39]

In the early twentieth century, a time of self-conscious belief in new possibilities for women, several women writers begin to see limitations in Shakespeare's characters. For example, Dorothy Richardson's Miriam thinks, "there was no reality in any of Shakespeare's women. They please men because they show women as men see them."[40] While acknowledging the presence of more articulate female characters, H.D.'s *By Avon River* includes a number of poems in the persona of Claribel, Alonso's recently married daughter, mentioned but never seen in *The Tempest* and thus a figure for female invisibility and silence. Virginia Woolf describes how little of women's reality she found in Lady Macbeth, Cordelia, and Ophelia,[41] and criticizes Shakespeare's lack of portrayal of female friendship and, indeed, of women in other roles than their relation to men; however, when arguing that women have had a more important place in literature than in history, she begins with Cleopatra, Lady Macbeth, and Rosalind.[42]

Even later, women writers could still give his female characters unambivalent praise; in 1958, Sylvia Townsend Warner could write that "Lady Macbeth, and Beatrice, and Helena in *All's Well* could almost be taken for women writers' heroines, they are so free and uninhibited, and ready to jump over stiles and appear in the drawing-room with muddy stockings, like Lizzie Bennet."[43] However, in Adrienne Rich's recent criticism, as Peter Erickson shows, the emphasis changes. While Rich's earlier poetry shows an identification with Cordelia, for her, Shakespeare's female characters are now dangerous models. Pointing out their limits, even at their most assertive, emphasizes the scope of the social transformation she seeks. Her view parallels the new perception of many post-1970 feminist Shakespeare critics that Shakespeare's women ultimately remain in patriarchal structures.[44]

Nevertheless, as we see in the essays about Joan Hutton Landis's conversations with Margaret Hutton, her mother, and about Natalie Strong's journal for Carolyn Swift's class, many women readers continue to identify with Shakespeare's female characters, whether to celebrate their achievements or to protest their plots. Like the other essays in this anthology, these suggest a need for alternatives to the most influential recent analyses of women's experiences in reading male authors. Patrocinio Schweikart, for example, makes a sharp dichotomy between feminist readings of male texts and feminist readings of female texts. When she imagines a positive feminist interpretation for a male text, it involves reversing the gender of the main characters; she neglects the possibility that a feminist might find a male-authored female character as worthy of identification.[45] As this volume documents, however, and as Carol Thomas Neely's epilogue emphasizes, many women have used identification with Shakespeare's female characters for feminist purposes. Furthermore, Madelon Sprengnether's essay especially provides a much more

complex analysis of women's identification with male characters than Judith Fetterley's attack on "immasculation"—her term for a process by
which women, reading a male author, are taught to identify with a male
point of view and a male system of values.[46] When Sprengnether identifies with a tragic hero, it is because of his vulnerability (just as when Emily
Dickinson identifies with Antony, Paula Bennett shows, it is because of
his visionary love). Contrary to Fetterley's claim, identifying with male
characters need not involve women readers, Sprengnether shows, in ste-
reotypical masculine values. Yet she explores other ways in which tragic
men's attitudes toward women are problematic for a female audience and
probes the implications and dynamics of her consciously resistant identification with Lady Macbeth. Women's responses to Shakespeare show that
our feminist theories of reading need much more development.

As I have suggested, these responses also show the need for more alternatives in our feminist theories of literary relations; yet my emphasis on
the tradition of women writers' identification with Shakespeare should
not negate the fact that women writers have expressed a kind of critical
distance from Shakespeare, as well as continuity with him, in their explicit
rewritings of his works. By including the *"Coriolanus"* chapter as well as
by other echoes, Brontë makes *Shirley* a revision of Shakespeare's play, to
give women more power, as Margaret Arnold shows; by many *As You Like
It* allusions, George Eliot encourages thought about why Gwendolen, in
her *Daniel Deronda,* fails to appropriate the power Rosalind possesses.
Both novels imagine a greater variety of possible roles for women than any
Shakespearean play possesses. Analogously, Mary Loeffelholz shows that
when the American playwright Charlotte Barnes uses *The Tempest* as a
model in her dramatization of Pocahontas's life she is emphatic about giving Pocahontas more historical vision and public concern than Miranda
has in Shakespeare.

Some contemporary feminist rewritings of Shakespeare make their
points partly by placing women in central roles Shakespeare gives men.
Margaret Laurence's *The Diviners,* Gayle Greene shows, imagines a female
Prospero, a woman writer concerned about her daughter and the meaning
of her life. Marilyn Hacker's *Love, Death, and the Changing of the Seasons*
echoes the language and themes of Shakespeare's sonnets in an often-
colloquial sonnet sequence about the growth and end of love between two
women of the 1980s.[47]

Other feminists more explicitly rewrite the plots of Shakespeare's female characters. In her recent novel *Nights at the Circus,* Angela Carter
takes aim at Shakespeare's presentation of women in love. One character
predicts that the novel will end like "the customary endings of the old
comedies of separated lovers. . . . Orlando takes his Rosalind. She says:

'To you I give myself, for I am yours.' And that goes for a girl's bank account, too." In response, the protagonist says, "But it is not possible that I should give myself. . . . My being, my me-ness, is unique and indivisible. . . . Surely he'll have the decency to give himself to me, when we meet again, not expect the vice versa!"[48] The novel ends not with a marriage ceremony but with Fevvers's cataclysmic laugh at having discovered, in conversation with her lover, that she has deceived him about her virginity. She laughs away all attempts to restrict and classify women's sexuality and thus releases the feminist potential in the jokes about cuckoldry so common in Shakespearean comedy.

In an afterword to her play *Pinball,* the Australian feminist Alison Lyssa discusses it as "a play where King Lear's daughter Cordelia (I called her Theenie) refused to let her father's madness continue until it led her to her death," and she further contrasts the mutual support of her female characters to the behavior of the sisters in *Lear.* Lyssa's emphasis on her changes from *Lear*'s plot resembles Rich's emphasis on the contrast between Shakespeare's worldview and contemporary feminism. But in revising Shakespeare's family picture, she also draws on the feminist potential of a device frequent in Shakespearean comedy: masculine disguise. Theenie's friend Vandelope helps her win child custody by disguising herself as a male doctor of laws. The trial scene is full of allusions to Portia's strategy in *The Merchant of Venice;* for example, punningly revising for Australia as well as for feminism, Vandelope pours Theenie a cup of tea and puts up a sign reading *"THE KOALA TEA OF MERCY IS NOT STRAINED."*[49]

These rewritings mark out a continuum of attitudes toward Shakespeare, with Brontë providing the most explicit tribute and the most underplayed criticism, and Carter and Lyssa most explicitly distancing themselves from his patriarchal structures. Yet Carter and Lyssa, while engaging with Shakespeare as a cultural icon, see the feminist potential of his comic women even as they transform it into actuality. These works, in different ways, are all ambivalent about Shakespeare, not just because of the "authorized transgression," both conservative and revolutionary, in the nature of *Pinball* and *Nights at the Circus* as parody,[50] but also because they find in Shakespeare's texts codes for their hopes for women as well as for the history of women's constraints.

These rewritings and rereadings of female characters show differences in the ideological and social possibilities for women at different historical points. Compare Jameson's analysis of Lady Macbeth with Sprengnether's, or the closing marriages of Mary Lamb's *Taming of the Shrew* and *Measure for Measure* with the relationship between Carter's Fevvers and her lover or with the different varieties of stress on ties between women in Rich, Laurence, and Lyssa. But even Lamb, in her image of Helena, constructs a witty, resourceful heroine with much in common, temperamentally, with Fevvers or Laurence's Morag or Margaret Hutton's Beatrice. Like the re-visionary images of Shakespeare the author, these rereadings and rewritings, pushing against cultural restrictions insofar as the time and place allow, use Shakespeare to authorize women, to authorize themselves.

If women writers and women readers have used Shakespeare against women's subordination, as Carol Thomas Neely stresses in the epilogue, so do the feminist critics who write in this anthology—not by claiming his agreement with what we believe, but by using the history of different constructions and revisions of Shakespeare to help our understanding of women's reading and writing, of women's contributions to criticism.

The conversation engaged in here can widen in many directions. Like the feminist literary history it rewrites, this anthology has concentrated on the texts of Anglo-American women, with exceptions in Swift's study of the journal of the Portuguese-American Natalie Strong and Erickson's treatment of Adrienne Rich's relation to her Jewish father. But women of many different ethnic groups and countries have read and watched Shakespeare's plays.[51] I am now working on a companion volume with a multi-cultural perspective, which will include discussions of responses by African-American, European, and Third-World women.[52] To the revisions of writers and "ordinary" readers, it will add study of the constructions of Shakespeare by women who have acted and directed.[53] Further essays might also consider some institutional contexts of women's Shakespearean readings, from informal study groups to universities and professional associations. I expect this wider scope to add discussion of both more antagonistic and less empowering responses. On one hand, Shakespeare's role as an icon of England, touched on here in essays by Loeffelholz, Greene, and Froula, will loom larger and more problematically in readings by some postcolonial Third-World women.[54] On the other, a study of the late-nineteenth-century Dallas Shakespeare Club would probably find that the majority gave a negative answer when the discussion of *Love's Labour's Lost* reached its final question: "The perfect independence of woman . . . is it to be desired?"[55]

"Until we can understand the assumptions in which we are drenched we cannot know ourselves," writes Adrienne Rich;[56] Shakespeare's plays have been interpreted and rewritten to drench women in assumptions about gender, but women have also interpreted and rewritten them to question those assumptions. The women discussed here, liking as much of the plays as pleased them, have produced a multiplicity of readings and rewritings which teach us about Shakespeare, the history of women's reading and writing, and ourselves.

NOTES

1. See Carol Thomas Neely, "Feminist Criticism in Motion," in *For Alma Mater: Theory and Practice in Feminist Scholarship*, ed. Paula Treichler, Cheris Kramerae, and Beth Stafford (Urbana: University of Illinois Press, 1985), 65–90.

2. Brian Vickers, ed., *Shakespeare: The Critical Heritage, 1623–1801*, 6 vols. (London: Routledge and Kegan Paul, 1974–81; G. B. Evans, ed., *Shakespeare: Aspects of Influence* (Cambridge, Mass.: Harvard University Press, 1976); Ruby Cohn, *Modern Shakespeare Offshoots* (Princeton: Princeton University Press, 1976).

3. Sandra Gilbert and Susan Gubar, *The Madwoman in the Attic* (New Haven: Yale University Press, 1979), 44.

4. In addition to selections in Vickers, see R. D. Stock, *Samuel Johnson and Neoclassical Dramatic Theory* (Lincoln: University of Nebraska Press, 1973). One female critic, Charlotte Lennox, criticized Shakespeare for lack of decorum in her *Shakespear Illustrated* (1753), a study of his relation to his sources.

5. Aphra Behn, "Preface to *The Dutch Lover*," in *Works*, 6 vols., ed. Montague Summers (1915; rpt. New York: Phaeton, 1967), 1:224.

6. Margaret Cavendish, "General Prologue" in *Playes* (London: A. Warren, for John Martyn et al., 1662). Brenda Ameter's essay " 'Yet Full Well He Writ': The Duchess of Newcastle's View of Shakespeare," informed me of this source.

7. Elizabeth Montagu, *An Essay on the Writings and Genius of Shakespear* (1769; rpt. London, 1796; rpt. New York: Augustus M. Kelley, 1970), 17–18.

8. See for example the discussions of Cavendish and Behn in Sara Heller Mendelson, *The Mental World of Stuart Women* (Amherst: University of Massachusetts Press, 1987), and Sylvia Myers's book on Elizabeth Montagu, forthcoming from Oxford University Press.

9. Sylvia Townsend Warner, "Women as Writers," in *Collected Poems*, ed. Claire Harman (New York: Viking, 1982), 271. The essay was originally delivered as a lecture and published in 1959; it has recently been discussed in Jane Marcus, "Still Practice, A / Wrested Alphabet: Toward a Feminist Aesthetic," in *Feminist Issues in Literary Scholarship*, ed. Shari Benstock (Bloomington: Indiana University Press, 1987), 91–95.

10. Townsend Warner, "Women as Writers," 272.

11. Margaret Cavendish, *CCXI Sociable Letters* (1664; rpt. Menston: Scolar Press, 1969), 245–46.

12. Elizabeth Montagu, letter of Sept. 10, 1760, to Lord Lyttelton, *Letters of Mrs. Elizabeth Montagu*, 4 vols. (1813; rpt. New York: AMS Press, 1974), 4:299. For knowledge of this letter, also quoted in n. 27, I am indebted to the late Sylvia Myers. With minor changes, this sentence also appears in Montagu's *Essay*.

13. See David Marshall, *The Figure of Theater* (New York: Columbia University Press, 1986), esp. 167–92.

14. Montagu's importance is stressed by Stock, *Samuel Johnson*, 45, and by Robert Babcock, *The Genesis of Shakespeare Idolatry 1766–1799* (1931; rpt. New York: Russell and Russell, 1964), 109.

15. Samuel Taylor Coleridge, *Biographia Literaria*, 2 vols., ed. J. Shawcross (Oxford: Oxford University Press, 1907), 2:20.

16. William Hazlitt, *Round Table and Characters of Shakespeare's Plays* (New York: E. P. Dutton, 1906), 346–47; "On Shakspeare and Milton," *Complete Works,* ed. P. P. Howe, 21 vols. (1930; rpt. New York: AMS Press, 1967), 5:47. Elaine Showalter, *A Literature of Their Own* (Princeton: Princeton University Press, 1977), discusses women's anxiety about whether the vocation of writer was too selfish.

17. Charlotte Brontë, *Shirley* (New York: Penguin, 1974), 116.

18. Sharon O'Brien shows that Cather, in different contexts, praises both Shakespearean and "virile" sensibilities, rather than contrasting them in the same passage as do Woolf and H.D. See *Willa Cather: The Emerging Voice* (New York: Oxford University Press, 1987), 147–63.

19. Woolf's 1918 diary, quoted in Gilbert and Gubar, *Madwoman,* 190.

20. Virginia Woolf, *A Room of One's Own* (New York: Harcourt Brace, 1929), esp. 102–7.

21. See especially articles on androgyny in *Women's Studies* 2, no. 2 (1974).

22. Hélène Cixous makes similar use of Shakespeare in her "Sorties," in Hélène Cixous and Catherine Clément, *The Newly Born Woman* (Minneapolis: University of Minnesota Press, 1986), 98. In French and French-influenced feminist criticism, the search for feminine elements in texts by male writers has been much more extensive than in the American tradition of feminist criticism I discuss.

23. Harold Bloom, *The Anxiety of Influence* (New York: Oxford University Press, 1973).

24. Nancy Chodorow, *The Reproduction of Mothering* (Berkeley: University of California Press, 1978). Mary Poovey uses Chodorow to make a similar point about appropriative creativity in *The Proper Lady and the Woman Writer* (Chicago: University of Chicago Press, 1984), 44. Chodorow's theories also help explain the ease at identifying with Shakespearean characters shown by most of the women discussed in this anthology.

25. C. L. Barber and Richard P. Wheeler, *The Whole Journey: Shakespeare's Power of Development* (Berkeley: University of California Press, 1986), 61. Ben Jonson's career as an actor was much shorter. Meredith Skura's work in progress, however, emphasizes the importance of actors' psychology for both of these playwrights. See also Jonas Barish, *The Antitheatrical Prejudice* (Berkeley: University of California Press, 1981), 132.

26. Earl R. Wasserman, "The Sympathetic Imagination in Eighteenth-Century English Theories of Acting," *Journal of English and Germanic Philology* 46 (1947): 264–72; John Russell Brown, "On the Acting of Shakespeare's Plays," in *The Seventeenth-Century Stage,* ed. Gerard Eades Bentley (Chicago: University of Chicago Press, 1968), 49.

27. Montagu, letter of Sept. 10, 1760, *Letters,* 4:301.

28. Philip Weissman, *Creativity in the Theater* (New York: Basic Books, 1965), 12, says the actor experiences "lack of differentiation of self from nonself."

29. Barish, *Antitheatrical Prejudice,* 89–106; Jean Howard, "Renaissance Antitheatricality and the Politics of Gender and Rank in *Much Ado about Nothing,*" in *Shakespeare Reproduced,* ed. Jean Howard and Marion O'Connor (New York: Methuen, 1987), 166–69.

30. Robert Greene, *Groatsworth of Witte* (1592), ed. G. B. Harrison (1922; rpt. New York: Barnes and Noble, 1966), 45. Shakespeare citations are from *The Complete Works,* ed. David Bevington, 3rd ed. (Glenview, Ill.: Scott, Foresman, 1980).

31. See my *Love's Argument* (Chapel Hill: University of North Carolina Press, 1984), 83–98, which also discusses other aspects of the woman/actor connection.

32. See Catherine Belsey, "Disrupting Sexual Difference: Meaning and Gender in the Comedies," in *Alternative Shakespeares,* ed. John Drakakis (New York: Methuen, 1985), 183; also Stephen Greenblatt, *Shakespearean Negotiations* (Berkeley: University of California Press, 1988), 91.

33. Margaret Cavendish, *Sociable Letters,* 246.

34. Montagu, *Essay,* 36, 201.

35. Elizabeth Griffith, *The Morality of Shakespeare's Drama Illustrated* (1775; rpt. New York: Augustus M. Kelley, 1971), 481.

36. Griffith, *Morality,* 140 (Kate's speech), 138 (Warburton).

37. For the history of contrasting male and female discourse on Ophelia, see Elaine Showalter, "Representing Ophelia: Women, Madness and the Responsibilities of Feminist Criticism," in *Shakespeare and the Question of Theory,* ed. Patricia Parker and Geoffrey Hartman (New York: Methuen, 1985), 80–94.

38. See for example Coleridge, *Shakespearean Criticism,* ed. Thomas Middleton Raysor, 2 vols. (New York: Dutton, 1960), 1:119–20; Hazlitt, *Round Table,* 180.

39. Nina Auerbach, *Woman and the Demon* (Cambridge: Harvard University Press, 1982), 207–17.

40. Dorothy Richardson, *Pilgrimage* (1910; London: J. M. Dent, 1967), 2:188, quoted in Carolyn Heilbrun's review of *The Woman's Part,* ed. Carolyn Ruth Swift Lenz, Gayle Greene, and Carol Thomas Neely (Urbana: University of Illinois Press, 1980), Marilyn French's *Shakespeare's Division of Experience* (New York: Summit Books, 1981), and Coppélia Kahn's *Man's Estate* (Berkeley: University of California Press, 1981) in *Signs* 8 (1982): 183.

41. Virginia Woolf, "Men and Women" (1920); rpt. *Books and Portraits,* ed. Mary Lyon (London: Hogarth Press, 1977), 28–29. I owe this reference to Alice Fox's paper "Reading Shakespeare and Writing Fiction: Virginia Woolf as Critic and Artist," presented at the 1983 MLA special session "Feminist Criticism of Shakespeare: Shakespeare and Women Writers." See also her *Virginia Woolf and the Literature of the English Renaissance* (New York: Oxford University Press, 1990).

42. Woolf, *Room of One's Own,* 86–87, 44.

43. Townsend Warner, "Women as Writers," 272.

44. See for example Clara Claiborne Park, "As We Like It: How a Girl Can Be Smart and Still Popular," in *The Woman's Part;* Peter Erickson, *Patriarchal Structures in Shakespeare's Drama* (Berkeley: University of California Press, 1985).

45. Patrocinio Schweikart, "Reading Ourselves: Toward a Feminist Theory of Reading," in *Gender and Reading,* ed. Elizabeth Flynn and Patrocinio Schweikart (Baltimore: Johns Hopkins University Press, 1986), 31–62.

46. Judith Fetterley, *The Resisting Reader* (Bloomington: Indiana University Press, 1978), xx.

47. Marilyn Hacker, *Love, Death, and the Changing of the Seasons* (New York: Arbor House, 1986).

48. Angela Carter, *Nights at the Circus* (New York: Penguin, 1984), 280–81.

49. Alison Lyssa, *Pinball,* in *Plays by Women,* vol. 4, ed. Michelene Wandor (New York: Methuen, 1985), 157–58, 150. Thanks to Jo O'Brien Schaefer for lending me this book.

50. Linda Hutcheon, *A Theory of Parody* (New York: Methuen, 1985), comments on the "dual drives of conservative and revolutionary forces" inherent in parody's "nature as authorized transgression," 26.

51. This anthology's focus on middle-class women should also be supplemented by the awareness that women of other classes have attended and read Shakespeare's plays: see Lawrence Levine, *Highbrow/Lowbrow: The Emergence of Cultural Hierarchy in America* (Cambridge: Harvard University Press, 1988), for a discussion of Shakespeare's popularity in nineteenth-century working-class America. Working-class women, of course, seldom wrote their responses to plays they saw.

52. For discussion of the problematics in Maya Angelou's reading of Shakespeare, see Christine Froula, "The Daughter's Seduction: Sexual Violence and Literary History," *Signs* 11 (1986): 636.

53. Pioneering here is Nina Auerbach, *Ellen Terry: Player in Her Time* (New York: Norton, 1987).

54. See Ania Loomba, *Gender, Race, Renaissance Drama* (Manchester: Manchester University Press, 1989).

55. Theodora Penny Martin, *The Sound of Our Own Voices: Women's Study Clubs 1860–1910* (Boston: Beacon Press, 1987), 108.

56. Adrienne Rich, "When We Dead Awaken: Writing as Re-Vision," in *On Lies, Secrets, and Silence* (New York: Norton, 1979), 35.

SUSAN J. WOLFSON

Explaining to Her Sisters:
Mary Lamb's Tales from Shakespear

In the 1807 Preface to *Tales from Shakespear,* Mary Lamb expresses a
desire "to make these Tales easy reading for very young children."[1] She really intends them chiefly for "young ladies," however, since "young gentlemen," having been "generally permitted the use of their fathers'
libraries at a much earlier age than girls are," know "the originals" and
"frequently hav[e] the best scenes of Shakespear by heart" well before
their sisters are even "permitted to look into this manly book" (2). Lamb's
girlhood reading was an exception: according to her brother, she suffered
no "prohibition" of manly texts and was free to browse among "good old
English reading" while happily neglecting "all that train of female garni-
ture, which passeth by the name of accomplishments."[2] Introducing
Shakespeare to girls thus has the look of a progressive reform—a practical
response to recent feminist calls, such as Mary Wollstonecraft's, to remedy
that "false system of education, gathered from the books written on this
subject by men."[3]

That response is cautiously managed, however, and its energy is frequently divided: although Lamb's project attempts reform, it is also
marked by conservative ideology. As in the work of other professionally
motivated women writers in the early nineteenth century, her tales display
contrary psychological tendencies and ambivalent social attitudes.[4] Some,
as we shall see, reveal a consciousness of cultural definitions and constraints so alert as to imply a critique of the ideologies of gender represented in the plays, while others reflect her compliance with, or even show
an elaboration of, certain conventional prescriptions. This ambivalence is
significant, not only because it anticipates the issues animating modern
feminist debates about Shakespeare's situation within patriarchal culture,
but also because it indicates the dilemma of feminist criticism situated
within that culture. On the one side, there are efforts to redeem Shakespeare from full complicity with patriarchy: Juliet Dusinberre, for instance, sees a concern in the plays "to dissolve artificial distinctions
between the sexes" that is "feminist in sympathy." Even those less confi-

dent about this sympathy are willing to discern a critique of patriarchy. Marianne Novy, for example, sees the plays focusing on "the politics of gender" and staging "symbolic transformations of ambivalence about gender relations"; similarly, Coppélia Kahn finds Shakespeare questioning "cultural definitions of sexual identity" and the structures of male dominance by which these are enforced. Yet they and other such readers do not deny what the editors of the first anthology of feminist Shakespeare criticism, *The Woman's Part*, recognize: the plays repeatedly demonstrate that while "women may strive to resist or to correct the perversions of patriarchy, they do not succeed in altering that order nor do they withdraw their allegiance from it." Thus adversarial critics such as Kathleen McLuskie insist that because Shakespeare's representations of gender are so inescapably informed by the social structures of Renaissance ideology and the Elizabethan theater, there is no way around "the patriarchal bard": "when a feminist accepts the narrative, theatrical and intellectual pleasures of this text she does so in male terms and not as part of the locus of feminist critical activity"; such activity, she urges, must read the plays to "reveal the conditions in which a particular ideology of femininity functions" in order to subvert "the hold which such an ideology has for readers both female and male."[5]

Extricating oneself from the ideologically compromised pleasures of the text is not an easy project, however. Indeed, the difficulty of locating an external, uncontaminated position from which to subvert the hold of "male terms" affects the voice of the most notable feminist of the 1790s, Mary Wollstonecraft, whose quotations of or allusions to Shakespeare in *A Vindication* show striking divisions of sympathy and exasperation. We see this in her first allusion: in the course of assessing the current devotion of women's education to "frivolous" accomplishments, she complains, "they dress, they paint, and nickname God's creatures—Surely these weak beings are only fit for a seraglio!—Can they be expected to govern a family with judgment?" (10). The voice, of course, is Hamlet's bitter denunciation of Ophelia and her sex: "You jig and amble, and you lisp, you nickname God's creatures, and make your wantonness your ignorance. . . . To a nunnery, go" (3.1.146–51).[6] Wollstonecraft speaks with Hamlet to name a problem, but doing so requires her to use the voice of male misogyny and, for the sake of her authority, to dissociate herself from "the present conduct of [her] sex": conceding Hamlet's point, she rewrites his differentiating "you" as a "they" from which she implicitly exempts herself. We see her working a similar distinction of pronouns again in the *Vindication* when she asks, "what have women to do in society? . . . surely you would not condemn them all to suckle fools and chronicle small beer!" (147–48); here she echoes another misogynist, Iago, to state the problem about "them," even though her argument is indirectly allied with Desdemona's protest against Iago's "most lame and impotent conclusion" (2.1.160–61), a voice she does not quote.[7] Throughout *A Vindication*, in fact, she tends to quote Shakespeare chiefly in voices of male misogyny, reading the plays, in effect, for statements of the problem rather than as resources for a solution.[8] This exemption of herself by virtue of her own "them" from the "you" marked by Hamlet and Iago is all the more compelling given the character of her private correspondence, which shows her repeatedly identifying emotionally and psychologically with the voices of Shakespeare's male tragic heroes—never his women—as she adopts their language in moments of personal crisis and despair, or reads herself into the figures of their agony.[9]

For Wollstonecraft, the latent but clearly emergent problem in coming to terms with Shakespeare has to do with her tendency to identify with his male voices—whether she is acknowledging what it is that provokes his misogynists or finding herself more attuned to the language of men, rather than women, in crisis. These effects, as McLuskie suggests, have to do with the way in which the emotional structure of the plays, as well as our involvement in the moral, emotional, or poetic satisfactions of the language Shakespeare gives certain of his male characters, implicitly require misogyny as a condition of sympathy.[10] Judith Fetterley has described this predicament as nearly inevitable for any woman reading a literature in which the hero is male and the antagonist female, or the center of subjectivity is male and the "other" female: "the female reader is coopted into participation in an experience from which she is explicitly excluded; she is asked to identify with a selfhood that defines itself in opposition to her; she is required to identify against herself."[11] For Lamb, the dynamics of reading Shakespeare are not so overtly antagonistic: the issue of mediating between female readers and his "manly book" emerges less in relation to male voices per se than as a play of ambivalences about what "young ladies" are to learn about themselves from the situation and careers of young ladies in these stories. Her ambivalence produces narratives that alternately resist and reinscribe conventionality. Reading Shakespeare as a woman and converting his texts into tales for younger women, Lamb is sensitive to the codes of gender, but at the same time she is cautious about identifying an ideological problem, either for herself or for her readers.

The circumspection is first evident in the way the language of her Preface implies that there are certain features in Shakespeare's "manly book" requiring careful mediation. It is not exactly clear what Lamb means by "manly book." The term may be no more than a reference to adult themes, what she calls "the histories of men and women." But the fact that it occurs in the same sentence that notes discrimination of access to the "fathers' libraries" has the effect of making the issue one of gender: who gets to read what, and on what terms? These questions are curiously exacerbated by the first plate in the 1807 first edition, which, in facing the title, assumes the quality of an emblem: Prospero, in the posture of an Old Testament patriarch, has his left arm raising a staff and his right extended across Miranda, his whole body in a posture that bars her from something which, one senses, he alone is empowered to address. In an edition of 1918, the first illustration is again of Prospero, arms spread, protecting his daughter, this time with a particularly beastly, menacing Caliban posing the threat.[12]

Such barriers seem to apply to Mary Lamb herself: she writes as the teller of another man's tales; the volume is supervised and co-authored by Charles; the title page in fact would name only him—her far more substantial role was never recognized in her lifetime and several years elapsed before her authorship was publicly known. This effacement may have reflected the mutual wishes of the authors and publishers to avoid recalling public attention to the scandal of the Lambs' personal life— namely, Mary's murder of her mother in a fit of insanity ten years before. Yet the question is not easily decided. At least one biographer thinks the title page evinces less mutual reticence than Charles's particular desire not to be linked with a woman writer, a desire all the more uncomplimentary since the *Tales* contributed to his "public fame . . . and helped to expand his growing literary reputation"—a benefit Mary might have enjoyed.[13] Charles, moreover, had first choice of tasks and claimed the great tragedies, or as Mary complains to her friend, Sarah Stoddart, all "the best stories."[14] Perhaps not coincidentally, these are the plays in which the power of patriarchal social order—both mystified and demystified—is most emphatically inscribed: *Lear, Macbeth, Hamlet, Romeo and Juliet, Timon, Othello.*

Mary Lamb's effacement behind male authority, of course, reflects general cultural attitudes. It is significant that her Preface appeals to men not only as co-mediators of Shakespeare but also as mediators whose authority may supplant her own on appropriate occasions. This self-deprecation is in part genuine humbleness. She makes a point of apologizing for the way her versions—whatever their educational value— necessarily downgrade the worth of the original: her words are "small and valueless coins . . . pretending to no other merit than as faint and imperfect stamps of Shakespear's matchless image. . . . the beauty of his language is too frequently destroyed by the necessity of changing many of his excellent words into words far less expressive of his true sense" (1). This apology seems to involve something more than discomfort with

"Prospero and Miranda." Frontispiece for the first edition of *Tales from Shakespear*, reprinted in *The Works of Charles and Mary Lamb*, ed. E. V. Lucas (London: Methuen, 1903), used here by permission of Methuen

"Prospero, Miranda, and Caliban." First illustration by Louis Rhead for *Tales of Shakespeare* (New York and London: Harper & Brothers, 1918) and used here by permission of Harper and Row

the inevitable limitations of paraphrase, however, for she implies that the loss of value incurred by her translations is to be recompensed, not just by recourse to the esteemed original, but also by the retellings of other men. The authority of male readers is enlisted to supplement and in effect expose her own imperfections: to assure her success, she "beg[s] [the] kind assistance" of "young gentlemen . . . in explaining to their sisters such parts as are the hardest for them to understand" and helping "them to get over the difficulties" (2).

That explanatory assistance is not simply a pedagogical matter of negotiating unfamiliar images and difficult syntaxes. It is also proprietary, for "the difficulties" brothers are asked to mediate have to do with young ladies learning about what the world requires of, and what it denies to, them: brothers are to acquaint their sisters with the original text by "carefully selecting what is proper for a young sister's ear." Mary's own brother, Charles, in fact, appends sentences to the Preface anticipating the time when girls will wish and "be allowed to read the Plays at full length." He seems to transcend the issue of gender by listing the benefits of Shakespeare for readers of both sexes: "Tales" and "true Plays" alike will provide "strengtheners of virtue, a withdrawing from all selfish and mercenary thought, a lesson of all sweet and honourable thoughts and actions, to teach you courtesy, benignity, generosity, humanity." The pedagogical object, "you," is not gender-specific, but following Mary's discrimination between sisters and brothers, it has the lingering effect of making the capacious values so enumerated seem ones prescribed more to the former than the latter.[15]

Assumptions about gender certainly inflect the two authors' investment in the project and their sense of themselves as subjects of professional scrutiny. Although the benefits Charles enumerated in the sentences that conclude the Preface seem to encode humanist generalities, he clearly felt embarrassed about his participation in the kind of pedagogy he associated, not at all favorably, with women's writing. Remarking to William Wordsworth that Mary's part of the Preface shows "a more **feminine** turn" of mind, he regretted the effect this turn had in presenting him—the one named on the title page—"as an instructor to young Ladies." Mocking the voice of coy maidenhood, he protests, "upon my modesty's honour I wrote it not" (2:256–57)—his eagerness to disclaim authorship of the Preface (if not the *Tales*) prompted both by his general antipathy to perverting juvenile literature into moral pedagogy and by a particular wish not to be grouped with those women writers, such as Sarah Trimmer and Anna Letitia Barbauld, adept at the mode.[16] For Mary, however, the prospect of joining this vigorous community of women writers seems to have been enabling—a prospect of more promise than the financial benefits she and Charles both expected. She took to her task with energy and discipline, completing six tales with no apparent trouble (2:225). According to Charles, she regarded this as "her great work" (2:233)—even though he was inclined to treat his own contributions as "humble amusements" (2:225).

It is difficult to imagine so tactful a project provoking objection, but it is revealing that it did, and precisely on the grounds on which the more vehement reactions to Wollstonecraft's *Vindication* were conducted. There was nothing like a consensus even about so modest a design as introducing Shakespeare to young women. The *Anti-Jacobin* devoted its brief notice to this issue, expressing its doubt that "the tales of Shakspeare, though told, as they are by Mr. Lamb, as decently as possible, are very proper studies for female children." They understood all too clearly the potential of the Preface's modest feminism: "we certainly object to the language of the preface, where girls are told, that there are parts in Shakspeare *improper* for them to read at one age, though they may be allowed to read them at another. This only serves as a stimulus to juvenile curiosity, which requires a *bridle* rather than a *spur*."[17] If the Lambs' Preface refers to gender to discriminate readers of the *Tales,* the *Anti-Jacobin* applies the discrimination to readers of the plays themselves.

The Lambs' publishers, the Godwins, were very alert to the value of gender in the marketplace, for to their ear, "the voice of the public" (the *Anti-Jacobin* aside) had clearly welcomed the first edition as a worthy resource for educating young ladies into proper womanhood. The "Advertisement" they affixed to the second edition of 1809 capitalized on this interest: in deference to "every reader of taste," they had "not suppress[ed] the former Preface," but they felt it was "not exactly applicable on the present occasion." What was applicable, apparently, was their announced design on young ladies alone: "It has been the general sentiment, that the style in which these Tales are written, is not so precisely adapted for the amusement of mere children, as for an acceptable and improving present to young ladies advancing to the state of womanhood." The *Tales,* that is, are now being marketed as a conduct manual, their stories "precisely adapted" in order that readers may in turn be adapted, or "improv[ed]," to "the state of womanhood" endorsed by cultural norms, and the Godwins assure the public that this vehicle has been "prepared with suitable elegance" (477).

If to appease reviewers such as the *Anti-Jacobin,* the Godwins promoted what was elegant over what was intelligent, Mary Lamb shows a kind of agitated sensitivity to those codes of social and familial life that denote what is acceptable and improving in young ladies' character and behavior. Some of her decisions about how to represent the lives of "young ladies" in the plays yield euphemisms and elisions that defend conventional proprieties; at other times, however, the results are less predictable, especially when she contends with material of a "more perplext and unmanageable" nature (2:234). This includes the bed tricks on which the plots of *Measure for Measure* and *All's Well That Ends Well* hinge and, more generally, Shakespeare's fascination with the dramatic possibilities and theatrical perplexities of female transvestism: "She complains of having to set forth so many female characters in boy's clothes," Charles tells William Wordsworth; "She begins to think Shakspear must have wanted Imagination" (2:233). Yet these perplexities, as will become clear, are not so much about Shakespeare's lack of ingenuity as about Lamb's own indecisiveness about the construction of women's roles, both social and theatrical.[18]

Although it would be misleading to argue that Lamb promoted a feminist critique of Shakespeare, her tales do reveal some of the feminist sensitivities of the post-Revolutionary, post-Wollstonecraft epoch in which they were first published. This quality may have been encouraged in part by a circumstance about which today's feminists agree—namely, that it is in the very plays that occupied Mary Lamb, the comedies, that female characters show greater freedom of action against the social restrictions of patriarchy. Lamb's engagement with these plays thus places her in a situation of testing the possibilities, and what emerges are narrative treatments ranging from optimistic openness to a conservatism narrower than that of the Shakespearean original. In her *All's Well*, quite surprisingly, not only is a young woman's initiative aided by patriarchal authority, but conventions of female conduct are expanded into models of resourcefulness, ambition, and success. *A Midsummer Night's Dream* opens a potential critique of patriarchy by foregrounding and making legible the social structures by which women, especially daughters, are constricted. By contrast, *The Taming of the Shrew, The Tempest,* and *Measure for Measure* refrain from even that critique as they naturalize conventional definitions of femininity and preserve orthodox interpretations of women's roles in society and the family—and do so by eliding the possible ironies of Shakespeare's own representations, as if to contain and stabilize for young women what the plays themselves leave problematic. Countering the disruptive potential of "so many female characters in boy's clothes" in other plays, Lamb refashions these plays to fit orthodox patterns of understanding.

Lamb's *Taming of the Shrew* is one of the clearest examples of such constraint. Her management of this story is noteworthy, not just because it maintains and idealizes a repressive ideology but, more particularly, because the plot of "taming" itself, as Elizabeth Segel points out in her recent study of children's literature, would emerge in the nineteenth century as a favorite paradigm in the market of girls' books (where the Lambs' *Tales* were an early and continuing presence). Victorian publishers produced story after story in which the girl "who resists the dictates of a genteel femininity must be 'tamed.' . . . The so-called happy ending . . . is that she herself stops rebelling and chooses the approved role in order to gain or to retain the love and approval of those around her."[19] Lamb's *Taming of the Shrew* not only perpetuates this prescription but touches on a potent personal circumstance. Its spectacle of a motherless woman aggressively out of control and virtually requiring strait-jacketing by the male establishment eerily coincides with the chief trauma of her adult life: her fatal attack on her mother in a fit of insanity. While she apparently never mentioned that event, reading and retelling this play may have evoked phantoms that she then worked to contain within the tradition of orthodox readings to which she could refer.

In 1815 Lamb would offer a pointed critique of women's subjection in the home, exemplified in particular by needlework, the debilitating and female-centered labor that triggered her matricidal madness. But in 1806 she tells the story of Kate's temper in a way that not only avoids a critical perspective on the project of taming but also suppresses Shakespeare's own frame for such a view, the prelude about Christopher Sly. This abridgment had ample support on the English stage: from 1756 to 1886, the favored text was not Shakespeare's but David Garrick's adaptation, *Catherine and Petruchio* (not until 1844 was Shakespeare's even restored to the English stage). The deletion of the Sly prelude, both on Lamb's part and Garrick's, is significant, because this is the scene that makes possible an ironic critique of shrew-taming: where the play names the woman given to fits of temper as a "shrew" in need of taming, the vignette underscores the value of gender, for here a drunken and disorderly man is allowed the comical character of an incorrigible "rogue." Erasing this frame also gets rid of any suggestion of problematic male self-interest in the spectacle of shrew-taming—namely, that the aggression it vents and the dream of domestic order it embodies are psychically governed, a scolded man's wish fulfillment.

Garrick and Lamb in fact do more than omit this prelude; they also suppress the early scenes in which Shakespeare makes obvious a father's favoritism of one daughter and marketing of both. True, Baptista insists that he will entertain no "specialities" with Petruchio about Kate until "the special thing is well obtained, / That is, her love; for that is all in all" (2.1.127–28), but he still holds to the system that makes "a daughter's love" an issue chiefly to be manipulated in the concerns of "business" (see 113–26).[20] One is persuaded by Coppélia Kahn's reading of Kate's shrewishness as a "desperate response to the prevailing system of female subjection" and of Petruchio's violence as a representation of "the system itself, its basic mechanisms displayed in exaggerated form."[21] Garrick's play severely foreshortens, if not altogether collapses, that perspective when it opens with Baptista cautioning Petruchio about "all the worst you are t'expect / From my shrewd daughter Catherine; if you'll venture . . . [to] . . . wed her."[22] Lamb authorizes this perspective with a tone of neutral narration that has the effect of naturalizing this interpretation, of eliding its psychological and ideological motivation. Entertaining no defense of Kate's behavior, her account presents her simply as a "loud-tongued scold" of "ungovernable spirit and fiery temper." Petruchio, on the other hand, is "a witty and most happy-tempered humourist, and withal so wise, and of such true judgment" that he is never suspected of being in less than perfect control, "for his natural temper was careless and easy" (109).

Lamb's bias against Kate responds to more than personal necessity; it also perpetuates the interpretation of the play codified in and by Garrick's version. Although one cannot be sure that Lamb had Garrick's play in mind as she worked out her tale, her supplements are remarkably similar. Both give unquestioned credit to Petruchio's judgment, an endorsement powerfully signaled for each in their respective handlings of Kate's politic agreement with Petruchio's insistence that the sun is the moon (4.5.1–22). Garrick in fact writes a new line for Kate that lays bare the ideology that governs taming in particular and marriage in general—and boldly contrasts with modern attempts, such as John C. Bean's, to see Kate emancipated by imagination and "the liberating power of laughter and play."[23] Garrick has her say only, "I see 'tis vain to struggle with my bonds; / So be it the moon, or sun, or what you please" (21). And Lamb makes it clear to her readers that the Kate who speaks thus is "no longer Katherine the Shrew, but the obedient wife" (114); when Petruchio insists that Kate address an old gentleman as if he were a young maid, Lamb remarks that a "now completely vanquished Katherine quickly adopted her husband's opinion" (115). Garrick goes even further, staging this reform with an interpolated family reunion:

> *Baptista:* Art not alter'd, Kate?
> *Catherine:* Indeed I am. I am transform'd to stone. . . .
> So good a master cannot chuse but mend me.
> *Bianca:* Was ever woman's spirit broke so soon!
> What is the matter, Kate? hold up thy head,

> Nor lose our sex's best prerogative,
> To wish and have our will—

(P. 22)

Garrick has Bianca's exhortation met immediately by Petruchio's counter-charge to Catherine to "tell this headstrong woman, / What duty 'tis she owes her lord and husband" (22; cf. 5.2.130–31). Catherine then recites a condensed version of Shakespeare's lines 136–54 before yielding to Petruchio who, after claiming to have abjured the role of "lordly husband" for a life "Of mutual love, compliance and regard," closes the play by pronouncing a slightly altered version of lines 161–64 in Shakespeare, there spoken by Kate: "How shameful 'tis when women are so simple / To offer war where they should kneel for peace; / Or seek for rule, supremacy, and sway, / Where bound to love, to honour, and obey" (22). Garrick's decision to give Petruchio the last word and end the play with the husband's ringing restatement of the institutionalized language of the marriage rite has its counterpart in Lamb's coopting as paraphrase Kate's final speech to the wives: "to the wonder of all present, the reformed shrewish lady spoke as eloquently in praise of the wife-like duty of obedience, as she had practised it implicitly in a ready submission to Petruchio's will" (117). Her decision merely to report the theme of Kate's speech, without quoting any of its language, and to assert the correlative of that theme in Kate's behavior applies the most conventional control imaginable to the unsettling spectacle of Kate's reformation, and Lamb reinforces that control with a final sentence of pure elaboration: "And Katherine once more became famous in Padua, not as heretofore, as Katherine the Shrew, but as Katherine the most obedient and duteous wife in Padua" (117).

Lamb's evasion of the language of Kate's final speech is a significant maneuver, for it releases her from having to deal with slippery ironies of tone and so leaves undisturbed the conservatism of her own conclusion. Yet even with their seemingly unequivocal emphases on Kate's transformation, both Lamb's tale and Garrick's adaptation offer good instances of how an apparent endorsement of the spectacle of shrew-taming and the social synecdoche thereby implied allows certain potent terms to remain unexamined. Lamb's casual but resonant phrase, "completely vanquished," suggests military victory or capitulation by force, rather than a happy access of psychic composure. And in Garrick's version, Catherine's confessed transformation "to stone," accompanied by her sister's observation of her broken spirit and posture of defeat, bears a queerly subversive force that exceeds the starkly orthodox conclusion he is intent to impose on Shakespeare's story. Garrick allows Bianca to express this reaction only under the expectation of having it corrected by the united force of Catherine and Petruchio, and *Catherine and Petruchio*. Yet it is no coincidence that the terms of Kate's transformation and of what Lamb judges to be "implicitly" the case about the depth and desire of Kate's "ready" practice of "wife-like duty" are exactly what focus modern debates. Does Kate's sermon demonstrate a depressing fulfillment of Petruchio's taming, or does it suggest Kate's canny manipulation of power within the marriage? Is it perhaps an ironic parody of the character others, including Petruchio, believe her to have achieved, or is it a sly and advantageous gaming conducted by them both against popular expectation? And if Kate believes herself ironically detached from the role she plays, might that belief signify the deepest taming of all—a treacherously subtle cooptation by and reinforcement of patriarchal authority under the illusion of free play, cooperation, or ironic control?

Some nineteenth-century critical accounts of the play tend to share Lamb's treatment of the story as an exemplum about the taming of the shrew into happy obedience. Hazlitt, for one, recommends Petruchio as "a character which most husbands ought to study" and finds the "concluding scene, in which trial is made of the obedience of the new-married wives (so triumphantly for Petruchio)" to be "a very happy one."[24] Sensitive to the ideology that fuels enthusiasms such as Hazlitt's, feminists today wrestle with that apparently "happy" result, variously calling attention to or disputing the force of male domination Lamb's retelling unproblematically endorses. Readers who want to save Shakespeare for feminism tend to suggest that Kate's taming looks worse than it is; it is really an education into cooperation, a necessary socialization that now has a secure base in a loving marriage of equal partners, and a therapy that redirects the energies of anger into imaginative play.[25] There is a quality of special pleading in these arguments, however, that does not quite succeed against Kate's summary advice to all wives to "place your hands below your husband's foot" (5.2.177). It is interesting that a feminist with no stake in claiming Shakespeare for the cause, Bernard Shaw, denounced the play's last scene as "altogether disgusting to modern sensibility. No man with any decency of feeling can sit it out in the company of a woman without being extremely ashamed of the lord-of-creation moral implied in the wager and the speech put into the woman's own mouth."[26]

Lamb's lack of quarrel with what would embarrass Shaw, let alone her lack of interest in offering the apologies modern feminists feel motivated to develop, suggests her desire to sentimentalize and idealize the ideology that sponsors shrew-naming and shrew-taming. The normative value such ideology has for her urges her to subscribe women's happiness to their capitulation to patriarchal authority. This tendency may also be read in her supplements to the ending of *Measure for Measure*. We hear first how "pleased was the good duke, when his own Isabel, from whom he expected all gracious and honourable acts, kneeled down before him" to ask for mercy for Angelo (138). Isabella's grace is made to seem a dutiful recognition of his benign authority, an implication Lamb enhances with the phrase "his own Isabel"—an easy appropriation that anticipates, or proleptically accomplishes, the terms of Lamb's conclusion, namely, Isabella's happy acceptance of the duke's proposal of marriage: "Isabel, not having taken the veil, was free to marry; and the friendly offices, while hid under the disguise of a humble friar, which the noble duke had done for her, made her with grateful joy accept the honour he offered her; and when she became the duchess of Vienna, the excellent example of the virtuous Isabel worked such a complete reformation among the young ladies of that city, that from that time none ever fell into the transgressions of Juliet, the repentant wife of the reformed Claudio. And the mercy-loving duke long reigned with his beloved Isabel, the happiest of husbands and of princes" (138–39). Not only is Isabel happy to marry the duke, but their union becomes a virtual force of redemption in fallen Vienna—an idealizing, in fact, that would become commonplace in patriarchal readings of the play.[27]

Lamb's willingness to elaborate the sections of Shakespeare's stories that bring independent women under the governance of stronger men, especially by marriage, has the paradoxical effect of calling attention to the instability of Shakespeare's own less determinate representations. Her commitment to conventional social emblems affects even the ordering of the *Tales,* which, reversing chronology, gives *The Tempest* privilege of first place, as if it were a paradigmatic tale for "young ladies."[28] That emphasis is more apparent in the narrative organization of the tale itself. Lamb omits Shakespeare's opening—the storm at sea and the revelation of Prospero's manipulation—and substitutes a naturalized, "objective" account of the circumstances: "There was a certain island in the sea, the only inhabitants of which were an old man, whose name was Prospero, and his daughter Miranda, a very beautiful young lady. She came to this island so young, that she had no memory of having seen any other human face than her father's"(3). What seems immediately worth noting, of course, is that this is not the case: in Shakespeare's text, Miranda contradicts her father's surmise that she cannot "remember / A time before we came unto this cell": "Certainly, sir, I can," she insists, adding that what she does remember is her life among women (1.2.38–39, 41).[29] Lamb's tale eventually reports this dialogue, but her decision to begin her tale by discrediting Miranda's memory has the effect both of granting Prospero's account the authority of neutral interpretation and of situating Miranda in relation to that authority. (And, of course, here is a young lady with no access to her father's library.) Prospero's authority is enhanced by Lamb's reporting the history of Prospero's wresting of power from the female-dominated family that complements him and Miranda—namely Sycorax and Caliban—in the voice of objective narration, rather than having this information emerge, as in Shakespeare's play, in another of Prospero's self-serving narratives.

Lamb's narratology is, of course, devised to orient young readers to the characters and their history at the outset of the story. But her emphasis on the father's imprisonment of a female political rival and his exercise of absolute authority over his daughter define a structure of power that she clearly wanted to make visible, for it is reiterated in the opening of the next tale of the volume, *A Midsummer Night's Dream*. Less mythologically than sociologically inclined here, Lamb gives an even fuller account of the patriarchal tyranny than Shakespeare does:

> There was a law in the city of Athens, which gave to its citizens the power of compelling their daughters to marry whomsoever they pleased: for upon a daughter's refusing to marry the man her father had chosen to be her husband, the father was empowered by this law to cause her to be put to death; but as fathers do not often desire the death of their own daughters, even though they do happen to prove a little refractory, this law was seldom or never put in execution, though perhaps the young ladies of that city were not unfrequently threatened by their parents with the terrors of it.
>
> There was one instance however of an old man, whose name was Egeus, who actually did come before Theseus (at that time the reigning duke of Athens), to complain that his daughter Hermia, whom he had commanded to marry Demetrius, a young man of a noble Athenian family, refused to obey him, because she loved another young Athenian, named Lysander. Egeus demanded justice of Theseus, and desired that this cruel law might be put in force against his daughter.
>
> Hermia pleaded in excuse . . . but [her] honourable reason for not obeying her father's command moved not the stern Egeus. (11–12)

The wry interjection about the risks of refractory behavior in daughters is the only light touch in paragraphs otherwise devoted to language detailing social and familial contests of power: compulsion, caprice, empowerment, threats, terror, execution, demands, commands, refusals, obedience, disobedience, justice. Though not overtly polemical, Lamb's narration clearly solicits sympathy for the daughter's reasons and judgment against the father's tyranny.

Less easy for Lamb to manage was *All's Well That Ends Well:* it "plagued" and "teazed me more than all the rest put together," she tells a friend (2:235). Given this aggravation, her determination to persist is provocative, especially since the necessity of telling this tale to young readers is at least arguable: the consensus was that it involved a cad of a hero and a distasteful story; since Shakespeare's day it had never been a stage favorite. The result helps explain Lamb's perseverance, however, for she was attempting a sympathetic portrait of a woman who persists in her aims against the conventional constraints of feminine propriety and passivity. It is as if Lamb had taken the opportunity of writing about Helena as a way to study the exercise of female ambition in a world of social restriction and written the tale to suggest to her "young ladies" what women can accomplish with wit, intelligence, and commitment.

This is a peculiar suggestion, I realize, to make about a play that for many eighteenth- and nineteenth-century readers admitted at least three impediments to enjoyment: Helena, Bertram, and the bed trick that secures their terms of endearment. The case of Helena is highly charged, not only by her own scheming but by her seeming cooperation with the tyranny exerted against a young man's freedom. Coleridge, for example, felt that Bertram, "just bursting into manhood, with all the feelings of pride of birth and appetite for pleasure and liberty natural to such a character so circumstanced," had "good reason to look upon the king's forcing him to marry Helena as a very tyrannical act," and he thought Helena "not very delicate."[30] For many, in fact, Helena's forwardness in demanding Bertram's hand (even Lamb uses the verb, 103) and her subsequent pursuit of him to Florence raised questions of propriety; her duplicity with the Countess (whom she told she was going on a pilgrimage to Spain—Florence happens to be on the way) further tainted her character, and her engineering of the bed trick proved her immorality.[31] Lamb manages these problems by using her role as narrator to fashion Helena into a paradoxical model of modesty and individual assertion. Her Helena is acutely sensitive to the obstacle posed by class: "so great the distance seemed to her between his height of dignity and her lowly fortunes" that she "dared not form any wish but to live his servant, and so living to die his vassal." It is only when she "form[s] an ambitious project in her mind to . . . undertake the cure of the king" and so gain a "legacy that should advance her fortune" that she entertains the "high dignity of being Count Rossilion's wife." Lamb actively solicits sympathy for the learning and initiative that fuel Helena's "firm hopes . . . of succeeding" in this venture "if she might be permitted to make the trial" (101), for her overcoming the "many difficulties" posed (103), and, after Bertram has rejected her, for the resiliency of her "ardent mind" in "conceiv[ing] a project (nothing discouraged of the ill success of her former one) to recover her truant lord" (106).

Lamb's repeated emphasis on Helena's initiative stands out against the mere expressions of sympathy offered by other readers. Hazlitt could speak of her only as a figure "of great sweetness and delicacy . . . placed in circumstances of the most critical kind," having "to court her husband both as a virgin and a wife: yet the most scrupulous nicety of female modesty is not once violated." Anna Jameson also focuses on Helena's "painful and degrading" situation: "She is poor and lowly: she loves a man who is far her superior in rank, who repays her love with indifference, and rejects her hand with scorn. She marries him against his will; he leaves her with contumely on the day of their marriage, and makes his return to her arms depend on conditions apparently impossible." It is a striking feature of her sixteen-page character sketch that it declines all mention of Helena's scheming, let alone her resourceful method for satisfying Bertram's seemingly impossible conditions. That demurral also appears in M. Leigh Elliot's twenty-three-page rhapsody on Helena, which merely remarks, with Victorian probity, "How she carries out her purpose and . . . what stratagems she is put to there, we need not dwell upon."[32] Shaw, predictably, does dwell upon Helena's methods, praising her "determination and courage" in the face of class prejudice and applauding Shakespeare's subversion of the male-generated "feeble romantic convention that the initiative in sex business must always come from the man"; in Shakespeare, he remarks, "the love interest is the interest of seeing the woman hunt down the man. . . . she is the pursuer and contriver."[33]

Of necessity, Lamb's case for Helena is more modestly construed. She meets the question of her man-chasing by making their convergence in Florence seem a matter of happy coincidence; she converts Helena's bed trick into a mere date-by-disguise—an adaptation assisted by altering Bertram's terms so that Helena need secure his ring only, not a pregnancy by him[34]—and she reforms Bertram. Getting rid of the bed trick allows Helena to succeed without compromising her modesty and without engineering a coldly mechanical ruse designed only to exploit the physical appetite of one partner and satisfy physical necessity in the other. Lamb's Bertram is released from lust, with the consequence that his courtship of "Diana" is affected by her arts of conversation alone. Helena's success has to depend on the sort of imaginative and verbal skills summoned by Portia, who in Lamb's rendering of *The Merchant of Venice* seems almost a prototype: "she began to think and consider within herself, if she could by any means be instrumental. . . . she did nothing doubt her own powers, and by the sole guidance of her own true and perfect judgment, at once resolved" to set matters aright (64).

As if to display such Portian powers in operation in *All's Well,* Lamb constructs the nighttime meeting between "Diana" and Bertram that

Shakespeare does not. Deleting the bed trick, of course, makes this easier, but it also gives Lamb the opportunity to show Bertram actually falling in love with Helena, and purely on the attractions of her personality. In the guise of Diana, in fact, Helena gets to draw attention to qualities hitherto unnoticed: "Bertram never knew how sensible a lady Helena was, else perhaps he would not have been so regardless of her" and the excellence "of her understanding." And Helena, animated by a sense that "her future fate, and the happy ending of all her love-projects, seemed to depend on her leaving a favourable impression on the mind of Bertram . . . exerted all her wit to please him; and the simple graces of her lively conversation and the endearing sweetness of her manners so charmed Bertram, that he vowed she should be his wife" (107). It is "mind," "wit," "conversation," and gracious "manners" alone, not tricky suits of paternity, that secure Helena's success. And this success gains force in the scheme of Lamb's narrative from its emphatic reversal of the result of their only previous conversation, when Helena's "humble speech . . . did not at all move the haughty Bertram to pity his gentle wife, and he parted from her without even the common civility of a kind farewell" (104).

That optimism about women succeeding through such powers inspires Lamb's conclusion, where, she assures her readers, Helena "was now the beloved wife of her dear Bertram" (109). Lamb's desire to confirm Helena's happiness corresponds to her extension of *Measure for Measure,* with the difference that Helena's marriage is treated as a reward for unconventional behavior rather than as a capitulation to conventional authority. But as in *Measure for Measure,* here, too, Lamb is more certain than Shakespeare about the terms of conclusion, a divergence that casts her palpable idealizing into strong relief. Shakespeare leaves Bertram without any confession of belated love for Helena and with a set of conditions addressed to the king: "If she, my liege, can make me know this clearly / I'll love her dearly, ever, ever dearly" (5.3.308–9).[35] Dr. Johnson was unforgiving: "I cannot reconcile my heart to Bertram; a man noble without generosity, and young without truth; who marries Helen as a coward, and leaves her as a profligate: when she is dead by his unkindness, sneaks home to a second marriage, is accused by a woman whom he has wronged, defends himself by falsehood, and is dismissed to happiness." Hazlitt seconded Johnson, finding in Bertram no more than "wilful stubbornness and youthful petulance."[36] Lamb's final paragraph evades all complications: Helena's marriage not only joins her to Bertram but happily unites lineage with luck, the orphaned daughter with a new mother and a renewed bond with her father, and the lowborn maid with an assured position in the aristocracy. Here is her last sentence: "Thus Helena at last found that her father's legacy was indeed sanctified by the luckiest stars in heaven; for she was now the beloved wife of her dear Bertram, the daughter-in-law of her noble mistress, and herself the countess of Rossilion" (109).

Lamb's *All's Well*, though responsive to conventional concerns of modesty and ultimately devoted to a conventional happy ending, takes advantage of narrative voice to sympathize with unconventional female desire and capability. Her version of this tale converts traditional constraints (modesty, marriage) into an opportunity to elaborate the middle space of Shakespearean comedy in which, as Carol Neely has observed, resourceful women, before they assume the submissive roles expected of them in marriage, are able to "assert verbal, social, and sexual power . . . to evade or manipulate financial pressures, fathers' commands, the intricacies of marriage contracts, and the stereotyping of themselves by romantic or misogynist lovers."[37] It is significant in this respect that although the world of *All's Well* is politically dominated by a king who strikes Bertram and his critical defenders as tyrannical, Shakespeare still represents this as a world of considerable female power: the king's actual physical power and social authority are restored by Helena's enterprises; and women's alliances prove effective. Moreover, it is the women, rather than the legally empowered men, who are more likely to contest the dispositions of nature and fate in social privilege and to advance a case for individual merit. The Countess's hopes for Helena's good depend first on what "her education promises" and second on the "dispositions she inherits" (1.1.35–38). Helena, too, is committed to the power of "merit" (1.1.223) and individual effort, and resists any notion that her fate is fixed: "Our remedies oft in ourselves do lie, / Which we ascribe to heaven; the fated sky / Gives us free scope; only doth backward pull / Our slow designs when we ourselves are dull. . . . my project may deceive me, / But my intents are fix'd, and will not leave me" (1.1.212–15; 224–25).

Her work in the play, in fact, is to turn men's scripts—the way her circumstances are scripted by them—to her own ends. Her first opportunity is the "prescriptions" left to her by her father, which she uses to heal the king and so engage his authority in behalf of her own designs on Bertram. A letter Mary Lamb writes to her closest friend, Sarah Stoddart, in the weeks before she agreed to take on the project of rendering *Tales From Shakespear* offers an odd, but provocative, parallel to Helena's situation. She complains of feeling oppressed by Charles's unsettled manner, "his feaverish teazing ways," and expresses her determination to gain "some little influence over myself—. And therefore I am most manfully resolving to turn over a new leaf with my own mind" (2:220). Her adverb, "manfully," implies a willingness to venture beyond conventional prescriptions for womanly behavior, motivated by a desire to distinguish the restlessness of her own mind from the infectious fever of her brother's behavior. It is revealing that the cure Lamb imagined turned out to be textual in character: a mental refiguring of her life as a text that she herself might influence. The image is soon realized in the task of translating Shakespeare's "manly book" in the new leaves of her *Tales*. The quiet claim for female authority in this resolve is enhanced by the fact that this project originated in the mind of another woman, Mary Jane Godwin, William Godwin's second wife and partner in publishing. Although despised by Charles and other of William Godwin's male friends, it was she, as everyone knew, who got the Godwins into the business of publishing juvenile literature and developed their list. The business that opened in 1806 bore her name: "M. J. Godwin & Co., at The Children's Library" (*Works* 3:474). Lamb reinforced the female encouragement actualized by M.J. Godwin with an instinctive turn to Sarah Stoddart as her muse: "I set you up in my fancy, as a kind of *thing* that takes an interest in my concerns, and I hear you talk-[ing] to me, and arguing [*sic*] the matter very learnedly when I give way to despondency" (*Letters* 2:220).

A little more than seven months later, she tells her that she has "been busy making waistcoats and plotting new work to succeed the Tales" (2:243). The conjunction of activities in this sentence is compelling in view of what Lamb writes in an essay she would publish six years later in 1815: "Needlework and intellectual improvement are naturally in a state of warfare." "New work" took shape in 1807 as other stories and poems for children, but that plotting of profession was habitually restrained both by her aversion to "affronting the preconceived habits of society" and by her sense that women were better off not aspiring to "situations now filled wholly by men."[38] Even so, telling the *Tales* seems to have given Lamb an opportunity to exercise her imagination toward ends other than that of fitting "herself to become a conversational companion" to men in their leisure time (so she complains about the customary aims of women's intellectual exertions), and the project seems to have stirred in her aspiration to something other than the performance of "feminine duties (that generic name for all our business)." Lamb's sensitivity to the constraints placed on women's lives, both in her own time and in the social worlds represented in the plays, is an important aspect of her reading Shakespeare under the encouragement of women as well as of her brother and with a sense of influencing future generations. Her tales offer a valuable perspective on the way one intelligent, well-read woman, conscious of the "disadvantages [her "sisterhood"] labour[ed] under from an education differing from a manly one," struggled with the ambiguous task of explaining to her sisters those issues of women's identity, relationships, social engagement, and sexuality with which Shakespeare's plays had agitated and challenged her own attention. It is no coincidence that the narratives she plotted anticipate, and in some cases correspond to, modern feminist explanations—especially those concerned to recognize in Shakespeare's plays an important stage for many of our culture's most deeply embedded attitudes about the roles men and women are given to play.

NOTES

For motivating and steadily improving this essay, I thank Marianne Novy; I have also benefited from generous scrutiny and savvy advice from Ronald Levao, Lawrence Danson, Emily Bartels, Elin Diamond, and William Galperin.

1. Preface to the first edition of *Tales from Shakespear. Designed for the Use of Young Persons* (1807). Quotations of the 1807 Preface, 1809 Advertisement, and the *Tales* follow vol. 3, *The Works of Charles and Mary Lamb,* ed. E. V. Lucas, 7 vols. (London: Methuen, 1903–5); hereafter *Works.* Lucas's text for the *Tales* is the second edition of 1809. Subsequent references appear in parentheses.

2. "Mackery End," *London Magazine,* July 1821; rpt. *Works,* 2:76.

3. Mary Wollstonecraft, *A Vindication of the Rights of Woman* (1792), ed. Carol H. Poston (New York: Norton, 1988), 7; references hereafter appear in parentheses. Lamb's acquaintance with William Godwin might have given her access to a more personal account of Wollstonecraft, both as a political theorist and as a theorist of children's, especially daughters', education.

4. For a perceptive study of Wollstonecraft's plight within the competing "demands of professional authorship" and "the cultural pressure to conform to the image of proper (or innate) femininity," see Mary Poovey, *The Proper Lady and the Woman Writer: Ideology as Style in the Works of Mary Wollstonecraft, Mary Shelley, and Jane Austen* (Chicago: University of Chicago Press, 1984); I quote from 241.

5. I quote, in order, Dusinberre, *Shakespeare and the Nature of Women* (New York: Barnes and Noble, 1975), 153, 5: Novy, *Love's Argument: Gender Relations in Shakespeare* (Chapel Hill: University of North Carolina Press, 1984), 3–4; Kahn, *Man's Estate: Masculine Identity in Shakespeare* (Berkeley: University of California Press, 1981), 20; *The Woman's Part: Feminist Criticism of Shakespeare,* ed. Carolyn Swift Lenz, Gayle Greene, and Carol Thomas Neely (Urbana: University of Illinois Press, 1983), 6; McLuskie, "The Patriarchal Bard: Feminist Criticism and Shakespeare," in *Political Shakespeare: New Essays in Cultural Materialism,* ed. Jonathan Dollimore and Alan Sinfield (Ithaca: Cornell University Press, 1985), 98, 106. This essay offers an interesting polemical overview of feminist approaches to the plays; for another report, see the editors' introduction to *The Woman's Part* (3–16).

6. Quotations follow the Arden *Hamlet,* ed. Harold Jenkins (London and New York: Methuen, 1981). Both the resort to Hamlet's terms of misogyny and the strategy of dissociation are anticipated in *A Vindication of the Rights of Men* (1790): Wollstonecraft accuses Burke of trying to convince women "that to be loved" ("woman's high end and great distinction!" she adds sarcastically), "they

should 'learn to lisp, to totter in their walk, and nick-name God's creatures'" (rpt. Gainesville, Fla: Scholars' Facsimiles and Reprints, 1963), 112–13.

7. Quotations follow the Arden *Othello*, ed. M. R. Ridley (1958; rpt. London and New York: Methuen, 1977).

8. See also Wollstonecraft's complaint against Dr. Gregory's advice to his daughters (in *A Father's Legacy to His Daughters* [1774]) that they dissemble about their learning in order not to provoke a "malignant" response from men: she borrows Hamlet's voice of anger against Gertrude to express her own disgust with the "system of dissimulation" in which "women are always to *seem* to be this and that—yet virtue might apostrophize them, in the words of Hamlet—Seems! I know not seems! Have that within that passeth show!" (99). It is significant that Wollstonecraft appropriates Hamlet's declarations of difference from the feminine ("I have that within which passeth show") and reverses the misogyny in order to urge fellow women to refuse the male-prescribed system of duplicity that necessarily degrades them in the name of dubious social advantage.

9. See *Collected Letters of Mary Wollstonecraft*, ed. Ralph M. Wardle (Ithaca: Cornell University Press, 1979), 176, 236, 242, 280, and 300 for incorporations of Hamlet's voice; 305 for Lear's; and 244 for Macbeth's.

10. I paraphrase Kathleen McLuskie (see n. 5), especially 98–100.

11. Judith Fetterley, *The Resisting Reader: A Feminist Approach to American Fiction* (Bloomington: Indiana University Press, 1978), xii.

12. The 1807 illustration, attributed to William Blake, seems to have acquired something of the status of an iconic signal. The illustration depicting Prospero, Miranda, and Caliban appears in *Tales from Shakespeare, By Charles and Mary Lamb, With Numerous Illustrations by Louis Rhead* (New York: Harper, 1918), facing page 2. I am grateful to Harper and Row for their permission to reprint Rhead's illustration. I am also grateful to Methuen and Company, London, for permission to reprint their reproduction of the frontispiece for the first edition of the *Tales*, which appears in *Works*, 3:3 (see n. 1).

13. See Katharine Anthony, *The Lambs: A Story of Pre-Victorian England* (New York: Knopf, 1945), 93–94.

14. *The Letters of Charles and Mary Anne Lamb*, 3 vols, ed. Edwin W. Marrs, Jr. (Ithaca: Cornell University Press, 1975), 2:235; references appear hereafter in my text.

15. By 1861, Mary Lamb's former Latin student, Mary Cowden Clarke, could present her edition of Shakespeare to boys and girls alike: "Shakespeare's works are a library in themselves. A poor lad, possessing no other book, might on this single one, make himself a gentleman and a scholar. A poor girl, studying no other volume, might become a lady in heart and soul. Knowledge, refinement, experience in men and manners, are to be gathered from these pages." Yet progress is still only partial: not only is there no prospect for girls analogous to "scholar," but the text itself is still being spoken of as something of a manly book. Moreover, Clarke's subsequent, conventional female gendering of "country" and "mother-tongue" notwithstanding, the most passionately animated linguistic politics in the Preface implicate a problematic sexual politics: Shakespeare, she urges her readers, offers a "standard for language" that is a "manly . . . purely English" antidote to

"the present rage for fineries of epithet, and fopperies of phraseology" (Preface, *Shakespeare's Works* [New York: D. Appleton, 1861]). I am grateful to Lawrence Danson for bringing this item to my attention.

16. As Joseph Riehl remarks in *Charles Lamb's Children's Literature* (Salzburg, Austria: Institut für Anglistik und Amerikanistik, 1980), by the mid-eighteenth century, the education of children, under the influence particularly of Rousseau and Locke, shifted in emphasis "from the instruction of learning to the forming of character" (11); women writers adept at turning tales into moral exempla were outselling Lamb at the book shops (14–15), much to his annoyance.

17. *The Anti-Jacobin Review* 26 (1807):298. The review is politically as well as ideologically motivated: the *Anti-Jacobin* had already attacked Charles in 1798 for his association with Coleridge and Southey's Jacobinism: Lamb had contributed to their *Annual Anthology* (see *Letters*, 1:153–54 n.9).

18. The spectacle of female transvestism, as Catherine Belsey points out, challenges patriarchy "by unsettling the categories which legitimate it" ("Disrupting Sexual Difference: Meaning and Gender in the Comedies," in *Alternative Shakespeares*, ed. John Drakakis [London: Methuen, 1985], 180).

19. "'As the Twig is Bent . . .': Gender and Childhood Reading," in *Gender and Reading: Essays on Readers, Texts, and Contexts*, ed. Elizabeth A. Flynn and Patrocinio Schweickart (Baltimore: Johns Hopkins University Press, 1986), 172. The "taming of the shrew" is also a familiar paradigm in the adult fiction of Lamb's own age. As Sandra Gilbert and Susan Gubar observe, it is Austen's favored plot (*The Madwoman in the Attic: The Woman Writer and the Nineteenth-Century Literary Imagination* [New Haven: Yale University Press, 1979], 154–55).

20. Citations and quotations of *The Taming of the Shrew* follow the edition of H. J. Oliver (New York: Oxford University Press, 1984).

21. *Man's Estate*, 104–6.

22. *Catherine and Petruchio. A Comedy. Altered from Shakespeare* (Taken from the Manager's Book at the Theatre Royal Covent-Garden; London: R. Butters, 1756), 3. Page references hereafter are given parenthetically in my text.

23. John C. Bean, "Comic Structure and the Humanizing of Kate in *The Taming of the Shrew*," *The Woman's Part*, 72.

24. William Hazlitt, *Characters of Shakespeare's Plays* (1817; rpt. London: George Bell and Sons, 1901), 219 and 222.

25. The evidence Irene Dash presents for Kate's achievement of "status and respect" is strained at best: "she has . . . heard her husband wager on her wit," and "she complies with delight" to his charge that "she lecture the other women on their 'wifely duties' ": "How sweet to be propelled into a seat of authority and favor," Dash remarks, hardly bothered by Kate's continued treatment as a commodity (*Wooing, Wedding, and Power: Women In Shakespeare's Plays* [New York: Columbia University Press, 1981], 61). Though much more attentive to "the ambiguous combination of patriarchy and play," Novy sees Kate achieving "a new and more tenable social role. . . . She speaks of marriage as an affectionate contract—a relationship in which both partners have a role" while recognizing their "mutual need and interdependence" (*Love's Argument*, 62, 68–69); Carol Thomas Neely goes further, reading Kate's final speech as a "celebration of reciprocity"

that "reconcile[s] patriarchal marriage with romantic love and mutual desire" (*Broken Nuptials in Shakespeare's Plays* [New Haven: Yale University Press, 1985] 30), and for John Bean, male tyranny has given way to "a nontyrannical hierarchy informed by mutual affection" ("Comic Structure," 70). Even Kahn, who critiques the subjection of women in the play's early scenes, is willing to hear in Kate's last speech a "contextual irony" that renders Petruchio "deluded" in his authority: he gains Kate's "outward compliance in the form of public display, while her spirit remains mischievously free" (*Man's Estate,* 115). Least accommodating is Richard Burt, for whom Petruchio's "charismatic authority ultimately disguises the fact that his taming process" is "coercive," a "social practice designed to discipline, control, and subordinate Kate"; he finds it significant that it is the men alone who celebrate Kate's reformation, while the women who resist their husbands' capricious bids become "socially acceptable targets of collective aggression" ("Charisma, Coercion, and Comic Form in *The Taming of the Shrew,*" *Criticism* 26 [1984]:299, 303).

26. Bernard Shaw, *Saturday Review,* 6 Nov. 1897; rpt. *Our Theatres in the Nineties,* 3 vols. (London: Constable, 1932), 3:240.

27. Edward Dowden and G. Wilson Knight, like many others, fantasize about what Shakespeare withholds. Dowden is certain "Isabella does not return to the sisterhood"; she has learned that "the vital energy of her heart can exert and augment itself through glad and faithful wifehood, and through noble station, more fully than in seclusion" (*Shakspere: A Critical Study of His Mind and Art* [1875; rpt. New York: Harper, 1918], 74). While Knight concedes "we are not told what will become of Vienna," he does not doubt the inevitability of marriage or its significance: "It is to be the marriage of understanding with purity; of tolerance with moral fervour" in which the Duke teaches Isabella "wisdom, human tenderness, and love" (*The Wheel of Fire: Interpretations of Shakespearian Tragedy with Three New Essays* [New York: Meridian, 1957], 95–96).

28. The Lambs' ordering may respond to that of the First Folio, where *The Tempest* is first—also the arrangement of Dr. Johnson's edition, the canonical one for the Lambs' age (*The Plays of William Shakespeare,* 21 vols. [5th ed.; London: J. Plymsell, 1803]). Yet if so, the Folio order is honored more in the breach than in the observance, for in no other respect do the Lambs follow it. I thank Marianne Novy for prompting me to investigate this issue.

29. Quotations follow the Arden edition of *The Tempest,* ed. Frank Kermode (1954; rpt. London and New York: Methuen, 1980).

30. *Coleridge's Shakespearean Criticism,* ed. Thomas Middleton Raysor (London: Constable, 1930), 356–57.

31. See, for example, Thomas Kenny (*The Life and Genius of Shakespeare* [London: Longman, Green, 1864]), who finds Helena difficult to sympathize with, both because her object hardly "deserve[s] her devotion" and because her stratagem shows "no very strong regard for rigid, unequivocating truthfulness" (207). To Dowden, even writing about the play was an "extreme difficulty, when regarded on the ethical side"; Helena was better than Bertram, but her methods lacked "moral force" (*Shakspere,* 75, 79). Frank Harris (*The Women of Shakespeare*

[London: Methuen, 1911]) preferred Bertram: sorry that Shakespeare had "damn[ed]" him "as an unspeakable cad" (139), he judged Helena's stratagem "a thousand times more revolting than the compulsion she has used to make him wed her" (130); "with as shameless a persistency as is shown by any of Bernard Shaw's heroines" (60)—with such deficiency "of feminine characterization" (123)—"no care could have made a girl charming, or even credible, who would pursue a man to such lengths or win him by such a trick" (131–32). As the reference to Shaw makes clear, such judgments are sensitive to the fact that, as Richard Wheeler puts it, "Helena can meet Bertram's mocking conditions . . . only by becoming more powerful and sexually aggressive" (*Shakespeare's Development and the Problem Comedies: Turn and Counter-Turn* [Berkeley: University of California Press, 1981], 55). This affront to the norms of feminine conduct is such that even Sylvan Barnet, who wants to defend her, can state the problem only as one of her impropriety ("she is too inclined to wear the pants") and plead her case only in terms of orthodox codes: "Helena is energetic yet thoroughly womanly"—as if one could not be both (Introduction, *All's Well That Ends Well* [New York: NAL, 1965], xxix–xxx).

32. Hazlitt, *Characters,* 202; Jameson, *Shakspeare's Heroines: Characteristics of Women, Moral, Poetical, and Historical* (1832; rpt. from the second, rev. edition of 1889, New York: AMS, 1971), 125; Elliot, *Shakspeare's Garden of Girls* (London: Remington, 1855), 257.

33. *Bernard Shaw: Collected Letters,* 3 vols., ed. Dan H. Laurence (London: Max Reinhardt, 1965–1972), 3:758, and the "Epistle Dedicatory" to *Man and Superman,* in *The Complete Prefaces of Bernard Shaw* (London: Paul Hamlyn, 1965), 155.

34. *Measure For Measure,* of course, allows for no such adjustments. Even with the circumlocution of "dishonourable solicitations," Lamb makes it clear that Angelo has required Isabella to "yield to him her virgin honour, and transgress even as Juliet had done with Claudio" (132). But she does apply a revision to balance this necessity and, in effect, legitimize the bed trick: Mariana is "the wife of Angelo" rather than his jilted fiancée (134).

35. Quotations follow the Arden edition of *All's Well That Ends Well,* ed. G. K. Hunter (1962; rpt. London: Methuen, 1967).

36. Samuel Johnson, *The Plays of William Shakespeare* (1765; rpt. *Johnson on Shakespeare,* ed. Arthur Sherbo, *The Works of Samuel Johnson,* 9 vols. [New Haven: Yale University Press, 1958–68], 7:404); Hazlitt, *Characters,* 204. As Oscar James Campbell remarks, the play ends with Bertram still an "immature, spoiled fellow . . . progressively more unworthy of Helena's inexplicable devotion" (*The Reader's Encyclopedia of Shakespeare,* ed. Oscar James Campbell [New York: Crowell, 1966], 16). Neely's assessment is cautious at best: this is not "a joyous lovers' union but . . . a compromised bargain . . . a precarious beginning" (*Broken Nuptials,* 65).

37. Neely, ibid., 21–22.

38. Lamb published her essay under the pseudonym of "Sempronia," as a letter to the editor of *The New British Ladies' Magazine,* 1 April 1815, 257–60,

which was sympathetic to calls for women's "intellectual improvement." I follow *Works* 1:176–80; subsequent references appear in parentheses. For a deft reading of this essay as "a contradictory and self-divided protest," see Jane Aaron, " 'On Needle-Work': Protest and Contradiction in Mary Lamb's Essay," *Romanticism and Feminism,* ed. Anne K. Mellor (Bloomington: Indiana University Press, 1988), 167–84.

CHRISTY DESMET

"Intercepting the Dew-Drop": Female Readers and Readings in Anna Jameson's Shakespearean Criticism

> *Medon:* Analysing the character of Cleopatra must have been some-
> thing like catching a meteor by the tail, and making it sit for its
> picture.
> *Alda:* Something like it, in truth; but those of Miranda and Ophelia
> were more embarrassing, because they seemed to defy all anal-
> ysis. It was like intercepting the dew-drop or the snow-flake
> ere it fell to earth, and subjecting it to a chemical process.
>
> Anna Jameson, *Characteristics of Women*

By devoting a book to the study of Shakespeare's heroines, Anna Jameson expands significantly the range of Shakespearean character criticism in the nineteenth century. Early reviewers praised her *Characteristics of Women* warmly, and between 1832 and 1925 the book went through at least eighteen editions; it was also translated into German.[1] Shakespearean enthusiasts, like the reviewers, ranked Jameson's criticism with that of Schlegel, Hazlitt, and Coleridge.[2] She also wrote on women's history, aesthetics, her travels, and European art. Although respected by her contemporaries, Jameson has since been relegated to the margins of Shakespearean criticism.[3] In *Woman and the Demon*, Nina Auerbach—one of the few recent critics to take Jameson seriously—writes that her *Characteristics of Women* frees Shakespeare's heroines "from the plays in which they are generally subordinate to the heroes and to the demands of the plot." Released from their "contexts of love and intrigue, marriage and death" by the female critic, the heroines can therefore live "a larger life than their plays allow."[4] The power of Jameson's Shakespearean criticism, however, derives from her ability to transform, rather than refute, the terms of nineteenth-century character criticism. She adopts from her male predecessors a psychology of reading that paradoxically helps her define her position as a female reader and writer. She inherits as well critical strategies that let her redefine the status of Shakespeare's heroines. Reading as a woman in an existing critical tradition, Anna Jameson anticipates one strain of contemporary feminist criticism of Shakespeare. More important, by establishing the female critic's relationship to her subject and audience, she makes for herself a place in the company of literary critics. Jameson submits to male authority in order to supersede it; for her, deference makes possible difference.

From the romantic tradition, Jameson drew the assumption that Shakespeare enjoys a superior grasp of all human nature; as Samuel Taylor Coleridge puts it, he is a Proteus who "lives in the universal" and knows "no self but that which is reflected not only from the faces of all around us, our fellow creatures, but reflected from the flowers, the trees, the beasts, yea from the very surface of the [*waters and the*] sands of the desert."[5] Participating in this tradition allows Jameson to claim a special kinship with Shakespeare's female characters. While earlier Shakespeareans were concerned with the morality of his characters, romantic critics, especially S. T. Coleridge and William Hazlitt, concern themselves with the interaction between reader and character. In Coleridge's criticism, for instance, the act of entering gradually into a character's passions—the dramatic experience—becomes inseparable from the act of analyzing that character: in a play "you meet people who meet and speak to you as in real life, interesting you differently, having some distinctive peculiarity which interests you."[6]

For Hazlitt and Coleridge, sympathy reinforces rather than undermines moral evaluation because reading combines egoistic identification with judgment. Coleridge works out most thoroughly the idea that reading is egoistic. According to his 1811–12 Shakespeare lectures, we learn about universalities by projecting ourselves into unfamiliar situations; in Shakespeare's plays, then, "every man sees himself without knowing that he sees himself."[7] For Coleridge, reading is like seeing an optical illusion in which we recognize ourselves but are physically and intellectually distanced. We perceive difference within similarity.

Jameson reiterates the belief that reading Shakespeare involves egoism in her preface to the *Characteristics of Women,* framed as a dialogue between Alda (the book's female "author") and Medon (a male interlocutor). Shakespeare's wicked women, says Alda at one point, "frighten us into reflection"; looking at his "amiable" women, on the other hand, "we are flattered by the perception of our own nature in the midst of so many charms and virtues: not only are they what we could wish to be, or ought to be, but what we persuade ourselves we might be, or would be, under a different and happier state of things, and perhaps some time or other *may* be."[8]

Every woman, like every man, can "see herself" in Shakespeare's characters, but for Jameson also, identification must be tempered by critical distance. Alda argues that Shakespeare's characters are "complete individuals, whose hearts and souls are laid open before us: all may behold, and all judge for themselves." When Medon objects that "all will not judge alike," Alda concurs that judgments about literary figures are colored by the reader's own nature: "We hear Shakespeare's men and women discussed, praised and dispraised, liked, disliked, as real human beings; and in forming our opinions of them we are influenced by our own characters, habits of thought, prejudices, feelings, impulses, just as we are influenced with regard to our acquaintances and associates" (*CW* 13). Alda explains, however, that because art permits distance as well as projection, literary characters make better objects for study than our friends and acquaintances: "We can do with them what we cannot do with real people: we can unfold the whole character before us, stripped of all pretensions of self-love, all disguises of manner. We can take leisure to examine, to analyse, to correct our own impressions, to watch the rise and progress of various passions—we can hate, love, approve, condemn, without offence to others, without pain to ourselves (*CW* 14). Learning about human nature through fictional characters is the "safer and the better way" because readers have the time and space to analyze, then revise, first impressions. Alda then offers an impromptu metaphor for art's relation to those passions it represents:

> But look, that brilliant rain-drop trembling there in the sunshine suggests to me another illustration. Passion, when we contemplate it through the medium of imagination, is like a ray of light transmitted through a prism; we can calmly, and with undazzled eye, study its complicate nature and analyse its variety of tints; but passion brought home to us in its reality, through our own feelings and experience, is like the same ray transmitted through a lens,—blinding, burning, consuming where it falls. (*CW* 14)

Representing the reader's experience through optical effects, Jameson confirms her kinship with the romantic critics, particularly Coleridge.

In her practical criticism, Jameson applies her romantic psychology of reading, identifying strongly with Shakespeare's heroines but tempering her advocacy with cool judgment. Coleridge does not distinguish readers according to gender, and in her more abstract statements about reading Shakespeare, neither does Jameson; in some portraits, however, her engagement with her subject demonstrates a particularly strong bond between Shakespeare's female characters and herself as female critic. In her portrait of Constance from *King John,* one of her most original, she supplements received opinion with detail from the historical Constance's life to flesh out Shakespeare's sketchy character. Although *King John,* with Sarah Siddons playing Constance, was popular during Jameson's lifetime, her male predecessors say little about Constance; Hazlitt, for instance, dislikes the play in general and stresses only Constance's lack of power.[9] Sarah Siddons, as leading interpreter of Constance's character, "thinks Constance more motherly than queenly," according to her niece, Jameson's friend Fanny Kemble.[10]

Jameson takes issue with Siddons's stress on Constance's motherhood. When we think casually of Constance, she admits, "it is in her maternal character. All the interest which she excites in the drama turns upon her situation as the mother of Arthur. Every circumstance in which she is placed, every sentiment she utters, has a reference to him; and she is represented through the whole of the scenes in which she is engaged, as alternately pleading for the rights and trembling for the existence of her son" (*CW* 312). If we contemplate Constance's character apart from the circumstances around her, however, we are struck by her "*power*—power of imagination, of will, of passion, of affection, of pride" (*CW* 314). Constance may lack self-control, but she is neither mad nor merely ambitious; Jameson concludes that imagination, rather than her meaner deficiencies, predominates in Constance's character: "she not only loves her son with the fond instinct of a mother's affection, but she loves him with her poetical imagination, exults in his beauty and his royal birth, hangs over him with idolatry, and sees his infant brow already encircled with the diadem" (*CW* 319–20). Working through her argument, Jameson synthesizes divergent views of Constance—as devoted mother, proud matriarch, and "poet" frenzied with passion—to arrive at a more complex description and more balanced evaluation of Constance's moral nature. In the process Constance acquires heroic grandeur; Jameson represents her, "when, deserted and betrayed, she stands alone in her despair," as a "mother-eagle, wounded and bleeding to death, yet stretched over her young in an attitude of defiance while all the baser birds of prey are clamouring around her eyrie" (*CW* 324). In Jameson's representation, Constance is not merely a mother or victim; she is a powerful and defiant ruler.[11]

Having called attention to Constance's regal stature, which transforms her motherly instincts into power, Jameson supports her interpretation with an account of the historical Constance's successes and tribulations, drawn from Holinshed and other dubious sources. Constance, widow to Geoffrey, son of England's King, ruled Brittany wisely after her husband's death; but her tyrannical father-in-law, Henry II, forced her to marry one of his earls, Randal de Blondeville, in order to keep Brittany subject to England. This new husband imprisoned Constance and her children; after her release, however, Constance divorced him and gave herself in marriage to a "man of courage and integrity" who helped her to protect her interests in Brittany and to resist England's rapacious assaults. Having lost her son and daughter to political ambitions of the English royal family—both died in captivity—Constance nevertheless married again and defended her dukedom.

Little of this information bears directly on Shakespeare's *King John,* since in the play Constance, represented only as Geoffrey's widow, dies offstage after her famous outpouring of grief for Arthur. Jameson claims that Shakespeare violates history only by failing to mention Constance's last marriage, a detail superfluous to the action and damaging to its "dramatic interest." So why does Jameson dwell so insistently on her life? By writing Constance's biography, she treats Constance as an individual and refutes oversimplifications of her character. Jameson's identification with Constance, however, may run deeper. This portrait might be read as a defense of Constance's unorthodox married life, since Jameson herself had an unusual marriage. Anna Brownell Murphy and the dashing Robert Jameson had a tense courtship, clouded by ambivalence on both sides. Real trouble began within the first week of their marriage, according to family lore, when on Sunday, Robert insisted on dining with his usual friends. Anna joined him reluctantly, and when it began to rain, he left her—dressed in her wedding white—to walk home alone (*LW* 27). The marriage continued to defy conventional expectations. Robert Jameson, leaving England for a government post in the West Indies and then in Canada, wrote his wife a few tender letters but sent her little money and discouraged her from joining him. In 1836 Anna undertook the long and perilous journey to Canada that ended with their legal separation. In light of Jameson's biography, Constance's perseverance, rewarded at last by divorce and a felicitous marriage, looks suspiciously like wish-fulfillment. By drawing on personal experience in the portrait of Constance, Jameson follows her romantic psychology of reading to its logical conclusion, demonstrating, if not openly declaring, that a special affinity links Shakespeare's female characters and his female readers.

Despite her empathy with Shakespeare's heroines, particularly with those overlooked or underestimated by previous critics, Jameson does not act merely as an advocate for them. In the portrait of Constance, in particular, she is careful to offer a balanced view of her subject's character. On certain issues, such as the wisdom of her third and last marriage, Jameson defends Constance: "it can hardly, considering her age and the circumstances in which she was placed, be a just subject of reproach. During her hated union with Randal de Blondeville, and the years passed in a species of widowhood, she conducted herself with propriety: at least I can find no reason to judge otherwise." Certainly Jameson knew how passing the years in "a species of widowhood" felt. But she also expects her biography of Constance, the long recitation of wrongs done against her, to demonstrate that "there must have existed in the mind of Constance, with all her noble and amiable qualities, a deficiency somewhere,—a want of firmness, a want of judgment or wariness, and a total want of self-control" (*CW* 312). The portrait thus becomes a cautionary tale for those who would exceed the bounds of feminine modesty. In her preface to the *Memoirs of Celebrated Female Sovereigns,* as well, Jameson worries about the appeal of powerful and unconventional figures. Why, she asks with exasperation, "are victories always *glorious,* always *splendid?* Why must our sympathies be always enlisted on the side of successful ambition? Why must criminal or all-grasping power be ever exhibited under an aspect of greatness, when surely there is a reverse of the impression producing a far deeper and more useful lesson?"[12] A balanced portrayal of Queen Constance is more instructive than a sensational one; Jameson therefore has an educational aim in showing both sides of Constance's nature.

While her gender helps Jameson identify with Shakespeare's heroines, it also complicates her relationship with her readers. In the preface to *Characteristics of Women,* Jameson deals explicitly with the problems of women's authorship. In *Madwoman in the Attic,* Sandra Gilbert and Susan Gubar argue that "the literary woman has always faced equally degrading options when she had to define her public presence in the world. If she did not suppress her work entirely or publish it pseudonymously or anonymously, she could modestly confess her female 'limitations' and concentrate on the 'lesser' subjects reserved for ladies as becoming to their inferior powers."[13] Like many women writers of the nineteenth century, Jameson hides her aspirations with a show of modesty. When Medon asks Alda whether anyone will read her book, Alda represents herself first in the role of a diarist and acknowledges the concerns of a professional author only secondarily: "This little book was undertaken without a thought of fame or money: out of the fulness [*sic*] of my own heart and soul have I written it. In the pleasure it has given me, in the new and various views of human nature it has opened to me, in the beautiful and soothing images it has placed before me, in the exercise and improvement of my own faculties, I have already been repaid: if praise or profit come beside, they come as a surplus" (*CW* 2–3).

Packaging her Shakespearean criticism as the private musings of an introspective woman, Jameson tries both to interest and disarm the critics and, ultimately, to attract the largest possible readership from both sexes. For unlike Alda, she had real financial concerns. Daughter to a poor Irish miniature painter and wife to an ardent suitor who became a neglectful husband, Jameson wrote for money. Even in childhood she assumed financial responsibility for her parents and sisters. Her literary labors were therefore designed to sell, and the financial ins and outs of publishing were often on her mind. When Anna finally went to Canada to join her husband, she took with her the plates she was engraving for a new edition of *Characteristics*. An American edition, Jameson hoped at the time, might bring her badly needed income; in letters to family and friends, the problems of getting those plates printed from provincial Toronto, the financial danger caused by her inability to find a courier who would take the plates to New York, and her hopes for revenue from the new edition were recorded along with details about the separation.[14]

Characteristics of Women therefore deals cautiously with feminist politics. When Medon teasingly suggests that Alda hopes to prove the superiority of her own sex, Alda reassuringly disclaims any intention of "speculating on the rights of women—nonsense! why should you suspect me of such folly?—it is quite out of date. Why should there be competition or comparison?" (*CW* 3–4). Nevertheless, concern for women's treatment in a society that marred their moral and intellectual faculties with bad education, trivial occupations, or stultifying work—concern that embraced women from Canada's Indian tribes as well as English governesses—was a constant theme of Anna Jameson's writing.[15]

Jameson not only comments on woman's social position, she thinks specifically about how her own writing can empower other women; in this way, she defines for herself an audience of women readers. Digressing into a condemnation of women's education in the preface to *Characteristics of Women*, Alda argues that the English system turns out "hard, clever, sophisticated girls, trained by knowing mothers and all-accomplished governesses, with whom vanity and expediency take place of conscience and affection." These girls, their "feelings and passions suppressed or contracted, not governed by higher faculties and purer principles," learn to follow opinion rather than the "light of virtue within their own souls." Women produced by such an educational system become self-caricatures: "Hence the strange anomalies of artificial society—girls of sixteen who are models of manner, miracles of prudence, marvels of learning, who sneer at sentiment, and laugh at the Juliets and the Imogens; and matrons of forty, who, when the passions should be tame and wait upon the judgment, amaze the world and put us to confusion with their doings" (*CW* 28). Reading Shakespeare, it seems, provides women with an alternative kind of education, schooling their moral faculties by deepening rather than suppressing their passions. Jameson frequently criticizes the education of English women and offers her own books as wholesome and substantial alternatives to the usual works designed for women. Thus, she addresses herself specifically to women without dismissing other readers.

As she defines her audience, singling out women as a special group, Jameson defines her role as critic. Her participation in the romantic tradition of Shakespearean criticism, by allowing her to claim a special kinship with Shakespeare's female characters, also lets her claim a special authority for her readings of them. In her preface to the *Characteristics of Women*, Jameson as critic mediates between woman characters and those male critics whom she wishes to replace as the reader's confidante and guide.

In the dialogue between Alda and Medon, Alda wields her authority as critic to defend Shakespeare's women but also uses the characters as talismans against the fraternity of established critics. Both movements in this complicated dance revolve around the male critic, whose authority Jameson appropriates even as she discredits him. Typically, Alda begins with a concession. When Medon reminds her that most critics think Shakespeare's women inferior to his men, Alda readily agrees: "In Shakespeare the male and female characters bear precisely the same relation to each other that they do in nature and in society—they are not equal in prominence or in power; they are subordinate throughout" (*CW* 15–16). Thus, Juliet's passion is mild compared to Othello's; Constance's frantic grief over her son takes second place to Lear's madness. Yet a few pages later, after a discussion of Shakespeare's "humorous" women, Alda qualifies herself, arguing that "on the whole, if there are people who, taking the strong and essential distinction of sex into consideration, still maintain that Shakespeare's female characters are not, in truth, in variety, in power, equal to his men, I think I shall prove the contrary" (*CW* 22). Alda—or Jameson—claims for herself a place in the critical tradition by shifting the grounds of her discussion. Her argument turns on the words "truth" and "power." Initially, Alda measures Shakespeare's women by their behavior: since the men suffer more hyperbolic fits of passion, the women have less "power." So far, Jameson accepts the position, articulated by William Richardson and implied by Coleridge, that Shakespeare fails to individuate his women because society gives women less scope for significant action than men. But in the second instance "power," now coupled with "truth," becomes an aesthetic standard; claiming that Shakespeare does distinguish his female characters, Jameson confers power on them.

While Alda rescues Shakespeare's women from masculine misconceptions, the characters also shield her from criticism. To argue that the characters are fit reading material for young girls, Jameson allows Medon (rather than Alda) to quote Coleridge's praise of Shakespeare's high moral character: "I think it is Coleridge who so finely observes, that Shakespeare ever kept the high road of human life whereon all travel, that he did not pick out by-paths of feeling and sentiment; in him we have no moral highwaymen, and sentimental thieves and rat-catchers, and interesting villains, and amiable, elegant adulteresses" (*CW* 24–25). Medon exploits this text for a sermon against those critics who, like Iago, "rip to pieces" Desdemona's reputation for virtue. Alda, having listened patiently to Medon's long discursus, wittily expresses a fear that she herself, as a writer, will suffer Desdemona's fate at the hands of Iago's critical counterparts: "Heavens bless me from such critics! Yet if genius, youth, and innocence could not escape unslurred, can I hope to do so?" she asks (*CW* 26). But Alda, despite her sarcastic timidity, surreptitiously strengthens her position, first by aligning herself with Coleridge, Shakespeare's venerable interpreter, then with Desdemona, Shakespeare's spotless heroine. Jameson's appeals to conventional pieties and her deference to male authority, filtered through the persona of Alda, allow her to assume authority under a mask of decorum.

In her attempt to place herself within the tradition of Shakespearean criticism, Jameson most nearly approaches contemporary women critics. For instance, in her feminist essay on *Othello,* Carol Thomas Neely positions herself as Jameson does, in opposition to the play's men and to the critics who resemble them. Neely identifies two kinds of critics for *Othello:* those who take Othello's perspective and those who take Iago's. Both groups badly underestimate Desdemona. Neely, taking a different standpoint, allies herself with Emilia. That Jameson identifies with Desdemona while Neely identifies with Emilia indicates the relative distance between Jameson's feminism and that of contemporary critics, especially with regard to attitudes toward sexuality.[16]

In all of her portraits, Jameson is shaping her own identity as Shakespearean critic. Writing, as we have seen, against both Siddons's emphasis on Constance's motherliness and Hazlitt's emphasis on her powerlessness, Jameson argues that Shakespeare shows intellect, sympathy, and moral fibre in refusing either to sentimentalize or to denigrate Constance; by using historical evidence to corroborate his characterization, she stresses her own intellect and moral sense.[17] In her portrait of Lady Macbeth, which concludes the *Characteristics of Women,* the power of Jameson's rhetoric comes from a particularly energetic interplay of critic, character, and male predecessors. She begins by satirizing vulgar opinion, which reduces Lady Macbeth to "a fierce, cruel woman, brandishing a couple of daggers, and inciting her husband to butcher a poor old king" (*CW* 369). But the impact of Jameson's portrait comes less from its conclusion than its method, and from the intimacy that develops between character and critic. For her examination of Lady Macbeth, Jameson moves from aesthetic to moral criteria, surreptitiously appropriating the authority of previous critics while she mitigates Lady Macbeth's guilt. Jameson finds her place in the critical tradition by discussing Lady Macbeth's verisimilitude, setting history against poetry in a debate that had been commonplace since the sixteenth century. Lady Macbeth belongs to the realm of poetry, not to history, Jameson argues: "She is Lady Macbeth; as such she lives, she reigns, and is immortal in the world of imagination. What earthly title could add to her grandeur?" (*CW* 367). More specifically, she is like an antique statue, whose figure is visible below her drapery: "We trace through the folds the fine and true proportions of the figure beneath: they seem and are independent of each other to the practised eye, though carved together from the same enduring substance; at once perfectly distinct and eternally inseparable" (*CW* 368). Her character, then, has an organic unity that makes it true to human nature; history forces us to infer character from events and misleading circumstances, but Shakespeare, by showing us what human nature *is,* enables us to judge the action from the individual, rather than the reverse. Thus he lifts us from mundane reality to the possible.

Beginning with a defense of Shakespeare's "truth to nature," Jameson establishes her credentials as a critic; because she prefaces the more controversial defense of Lady Macbeth with a familiar argument from aesthetics, she deflects potential antagonism from herself and from Lady Macbeth. Next she dissects Lady Macbeth's moral nature, for she wants to argue that Lady Macbeth is more than a beautifully crafted object; she is a woman who represents our own passions magnified. "Those who can feel and estimate the magnificent conception and poetical development of the character," she says, nevertheless "have overlooked the grand moral lesson it conveys; they forget that the crime of Lady Macbeth terrifies us in proportion as we sympathise with her; and that this sympathy is in proportion to the degree of pride, passion, and intellect we may ourselves possess" (*CW* 369). In this way, aesthetic appreciation leads both to sympathy and to moral judgment.

As usual, Jameson's argument begins with the conventional wisdom: "True it is, that the ambitious women of these civilized times do not murder sleeping kings: but are there, therefore, no Lady Macbeths in the world? no women who, under the influence of a diseased or excited appetite for power or distinction, would sacrifice the happiness of a daughter, the fortunes of a husband, the principles of a son, and peril their own souls?" (*CW* 369).[18] This indictment of women is misleading, however, for it becomes the linchpin of Jameson's defense of Lady Macbeth against Hazlitt's strictures against her in his essay on Macbeth. Jameson re-evaluates Lady Macbeth first by asserting her humanity, then by examining external influences on her, and finally by highlighting her conventionally "feminine" qualities. Hazlitt thinks of her as a "great bad woman, whom we hate, but whom we fear more than we hate" (*CSP* 18). Jameson objects to the easy assumption that Lady Macbeth lacks both humanity and the power to arouse empathy, for an extended treatment of a

Shakespearean character in the nineteenth century depends on these two conditions. Jameson argues that although Lady Macbeth may be a "terrible impersonation of evil passions and mighty powers," she is never "cast beyond the pale of our sympathies" (*CW* 372). Nor does she become inhuman; Lady Macbeth remains within her sex and within humanity in general. Jameson then turns to Macbeth himself. Since Hazlitt refers Macbeth's downfall to his wife's strong influence over him, Jameson lays some blame at Macbeth's feet, for the idea of murdering Duncan occurs first to Macbeth, before his reunion with his wife. His letter, in fact, affects her as the Weird Sisters' prophecy affects him; "the guilt is thus more equally divided than we should suppose, when we hear people pitying 'the noble nature of Macbeth,' bewildered and goaded on to crime, solely or chiefly by the instigation of his wife" (*CW* 373).

Establishing that Macbeth is responsible for his own destruction, Jameson can then counter the related assumption that Lady Macbeth exhibits a perversely "masculine" nature; Hazlitt, for instance, links Lady Macbeth's ascendancy over her husband to her "masculine firmness" of will. Jameson insists that although Lady Macbeth is ruled by "strong-nerved ambition," a phrase she adopts from Hazlitt, Lady Macbeth's character retains always a "touch of womanhood" (*CSP* 18). Having suggested in the beginning of her essay that real women can behave as monstrously as Lady Macbeth does, Jameson now suggests that Lady Macbeth retains some qualities of ordinary women. Hazlitt contends that Lady Macbeth's fault is a "strong principle of self-interest and family aggrandisement" that destroys her sense of compassion and justice; Jameson, on the other hand, thinks that Lady Macbeth is ambitious less for herself than for her husband. She also examines Lady Macbeth's behavior after the murder of Duncan, when she suffers from nervous weakness even while she struggles to sustain her husband. The final descent into madness proves not that she has lost her humanity but rather that conscience remains powerful within her. In this chapter, which concludes her book, Jameson seeks not so much to exonerate Lady Macbeth as to discover mitigating circumstances that make her a complex character, and she succeeds.[19]

Although Jameson wants to join the ranks of respectable critics, and for this reason mingles deference with defiance, not all of her negotiations with critical tradition and with her own pedagogical imperative involve accommodating herself to social and literary authority. In her portrait of Isabella, in particular, Jameson defies critical opinion: first, by transferring to Isabella qualities generally associated with Shakespeare's heroes and, second, by using the male critics' own language against them. In this, perhaps her most radical portrait, Jameson begins by critiquing the general lack of appreciation for Isabella: "Johnson, and the rest of the black-letter crew, pass her over without a word. One critic, a lady-critic too, whose name I will be so merciful as to suppress, treats Isabella as a coarse vixen." The lady-critic was probably Charlotte Lennox, but Jameson's real target is Hazlitt, who "with that strange perversion of sentiment and want of taste which sometimes mingle with his piercing and powerful intellect, dismisses Isabella with a slight remark, that 'we are not greatly enamoured of her rigid chastity, nor can feel much confidence in the virtue that is sublimely good at another's expense.' What shall we answer to such criticism?" (*CW* 75).

Jameson's reply is an oblique attack on the romantic preference for Shakespeare's chaste, but passive, daughters. For Coleridge, for instance, Miranda epitomizes Shakespearean womanhood. In her we find "the sweet, yet dignified feeling of all that *continuates* society, as sense of ancestry and of sex, with a purity unassailable by sophistry" (*SC* 1:119). For Coleridge, Miranda typifies cultural and moral virtue; she is a perfect mirror of social ideals. Isabella, in Hazlitt's view, puts herself before others and so falls short of this romantic standard for perfection. Jameson counters by claiming that Isabella's qualities are perfectly combined and modulated; although she has no marked eccentricities to make her ridiculous, Isabella is distinguished particularly by her "fine powers of reasoning, and that natural uprightness and purity which no sophistry can warp, and no allurement betray" (*CW* 70). Adapting Coleridge's phrase for Miranda when she praises Isabella's "purity which no sophistry can warp," Jameson calls attention to her softer female virtues as well as to her intellect.

Having evoked Isabella's "femininity," however, Jameson then proves her to be capable of passion, which Victorians generally considered unfeminine. To illustrate the paradoxical union of opposites in her subject, Jameson turns to the Coleridgean model for Shakespeare's tragic heroes, most carefully developed in his characterization of Hamlet. While Hamlet's excessive meditation smothers his passions and slows his revenge, Isabella's religious rigor restrains her passions until at last they break out forcefully, first against Angelo, then against her brother. It is "the strong undercurrent of passion and enthusiasm flowing beneath this calm and saintly self-possession, it is the capacity for high feeling and generous and strong indignation veiled beneath the sweet austere composure of the religious recluse, which, by the very force of contrast, powerfully impress the imagination" (*CW* 73). So just as Hamlet's love for Ophelia finally "blazes out" in Coleridge's interpretation of that play, Isabella pleads for her brother's life in broken sentences "poured from the abundance of her heart"; and later, when her brother begs Isabella to accept Angelo's terms, "her scorn has a bitterness and her indignation a force of expression almost fearful" (*SC* 1:33; *CW* 68, 74). In this way, Jameson's Isabella breaks with literary and social stereotype.[20]

Anna Jameson offers by far the most complex reading of Isabella from the period. To represent her nature adequately, Jameson turns to a landscape metaphor. She identifies many characters by such a metaphor, but this is her most striking. Distinguishing Isabella from Portia, Jameson identifies Portia as a radiant, fruitful orange tree; Isabella, by contrast,

> is like a stately and graceful cedar, towering on some Alpine cliff, unbowed and unscathed amid the storm. She gives us the impression of one who has passed under the ennobling discipline of suffering and self-denial: a melancholy charm tempers the natural vigour of her mind: her spirit seems to stand upon an eminence, and look down upon the world as if already enskyed and sainted; and yet, when brought in contact with that world which she inwardly despises, she shrinks back with all the timidity natural to her cloistral education. (*CW* 66)

Jameson builds her extended metaphor from Lucio's brief tribute to Isabella as a thing "enskyed and sainted." But although she often uses Shakespeare's language for her descriptions, the comparison between Isabella and an alpine cedar relates less to Shakespeare's play than to romantic encomiums of Shakespeare or of his tragic heroes. Coleridge uses a comparable analogy for Shakespeare, describing him as a "self-sustaining pine, the monarch of some Norwegian precipice, now mourning with a sea-like, almost soul-like voice, as if the spirit of the calm were wooing the breezes in its branches" (*SC* 1:215).[21] Hazlitt, similarly, sees King Lear as being like a "sharp rock circled by the eddying whirlpool that foams and beats against it, or like the solid promontory pushed from its basis by the force of an earthquake" (*CSP* 154).

The use of nature metaphors to praise Shakespeare's genius is standard critical procedure. But Hazlitt, for instance, chooses metaphors that resonate with *King Lear's* plot, alluding both to the tempest on the heath and the cliff from which Gloucester attempts suicide. By picturing Isabella as a "stately cedar"—using an image divorced from *Measure for Measure's* action but associated with Shakespeare and his noble heroes—Jameson lifts her above the social stereotypes perpetuated by other critics of the period. Jameson therefore uses allegory to tip the balance between opposites in Isabella's character. She has "firmness of character" but, in a crisis, shrinks back with the timidity imposed by her cloistral education. Yet in the passage describing Isabella as a blasted cedar on the cliff, only her strength and will are actually figured; we are told of her timidity but cannot visualize it.[22] As Jameson ennobles Isabella, she strengthens her own identity as critic by revising the insights and language of her masculine rivals.

Although her "re-visions" of Shakespeare's heroines ensure her a place in the history of Shakespearean criticism, Jameson's work is less important for *what* she says than *how* she says it. In Shakespeare's plays, "every man sees himself without knowing that he sees himself," says Coleridge. In Shakespeare's plays, Anna Jameson sees herself dignified and transformed, but she seems to achieve a greater self-consciousness about the relationship between character and critic than her male counterparts do. Alda, in the preface to the *Characteristics of Women,* remarks that analyzing some of Shakespeare's heroines is "like intercepting the dew-drop or the snow-flake ere it fell to earth" and like "subjecting it to a chemical analysis." Although Alda relishes the opportunity to dissect and analyze these ephemeral women, her reaction is complex: she respects the integrity of those women she discusses—they are formed as perfectly as snowflakes or dewdrops—even as she celebrates her own power as critic.

Working within the constraints of her received rhetoric, Anna Jameson revises traditional judgments of better-known Shakespearean heroines and brings new figures to the foreground. She anticipates and makes possible later feminist criticism, although she sees more in these characters than we do: today feminists are more likely to view Isabella and Lady Macbeth as the pawns of patriarchy, and Shakespeare's willful queens are largely ignored. Jeanne Addison Roberts, who shares Jameson's pedagogical anxieties, argues that in the Shakespearean plays usually studied "our school systems institutionalize for secondary school students a painfully constricted view of possible female roles."[23] Jameson, within her own cultural context, does much to expand the repertoire of available female roles. In her most vigorously argued essays, she not only recreates Shakespeare's characters in her own image, she invites female readers to recreate themselves. Through her artistry, Anna Jameson makes Shakespeare a province for women.

NOTES

Research for this essay was completed with a fellowship from the University of Georgia Humanities Center.

1. Clara Thomas, in her biography of Jameson, writes that the *Characteristics of Women* went through ten editions before Jameson's death in 1860 and through twenty editions by 1920 (Clara Thomas, *Love and Work Enough: The Life of Anna Jameson* [Toronto: University of Toronto Press, 1967], 72. Future references to this work, abbreviated as *LW,* will be incorporated into the text.) Tabulating the editions of Jameson's book is complicated by its appearance under the title *Shakespeare's Heroines* and by the presence of American editions, some of which derive from the 1837 American edition printed under Jameson's direction,

others from the third and fourth London editions. My own perusal of the *National Union Catalogue* suggests that at least eighteen separate editions appeared before 1925.

2. See, for instance, Gerard Manley Hopkins, "Letter to Alexander Baillie," Sept. 6, 1863, in *A Hopkins Reader*, ed. John Pick (London: Oxford University Press, 1953), 71, and *One Touch of Shakespeare: Letters of Joseph Crosby to Joseph Parker Norris, 1875–1878*, ed. John W. Velz and Frances N. Teague (Washington, D.C.: Folger Library, 1986), 88.

3. Most histories of Shakespearean criticism do not pay much attention to Jameson. Perhaps her critical fortunes will now change: Harry Levin, in an essay on "Critical Approaches to Shakespeare from 1660 to 1904," mentions Jameson as an early female Shakespearean, noting neutrally her feminist agenda (*The Cambridge Companion to Shakespeare Studies*, ed. Stanley Wells [Cambridge: Cambridge University Press, 1986], 225–26).

4. Nina Auerbach, *Woman and the Demon: The Life of a Victorian Myth* (Cambridge: Harvard University Press, 1982), 211.

5. Samuel Taylor Coleridge, *Philosophical Lectures* (London: Pilot Press, 1949), 179.

6. Samuel Taylor Coleridge, *Shakespearean Criticism*, ed. Thomas Middleton Raysor, Everyman's Library, 2 vols. (London: Dent; New York: Dutton, 1960), 2:252. Future references to this work, abbreviated as *SC*, will be incorporated into the text. See also William Hazlitt, *Characters of Shakespear's Plays*, 2nd ed. (London: Taylor and Hessey, 1818), 42–43. Future references to this work, abbreviated as *CSP*, will be incorporated into the text. For my understanding of Hazlitt's ideas about character, I am indebted to Joel Haefner's essay, " 'The Soul Speaking in the Face': Hazlitt's Conception of Character," *Studies in English Literature* 24 (1984): 655–70.

7. *Coleridge on Shakespeare: The Text of the Lectures of 1811–12*, ed. R. A. Foakes (London: Routledge and Kegan Paul, 1971), 102.

8. Anna Jameson, *Characteristics of Women: Moral, Political, and Historical*, new ed. (London: George Bell and Sons, 1879), 19. Future references to this work, abbreviated as *CW*, will be incorporated into the text.

9. For *King John*'s stage history, see Eugene Waith, "*King John* and the Drama of History," *Shakespeare Quarterly* 29 (1978): 192–211.

10. Frances Ann Kemble, *Records of a Girlhood*, 2nd ed. (New York: Henry Holt, 1879), 517.

11. Jameson may also be drawing on conversations with Fanny Kemble. Kemble writes that Constance's maternal love is mixed with a love of power, since Arthur represents the continuation of Constance's reign: "he was her royal child, and that I do not think she ever forgot till he was, in her imagination, her dead child" (Kemble, *Records of a Girlhood*, 517). Jameson herself must have felt that Kemble was a powerful influence on the *Characteristics of Women*, because she dedicated the book to her actress friend.

12. Jameson, *Memoirs of Celebrated Female Sovereigns*, 2 vols. (New York: J. J. Harper, 1832), 1:xvi, microfilm.

13. Sandra M. Gilbert and Susan Gubar, *The Madwoman in the Attic: The Woman Writer and the Nineteenth-Century Imagination* (New Haven: Yale University Press, 1979), 64. Elaine Showalter makes the related point that Victorian women writers, faced with a "critical double standard," reinforced it "by playing down the effort behind their writing, and trying to make their work appear as the spontaneous overflow of their womanly emotions," a tactic used also by Jameson's Alda. (Elaine Showalter, *A Literature of Their Own: British Women Novelists From Brontë to Lessing* [Princeton: Princeton University Press, 1977], 83).

14. Thomas, *Love and Work Enough*, 98–126 passim; [Beatrice C.] Erskine, *Anna Jameson: Letters and Friendships (1812–1860)* (New York: E. P. Dutton, n.d.), 129–60 passim.

15. In *Winter Studies and Summer Rambles in Canada* (1838), Jameson compares the status of Indian women with that of European women; in *Memoirs of the Beauties of the Court of Charles II* (1831), she considers the degradation of women to "objects of pleasure" in that court. Her *Memoirs and Essays* (1845) contains two pieces on women's rights, "Women's Mission and Women's Position" and "The Relative Position of Mothers and Governesses."

16. Carol Thomas Neely, "Woman and Men in *Othello*: 'What Should Such a Fool / Do with So Good a Woman?'" in *The Woman's Part: Feminist Criticism of Shakespeare*, ed. Carolyn Ruth Swift Lenz et al. (Urbana: University of Illinois Press, 1983), 211–39; revised in *Broken Nuptials in Shakespeare's Plays* (New Haven: Yale University Press, 1985), 105–35. Many of the essays in *The Woman's Part* revise existing readings of Shakespeare by adopting the perspective of women characters within the plays.

17. Given her infatuation with the Kemble family—Fanny Kemble was Sarah Siddons's niece—but also given the fact that she had lost to Thomas Campbell the opportunity to write Siddons's biography, Jameson must have regarded Siddons's opinions with mixed feelings.

18. Here Jameson seems to be working from Hazlitt's observation that Lady Macbeth's "fault seems to have been an excess of that strong principle of self-interest and family aggrandisement, not amenable to the common feelings of compassion and justice, which is so marked a feature in barbarous nations and times" (*Characters of Shakespear's Plays*, 21).

19. Jameson's essay makes an interesting comparison with Joan Larsen Klein's essay on Lady Macbeth. Like Jameson, Klein blames Macbeth for his own downfall, and like Jameson, she sees traditionally womanly qualities in Lady Macbeth. (Klein refers to Coleridge rather than to Jameson, however.) They differ in that Klein sees Lady Macbeth as more thoroughly shaped by traditional Renaissance views of the wife's role than Jameson does, and in that Klein sees Lady Macbeth's disintegration as more complete. Jameson thinks that even in madness Lady Macbeth feels the prompting of conscience (Joan Larsen Klein, "Lady Macbeth: 'Infirm of Purpose,'" in *The Woman's Part*, 240–55.)

20. Again, the value of chastity for Jameson's Victorian feminism, by contrast with 1980s feminism, emerges in the lack of a recent feminist defense of Isabella. Kathleen McLuskie imagines how a feminist production could deny the lively sexuality of *Measure for Measure*'s pimps and bawds and "celebrate Isabella's chastity

as feminist resistance," but says that this would "require a radical rewriting both of the narrative and of the way the scenes are constructed" ("The Patriarchal Bard: Feminist Criticism and Shakespeare: *King Lear* and *Measure for Measure*," in *Political Shakespeare: New Essays in Cultural Materialism*, ed. Jonathan Dollimore and Alan Sinfield (Ithaca: Cornell University Press, 1985), 88, 97). See also Marcia Riefer, " 'Instruments of Some Mightier Member': The Constriction of Female Power in *Measure for Measure*," *Shakespeare Quarterly* 35 (1984): 157–69.

21. Although Raysor identifies this fragment as an introduction to Coleridge's fourth lecture of 1818, he also says that it was not published prior to his own collection of Coleridge's criticism.

22. In a sketch written shortly after the actress's death, Jameson uses metaphor in a similar way to describe the legendary Sarah Siddons: "I remember that the first time I found myself in the same room with Mrs. Siddons (I was then about twenty), I gazed on her as I should have gazed at one of the Egyptian pyramids—nay, with a deeper awe, for what is material and physical immensity, compared with moral and poetical grandeur?" (Jameson, *Visits and Sketches, at Home and Abroad*, 2 vols. [New York: Harper and Bros., 1834], 1:279). Sarah Siddons, as a "pyramid," has the same presence and permanence that Jameson attributes to Isabella, that Hazlitt attributes to Lear, and that Coleridge attributes to Shakespeare. Thus, Jameson appropriates masculine metaphors of endurance and monumentality for these exceptional women.

23. Jeanne Addison Roberts, "Making a Woman and Other Institutionalized Diversions," *Shakespeare Quarterly* 37 (1986): 367.

MARY LOEFFELHOLZ

Miranda in the New World:
The Tempest *and Charlotte Barnes's*
The Forest Princess

Born in 1810, daughter of theatrical parents, Charlotte Mary Sanford Barnes made her debut on the American stage in 1834 at Philadelphia's Arch Street Theater, playing Juliet to her mother's Romeo. In 1847 she married the actor E. S. Connor, whose acting experience encompassed several of the larger (if seldom quite the leading) male Shakespearean parts, among them Iago, Macduff, Laertes, and Edgar.[1] Charlotte's own acting attracted less notice in her lifetime than did her two major plays, which she collected and published along with other works in her *Plays, Prose and Poetry* (1848). *Octavia Bragaldi,* a verse revenge drama in five acts, was "performed more than fifty nights in the United States, and in London and Liverpool," following its 1837 opening in Philadelphia, according to Barnes's own publication blurb.[2] *The Forest Princess; or, Two Centuries Ago,* although never so successful as *Octavia Bragaldi,* played in Liverpool in 1844 and opened in Philadelphia in 1848, with Barnes herself starring as Pocahontas and her husband in the role of Powhatan.[3] Both verse dramas bear the imprint of Barnes's experience with Shakespeare on the American stage, at a time when Shakespeare as an ideological property was undergoing a complex conversion in the United States— from pre-Revolutionary Tory to something like an American national romantic. That conversion is too complicated and as yet too little known to sketch in this space,[4] but it surely informs Barnes's own playwriting practice, which both called upon and helped reproduce the prestige of "Shakespeare" for the mid-nineteenth-century American drama.

The Forest Princess is (among other things) Barnes's revision of *The Tempest*—the earliest of the spate of "Indian plays" in the nineteenth-century United States, so far as I know, to bear a fairly distinct relation to Shakespeare's text.[5] Its transatlantic production history is anything but incidental to Barnes's revisionary themes, for *The Forest Princess* represented a consolidated American national identity, forged from "native" as well as colonial materials, to the play's English audience as much as to the United States' theater-going public. Barnes's Pocahontas/Miranda is a good-will ambassadress from the new nation to the old kingdom. In her introduction to *The Forest Princess,* Barnes claims that "but for the benefactions of Pocahontas, Virginia would have been lost to England": "How far the aspect of civilization, of national character and government, of literature and science, in America, would have been affected, had other lands given customs, laws, and language to so extensive and central a portion of our continent, is a question well worthy of consideration, and in justice to Pocahontas, should ever be associated with her name" (148). Pocahontas, Barnes might have said, made America safe for Shakespeare. Her romance perpetually compliments the parent culture while ennobling the new.

The Forest Princess looks homeward, though, as well: its composition and performance history coincide not only with a particular moment in American-British relations, but with a tragic epoch in the diaspora of the American Indian population, and a fundamental shift in white American thinking about the American Indian peoples. The mass forced removals of American Indians from the eastern United States had begun in the 1830s and were still proceeding, against the few remaining southeastern pockets of Indian settlement, in the 1840s. Popular sympathy for the Indians was fairly widespread in the northeastern states, where—as Southerners and Westerners did not fail to point out—the native Indian population had long ago been exterminated or driven away. Even among relatively sympathetic white observers, however, the notion that American Indians were destined to racial extinction gained currency in the 1830s and 1840s. "Indian Removal represented a major victory for ideas which, though long latent in American society, became fully explicit only after 1830." These new ideas made themselves felt in literary representations of American Indians: "there was a common assumption that the Indian was doomed to inevitable extinction."[6]

The rarer actual American Indians became in the United States, however, the more accessible their history became to appropriation by a national culture in search of legitimating traditions of identity. By the 1840s both Shakespeare and the American Indians could be pressed into the service of American romantic cultural nationalism. In Barnes's rewriting of *The Tempest,* the characters of Shakespeare's play and the contemporary figure of the vanishing American Indian collaborate in the expression of American post-Revolutionary "national character."[7] And Barnes's gendered interests in rewriting Shakespeare, her romantic reconstruction of Pocahontas/Miranda's crucial "instrumentality on earth" (147) firmly link American *womanhood* to American post-Revolutionary national identity.[8] *The Forest Princess* represents and renegotiates issues of gender in *The Tempest* along with those of race, colonialism, and nationality.

Barnes's introduction to *The Forest Princess* stresses her historical research into the Smith-Pocahontas story and her own fidelity to the historical record, even at the cost of coherent dramatical construction. The "charm" of Pocahontas's story, she writes, lies in the "certainty and truth" of all the particulars of her biography. This factual certainty Barnes claims to have preserved, despite the problems posed by the story's "unconquerable" lack of dramatic unity: Pocahontas saves John Smith yet marries John Rolfe, yielding a plot split down the middle rather than a coherent romance (147–48). Barnes's diagnosis of her play's structural problems is disarmingly accurate; her claims to historical fidelity are untenable (even though she does resist the perennial temptation to rewrite history by turning John Smith into Pocahontas's romantic lead).[9] Barnes in fact, I will argue, evolved her characters and shaped her play into what conventional unity it enjoys partly through reference, conscious or unconscious, to the plot and characters of *The Tempest*—perhaps not the first reader to yield to or exploit the "tempting fancy" of linking Miranda with Pocahontas, and certainly not the last.[10] Barnes's play evokes at its margins the still-tangled interplay between colonial history, documentary sources, and *The Tempest*. Her unnoted departures from the historical record (partly fictional as that itself may or may not be), her account of the father-daughter relationship between Powhatan and Pocahontas, her invented love scenes, and her emphases within the available historical material, swing Barnes's Indian drama into the orbit of Shakespeare's.

The Forest Princess's three-part structure reflects the incorrigible lack of unity of which Barnes complained in the Pocahontas story. The first act tells the famous story of Pocahontas's intervention to save the life of John Smith; the second act relates the John Rolfe–Pocahontas courtship and Powhatan's concession of Virginia to England; the final act, set in England, brings Pocahontas to her deathbed vision of peace—a sort of masque or tableau vivant that recalls the stage-magic of *The Tempest*.

Divided into three scenes, the first act of *The Forest Princess* distantly echoes the dramatic structure of the opening two acts of *The Tempest*. We are introduced to the group of English colonists in the first and second scenes and then join the royal Indian father-daughter pair, Powhatan and Pocahontas, in the third, to learn of their reactions to the intruders' arrival. Like Miranda in *The Tempest* (1.2), Pocahontas is naturally disposed to be the foreigners' advocate. Powhatan would ask that "The God / Of ill rain curses" on the "pale-faced men" whose "white winged canoes" once more stand off the Virginia shore; Pocahontas, like Miranda attracted to a "brave vessel" with "some noble creature in her" (*Tempest* 1.2.6–7), urges mercy.

> *Pocahontas:* Though some were false.
> My father will not judge all harshly. Think!

Even amongst our own and other tribes
There oft are wicked and deceitful men—
So may it be with these. Remember too,
'Mongst those who landed here, and since went home
O'er the big waters, years ere I was born,
I've heard my father praise—ay! more than one—
Many for bravery stood eminent.

Powhatan: Thy voice breathes kindness ever. Pocahontas
Is her father's dearest child.

(1.3.167)

Just as for Miranda and Prospero in the parallel scene of *The Tempest,* Pocahontas and Powhatan's reactions to the intruders' arrival are constructed around a pre-history of injustice and usurpation, one that precedes the daughter's own firsthand knowledge or ability fully to recall. The nobility of certain individual men in the colonial parties notwithstanding, the intruders have been, and ever shall be, usurpers. Yet the daughter's gratuitous generosity towards them is necessary, even cultivated (with reservations) by her father—necessary for the romance plot of *The Forest Princess,* necessary for the fictive resolutions of political struggles (in both the past and present) that the play offers.

When Smith arrives in the Indian settlement, eager to strike a bargain with them to ensure the colonists will have food for the coming winter, Powhatan has him seized and threatens to kill him in the hopes of "driv-[ing] all rash intruders hence." Pocahontas pleads again for mercy, leading Powhatan again to rehearse (with anxious Prospero-like injunctions to "Mark me!") the past treachery of the colonists, adding a prescient warning about the future:

Powhatan: Thy father hates these strangers.—Mark me well.
They came in numbers ere thyself wast born.
Their deeds, their history, their conduct, *then,*
To our tribes will *ever* be the same.
The time will come they'll spread o'er all the land.
Foul tyranny and rapine they'll return
For friendly welcome and sweet mercy shown.
Defrauding or exterminating still
Our ancient race, until the red man's name
Will live but in the mem'ry of the past,
Or in some exile powerless, who sells
For a few ears of corn his father's land,
Lord of that soil where then he'll beg a grave.

Pocahontas: And *should* our race thus pass from earth away,
The shame will not be theirs, but their oppressors.
Who then, amidst the chronicles they keep,
This act of mercy by a forest-king
Full surely must record. Oh! spare him, father!

(1.3.173–74)

At a time when the English colonists still had to beg their subsistence from the native inhabitants, Powhatan comprehensively foresees the fate dealt out to the American Indians in the 1830s—exile from their lands—and its anticipated end: racial extinction. This is the first instance of Indian prophecy in *The Forest Princess*. Barnes employs the device liberally hereafter, as we shall see. It is a power that Powhatan and his daughter possess almost by way of compensation for their status as history's victims. Father and daughter deploy this power differently, however. Powhatan foretells his people's extinction; Pocahontas foretells their recuperation into white men's histories. She mediates, here and hereafter, between Indian oral prophecy and English written culture, the old regime and the new.

The historical Pocahontas's generosity towards the strangers in general, and John Smith in particular, is the single most salient point of correspondence between the characters of Pocahontas and Miranda and has often been remarked on. Barnes plays on this likeness and adds to it in *The Forest Princess,* assimilating her other characters into roles out of *The Tempest*. Powhatan's prophetic foresight links him to Shakespeare's Prospero, with the crucial difference that Powhatan lacks the power to shape the events he foretells.[11] We will hear more of Powhatan's extraordinarily prescient interpretations of the Englishmen's designs on Virginia in the second act. First, however, we must consider Barnes's departure from both the historical record and *The Tempest*'s dramatic pattern in her construction of *The Forest Princess*'s first two scenes, which introduce the English colonists.

In Barnes's play, John Smith's party—unlike Alonso's in *The Tempest*—arrives on Virginia's shores intact, and numbers among its members the very John Rolfe who would later marry Pocahontas. As a matter of historical fact, John Rolfe didn't arrive in Virginia until 1609, two years after the date of Pocahontas's intervention on Smith's behalf. His presence in the first scene is a departure not only from the historical record but also in a way from *The Tempest*'s dramatic pre-text, its underlying template for *The Forest Princess*'s romance: there Ferdinand, Miranda's destined husband, was separated from his father and the other voyagers by the storm and Prospero's magic; here Rolfe, Pocahontas's destined husband, is (historically speaking) prematurely a member of the 1607 English party. Yet for the purposes of her romance plot, it would seem that Barnes needed to defy historical fidelity, in this introductory scene, precisely in order to set up the (dramatically speaking) "correct" relationship between Smith and Rolfe, rewriting Rolfe's historical character into a version of Ferdinand's.

> *Smith:* Fair praise is merited by Master Rolfe.
> Who, all unused to labour, still hath toiled
> Without reward, hard as paid artisan,
> And from the savage brought to Britain young,
> Learned e'en as much as I.
>
> *Rolfe:*   You wrong me there.
> You are my elder and my better too:
> A soldier prudent, brave and tried, while I
> Wild for adventure, only hope to see
> The Indian countries noble Ralegh named,
> And with my sword to carve my way to fame
> And fortune—if I *can*.
>
> (1.1.152–53)

In this exchange, Barnes casts Rolfe vis-à-vis Smith as the much younger, wilder, and more romantic man, who (like Ferdinand on Prospero's island) undergoes a maturing trial of labor, for which he (like Ferdinand) will later be rewarded by love. Smith praises Rolfe for the discipline he has already attained, which Rolfe modestly disavows. Yet Rolfe has apparently distinguished himself enough already for Smith to mark him out from among the other colonists, and Rolfe will—modesty notwithstanding—distinguish himself further as a disciplined leader. This exchange and subsequent events in effect nominate Rolfe as Smith's natural heir, the second-in-command in the English party. The actual John Rolfe was neither so romantic, nor so prominent a colonial leader on his first arrival, nor so very youthful as he is repeatedly called in *The Forest Princess*.[12] Barnes remakes the historical John Rolfe as a romantic lead on Ferdinand's pattern, and as we shall see, he will later woo Pocahontas very much on Ferdinand's model.

The first two scenes of *The Forest Princess* also embroider on the historical record and borrow from events in *The Tempest*, introducing a usurpation subplot among the English colonists that roughly parallels the intrigue lauched by Sebastian and Antonio against Alonso, and the comic conspiracy of Trinculo, Stephano, and Caliban. When Smith departs for the Indian settlement, leaving Rolfe in charge, the lesser English colonists reveal their true natures. Todkill and Francis, like Trinculo and Stephano, fear the New World's dangers and only want to secure some vinous courage with which to confront them. Todkill flees from bears, Francis steals a flagon of wine, and they share a drink, regretting the England left behind them. They remain, however, fundamentally loyal to Rolfe and Smith. Only Volday, "a Switzer" (as the "Persons of the Drama" identifies him), seriously contemplates revenging himself on the colony's leaders. Smith has earlier rebuked him for trying to cheat the Indians; as Smith's deputy, Rolfe tells Volday that "of all / The lawless spirits here (and they are many,) / Thou art the hardest to control" (1.2.157). Volday challenges Smith's right to "lord it o'er the rest," to which Rolfe replies that Smith's demonstrated merits "give him right to rule o'er me, and thee." If we look for a Caliban in *The Forest Princess*, we will find him not with the American Indians but here: Volday is the only character in the play whose vision of freedom refuses to acknowledge "natural" law, nature's nobility, the only character who is truly and irredeemably foreign.

The first act of *The Forest Princess* ends with Pocahontas's rescue of Smith, leaving Volday's usurpation plots to carry into the ensuing action. The second act, which Barnes dates in 1609, actually conflates historical events from 1609—when Rolfe arrived in Virginia and John Smith left for England after being injured in a shipboard explosion—through 1613–14, when Pocahontas was captured by the English colonists, instructed in Christianity, and finally married to John Rolfe. As the second act opens, the English colonists are in desperate straits for food. Smith and Rolfe are once again allied in keeping order, and Volday conspires both to revenge his humiliations at their hands and to establish himself as ruler over the Indians:

> *Volday [apart]*: Were not these fools so tame,
> So swayed by Smith and Rolfe, I know that some
> Would back me in the strife. So let it be.
> The secret messages I've sent unto
> The savage king, have prospered, and he knows
> The fitting time for ambush and surprise.
> These patient victims then will fall, and I,
> Rewarded, honoured by the savages,
> In time in lawless luxury may live
> And reign amid these forests.

> (2.1.182)

Volday's "lawless" ambitions again stamp him as the Caliban of Barnes's forest—a "monster," as his temporary ally Powhatan will later call him (206). (His later willingness to spill the blood of his "own people" in achieving his ambitions, however, links him as well to *The Tempest's* Antonio, arguably the more unsympathetic character, who conspires against his own king.) Volday's plan, like his displaced "Switzer" ethnic identity, signals his Calibanish status as an outsider and transgressor of cultural boundaries. Alone among the play's Europeans, he envisions a kind of "crossing over," "going native"—although of course only as king of the hill.[13] His plotted transgression, of course, is precisely the monstrous mirror image of Pocahontas's romantic saga: only a monstrous European would imagine becoming an Indian, only a saintly Indian maiden could become an English lady. While Barnes's play on its face ennobles the Indians, refusing to cast them as Calibans, her romance plot (perhaps inevitably) endorses this Anglocentric evaluation of cultural boundary-crossings. Volday symbolically becomes the Calibanish "bad Indian" (treacherous, shifty, sensual, greedy) and very nearly seduces the "good Indian," Powhatan, into collaborating with him.

While Volday plots against Virginia's rightful rulers—both Indian and English—John Rolfe at last meets, woos, and wins Pocahontas. The "Indian Ceres" (as Rolfe calls her[14]) sends a party with relief supplies to the English settlement; Rolfe volunteers to stand guard by the famine-devastated fort as the supplies are distributed. Dreaming of Pocahontas, with whom he declares himself already "half in love," he spies and shoots a panther about to seize upon the "recumbent form" of an unknown Indian woman. She rewards him with a string of shells, telling him, "Whate'er thy peril, send the forest maid / That little chain, her tribe will free thee straight" (185). Rolfe receives this token of reciprocal obligation in European fashion, as would a courtly lover, and asks his lady's name:

> *Rolfe:* No sainted relic e'er was treasured more
> Than this shall be for sake of her who gave it.
> But may I ask the gentle donor's name?
>
> *Pocahontas:* Matoka is my *name*. Virginia's tribes
> Know me as Pocahontas.

(2.1.185)

The European rhetoric of courtly romance and the Indian structure of reciprocal obligations and fictive kinship meet and mesh. This moment has no historical warrant in Barnes's sources, but it does have a dramatic precursor in *The Tempest*.[15] As in *The Tempest,* the exchange of a given name marks a decisive moment in Miranda / Pocahontas's Oedipal romance. Pocahontas takes Rolfe into the secrecy of her private family name, as Miranda in telling her name breaks for the first time her obedience to her father:

Ferdinand: I do beseech you,—
Chiefly that I might set it in my prayers,—
What is your name?

Miranda: Miranda,—O my father,
I have broke your hest to say so!

(*Tempest* 3.1.34–37)

The historical John Rolfe, a good Puritan, might not have relished the comparison between his lady's love-token and "sainted relics"; indeed, what little we know of his wooing suggests that courtly love was in no wise his idiom.[16] This scene with its exchange of names, however, evens up the mutual obligations between the English and the Indian parties. Having rescued Smith, Pocahontas is rescued by Rolfe, who thus in effect repays his father's debt to her—as Ferdinand in a sense repays his father's debt to Miranda.

Pocahontas and Rolfe's bond—composed in equal parts of imported romance and native reciprocal obligation—resolves the impending political crisis between the Indians and the colonists. Going to the English fort to warn the colonists of Volday's treachery, Pocahontas finds herself detained as a hostage until Powhatan shall sign a peace. By this point, the colonists and the Indians are both guilty of mutual trespasses against each other's peace; each has seized hostages and property from the other. The only true villain in the lot, however, proves to be Volday, who tries to play both sides. (The genuinely English colonists seem benevolent even in their trickery.) Volday is at the point of killing Rolfe, who is headed back to the fort to protest Pocahontas's capture, when Powhatan stays his hand. Powhatan intends to slay Rolfe himself—until he sees Pocahontas's token around Rolfe's neck and demands, "Stranger, speak! my child / Has left her father's home" (words truer than Powhatan can yet know). Knowing that Pocahontas is a prisoner, and realizing that the web of mutual obligation between the Indians and the colonists is too elaborated to disentangle, Powhatan arrives at a truce with the English.

The rest, as the saying goes, is history. The English colonists propose to knit up the peace with the marriage of Pocahontas to John Rolfe, a proposal obviously not unwelcome to the couple. Like Miranda and Ferdinand, they plight their troth in front of the whole reunited society, English and Indian. Sir Thomas Dale, the (rather Gonzalo-like) courtier, pronounces the predictable blessing: "This deed unites / In peace and love the Old World and the New." But the last, prophetic words belong to Powhatan, as they belong to Prospero in *The Tempest*. Powhatan delivers an epilogue on behalf of himself and his people. "The king / Of Powhatan's twelve tribes," he boasts, "can send his child / Well portioned to the stranger's wigwam" (2.4.223). For himself, however, he anticipates the time when

> her father's eyes
> Are closed, her kindred driven from the earth,
> As soon they will be, 'neath the crushing strikes
> Of thy vast nation. And when Powhatan,
> Like a true brave, his death-song calmly sings
> Amid his greatest feats of war, he'll proudly boast
> His richest trophy was his daughter's love.
>
> (2.4.223–24)

With Prospero's magical foresight, but without his ability to orchestrate events, Powhatan yields himself up to history, his daughter up to the romance of "nature's law," which declares that "The birds, when *fledged,* go forth—they meet their mates / And ne'er unto the parent nest return" (2.4.219–20).

From the standpoint of the romance plot, the final act of *The Forest Princess* is supererogatory, the story of what happens after Rolfe takes Pocahontas to live happily ever after. *The Tempest,* after all, concludes with Prospero's epilogue, not with Ferdinand and Miranda's unification of Milan and Naples. And Barnes's stagecraft, in these final scenes, is murkier than in the first two acts. All the Virginia characters return, running true to their previous form. The comic miscreant Todkill turns up in England, rehabilitated as a tavernkeeper (for whom Barnes writes some dialogue straight out of Shakespeare's *Henriad;* there seems no other motivation for his return). Volday reappears at Todkill's tavern, still hatching conspiracies—this time, implicating John Rolfe with Sir Walter Raleigh in a plot to turn Virginia into an independent dominion. On the strength of Volday's fabrications, Rolfe is imprisoned in the Tower; John Smith brings word of his seizure to Pocahontas. Appealing directly to Queen Anne and the Prince of Wales, Pocahontas wins her husband's release before finally expiring of homesickness in his arms.

If uncertain dramatically, however, and quite without historical foundation for its major events,[17] the final act is nevertheless fascinating, for in it Barnes offers a variety of displaced representations of the American war of independence. Indeed, Barnes's dramatic uncertainty here witnesses to the ideological difficulty of legitimating the American revolution for both British and American audiences. Barnes resolves her difficulties—dramatic and ideological—by conferring upon Pocahontas a final deathbed vision of peace, a vision that replaces her father's parting prophecies of racial extinction with a new romance of history and more distantly recalls Prospero's wedding masque for Miranda and Ferdinand in *The Tempest*. Barnes assigns the last word in visionary power to Miranda rather than Prospero, giving Miranda/Pocahontas the ambiguous power of scripting the play's romantic and political resolution.

The treasonable "conspiracy" for which Rolfe is arrested—"to establish an independent kingdom in Virginia" (245)—had of course already been accomplished, in a different form, by the time Barnes wrote *The Forest Princess*. In the play, the conspiracy is a trumped-up fiction. The only character guilty of actually conspiring to establish an independent kingdom in Virginia is, as we have already seen, Volday himself, who reports the alleged conspiracy to the king. Like Caliban's aspirations, Volday's dreamt-of kingdom is sensual, "lawless," savage, and doomed. Revolutionary conspiracies come from the world "outside" (Volday the "Switzer"), not from Englishmen. When will this change? How can Barnes's play represent—or anticipate—a successful revolution made by Englishmen against England herself?

I use the sexual trope for revolution—English*men* against the mother country— advisedly. The final act of *The Forest Princess* uneasily navigates the ideological gulf between an illicit, treacherous conspiracy and a natural, legitimate revolution; Barnes crosses these waters with the help of all the figurative possibilities of Pocahontas's gender. Pocahontas not only marries the New World to the Old; she symbolically dies while giving birth to the "Island-Mother" 's revolutionary progeny, "her Giant Child."

Barnes anticipates Pocahontas's dying vision of peace with an earlier moment in which Pocahontas implicitly lays claim to her father's power of prophetic insight. Pleading with Queen Anne and the Prince of Wales for Rolfe's release, Pocahontas addresses herself to Charles:

> *Pocahontas:* Sweet prince! death since hath claimed thy brother dear,
> Thou wilt be king. Then think. (For who can read
> The future!) Clouds may dim thy reign, and woes
> Arise, such as crowned heads but rarely know.
> Should troubles swarm, and death close up thy path,
> The thought that thou hast e'er the wretched soothed,
> Redressed a wrong, protected virtue—cheered,
> Sustained the weak, will more avail thee then
> Than all the thousands who thy crowning hail
> With—"Long live Charles the First!"
>
> *Charles:* Cease, lady, cease!
> Thy words prophetic seem and touch my soul.

(3.4.252–53)

Plainly, Pocahontas *can* read the future, and she has a particular aptitude for sensing impending revolutions and transfers of power. Revolutions can and will happen even among English subjects, indeed even on English soil. Rolfe will (in Barnes's fiction) be freed, but Raleigh (we know) will one day be revenged upon the Stuarts.

Compared to this dimly anticipated episode in English history, what Pocahontas foresees of the American revolution is wholly benign. Like the masque Prospero arranges for Ferdinand and Miranda in *The Tempest*, it is a vision of peace and plenty; unlike that masque, it reaches its triumphant conclusion. *"A strain of invisible music is heard, and thin clouds obscure the view from the casement."* The stage panorama then unfolds to take the audience back to Virginia: *"on the bank stands Powhatan, awaiting his daughter's arrival."* More clouds; they disperse *"to disclose in the distance, the form of Washington—the Genius of Columbia stands near him. Time hovers near, and Peace encircles with her arms the Lion and the Eagle"* (3.5.262–63). Pocahontas herself, as her vision concludes, supplies the authoritative interpretation of its allegory. "From that beloved soil where I drew breath / Shall noble chiefs arise," foremost among them he who shall be called " 'The Father of his Country!' " Pocahontas's interpretation completes the vision's familial allegory of revolution: "By ties of love and language bound, I see / The Island-Mother and her Giant Child" (264). Metaphors of nature and family, gigantically united in the soon-to-be United States, combine to yield a triumphantly inevitable logic of history: "Like the Great River of far Western wilds, / Improvement's course, *unebbing,* shall flow on."

Though benign on the face of it, this interpretation, symbolically speaking, costs Pocahontas her life in childbirth. Her vision represents the American revolution as bloodless—meaning that the only sacrifice it demands is her own. *"As the prophetic enthusiasm dies away, Pocahontas sinks exhausted in the arms of her wondering attendants."* Her own death is not long to follow. Learning from John Smith that Volday's fabrications have been exposed and her husband released, Pocahontas offers him "The thanks of one whose name and race will die / Together!" Protesting, Smith tells her

> No! thy country's sons will task
> The sculptor's and the limner's art to pay
> Hereafter homage to thy memory.
> In Britain too, whole ages hence, the tale
> Of Pocahontas' noble life and death
> Will love and admiration claim from all.
> Thy name will live forever!
>
> (3.5.265)

By "thy country's sons," Smith presumably means (white) *American* sons, since he tacitly agrees with Pocahontas that her own race will die. Smith speaks as if he had already seen Pocahontas's vision accomplished in reality; once the romantic logic of history is revealed, the revolution has always already happened. Peace is here, and it shall be guaranteed by the figurative sacrifice of Pocahontas's speaking body to statuary art: *The Forest Princess* closes with a frozen tableau vivant—vivant, at any rate, for Rolfe and Smith, mourning over Pocahontas's dead body. Pocahontas's apotheosis and the creation of an American national identity are, symbolically speaking, one and the same event in the play:—both demand the literal death of Pocahontas and her people.

How can we now, from our own historical vantage point, evaluate Charlotte Barnes's revisions of Shakespeare in *The Forest Princess*? It seems to me that Barnes revises *The Tempest* self-consciously from a "woman's" point of view: strengthening Shakespeare's Miranda in her own characterization of Pocahontas, insisting that Pocahontas did not act solely from romantic motives, conferring visionary powers on Pocahontas, and asserting (what we might call) the world-historical importance of Pocahontas's life. Just as clearly, however, Barnes revises *The Tempest* from a point of view that is both nationalistic and Anglocentric, so that *The Forest Princess* uses the story of Pocahontas and the subtext of *The Tempest* to ratify the central and abiding importance of English culture for American nationalism. There is no detaching Barnes's existence and interests as a woman from her other historical circumstances and ideological interests, including her own situation specifically as a northern American white woman of English descent. While *The Forest Princess* evinces a deep and (I think) intellectually cogent sympathy for the plight of American Indians in the 1840s, the play envisions the Indian diaspora, and eventually American Indian racial extinction, as inevitable, bloodless, and romantic—inevitable and romantic in the same way that a beautiful daughter's leaving her father for a stranger-husband is inevitable, under the logic of romance. Powhatan, Barnes makes clear, is no Caliban. (And Barnes casts Volday, who unthinkingly calls Powhatan a savage, in Caliban's place—as a kind of stand-in for the possible racism of her audiences?) He has too much in common with the Prospero whose "Every third thought shall be my grave," who foresees his own supersession. The logic of romance becomes the logic of history; victimage, oppression, and even genocide are rewritten into the foreclosed forms and metaphors of family, courtship, after-the-fact "prophecy," and symbolic restitution.

It's not possible to argue that Barnes's interests as a woman supersede her other cultural allegiances; nor is it possible to argue that Barnes's interests as a woman revising Shakespeare somehow fully anticipate those of feminist critics of this century. Barnes does assign Pocahontas an important part in history—as did many other of her contemporaries, male and female, who were fascinated with the Pocahontas story. And in denouncing those who "employ the torch of Hymen, or Cupid's 'purple light' to replenish the celestial flame" of Pocahontas's reputation, Barnes makes an effort to detach some of the major events of her life (major from an Anglocentric point of view)—her intervention on Smith's behalf and the Indian generosity toward the English colonists—from narrowly romantic motivations (Barnes, 148). Yet the model of historical agency that Barnes ascribes to Pocahontas in place of such narrowly romantic motivations is recognizably drawn from nineteenth-century conventions of True Womanhood.[18] Miranda the loving daughter, in Barnes's revision of *The Tempest*, becomes Pocahontas the social mother—the woman whose active agency in the world beyond the domestic sphere is modeled on, and legitimated by, her familial role and the character traits associated with it. Pocahontas's life, Barnes writes, "was pure, active, and affectionate: her 'beautiful, godly and Christian death' was a theme of praise to all beholders." She "stands forth from first to last the animated type of mercy and peace, unselfishness and truth" (147), radiating the "pure disinterestedness of a woman's fame" (148).

As would much later nineteenth-century feminist Ideology, *The Forest Princess* goes some way toward turning "woman"—Miranda/Pocahontas—into a genuinely *political* female subject, one possessed of wide historical vision and moved by more than sheerly private concerns. (The year before Barnes wrote *The Forest Princess*, Margaret Fuller had given *her* wished-for, self-sufficing womanly ideal the name of Miranda and connected her, suggestively, to an Indian custom through which an independent woman could become the bride of the Sun.[19]) At the same time, however, Barnes's conception of Pocahontas severely qualifies "woman" as a political subject, at least from the standpoint of much twentieth-century feminism. Barnes's Pocahontas knows more, in a sense, than Miranda. Yet Pocahontas's historical vision comes to her all too *literally* as a vision—part of her racial heritage, not under her conscious desiring control, and certainly not a kind of knowledge to be formulated consciously with other women. (Like Miranda, Pocahontas for all practical purposes stands alone in a world of men.) And in her anxiety to refute the notion that Pocahontas acted solely from motives of private desire for John Smith, Barnes resorts to an ideal of womanly "disinterestedness" that implicitly denies the legitimacy of any active, self-centered desire on Pocahontas's part. Not only is Pocahontas thereby rendered asexual ("Vesta's fire" still burns on her shrine despite her marriage to Rolfe[20]), but *inter-*

estedness itself, that basic attribute of political subjects, is taken to be constitutively lacking in "woman." As "woman," Pocahontas does not act on the world-historical stage to represent her own interests, or even finally those of her people. Her womanly altruism is so generalized as to transcend all specific loyalties, be they familial, erotic, or ethnic. Fittingly, then, she becomes the signifier of other people's interests. She dies giving symbolic birth to a vision of future peace; her reward (as Smith tells her) is to become a symbol herself, in effect to join her own allegory.

What is today's feminist criticism to make of Barnes, then—Barnes, the Shakespearean actress and playwright, playing her own Pocahontas, re-presenting history's Pocahontas, revising Shakespeare's play of the New World, *The Tempest?* Whatever our literary evaluation of Barnes's play, the very least we can grant her is the recognition that *The Forest Princess,* in its time, did "cultural work" (to borrow Jane Tompkins's term) of real importance for shaping an American national identity. Against the grain of Barnes's own characterization of "woman," I have tried for my part to restore, along with the complexity of *The Forest Princess*'s cultural contexts and pre-texts, some of the complexity of Barnes's own *interestedness*—in which gender, race, and nationality inseparably make their insistence felt.

NOTES

1. See Arthur Wilson, *A History of the Philadelphia Theatre 1835 to 1855* (1935; rpt. New York: Greenwood Press, 1968), for information on Barnes and Connor's acting careers. In most reference books, Barnes must be traced under her married name, as Mrs. E. S. Connor.

2. Barnes, *Plays, Prose and Poetry* (Philadelphia: E. H. Butler, 1848), iii. All further citations of Barnes's work will be taken from this collection and identified in the text.

3. For *The Forest Princess*'s performance history, see Wilson, *History,* 372, and Brenda Jean Anderson, "The North American Indian in Theatre and Drama from 1605 to 1970," (Ph.D. diss., University of Illinois at Urbana-Champaign, 1978), 81, 100n.16.

4. The acceptance of theater in general into American cultural life was still shaky in the early nineteenth century. A few years before Barnes wrote *The Forest Princess,* the financial panic of 1837 had revived old jeremiads against the theater. As one diarist wrote, "Shakespeare and Jim Crow come in equally for their share of condemnation, and the stage is indiscriminately voted immoral, irreligious, and what is much worse, *unfashionable*" (cited in Page Smith, *The Nation Comes of Age* [New York: McGraw-Hill, 1981], 177). Esther Cloudman Dunn's *Shakespeare in America* (1939; rpt. New York and London: Benjamin Blom, 1968) began to develop the particular history of Shakespeare's reception.

5. Philip Young implies that John Esten Cooke's novel *My Lady Pocahontas* (1885) is the first item of our "Pocahontas literature" to draw upon *The Tempest;*

he does not remark upon the similarities between Barnes's play and *The Tempest*. See "The Mother of Us All: Pocahontas," in *Three Bags Full* (New York: Harcourt Brace Jovanovich, 1971), 191.

6. Reginald Horsman, *Race and Manifest Destiny: The Origins of American Racial Anglo-Saxonism* (Cambridge, Mass.: Harvard University Press, 1981).

7. By the time Barnes wrote *The Forest Princess*, it had become fashionable in Virginia aristocratic circles to claim Pocahontas as an ancestor. The prestige of her bloodline was later written into Virginia law, which provided that "persons who have one-sixteenth or less of the blood of the American Indian and have now other non-Caucasic [*sic*] blood shall be deemed to be white persons"—from the standpoint of the anti-miscegenation statute of the Virginia Code. This exception was justified, in the Code, by "the desire of all to recognize as an integral and honored part of the white race the descendants of John Rolfe and Pocahontas" (Section 20–54 of the Virginia Code, cited in Loving *v.* Virginia, 338 U.S. 1 [1967], in which opinion the anti-miscegenation statute was ruled unconstitutional).

8. Barnes's earlier and rather more popular *Octavia Bragaldi* (first performed in 1837) had similarly tried to make a space for women's active agency in the genre of the revenge tragedy, and had linked this revisionary impetus to a specifically American project of justifying bourgeois society (especially bourgeois sexual relations) against aristocracy. Her preface to *Octavia Bragaldi* stressed that the actual incidents of this verse drama—its Italian renaissance setting notwithstanding—were drawn from a murder that "occurred in the city of Frankfort, (Kentucky,) in 1825" (iv).

9. For insightful comments on the provenance and validity of the historical documents, see Young, "Mother of Us All," and Peter Hulme's *Colonial Encounters: Europe and the Native Caribbean, 1492–1797* (London and New York: Methuen, 1986).

10. Geoffrey Bullough, cited in Hulme, *Colonial Encounters*, 138. For later instances, see n. 3, above.

11. As Barnes would have remembered, of course, many other Shakespearean characters utter prophecies. The histories are rife with predictions of victory and defeat, downfall and change; the most interesting parallel, however, may be to *Cymbeline* (a romance ending, like *The Forest Princess*, in a promise of peace), in which the Roman soothsayer deciphers the message left on Posthumus's chest after his prophetic dream. What Britain is to Rome in *Cymbeline*, America is to Britain in *The Forest Princess*, as Pocahontas's dying vision of peace will make plain.

12. Rolfe brought his first wife and their child to Virginia in 1609; they were in fact among the British party shipwrecked in the Bermudas (reported from which later made their way into *The Tempest*), where the child was born. His wife died shortly after their arrival, so he had been widowed some four years by the time he met Pocahontas. To judge from his writings, he was well-educated and Puritan in his upbringing. See John Melville Jennings's "Biographical Sketch" in John Rolfe's *True Relation* (Charlottesville: University Press of Virginia, 1971) for a brief account of what is known about Rolfe's background.

13. As Peter Hulme points out (142–43), far more European colonists in fact defected to the Indians than the other way round, especially under the starva-

tion conditions of the early years of their settlements. The story of Pocahontas was all the more valuable, therefore, as a kind of inoculation against this uncomfortable fact.

14. Prospero's betrothal masque for Miranda and Ferdinand also invokes Ceres; Rolfe perceives the New World, again, through *The Tempest*'s mythology.

15. Miranda's gift of a necklace also recalls Rosalind's gift to Orlando in *As You Like It* (1:2); later Orlando will save his brother Oliver from a lioness, an episode Oliver recounts in 4:3. If the specific verbal exchange in the scene from *The Forest Princess* seems derived from *The Tempest*, the conventions of gift-giving and saving an "enemy" from a wild animal are common traditions of pastoral literature.

16. See Rolfe's famous 1614 letter to Sir Thomas Dale, in which he describes his wife-to-be as a woman "whose education hath byn rude, her manners barbarous, her generation Cursed, and soe discrepant in all nutriture from my self" (cited in Hulme, *Colonial Encounters*, 145).

17. John Rolfe seems to have been a contentious, rigid man and sometimes quarrelled with his fellows in the Virginia Company, but he was never imprisoned on any charges of collusion with Raleigh. Barnes's invention serves to yoke Rolfe with Raleigh's great romantic popularity, with nostalgia for the Elizabethan age, and discontent with Stuart rule—the discontent that, as Pocahontas foretells, would turn into outright revolution in England, prefiguring the happier revolution in America. See Jennings (n.13 above) for more information on Rolfe's activities in the Company before, during, and after his marriage to Pocahontas.

18. Barbara Welter's pioneering article, "The Cult of True Womanhood: 1800–1860," *American Quarterly* 18 (Summer 1966), inaugurated feminist discussion of this nineteenth-century ideological topos.

19. Margaret Fuller, "The Great Lawsuit: Man versus Men: Woman versus Women," first published in the *Dial* 4 (July 1843):1–47, revised the following year into *Woman in the Nineteenth Century* (New York: Greeley and McElrath, 1845).

20. Barnes's preface, which stresses Pocahontas's lack of sexual motivation for her generalized benevolence, is in some respects at odds with the play's betrothal scene, in which Powhatan insists that Pocahontas marry Rolfe only if she freely loves him. Yet the love Pocahontas confesses to does not seem particularly sexual, nor does *The Forest Princess* make an issue either of premarital chastity, the "fire in th' blood" against which Prospero warns Ferdinand (4.1), or the legitimate wedded pleasures to follow. In terms of nineteenth-century ideology, Pocahontas is "passionless" insofar as her "sexual appetite contributed a very minor part (if any at all) to [her] motivations" (Nancy Cott, "Passionlessness: An Interpretation of Victorian Sexual Ideology, 1790–1850" [*Signs* 4.2:220). As Cott stresses, "passionlessness" could cut two ways: divesting women of sexual power on one hand, but also replacing a "sexual/carnal characterization of women with a spiritual/moral one, allowing women to develop their human faculties and their self-esteem" (233). Through her "passionless" interpretation of Pocahontas's motives, Barnes defends Pocahontas not only against the romanticized interpre-

tation of her rescue of John Smith but also against the colonial texts, John Smith's included, that referred to her as a "wanton" young woman. For a discussion of the "Virgin-Whore paradox" as inflected by race conflict and national identity for American Indian women, see Rayna Green's "The Pocahontas Perplex: The Image of Indian Women in American Culture," *Massachusetts Review* 16 (1975):698–714.

MARGARET J. ARNOLD

Coriolanus Transformed:
Charlotte Brontë's Use of Shakespeare
in Shirley

Charlotte Brontë shows a broad knowledge of Shakespearean characters and language throughout her fiction and letters, but she emphasizes
the figure of Coriolanus, using the play and its martial hero in the structure and characterization of her second published novel, *Shirley*.[1] In fash-
ioning her hero, Robert Moore, she creates a middle-class exemplar of
many of the Roman hero's qualities, setting a lonely industrial warrior in
the context of a society of well-fed tradesmen and pitting a group of starving mill-hands against him. When Robert Moore and Caroline Helstone
read Shakespeare's play together in chapter 6, Brontë clarifies the central
moral and personal questions of the novel. In place of Coriolanus's mother
and wife, however, she develops women characters ambivalent about
Robert's egoism, capable of forming friendships, opinions, and fantasies
they share with each other but need not share with members of the dominant patriarchal society. Chiefly because of the responses of Caroline
Helstone and Shirley Keeldar, Robert has the opportunity to become a
domestic, more benevolent adult in contrast to Coriolanus's lonely end
with the taunt of "Boy" (5.6.211) in his ears.[2]

Why choose this play and this hero, less popular than *Hamlet* for most
Victorian readers? Brontë's respect for integrity and martial valor like Coriolanus's appears in childhood when she begins the Brontë children's
"Young Men" play by naming one of Branwell's toy soldiers "Duke of
Wellington." Later, at the Pensionnat Héger, her essay "Sur le nom de Napoléon" characterizes Bonaparte as a modern Prometheus, defiant and
chained, a human instrument whose ambition overrides all in his drive for
power. Wellington, on the other hand, "le moderne Coriolan," sternly
braves massive opposition, respecting only the dictates of his conscience:
"Napoléon flattait le peuple; Wellington le brusque; l'un cherchait les ap-
plaudissements, l'autre ne se soucie que du témoignage de sa conscience;
quand elle approuve, c'est assez; toute autre louange l'obsède."[3]

Charlotte clearly expresses her unqualified admiration for Well-
ington-Coriolanus at a time when she was isolated in Brussels. In *Shirley*,
however, she no longer portrays Coriolanus as a totally admirable hero.

Caroline Helstone voices words of admiration for the Coriolanian Robert, but Caroline is also aware of his flaws. Brontë's later ambivalence about heroes like Coriolanus and Wellington reflects her long struggle between romantic egoism and domestic realism, most clearly suggested by Donald Stone.[4] In *Jane Eyre,* for instance, St. John Rivers most resembles Coriolanus as a heroic figure who is militant, true to his lonely integrity but difficult to domesticate. Although Rochester possesses a powerful ego and a desire to live by his own personal rules, he must suffer dependence to prepare him for domestic life. Robert Moore represents Brontë's cold and militant hero—the brave mill owner willing to stand alone—in an attempt to make *Shirley* a more realistic novel than *Jane Eyre.* In *Jane Eyre* a cold, proud figure like Rivers, a secondary character, could be allowed to pursue his lonely path. Robert, on the other hand, cannot remain cold, proud, and alone. He holds a social position in which inflexibility is inappropriate and must be educated, finally, to suit a social and domestic setting.

Brontë's Yorkshire transformation of Coriolanus not only replaces the proud Roman aristocrat with a proud mill owner but also changes the milieu of Shakespeare's play to a middle-class one, torn by resentment among social classes. She sets the novel in a neighborhood near Miss Wooler's school, drawing upon the kinds of people she knew, the stories handed down about the Luddites, and the records of the *Leeds Mercury.* Since Charlotte has observed men of business and of the clergy from Haworth and from larger cities, it is not surprising that she chooses a mill owner as a nineteenth-century Coriolanus. She holds the opinion that such figures are the aristocrats and heroes of her day. A parson's daughter and no stranger to observations of poverty, she nevertheless recognizes the power of "trade." As she writes to George Smith, whom she has met as a publisher and with whom she has continued a long correspondence, on March 8, 1851, "May not Trade have its Alexanders as well as War?—and does not many a man begin with a modest Macedon in the City and end by desiring another world for his speculations?"[5]

Having established a modern industrialist as a worthy subject for echoing the world of *Coriolanus,* Brontë draws remarkable parallels in setting and character. Like Shakespeare she creates a society in which the ruling classes face mobs of hungry citizens. In this setting Robert Moore shares Coriolanus's martial dedication and inflexibility, qualities she and her heroines can respect even if they urge greater moderation. She can point to his flaws as well—arrogant egoism and intolerance—often through the observations of Caroline Helstone and Shirley Keeldar.

As analogies to the class struggles in *Coriolanus,* Brontë develops the poverty and class divisions of nineteenth-century Yorkshire. The Roman dearth of corn is paralleled by the displacement of starving men by machines: "Misery generates hate: these sufferers hated the machines which they believed took their bread from them: they hated the buildings which contained those machines; they hated the manufacturers who owned these buildings."[6] As a sympathetic niece of Rector Helstone, Caroline is aware of this discontent. Robert, on the other hand, disregards it or thinks he must defend his livelihood with any necessary measures.

Both the patricians in Rome and the property owners in Yorkshire are complacent and single-minded when they confront lower-class sufferers. Menenius presents the Roman structure as an indestructible power when he tells the citizens:

> For your wants,
> Your suffering in this dearth, you may as well
> Strike at the heaven with your staves as lift them
> Against the Roman state, whose course will on
> The way it takes, cracking ten thousand curbs . . .
>
> (1.1.62–68)

In Yorkshire, the narrator observes a similar complacency and pride of place, the assumption that power will remain fixed and that the monied classes are so thoroughly obsessed with their own commerce that they have left no space for private honor or compassion (132). As Margaret Blom puts it, "The society thus stricken is innately corrupt. Having placed its faith in material values, starved the affections, and ignored the soul, the citizenry lacks the means and the will to control the fear which sweeps over it when the system it has willingly perpetuated begins to break down."[7] Shirley and Caroline, in contrast to the women in *Coriolanus,* pay intelligent attention to this class division and the potential for a mob uprising. Shirley admits that, when confronted with a mob, she would have to take an aristocratic stance, but she tries to use her own wealth and endeavors to ameliorate the conditions of the starving workers.

Shakespeare's mob contains both the self-serving tribunes and decent people like the Second Citizen: "Consider you what services he has done for his country?" (1.1.26–27). Brontë's mob also contains both elements, from the inveterate ringleaders like Moses Barraclough and Noah O'Tims to a patient, decent man like William Farren. The narrator emphasizes that "there was no ferocity, no malignity in his countenance: it was wan, dejected, austere, but still patient. How could Moore leave him thus, with the words 'I'll never give in,' and not a whisper of goodwill, or hope, or aid?" (109).

Even more important than the careful delineation of class struggle stands Brontë's characterization of Robert Moore, the Yorkshire Coriolanus. Before Shirley and Caroline intervene, he resembles the young Roman in many ways. He is like Coriolanus in his isolation and lack of self-knowledge; he holds a heroic stature among mill owners; he is as single-minded about his business as Marcius is about war; he is reticent about love; he is capable of defiance, hatred, and revenge; he is diffident about politics and public acclaim; he exhibits an aristocratic lack of concern for the common people; and he revels in the martial aspects of the defense of his mill. Some concrete details indicate how closely Brontë had Shakespeare's hero in mind.

Just as Coriolanus is proud of battling the Volscians alone when he says, "O, me alone! Make you a sword of me?" (1.6.76), Moore is willing to defend his mill in isolation. When Peter Malone arrives to wait at night for the frames which may need defense, Moore protests that he needs no help. Even when the mob directly approaches the mill, he asserts to his companions, "*You* need not appear. I shall meet them in the yard when they come; *you* can stay here.... Give way, if you please.... leave me to myself; I have no objection to act alone: only be assured you will not find safety in submission" (102).

Coriolanus does not know the degree to which he is hated until Rome banishes him. Moore is similarly blind, underestimating the hatred of the unemployed workers. Matthewson Helstone speaks of his refusal to take precautions against attacks on his person, sitting in the mill with the shutters open and freely wandering about the countryside at night. When Robert and Caroline discuss *Coriolanus,* in a pivotal chapter discussed below, he fails to see why Coriolanus was hated and banished. Like Coriolanus he lacks the self-knowledge to see the traits in his own character which elicit hatred from his fellow men.

Moore is elevated to a heroic stature among mill owners. Others fear mob violence; he is the only one who defies the mob and seeks to prosecute the ringleaders. Mike Hartley, the Antinomian weaver, singles him out as a target, "a sacrifice, an oblation of a sweet savour" (10). One recalls the First Citizen's focus on Coriolanus although other patricians are equally guilty: "Let us kill him, and we'll have corn at our own price. Is't a verdict?" (1.1.9–10). Both heroes personify the qualities of the hated superiors in distilled form.

Moore is as single-minded and ambitious about his business as Coriolanus is about war. He tells his "mob" that he will persist in getting new frames even if they break the ones he has. In fact, both heroes subordinate private relationships to their public obsessions. Coriolanus quietly greets his "gracious silence" (2.1.165) but quickly turns to the affairs of the Capitol. Moore likes to look at Caroline Helstone and is warm toward her when they read together, only to replace his warmth with coolness the next day. He denies that he has time to think of love and feels he lacks the wealth to marry the Rector's niece, who would bring no dowry to the match.

Moore also shares Coriolanus's defiance of the mob and his determination to seek revenge. Coriolanus is willing to wage war on Roman citizens:

> Would the nobility lay aside their ruth,
> And let me use my sword, I'd make a quarry
> With thousands of these quartered slaves as high
> As I could pick my lance.
>
> (1.1.192–95)

Moore, with pistol in hand, is also willing to wage war against his own "people":

> Here I stay; and by this mill I stand; and into it will I convey the best machinery inventors can furnish.... The utmost you *can* do—and this you will never *dare* to do—is to burn down my mill, destroy its contents, and shoot me.... Hear me!—I'll make my cloth as I please, and according to the best lights I have. In its manufacture I will employ what means I choose. Whoever, after hearing this, shall dare to interfere with me, may just take the consequences.... Both barrels are loaded.... I'm quite determined!—keep off! (107)

He speaks of his hatred of the leaders of the group who broke his frames and resolutely seeks revenge upon them by bringing them to justice. It is no wonder that, as the narrator tells us, "With the revenge of Caius Marcius, Moore perfectly sympathised; he was not scandalised by it; and again Caroline whispered, 'There I see another glimpse of brotherhood in error'" (71).

Like Coriolanus, Moore thrives on points of conflict and feels uncomfortable with political matters and public appearances. He admits that he is "baffled" (17) by the Orders in Council, which prohibit the sale of goods to French-controlled territory. He owes little allegiance to the British government, commenting that his hatred is so consuming for the "fellows who had broken my frames, that I have little to spare for my private acquaintance, and still less for such a vague thing as a sect or a government" (43).

Both Coriolanus and Moore are reticent about accepting praise for doing what they see as duties. Coriolanus's response to commendation is "No more of this; it does offend my heart./ Pray now, no more" (2.1.158–59). Moore shows a similar discomfort upon a similar occasion: "Often had Moore gazed with a brilliant countenance over howling crowds from a hostile hustings: he had breasted the storm of unpopularity with gallant bearing and soul elate; but he drooped his head under the half-bred tradesmen's praise, and shrank chagrined before their congratulations" (416).

Both heroes display an aristocratic contempt for the common people. Coriolanus greets them,

> What's the matter, you dissentious rogues,
> That, rubbing the poor itch of your opinion,
> Make yourselves scabs?
>
> (1.1.159–61)

He also thinks of the plebeians as a "mob," failing to allow for individual differences. Robert again identifies with Coriolanus when he reads the part with Caroline and fails to consider individuals: "He delivered the haughty speech of Caius Marcius to the starving citizens with unction; he did not say he thought his irrational pride right, but he seemed to feel it so" (70–71). Like Coriolanus he fails to see the decency of individuals within the mob and is just as harsh and defiant to William Farren as he is to the more culpable ringleaders. The narrator also observes, "he did not sufficiently care when the new inventions threw the old workpeople out of employ: he never asked himself where those to whom he no longer paid weekly wages found daily bread" (21). Coriolanus shows a similar scorn for the common people's nurture: "The Volsces have much corn. Take these rats thither/To gnaw their garners" (1.1.244–45).

Brontë goes to some length in detailing Moore's martial interests. When he reads *Coriolanus,* he delights in the encounter between Marcius and Tullus Aufidius. Like Coriolanus he participates in strictly patriarchal, military networks. For example, he keeps secret even from Shirley, who owns the property, his plan to bring in the redcoats and organize male neighbors for the battle at the mill. She refers to him as "Captain Gérard Moore, who trusts much in the prowess of his own right arm, I believe" (194), and jokes with Caroline about his pride and supremacy as if he were a biblical patriarch at the school feast: "He looks amidst the set that surrounds him like Eliab among humbler shepherds—like Saul in a war-council: and a war-council it is, if I am not mistaken" (247). In a traditional pattern, the women watch the fierce struggle, realize that they must not intervene, and care for the wounded in the morning.

Although they do not intervene in the battle, in the novel as a whole Caroline and Shirley are crucial in Brontë's redirection of Coriolanus's character and environment. Just as Moore, a mill owner, replaces Coriolanus as an exemplar of egoism, the women of *Shirley*, representing intelligent middle-class women from a society Brontë knew, replace the aristocratic Volumnia, Virgilia, and Valeria of Coriolanus's world. By giving her heroines ties with each other and the abilities to form and give voice to independent valuations, Brontë domesticates the potentially tragic outcome of Robert's Coriolanus-like pride and inflexibility. In addition, she lets the heroines voice a radical critique of a harsh patriarchal structure, which oppresses women as well as mill workers. Because Brontë's women develop separate identities and shared interests independent of men, they have opportunities to discuss the importance of useful work for both sexes, to deplore the distorted images of women men often hold, and to build theologies not dependent on patriarchal tradition.[8] Such discussions Brontë herself could imagine from her close relation to her sisters and her life-long friendship with the conventional Ellen Nussey and the more "radical" Mary Taylor. Later, she formed strong attachments to fellow women writers like Elizabeth Gaskell and Harriet Martineau, even though their political and religious views differed from her own. Caroline and Shirley do love the Moore brothers, but they also sympathize with the poor. When she gives her women the compassion the patriarchal world lacks, Brontë is expressing her own belief. Patrick Brontë, in a letter to Elizabeth Gaskell on 27 August 1855, speaks of Charlotte's view: "She jocularly replied 'In deeds of charity men reason much and do little; women reason little and do much, and I will act the woman still.'"[9] Writing to her former teacher Margaret Wooler in 1848, Charlotte commends Charles Lamb, who, in her account, devoted his life to the care of his sister Mary in her insanity, seeing his behavior as unusual in the "coarser sex."[10]

The women in Shakespeare's play live through and for Coriolanus. No female voice mitigates his pride until Volumnia, too late, succeeds in saving Rome but losing her son. There is also no female space and no critique of the patriarchal religion, family, or state. Volumnia has raised her son for patriarchal "honor," sending him "To a cruel war,... from whence he returned, his brows bound with oak" (1.3.9–16). She rejoices in his wounds and, with Valeria, is proud of a grandson whose treatment of butterflies promises a military future. Virgilia is also dependent on Coriolanus, waiting silently for his return and never speaking of his flaws. Unlike Shirley and Caroline, Volumnia and Virgilia are not personal friends.

Caroline and Shirley, on the other hand, are conscious of male power and try to develop their places within the social structure and within the imaginative worlds they are able to build. Caroline knows that, had she been male, she could have worked with Robert. Unlike Virgilia, with whom she shares a gentle nature, she cannot bear a life of occasional social duties and needlework. In neither text are women represented as working for a wage, but Caroline and Shirley voice their discontent. Shirley asks,

> "Caroline . . . don't you wish you had a profession—a trade?"
> "I wish it fifty times a day. As it is, I often wonder what I came into the world for. I long to have something absorbing and compulsory to fill my head and hands, and to occupy my thoughts." (179)

Here, friends share common concerns apart from the men in their lives. It is nearly impossible to fit this kind of interchange into the world of the Roman women.

In *Shirley* close female friendship permits Caroline and Shirley to open their thoughts to each other in the female space of the woods, away from men and close to the natural world. The grove balances the *Coriolanus*-like social structure with a temporarily matriarchal context. They, not men, may safely behold a mermaid. In this female world, they venture a critique of the distorted images of women men have created in literature and life. For example, Shirley comments that men underestimate women, adding, "If men could see us as we really are, they would be a little amazed; but the cleverest, the acutest men are often under an illusion about women: they do not read them in a true light: they misapprehend them, both for good and evil: their good woman is a queer thing, half doll, half angel; their bad woman almost always a fiend" (278).[11] Shirley's most radical revision of the patriarchy is her rewriting of theology to rehabilitate Eve, repudiating both Genesis and Milton: "Milton tried to see the first woman; but, Cary, he saw her not. . . . It was his cook that he saw; or it was Mrs. Gill. . . . I would beg to remind him that the first men of the earth were Titans, and that Eve was their mother: from her sprang Saturn, Hyperion, Oceanus; she bore Prometheus—. . . . I saw—I now see—a woman-Titan: her robe of blue air spreads to the outskirts of the heath. . . . So kneeling, face to face she speaks with God. That Eve is Jehovah's daughter, as Adam was His son" (252–53).[12] The mother goddess appears in the mythology Greeks and Romans recorded, but no one in *Coriolanus* steps aside to affirm woman's spiritual powers. The fact that Brontë's women do so permits the reader to contemplate a visionary alternative to the masculine world of the novel, a world so much like that of *Coriolanus*. Shirley's vision does not change society, but she and Caroline gain comfort and inspiration from its imaginative power.

The greatest impact Caroline and Shirley have on their society comes from their effect on Robert Moore. Coriolanus ends his life tragically, still immature. Robert Moore, like Coriolanus, is young, originally proud, and weak in self-knowledge. Largely because of Shirley and Caroline, he achieves a more comprehensive manhood. Brontë believed that men were not educated to understand the risks and joys of domestic life. In *Jane Eyre* Jane educates Rochester so that he accepts her as an equal and as a real woman rather than an angel, elf, or sprite.[13] Lucy Snowe convinces Paul Emanuel to accept her as an independent person and a Protestant.[14] Both Caroline and Shirley educate Robert Moore so that he achieves a clearer vision of himself, women, and his place in the social order.

No one curbs Coriolanus's contempt for the plebeians. Robert Moore, however, hears Caroline, who knows the poor as individuals, suggest that he is over-haughty "In—(courage! let me speak the truth)—in your manner—mind, I say only *manner* to these Yorkshire workpeople" (55). Chapter 6, "Coriolanus," is pivotal to the work because it opposes Caroline's values to Robert's pride and self-ignorance. She exposes him to *Coriolanus* because she wants him to see his own strengths and weaknesses in the Shakespearean character: her purpose is not only to entertain but to educate. In this chapter both Caroline and Robert reveal themselves through responses to literature without fully understanding the reasons the works appeal to them. Their mutual reading of *Coriolanus* is followed by allusions to and a partial recitation of Caroline's favorite French poem, André Chénier's "La jeune captive," the lament of a very young woman sentenced to death during the French Revolution, mourning the loss of a longer, richly fulfilled life. Caroline at eighteen does not know why she prefers Chénier to the great neoclassical writers, but the reader comes to understand her desire to live a life containing love and purpose rather than the symbolic death-in-life she will face in a society which denies her marriage and useful work.

She hopes that *Coriolanus* will alert Robert to the potentially tragic consequences of his arrogance and callousness toward his "mob" of unemployed workers; fearing that they will be harmed, she also sympathizes with their sense of grievance. She introduces *Coriolanus* in order to show Robert himself and to arouse his feelings about a figure like himself: "Yes, an old English book, one that you like; and I will choose a part of it that is toned quite in harmony with something in you. It shall waken your nature, fill your mind with music: it shall pass like a skilful hand over your heart, and make its strings sound. . . . It is to stir you; to give you new sensations. It is to make you feel your life strongly, not only your virtues, but your vicious, perverse points" (69). When Robert reads Coriolanus's speech to the mob with dramatic power, Caroline can interpose a choric comment: "There's a vicious point hit already . . . you sympathise with that proud patrician who does not sympathise with his famished fellowmen, and insults them" (71). His enthusiasm suggests that he is blind to his own arrogance; he readily gives up reading the "comic" scenes to Caroline, because he sees no humor in his own situation. When Caroline asks him about Coriolanus's faults, he turns the question back to her: Caroline echoes Aufidius's analysis (4.7.37–45) and quickly moves to Robert's own faults: "It was a spice of all; and you must not be proud to your workpeople; you must not neglect chances of soothing them, and you must not be of an inflexible nature, uttering a request as austerely as if it were a command" (72). She further urges him to see each worker as an individual and not as a member of a "mob." When she adds that "kindness is more likely to win their regard than pride" (73), she proposes a constructive alternative to his flawed heroism. When Caroline actually points to the lesson she hopes Robert will learn, he says only, "That is a moral you tack to the play" (72). Only later, after his isolation from Caroline and Shirley, does he echo Caroline's idea that he needs to regard people as individuals.

Shirley strikes an important blow to Robert's pride because she sees his egoism clearly, finally motivating the journey which teaches him more about others and about his place in society. Early in her residence at Fieldhead, she speaks to Hiram Yorke directly about the male egos of landowner, Rector, and mill owner alike: "Moore, although juster and more considerate than either you or the Rector, is still haughty, stern, and in a public sense, selfish" (293). But she affects Moore most deeply when he makes the mistake of assuming that friendly collegiality is a romantic overture making her responsive to a marriage proposal. When she refuses his offer, responding "You spoke like a brigand who demanded my purse, rather than like a lover who asked my heart" (420), Moore gains new insight into himself and into relationships between men and women, resolving, "I'll do it no more . . . never more will I mention marriage to a woman, unless I feel love. . . . No woman shall ever again look at me as Miss Keeldar looked—ever again feel towards me as Miss Keeldar felt: in no woman's presence will I ever again stand at once such a fool and such a knave—such a brute and such a puppy" (423).

Caroline prompts thoughts about his pride; Shirley strikes such a serious blow that he extends his trip out of the area long after he has seen the conviction of the uprising's leaders, taking the opportunity to observe how other people suffer. He can then remember Caroline's advice. It is difficult to gain self-understanding without exposure to the sufferings of others. Coriolanus dies without insight into his own martial pride; no one prods him to walk in another person's shoes. He remains a proud boy, clinging to his memory of his isolated power against the "Volscians in Corioles" (5.6.114). Robert Moore is on his way to adult manhood. His observations demonstrate his broader thought and his growth in understanding and feeling for others. Thus his words reveal new self-understanding: "I went where there was want of food, of fuel, of clothing;

where there was no occupation and no hope. I saw some, with naturally elevated tendencies and good feelings, kept down amongst sordid privations and harassing griefs. I saw many originally low, and to whom lack of education left scarcely anything but animal wants, disappointed in those wants, ahungered, athirst, and desperate and famished animals: I saw what taught my brain a new lesson, and filled my breast with fresh feelings" (426). A man different from the arrogant youth who showed contempt to William Farren speaks here. Although he adds that he would still bring the ringleaders to justice, Robert gives voice to a new self-image, substituting self-respect for hybris: "To respect himself, a man must believe he renders justice to his fellow-men. Unless I am more considerate to ignorance, more forbearing to suffering, than I have hitherto been, I shall scorn myself as grossly unjust" (427).

Nevertheless, like Rochester's, Moore's resolve needs to be strengthened by feeling for himself the helplessness Caroline and the workers have learned to know. Mike Hartley's gunshot results from feelings a younger Moore has stirred. The outcome could have been tragic, but Robert verges on the comic little boy when he suffers some inconveniences women might face: his visitors are restricted, and the formidable Mrs. Horsfall dictates intimate details of his daily life. To Martin Yorke and to Robert, Caroline Helstone proves a true and loving "wood nymph," helping to move the dénouement toward domestic comedy. Robert shows that he has learned compassion for workers when he refuses to prosecute Mike Hartley, later helping his widow to bury him.

In his readiness to enter an adult marriage for love, he includes Caroline in a relationship of mutual respect and communication: "I *will* do good; you shall tell me how: indeed, I have some schemes of my own, which you and I shall talk about on our own hearth one day. I have seen the necessity of doing good: I have learned the downright folly of being selfish" (508).

Thus Moore has overcome his inflexible, aristocratic, Coriolanus-like pride. Although he and Caroline plan to comfort the poor together, the novel ends with a certain elegiac bitter-sweetness. The "mighty mill and chimney, ambitious as the tower of Babel" (511), replace the grove, where fairies no longer roam and where Shirley and Caroline had built their feminist alternatives to the patriarchal world in which each now has her place.

Brontë has, thus, taken her favorite Shakespearean tragedy and transformed it into, finally, a new domestic setting. She has placed the poverty and class struggle of *Coriolanus* in the industrial world she and her readers understand and has invited them to note the parallels between a young, militant business "hero" and the isolated, proud soldier of Shakespeare's tragedy. Her own ambivalence about Coriolanus is apparent, but her major transformation of the Shakespearean play lies in her creation of Caroline Helstone and Shirley Keeldar, who criticize male egoism, build mental alternatives to nineteenth-century patriarchal structures, and help a potentially tragic "boy" to achieve a mature self-understanding and a mutual relationship with a woman who loves him.

NOTES

1. Brontë, at the age of eighteen, referred directly to Shakespeare's *Henry VIII, Richard III, Macbeth, Hamlet,* and *Julius Caesar* as plays profitable for the mind and character, in a letter to Ellen Nussey written on July 4, 1834, collected in T. J. Wise and J. A. Symington, eds., *The Brontës: Their Lives, Friendships, and Correspondence in Four Volumes* (Oxford: Shakespeare Head Press, 1931–38), 1:122. In subsequent notes this collection will be cited as *SHB*. She signs another letter to Ellen, dated "Aug. 20, —40," as "Caliban," *SHB*, 1:215. Although she preferred reading Shakespeare to seeing a performance, she refers to Macready's *Macbeth* and *Othello* in letters to her father (Dec. 4, 1849) and Margaret Wooler (Feb. 14, 1850), *SHB*, 3:34, 76. She was impressed with Elizabeth Gaskell's daughter Julia and mentions seeing *Twelfth Night* with them in a letter dated July 9, 1853 (*SHB*, 4:77). The most complete list of literal allusions appears in F. B. Pinion, *A Brontë Companion: Literary Allusions, Background, and Reference* (London: Macmillan, 1975), 380.

Other *Shirley* readers who have referred to *Coriolanus* include Wendy Anne Craik, who calls Moore "Coriolanus in a cottage" but does not develop the parallels in *The Brontë Novels* (London: Methuen, 1968), 146. F. B. Pinion speaks of the "Coriolanian Robert Moore," *A Brontë Companion*, 130. Harriet Bjork in *The Language of Truth: Charlotte Brontë, the Woman Question and the Novel* (Lund: Gleerup, 1974) says, "Like the eternal truths of *Coriolanus,* the literary parallel in *Shirley,* the 'dawn' of the century, the England of 1812, reflects 'present years' " (100). Cynthia Linder in *Romantic Imagery in the Novels of Charlotte Brontë* (New York: Barnes and Noble, 1978) mentions the "Coriolanus" chapter, saying, "the scene is essential, both structurally and thematically, to the novel as a whole. The inclusion of the shooting incident, when Moore is injured by one of his hands, Michael Hartley, whom he persecuted for breaking his frames, is an illustration of the point that Caroline tried to make Moore understand when he read *Coriolanus:* that an employer who will have no 'truck' with his labourers, and who refers to them as 'the mob,' is likely to engender a violent reaction from 'the mob.' Caroline's warning was not heeded by Moore, with the result that he was attacked" (78–79). Although she notes the structural importance of the scene, Linder does not develop the parallels between Coriolanus and Robert Moore.

2. William Shakespeare, *Coriolanus,* ed. Harry Levin, *The Pelican Shakespeare,* general ed. Alfred Harbage (Baltimore: Penguin Books, 1956). References to *Coriolanus* will be to act, scene, and line from this edition.

3. "Napoleon flattered the people; Wellington is curt with them. One sought their commendation; the other seeks only the testimony (or witness) of his conscience. When it approves, that is enough; all other praise disturbs him" (my

translation), quoted in Elizabeth Gaskell, *The Life of Charlotte Brontë*, 2 vols. (London: Smith, Elder, 1857), 1:293–94.

4. Donald Stone, *The Romantic Impulse in Victorian Fiction* (Cambridge: Harvard University Press, 1980), Stone discusses this ambivalence most directly in chapter 4. I disagree in part because Robert is more like Wellington than the Byronic Bonaparte and because, even though there is no movement for social reform, he becomes a domestic figure determined to show benevolence toward all who approach him for employment.

5. *SHB*, 3:211.

6. Charlotte Brontë, *Shirley* (London: Dent; New York: Dutton, 1908), 22. Subsequent citations from *Shirley* will be designated by page number from this edition.

7. Margaret Blom, *Charlotte Brontë* (Boston: Twayne, 1977), 111.

8. Linda C. Hunt examines the young women's friendships in "Sustenance and Balm: The Question of Female Friendship in *Shirley* and *Villette, Tulsa Studies in Women's Literature* 1, no. 1 (Spring 1982): 55–66. A helpful essay relating the personal oppression of single women to larger social problems is by Rosalind Belkin, "Rejects of the Marketplace: Old Maids in Charlotte Brontë's *Shirley*," *International Journal of Women's Studies* 4 (1981): 50–66. Charlotte expressed her own views about the importance of employment for women in letters to W. S. Williams about his daughters in *SHB*, 2:220, and 3:5.

9. *SHB*, 4:295.

10. "An instance of abnegation of self scarcely, I think, to be paralleled in the annals of the 'coarser sex,'" *SHB*, 2:249.

11. Clara Helen Whitmore, *Women's Work in English Fiction* (New York: G. P. Putnam and Sons; London: Knickerbocker Press, 1910), also notices this point, 268.

12. For a development of the revision of the Eve story, see Carol Ohmann, "Charlotte Brontë: The Limits of Her Feminism," *Female Studies* 6 (1972): 160–64, and M. A. Blom, "Charlotte Brontë: Feminist Manquée," *Bucknell Review* 21 (1973): 95–99.

13. See Susan Siefert, *The Dilemma of the Talented Heroine: A Study of Nineteenth-Century Fiction* (St. Albans, Vt.: Eden, 1977): "At this moment Jane has attained the fulfillment of the self-definition to which she had aspired. Mr. Rochester recognizes both her humanity and her freedom. She is no longer an 'elf,' 'fairy,' or 'sprite' to him but 'altogether a human being,'" 126.

14. Robert Bernard Martin writes in *The Accents of Persuasion: Charlotte Brontë's Novels* (London: Faber and Faber, 1966): "Lucy Snowe is both schoolmistress and pupil, but M. Paul learns from her as much as he is able to teach her," 30. Patricia Beer in *Reader, I Married Him: A Study of the Woman Characters of Jane Austen, Charlotte Brontë, etc.* (London: Macmillan, 1974), adds: "Yet there is equality here, too. She is now a prosperous headmistress; she counts in Villette. And, more important, her religion has been formally recognised. Paul writes that he wishes her to remain a Protestant as it is right for her. He speaks civilly of Protestantism, too, in a way he has never done before," 107.

MARIANNE NOVY

Daniel Deronda *and George Eliot's Female Re-Vision of Shakespeare*

U. C. Knoepflmacher noted in 1961 that *"Daniel Deronda*, George Eliot's last work of fiction, is the most consciously Shakespearean of all her novels." Knoepflmacher points to a "deliberate process of imitation on the part of the novelist" and suggests that she incorporates "the playwright and his works into the novel itself as an original means of characterization and differentiation."[1] Much feminist criticism written in the years since has suggested that such use of a male model is problematic for the woman writer. As a reader of male texts, argues Judith Fetterley, she undergoes a process of "immasculation" unless she sympathizes with their female characters and thereby becomes a "resisting reader."[2] Such resistance, and the related attitudes found in women writers by Sandra Gilbert and Susan Gubar, would seem to preclude conscious imitation of the male writer, except to mock or subvert him.[3] In this view, if George Eliot did identify with Shakespeare, it seems a sign of alienation from her sex.

However, these alternatives are too simple. As Mary Poovey has suggested, "Confrontation is not the only profitable way of formulating women's relationship to their literary fathers."[4] More specifically, the claim in *The Madwoman in the Attic* that canonical male writers portray women only as "extreme stereotypes (angel, monster)" does not fit Eliot's view of Shakespeare's women.[5] George Eliot read Shakespeare with distinct though not exclusive interest in his female characters, as did many Victorians, but unlike many Victorians, she emphasized his female characters' autonomy. I suggest that she enjoyed Shakespeare partly because she saw him as a creator of powerful women and that she saw herself as writing both in his tradition and from a female viewpoint.

The contrast between Eliot's attitude to Shakespeare and the Fetterley-Gilbert-Gubar model is partly a result of the difference between Shakespeare on the one hand and Milton and male American novelists on the other. It also results from two aspects of Victorian culture that Gilbert and Gubar do not mention—its praise of Shakespeare for the wide range of his sympathy, a trait considered particularly accessible to women, and its celebration of his female characters, discussed recently by Nina Auerbach in *Woman and the Demon*.[6] These factors may have made the Shakespearean tradition more accessible to women writers than the Miltonic one at issue in *The Madwoman in the Attic*.

George Eliot's writings give an especially extensive record of interest in Shakespeare, and the Shakespearean allusions in *Daniel Deronda* gain resonance when we can situate them in a context that is both personal and cultural. Gwendolen's identification with Rosalind looks back to Eliot's own past; however, Eliot stresses the contrast between Rosalind's plot in *As You Like It* and Gwendolen's in *Daniel Deronda,* and points up the aspects of women's experience that do not fit into Shakespeare's comedy. In her characterization of Deronda himself, she emphasizes his wide-ranging sympathy—important both in her culture's image of Shakespeare and in her own aesthetic—and relates it to irresolution, important in her culture's image of Hamlet. One way of describing the contrast between the plots of *Daniel Deronda* is as a contrast between a realistic rewriting of *As You Like It* and a romantic rewriting of *Hamlet*. In these rewritings, Shakespeare provides materials for her interest in Victorian ideals of womanhood and womanly qualities, ideals that she partly shared and partly criticized, as well as for her attempt, as an author, to transcend the limitations her culture associated with her gender.

Long before she wrote *Deronda,* long before she became a novelist, George Eliot read Shakespeare with a special interest in his female characters.[7] Her letters, especially the first volume (written between the ages of sixteen and twenty-two), abound in Shakespearean references. Ten of the more than twenty in that volume are from *As You Like It,* and throughout her life it is the play she most often alludes to in her correspondence.[8] The friendship between Rosalind and Celia is often a model for her own friendship with other women. To Maria Lewis, she writes, "I heartily echo your kind wish that we should be 'like Juno's swans' coupled together" (1:51; *AYLI* 1.3.75). To Martha Jackson, "I have as many queries rising to my lips as, if you were here to have them orally delivered, would make you wish, like Rosalind, that the answers were corked up in you like wine in a bottle" (1:92; based on *AYLI* 3.2.197–200). To Sara Sophia Hennell, "Not a word more to throw at a dog. So said Rosalind to Celia and so says one to thee, who loves thee as well as Rosalind did her Coz" (1:203; based on *AYLI* 1.3.3). In some of her other letters from this time she playfully puts on a male identity to express this affection, suggesting another dimension of her interest in the cross-dressed Rosalind and anticipating her later use of a male pseudonym. "I have not been beyond seas long enough to make it lawful for you to take a new husband—therefore I come back to you with all a husband's privileges and command you to love me whether I shew you any love or not" (1:279). These letters place her relationships within the tradition of romantic friendship discussed by Lillian Faderman.[9] Yet the *As You Like It* allusions make the note of playfulness more explicit.

Eliot's longest discussion of Shakespeare focuses on his representation of women. In 1855, writing criticism for the *Leader,* she uses Shakespeare's women as models to attack what she calls "the doctrines of modern propriety."[10] Discussing Girardin's *Cours de Litterature Dramatique,* she energetically refutes the claim that Shakespeare's women, unlike those of ancient dramatists, declare their love only after a lover has declared himself to them. On the contrary, "Shakespeare's women have no more decided characteristic than the frankness with which they avow their love, not only to themselves, but to the men they love." By contrast to Hazlitt's view that these characters show "weakness leaning on the strength of its affections for support,"[11] note the active power that George Eliot finds: "If Romeo opens the duct of love with a few notes solo, Juliet soon strikes in and keeps it up in as impassioned a strain as he. Sweet Desdemona, 'a maiden never bold,' encourages Othello, not only by a 'world of sighs,' but by the broadest possible hint that he has won her heart. Rosalind, in her first interview with Orlando, tells him that he has 'overthrown more than his enemies;' Portia is eloquent in assurances of her love before the casket is opened. . . . Curious it is to contrast these Shakspearean heroines with some of Walter Scott's painfully discreet young ladies." She sees the "respectability" of Scott's ladies as a violation of nature: "they are like trees trained in right lines by dint of wall and hammer." At the end of the paragraph she explicitly uses the concurrence of Shakespeare and Greek dramatists in portraying "feminine frankness" as evidence that "it must be simply a natural manifestation which has only been gradually and partially repressed by the complex influences of modern civilization."

Her enthusiastic emphasis on the initiative of Shakespeare's women was unusual. Hazlitt's picture of Shakespeare had influenced her greatly, as we shall see, yet her view here differs markedly from his. For many Victorian critics, as Russell Jackson has shown, "Rosalind, Beatrice, and Viola, for all the affection they attracted, could not be accepted without some special pleading. They enjoyed a freedom of speech and mind beyond what was proper in a well-brought-up Victorian girl."[12]

In her notebook, Eliot herself commented on this peculiarity of Victorian criticism: "It is remarkable that Shakespeare's women almost always *make love,* in opposition to the conventional notion of what is fitting for woman. Yet his pictures of women are belauded" (11).

However, she can also criticize women's roles in Shakespeare's plots. In her journal the same year (March 16, 1855), she writes, "After dinner

read 'Two Gentlemen of Verona'. . . . That play disgusted me more than
ever in the final scene, where Valentine, on Proteus's mere begging par-
don, when he has no longer any hope of gaining his ends, says 'All that
was mine in Silvia, I give thee!' Silvia standing by."[13]

Each of these Shakespearean allusions has a strong personal resonance
for Eliot. She borrows phrases from the dialogues between Rosalind and
Celia when female friendships are the most important ones in her life;
when her defining relationship becomes her love of G. H. Lewes, she
writes on Shakespeare's portrayal of unconventional, frankly passionate
women. She objects to a Shakespearean woman's passive role while Lewes
is away, apparently to determine whether his marriage with Agnes is irre-
trievably broken.[14]

In her first published fiction, *Scenes of Clerical Life*, after drawing on
memory to a large extent for "The Sad Fortunes of Reverend Amos Bar-
ton," she wrote "Mr. Gilfil's Love Story," which borrows from a number
of Shakespeare's plays.[15] Like Helena in *All's Well That Ends Well*, mentioned in the Girardin review, the main female character is a ward in love
with a man of higher position. Eliot's narrator modulates a comment on
Caterina's educational limitations into a claim that puts her explicitly in
the tradition of Shakespeare's tragic heroines. "It is very likely that to her
dying day Caterina thought the earth stood still, and that the sun and
stars moved round it; but so, for the matter of that, did Helen, and Dido,
and Desdemona, and Juliet; whence I hope you will not think my Caterina less worthy to be a heroine on that account. The truth is, that, with
one exception, her only talent lay in loving; and there, it is probable, the
most astronomical of women could not have surpassed her" (*Scenes* 110).

Caterina is Eliot's most explicit experiment in portraying the frank
passion in women that she so enjoyed seeing in Shakespeare, and her publisher was rather taken aback (*Letters* 2:297). As Blackwood and Eliot discuss the story, they re-enact the conflict between civilized respectability
and passion that Eliot sees exemplified in the contrast between Scott's
women and Shakespeare's. Although most of Eliot's other female characters in later works show more of "the complex influences of modern civilization," a critique of those influences is one of her continuing concerns.

The passion Eliot noted and valued in Shakespeare's female characters, I argue, is closely linked with the strong emotions she experienced
while watching his plays. A letter she wrote in 1859 indicates how central
to Eliot's image of Shakespeare is this experience. "In opposition to most
people who love to *read* Shakespeare I like to see his plays acted better
than any others: his great tragedies thrill me, let them be acted how they
may. I think it is something like what I used to experience in the old days
in listening to uncultured preachers—the emotions lay hold of one too

strongly for one to care about the medium. Before all other plays I find myself cold and critical, seeing nothing but actors and 'properties' " (*Letters* 3:228).

But, somewhat as in the woman's poetics theorized by Lawrence Lipking, Eliot valued Shakespeare's plays not only for the emotions they created in her but also for the sympathy they aroused.[16] As Knoepflmacher has noted (27), wide-ranging sympathy was one similarity many Victorians saw between Eliot and Shakespeare, and I believe that this aspect of his cultural image, combined with an emotional response that included a personal concern with his female characters, contributed to her choice of Shakespeare as an important model in her writing. To her, Shakespeare's plays meant both emotion and sympathy—passion becoming compassion—and such conversion she gave central importance in her life and work.

Her culture's image of the sympathetic Shakespeare, developed especially by Keats and Hazlitt, is crucial for Eliot's imaginative use of him. Putting the self aside or projecting it into a variety of other characters, this Shakespeare proved that sympathy and identification, rather than egotism, could produce greatness.

Keats opposed Shakespeare as the "camelion poet" with "no self" to the "wordsworthian or egotistical sublime."[17] Hazlitt wrote that Shakespeare "seemed scarcely to have an individual existence of his own, but to borrow that of others at will, and to pass successively through 'every variety of untried being'. . . . His talent consisted in sympathy with human nature, in all its shapes, degrees, depressions, and elevations. . . . He was the least of an egotist that it was possible to be."[18]

This view of the great writer as sympathetic rather than egotistical was particularly important because Eliot, influenced by Victorian constructions of womanhood, was extremely anxious about egotism.[19] She calls herself too egotistical at least sixteen different times in the first volume of her letters—usually with regard to writing too much about herself. As Ruby Redinger shows, she frequently felt uneasy about an interest in herself that she could not suppress; indeed that very uneasiness added to her self-consciousness (42).

Writing to her friends from Geneva in 1848, she begs for letters on the grounds that she has both too much identity and too little, with one allusion to a Shakespearean text (*Macbeth* 3.4.24) and one to the animal that was one of Keats's images of Shakespeare.[20] "My nature is so chameleon I shall lose all my identity unless you keep nourishing the old self with letters" (*Letters* 1:302); "When one is cabin'd, cribbed, confined in oneself, it is good to be enlarged in one's friends" (1:324). The cumulative effect of her letters suggests that these comments are not simply jokes but also reflections of an uncertainty about identity rather similar to that discussed by Erik Erikson in *Young Man Luther.*[21]

In Erikson's interpretation, Luther resolved his crisis by writing lectures on the Psalms and by reformulating his theology; Eliot helped herself resolve this crisis by her work as an essayist and translator and by formulating views about both life and fiction in which the growth out of egotism into sympathy is seen not simply as a need of her own but as a process of maturing more generally important, and one in which the role of the artist is especially important. "When we are young we think our troubles a mighty business—that the world is spread out expressly as a stage for the particular drama of our lives and that we have a right to rant and foam at the mouth if we are crossed. I have done enough of that in my time. But we begin at last to understand that these things are important only to one's own consciousness" (*Letters* 2:156).

In "The Natural History of German Life," July 1856, she declares, "The greatest benefit we owe to the artist, whether painter, poet, or novelist, is the extension of our sympathies" (*Essays* 270). Yet she found no English novelist really adequate in presentation of the life of the people. Dickens is her best example, but, when dealing with "the emotional and tragic," he is "transcendent in his unreality" (271). Praising him, however, she grants him "the same startling inspiration in his description of the gestures and phrases of 'Boots', as in the speeches of Shakespeare's mobs or numbskulls." Implicit in this essay is the image of the sympathetic Shakespeare as the quintessential artist.

By the end of her career, descriptions of the impression she created in person as well as in her novels often resemble the Victorian image of Shakespeare. When Lewes contrasts Shakespeare to Goethe, for example, he writes, "He uttered no moral verdict; he was no Chorus preaching on the text of what he pictured. Hence we cannot gather from his works what were his opinions."[22] Cross's summary at the end of *Life and Letters* makes a similar point: "And it was this wide sympathy, this understanding of so many points of view, that gained for her the passionate devotion not only of personal friends, but also of literary admirers from the most widely sundered sections of society. . . . This many-sidedness, however, makes it exceedingly difficult to ascertain, either from her books or from the closest personal intimacy, what her exact relation was to any existing religious creed or to any political party" (3:344–45).

To the reader of *Daniel Deronda,* this description may recall not only the Victorian image of Shakespeare but also the initial presentation of Daniel himself, where many-sided sympathy has its drawbacks. In his characterization, Eliot treats her ideal of compassion in a self-conscious way. Partly because of the link between aesthetic manysidedness and inactivity, nineteenth-century critics often identified Shakespeare and Hamlet; I will show that Daniel has something of what they saw in both.[23]

Like Rosalind, Hamlet interested George Eliot throughout her career, but while the greatest concentration of *As You Like It* allusions in Eliot's correspondence is early, her *Hamlet* allusions, the second most numerous overall, increase as time proceeds. Any cultured Victorian probably knew this play well, but Eliot's interest in it can be related to her particular situation within her culture. I suggest that she often sees *Hamlet* from a woman's viewpoint, in several different ways.

In *The Mill on the Floss,* her narrator turns a cold, demythologizing eye on its hero and takes critical note of his attitude toward Ophelia. "Hamlet, Prince of Denmark, was speculative and irresolute, and we have a great tragedy in consequence. But if his father had lived to a good old age, and his uncle had died an early death, we can conceive Hamlet's having married Ophelia and got through life with a reputation of sanity notwithstanding many soliloquies, and some moody sarcasms towards the fair daughter of Polonius, to say nothing of the frankest incivility to his father-in-law."[24] The narrator of *Middlemarch* refers to Hamlet in a rather different context: when Dorothea returns with a "triumphant power of indignation" from the visit in which she sees Rosamond with Ladislaw and moans, "Oh, all the troubles of all people upon the face of the earth," Celia is "uneasy at this Hamlet-like raving" and asks, "Dear me, Dodo, are you going to have a scheme for them?"[25] This association in Celia's mind suggests that Eliot finds in Hamlet the universal sympathy she sees in his creator, a quality congenial to the self-image of an idealistic Victorian woman, if not to the pragmatic Celia.

In Hamlet, Eliot chose a hero whose manhood is often questioned by himself and others. David Leverenz, who writes that Hamlet is "as Goethe was the first to say, part woman," has shown how often Hamlet and other characters use female imagery of him:[26] Claudius calls his grief "unmanly" (1.2.94) and Hamlet associates his powerlessness with that of a whore or a drab. According to Bernard Grebanier, starting with Sarah Siddons in 1775, more than fifty women have played Hamlet, many in the nineteenth century. Like Eliot, they were interested in transcending the limits usually set on women, but their particular focus on Hamlet, like hers, I would argue, resulted from seeing him as a figure who also transcended the bounds of gender.[27]

Many male critics of the nineteenth century used words such as "sensitivity," with feminine associations, to apply to Hamlet. What is unusual in the *Middlemarch* passage is the implied association of Hamlet with sympathy—a word much harder to find in nineteenth-century descriptions of Hamlet.[28]

Hamlet is the one Shakespearean character for whom Eliot tells us directly a character of hers is named: "A College Breakfast-Party" begins with "Young Hamlet, not the hesitating Dane, / But one named after him."[29] This character is "held inert / 'Twixt fascinations of all opposites.... Having no choice but choice of everything." Speculative and irresolute indeed! He asks a priest:

> I crave direction, Father, how to know
> The sign of that imperative whose right
> To sway my act in face of thronging doubts
> Were an oracular gem in price beyond
> Urim and Thummim lost to Israel.
> That bias of the soul, that conquering die
> Loaded with golden emphasis of Will—
> How find it where resolve, once made, becomes
> The rash exclusion of an opposite
> Which draws the stronger as I turn aloof.
>
> *(Poems* 420)

Ruby Redinger comments on the poem, "She herself had known well the Hamlet-road of quest and questioning" (366). It was published in 1874, an incidental project while she was writing, in her last novel, about another character whose "sensibility and reflectiveness had developed into a many-sided sympathy, which threatened to hinder any persistent course of action."[30] This blending of Hamlet characteristics with the Shakespeare characteristic most associated with "female" values is one of the main ways that *Daniel Deronda* shows Eliot reading and revising Shakespeare from a woman's point of view.

The two main characters in *Daniel Deronda* are, in different ways, rewritings of these two Shakespearean figures Eliot found so interesting— Rosalind and Hamlet. The identification of Gwendolen with Rosalind is the most explicit, although, as Knoepflmacher observes, the effect is ironical (28). It is partly because George Eliot loves the frank passion that she sees in Shakespeare's women that she recalls them so emphatically in the creation of a character as far removed from frank passion as Gwendolen. On a festive day in the forest, "It was agreed that they were playing an extemporized 'As you like it;' and when a pretty compliment had been turned to Gwendolen about her having the part of Roasalind, she felt the more compelled to be surpassing in liveliness" (135). Gwendolen has Rosalind's charm, commanding personality (except with Grandcourt), and love of role-playing, but she lacks the affection toward others that is one of the most salient characteristics of Rosalind in Eliot's allusions to her.

When Gwendolen says to Anna, "You are a dear little coz" (50), she echoes Rosalind's words to Celia and recalls the relationship that Eliot enjoyed evoking in her early letters. But Gwendolen lacks Rosalind's easy sisterly communication and thus seems more isolated.

Comparison to a scene in *As You Like It* points up the emphasis in two early incidents on how much stronger Gwendolen's feeling for herself is than her feeling for others. During Rosalind's time disguised as a boy, she is accosted by Orlando's brother Oliver, who explains that Orlando has saved him from a starved lioness and flourishes a cloth stained with his brother's blood. At this sight Rosalind faints, revealing the depth of the feeling under her disguise. However, she tries to cover this up by claiming that she was acting: "I pray you," she says to Oliver, "tell your brother how well I counterfeited" (4.3.165–66).

Early in *Daniel Deronda*, Gwendolen acts in a Shakespearean tableau: she plays Hermione in the statue scene from *The Winter's Tale*. When Paulina calls for music and Herr Klesmer, the musician, plays a chord on the piano, a panel flies open to reveal a dead face, and Gwendolen is terrified. Obviously her terror is not an intended part of the performance, but Herr Klesmer pretends it is: he twice praises it as a "bit of *plastik*" (54,55). In both scenes, self-possessed characters are momentarily shocked out of their poise. Rosalind's shock comes out of her feeling for Orlando, and she has enough aplomb to invent a quick excuse for herself; Gwendolen's shock comes out of a more primitive fear of death; she is not resourceful enough to invent an excuse and is so self-deceived that she thinks Herr Klesmer really means the praise of her acting that he offers.

But if Gwendolen's fear is heart-felt, Eliot shows her acting soon after. Her uncle Gascoyne tells her about her cousin Rex's fall on a riding expedition from which Gwendolen has returned with great success. Gwendolen's response is " 'Oh, poor fellow! he is not hurt, I hope?' with a correct look of anxiety, such as elated mortals try to superinduce when their pulses are all the while quick with triumph" (68). Gascoyne is carefully watching Gwendolen to determine what she feels about his son; when he explains that Rex has put his shoulder out and is bruised, "Gwendolen, instead of any such symptoms as pallor and silence, had only deepened the compassionateness of her brow and eyes, and said again, 'Oh, poor fellow! it is nothing serious, then?' " As he deliberately emphasizes the incongruity of his description, Gwendolen gives up attempts at a sympathetic face and bursts into laughter. Comparison with Rosalind, who can't help fainting when she hears about Orlando's injury, emphasizes Gwendolen's lack of feeling for Rex and, by extension, for other people in general. As Bonnie Zimmerman has shown, many details place Gwendolen as a type of the "new woman" of the 1860s and 1870s, the "Girl of the Period," whose highest priority, in the critical view of Eliza Lynn Linton, was fun.[31] By contrast, the sympathetic qualities of Rosalind were emphasized by the Victorians, including Eliot's friend, the actress Helen Faucit, who helped moved the character "from an eighteenth century hoyden, a comic breeches part, into the sentimental 'womanly woman.' "[32]

Gwendolen's most disastrous act is a further contrast to Rosalind. Rather than choose a husband she loves, as Rosalind does with the frankness Eliot praises in her essay on Girardin, Gwendolen marries Grandcourt. To others, this appears the climax of a romantic courtship: on the day of the forest party, for example, the earl interprets Grandcourt's lateness as if it belonged to a character like Orlando—"a lover so absorbed in thinking of the beloved object as to forget an appointment which would bring him into her actual presence" (134–35). When Gwendolen is asked if she has met him on a walk, she replies, "No. . . . And we didn't see any carvings on the trees either" (138).

What she has seen shows how much darker the world of *Deronda* is than the world of Shakespeare's comedy, even when both are dealing with marriage. In the play, infidelity is something to be laughed at ("Wilt thou have me?" "Ay, and twenty such" 4.1.11–12) and the emphasis is on cuckoldry—the husband's perspective on a wife's behavior. In the novel, infidelity results in children and has more serious consequences for women: Gwendolen meets Lydia Glasher, who has left her husband for Grandcourt and has then been rejected by *him*. In *As You Like It*, realism is making fun of Petrarchan convention; here the inadequacy of literature goes deeper: "Gwendolen's uncontrolled reading, though consisting chiefly in what are called pictures of life, had somehow not prepared her for this encounter with reality" (140).

Gwendolen's strongest passion is for self-assertion, and she uses the plays for this purpose. In the *Winter's Tale* tableau, she changes the staging from Shakespeare's text so that she will be paid the tribute of a kneeling Leontes. "This awakened Hermione is to maintain the remoteness and detachment of the carved figure."[33] The scene interests her because of the opportunity of appearing in a statuesque pose in her Greek dress. Elsewhere she quotes—slightly misquotes—Othello's lines about Desdemona (3.3.92–93) only to make fun of her suitor's lack of expression: "If he had to say 'Perdition catch my soul, but I do love her,' he would say it in just the same tone as, 'Here endeth the second lesson.' " (49). (It is ironic that after this dismissal of Mr. Middleton she marries a man whose emotionless manner is much more ominous.) She often sees life in terms of theater, but without understanding the demands of either. "She had never acted—only made a figure in *tableaux vivans* at school; but she felt assured that she could act well," and she wondered "whether she should become an actress like Rachel, since she was more beautiful than that thin Jewess" (48). In calculating her chances for success, she uses arguments which recall Sarah Siddons's writings about Lady Macbeth's femininity: "I think a higher voice is more tragic: it is more feminine; and the more feminine a woman is, the more tragic it seems when she does desperate actions" (48).[34] Though these lines hint something of Gwendolen's future in this book, at this point she knows nothing of tragedy or desperation.

The *As You Like It* allusions suggest a doubleness in the way Eliot now takes a woman's viewpoint on Shakespeare: she enjoys his representation of women who could combine power and love, and recalls it to criticize Gwendolen; but she associates Gwendolen's illusions about her power as a wife with Gwendolen's interest in the power of Shakespeare's women, and thus she criticizes a reading of the comedies to foster romanticism about marriage.

Gwendolen has less feeling for others and more ambition than her culture's ideal of woman. Eliot juxtaposes her with Daniel, who has more feeling and apparently less ambition than his culture's ideal of man. The narrator makes it explicit that Daniel transcends traditional gender expectations—he is "moved by an affectionateness such as we are apt to call feminine, disposing him to yield in ordinary details, while he had a certain inflexibility of judgment, an independence of opinion, held to be rightfully masculine" (295).

In a different way from the associations of Gwendolen and Rosalind, the *Hamlet* allusions in this novel also show Eliot reading Shakespeare as a woman. Like Hamlet, Gwendolen and Daniel in turn each receive a "ghastly vision" (137) and "a new guest who seemed to come with an enigmatic veiled face, and to carry dimly-conjectured, dreaded revelations" (152). Both Gwendolen's literal visitor, Mrs. Glasher, and Daniel's metaphorical one, the idea of his illegitimacy, carry secret messages connected with another's sexual behavior. For both characters, Eliot is rewriting Hamlet's ghostly visitation, except that the message in *Deronda* is presented more as the wrong done to women and children than, as in *Hamlet*, wrong that inspires disgust with women.

Daniel is like the Victorian Hamlet and the Hamlet of "A College Breakfast-Party" because of his "reflective hesitation" (164). He returns to England after studying on the continent "questioning whether it were worth while to take part in the battle of the world" (169). Like Hamlet he has a Polonius-like foil in Sir Hugo. When he asks permission for his continental studies, Sir Hugo says, with both the superficiality and the interest in selfhood in Polonius's famous speech to Laertes: "For God's sake, keep an English cut, and don't become indifferent to bad tobacco! And—my dear boy—it is good to be unselfish and generous; but don't carry that too far. It will not do to give yourself to be melted down for the benefit of the tallow trade; you must know where to find yourself" (168). But unlike Hamlet's "incivility" to Polonius, Deronda maintains a tolerant affection for his uncle.

Deronda is given an Ophelia as well as a Polonius. He meets his future wife for the first time as she is on the point of drowning herself. The willows in the background recall the setting of Ophelia's drowning as described by Gertrude—a frequent subject for painting and other allusions in the nineteenth century. It is as if Eliot's rewritten Hamlet must reverse the course of the original in dealing with women and so become even more idealized. Shakespeare's Hamlet moves from disgust with his mother—"Frailty, thy name is woman" (1.2.146)—to rejection of Ophelia—"If thou wilt needs marry, marry a fool, for wise men know what monsters you make of them" (3.2.138). Deronda, seeing Mirah's misery, thinks, "Perhaps my mother was like this one" (175) and saves her from drowning.

Deronda is more like Hamlet and like the Shakespeare of the sonnets in his intense involvement with male friendship. At the university he gives up much of his own study time to help his friend Hans Meyrick, but he longs for a friend to whom he can confide more about himself, toward whom he feels more of an equality. His friendship with Mordecai, who communicates mystical visions of Zionism, is presented in language echoing that of the idealizing sonnets, without their tensions or disillusionment. When they are about to have their first conversation, the two have "as intense a consciousness as if they had been two undeclared lovers" (462).[35]

In general, Daniel's Shakespearean associations idealize him. While with Gwendolen we repeatedly find less sympathy than her Shakespearean prototype, with Daniel we find more.[36] By contrast with Gwendolen, he reads with empathy, forgetting "his own existence in that of Robert Bruce" (154). The narrator repeatedly suggests that "many-sided sympathy" is the cause of his inaction (335–36). Like the revision of Hamlet's disgust with women into Deronda's "interest in the fates of women" (174), this interpretation shows Eliot writing from a female perspective. Preëminence in sympathy links Deronda not only to Hamlet but to Shakespeare himself. Eliot calls it "an activity of imagination on behalf of others" (162) and gives an explicitly Shakespearean reference point for this sympathy when "Grandcourt held that the Jamaican negro was a beastly sort of baptist Caliban; Deronda said he had always felt a little with Caliban, who naturally had his own point of view and could sing a good song" (303–4). Although he is not a poet, the imagery presenting him often compares him to one; the narrator calls his "meditative interest in learning how human miseries are wrought . . . as precocious in him as another sort of genius in the poet who writes a Queen Mab at nineteen" (163).

Reading Shakespeare with Eliot's passion, imagining others' sorrows as she saw her own art as doing, Daniel becomes identified not only with Hamlet and Shakespeare but also with Eliot's own public image. Consider, for example, the account of a meeting with Eliot late in life that her childhood friend Mary Sibree Cash wrote to Cross: "It touched me deeply to find how much she had retained of her kind interest in all that concerned me and mine, and I remarked on this to Mr. Lewes. . . . When I added, inquiringly, 'The power lies there?' 'Unquestionably it does,' was his answer; 'she forgets nothing that has ever come within the curl of her eyelash' " (Cross 1:385). Compare these descriptions of Daniel:

> What he felt was a profound sensibility to a cry from the depths of another soul; and accompanying that, the summons to be receptive instead of superciliously prejudging. Receptiveness is a rare and massive power, like fortitude; and this state of mind now gave Deronda's face its utmost expression of calm benignant force. (463)

> His eyes . . . were a dark yet mild intensity, which seemed to express a special interest in every one on whom he fixed them, and might easily help to bring on him those claims which ardently sympathetic people are often creating in the minds of those who need help. (304)

Critics have found a number of autobiographical elements in Gwendolen's early life. Many of the passages I cite here suggest ways in which Daniel is also a projection of Eliot's own experience. Eliot links them both with Shakespearean figures important to her: the novel's Shakespearean dimension is closely related to its personal dimension because Shakespeare was so much a part of Eliot's personal mythology. Eliot's letters and her narrators' voices speak of maturity as a conversion from self-concern to sympathy. But both self-concern and sympathy, as Eliot imagined them in Gwendolen and Daniel, possess the intense feeling that Eliot associated with Shakespeare. Daniel gently urges to Gwendolen the conversion that Eliot enacted in her own life: "I suppose our keen feeling for ourselves might end in giving us a keen feeling for others, if, when we are suffering acutely, we were to consider that others go through the same sharp experience" (420).

The conclusion of both plots in *Daniel Deronda* rewrite literary tradition. Gwendolen's expectations that Daniel will stay in her life as, at least, a mentor coalesce with novelistic and comic conventions that, like a Mr. Knightly or a Felix Holt, having educated her, he will marry her. But there is no comic ending for Gwendolen. She is left in an openness and uncertainty that recalls something of Deronda's situation near the beginning.

The epigraph of chapter 32 implies that writing about Daniel's love in relation to his intellectual worldview is rewriting the great love stories of literature in another way. The reversal in emphasis from the passage in *Clerical Life* which declares Caterina's astronomical ignorance irrelevant to her talent for loving suggests how much more ambitious Eliot had become about the scope of her fiction: "In all ages it hath been a favourite text that a potent love hath the nature of an isolated fatality, whereto the mind's opinions and wonted resolves are altogether alien: as, for example, . . . Romeo in his sudden taking for Juliet, wherein any objections he might have held against Ptolemy had made little difference to his discourse under the balcony. Yet all love is not such, even though potent; nay, this passion hath as large scope as any for allying itself with every operation of the soul: so that it shall acknowledge an effect from the imagined light of unproven firmaments, and have its scale set to the grander orbits of what hath been and shall be." (332)

Daniel chooses to commit himself to making a Jewish nation in terms that, as Bonnie Zimmerman has pointed out, idealize Judaism as the "heart of mankind, . . . the core of affection" (492).[37] From one point of view, this suggests the breakdown of the public/domestic dichotomy in his final vocation; from another, it suggests how visionary is his and Eliot's final image of public life. His valuation of Judaism for its transmission of emotion is rather like the valuation that Eliot places on "that exquisite type of gentleness, tenderness, possible maternity suffusing a woman's being with affectionateness, which makes what we mean by the feminine character" (*Letters* 4:468). Thus, in his membership in an oppressed group as well as in his temperament, Daniel's viewpoint is close to what Eliot sees as a woman's.

Eliot's "Notes on the Spanish Gypsy and on Tragedy in General" emphasizes the role of hereditary conditions in tragedy, using as main examples Othello and the Virgin Mary, designated because of her heredity for a fate different from "the ordinary lot of womanhood" (Cross 3:32). But that "ordinary lot," or what remains of it even for an atypical woman, is itself a hereditary condition in a different sense.

Eliot herself had dealt with the conflict between the ideal of female domesticity and her interest in accomplishing something in the larger world. Her discovery of herself as a fiction writer coincided with her discovery that her own life had given her subject matter in the lives of women as well as the lives of her former neighbors whose provinciality had seemed a burden to her. Her attitude toward being a woman eventually came to be rather like Deronda's attitude toward being a Jew: ultimately she gloried in defining herself as "wife" and "mother" and wrote to other women in ways that assumed much more community with them in these roles than contrast.[38] If she saw her writing as an act of sympathy, it was consistent with the ideals she saw in womanhood and thus very different from the art of Alcharisi, who could not combine her role as an artist with her role as a mother.

But Eliot was no longer simply the interested correspondent and good listener, or even the translator and anonymous journalist. She was the internationally known novelist-sage whose novels dealt with events in world history. Shakespeare's female characters, though she early found them models of autonomy, did not exhaust the plots of women's lives, as her portrayal of Gwendolen emphasizes, and could not be models for her in making that transition. Instead she behaved somewhat as Carolyn Heilbrun urges contemporary women to do and reinterpreted male literary figures for her own purposes.[39] The romantic and Victorian Hamlet, with his concern for the world's wrongs and his contemplative nature, was a suggestive model, though imperfect, and the romantic and Victorian Shakespeare, whose writing was motivated by his universal sympathy, was an even better one. And both because she felt that "woman has something specific to contribute" to art and literature (*Essays* 53) and because he had written so many years previously, he was the kind of model that left her much of her own to say, somewhat as Daniel leaves Gwendolen to find her own work.

Thus in *Daniel Deronda* Eliot was rewriting Shakespeare in several ways. Gwendolen's story ends more sadly than Rosalind's because of Gwendolen's own limitations as well as because of the greater harshness of the world where Eliot places her. Daniel, on the other hand, is a Hamlet idealized enough to represent Eliot's own ego-ideal. In Gwendolen's plot we can see Eliot's interest in Shakespeare's women turning into a concern to represent the experiences of women more realistically; in Daniel's plot we see Eliot claiming both Shakespeare and Hamlet as figures that she could identify with partly because of their possession of qualities that she associated with women. Her interest in women as a distinct and diverse group, sharing many social restrictions, predominates in the realistic mode of Gwendolen's plot; her interest in traditionally female values predominates in the idealizing mode of Daniel's plot. Comedy revised toward realism, tragedy revised toward romanticism—this description of the two plots may help to account for the disjunction many readers have felt between them.[40]

Eliot's reading was vast, and the number of writers who stirred her imagination was not small. Ellen Moers has shown her interest in such women writers as Jane Austen, Charlotte Brontë, George Sand, and Harriet Beecher Stowe; Gillian Beer has added Geraldine Jewsbury and Fredrika Bremer.[41] But Shakespeare played a special role for her, as he would for such twentieth-century writers as Virginia Woolf and H.D.[42] Paradoxically, taking him as a model permitted her to affirm her aspirations and deny self-centeredness at the same time. Reading Shakespeare from a woman's viewpoint, emphasizing qualities in him and in his characters that crossed gender boundaries, Eliot reimagined a literary tradition that she could claim as her own.

NOTES

This essay is a shorter version of one published in *Studies in English Literature* 28 (1988): 671–92. I am grateful for helpful comments on earlier versions of this paper from Jonathan Arac, Shirley Nelson Garner, Harriet Gilliam, Helene Moglen, Liane Ellison Norman, Josephine O'Brien Schaefer, Elizabeth Segel, William J. Sullivan, and Richard Tobias.

1. U. C. Knoepflmacher, "*Daniel Deronda* and William Shakespeare," *Victorian Newsletter* 19 (1961): 27, 28.

2. Judith Fetterley, *The Resisting Reader* (Bloomington: Indiana University Press, 1978), xx–xxii.

3. Sandra Gilbert and Susan Gubar, *The Madwoman in the Attic* (New Haven: Yale University Press, 1979).

4. Mary Poovey, *The Proper Lady and the Woman Writer* (Chicago: University of Chicago Press, 1984), 44.

5. Gilbert and Gubar, *The Madwoman in the Attic*, 48.

6. Nina Auerbach, *Woman and the Demon* (Cambridge: Harvard University Press, 1982), 207–17. Auerbach writes that "for Victorian audiences Shakespearean characters represented the apotheosis of selfhood and a glorification of womanhood in particular" (207).

7. Throughout I will use the name George Eliot, although my discussion includes works written before her adoption of this pseudonym and letters signed, for example, Marian Lewes, as well as the novels. The persistence of her pseudonym, as distinguished, for example, from Charlotte Brontë's, seems in part a sign of the "created" nature of her identity; see Ruby Redinger, *George Eliot: The Emergent Self* (New York: Alfred A. Knopf, 1975).

8. See *The George Eliot Letters*, ed. Gordon S. Haight, 9 vols. (New Haven: Yale University Press, 1954–78). Further references to these volumes (*Letters*) will be parenthetically included in the text. The letters include eighteen references to *AYLI*, and she frequently includes it in short informal lists of Shakespeare's works, for example in 6:113. *AYLI* 1.3.12 is the source of what she calls "my favorite little epithet 'this working day world' " (1:44), a phrase which appears frequently in her essays and novels; see her *Essays*, ed. Thomas Pinney (New York: Columbia University Press, 1963), 302n. Shakespeare citations are from *The Complete Works*, ed. David Bevington, 3rd ed. (Glenview, Ill.: Scott, Foresman, 1980).

9. Lillian Faderman, *Surpassing the Love of Men* (New York: Morrow, 1981).

10. George Eliot, *A Writer's Notebook 1854–1879 and Uncollected Writings,* ed. Joseph Wiesenfarth (Charlottesville: University Press of Virginia, 1981), 255. The *Leader* was Lewes's journal and it was just the previous year that she had chosen to violate "propriety" by living with him. Of course the review, like most journalism then, was published anonymously. For an earlier violation of propriety, see her passionate letter to Herbert Spencer (8:56–57).

11. William Hazlitt, *Round Table and Characters of Shakespeare's Plays* (New York: E. P. Dutton, 1836), 180.

12. Russell Jackson, " 'Perfect Types of Womanhood': Rosalind, Beatrice and Viola in Victorian Criticism and Performance," *Shakespeare Survey,* ed. Kenneth Muir (32 [1979]: 16). Jackson shows such unease even in Mary Cowden Clarke and Anna Jameson, two of Auerbach's major examples of the Victorian celebration of the individuality of Shakespeare's women. The mythic female power Auerbach finds in such Victorian Shakespeare criticism, as elsewhere in Victorian culture, must be distinguished from Eliot's interest, social assertiveness.

13. J. W. Cross, ed., *George Eliot's Life as Related in Her Letters and Journals,* 3 vols. (Boston: Dana Estes; rpt. Grosse Pointe., Mich.: Scholarly Press, 1968), 1:287–88.

14. Elizabeth D. Ermarth, *George Eliot* (Boston: Twayne, 1985), 14.

15. Characters love at cross-purposes somewhat as in *AYLI:* Captain Wybrow uses a phrase from this play when he says, "I've a fellow-feeling for a poor devil so many fathoms deep in love as Maynard"; see *Scenes of Clerical Life,* ed. Thomas A. Noble (Oxford: Clarendon Press, 1985), 146; *AYLI* 4.1.198. But he is arguing in favor of moving up an arranged marriage, which precipitates a disaster somewhat as in *Romeo and Juliet.* Maynard fears Caterina has drowned and "seems to see part of her dress caught on a branch, and her dear dead face upturned" (165), like Ophelia. On the obsession with Ophelia's drowning in nineteenth-century art and literature, see Auerbach, *Woman and the Demon,* 94–96, and Elaine Showalter, "Representing Ophelia: Women, Madness, and the Responsibilities of Feminist Criticism," in *Shakespeare and the Question of Theory,* ed. Patricia Parker and Geoffrey Hartman (New York: Methuen, 1985), 83–85.

16. Lawrence Lipking, "Aristotle's Sister: A Poetics of Abandonment," in *Canons,* ed. Robert von Hallberg (Chicago: University of Chicago Press, 1984), 85–105.

17. John Keats, *Selected Letters,* ed. Lionel Trilling (New York: Farrar, Straus, and Young, 1951), 152.

18. William Hazlitt, "On Shakespeare and Milton," in *Complete Works,* ed. P. P. Howe, 21 vols. (1930; rpt. New York: AMS Press, 1967), 5:47.

19. Anxiety about whether the vocation of writer was too selfish was, as Elaine Showalter shows, generated by the nineteenth-century construction of women's role; see *A Literature of Their Own* (Princeton: Princeton University Press, 1977). However, Eliot's letters mention anxiety about egotism much more than those of such other authors as Charlotte Brontë or Elizabeth Gaskell.

20. On her 'chameleon' nature and her ambivalence about it, see Nina Auerbach, *Romantic Imprisonment* (New York: Columbia University Press, 1985), 257.

21. Erik Erikson, *Young Man Luther* (New York: W. W. Norton, 1958).

22. G. H. Lewes, *Life of Goethe,* 2nd ed. (London: Smith, Elder, 1864), 54.

23. Jonathan Bate, *Shakespeare and the English Romantic Imagination* (Oxford: Clarendon Press, 1986), 19. The similarity between Hamlet and Deronda has also been noted by Linda Bamber in *Comic Women, Tragic Men* (Stanford: Stanford University Press, 1982), 89.

24. George Eliot, *The Mill on the Floss,* ed. A. S. Byatt (Baltimore: Penguin Books, 1979), 514.

25. George Eliot, *Middlemarch,* ed. W. J. Harvey (Baltimore: Penguin Books, 1965), 833.

26. David Leverenz, "The Woman in Hamlet: An Interpersonal View," in *Representing Shakespeare,* ed. Murray Schwartz and Coppélia Kahn (Baltimore: John Hopkins University Press, 1980), 110–128; quote is from 111.

27. Bernard Grebanier, *Then Came Each Actor* (New York: David McKay, 1975), 253–54. Grebanier suggests that the common belief in Hamlet's sensitivity encouraged actresses to think of him "as a sister under the skin" (253).

28. See for example *Readings on the Character of Hamlet,* ed. Claude C. H. Williamson (London: Allen and Unwin, 1950).

29. George Eliot, *Poems,* in *Works,* 10 vols. (New York: Bigelow, Brown and Co., 1908), 8:416.

30. George Eliot, *Daniel Deronda,* ed. Graham Handley (Oxford: Claredon Press, 1984), 335.

31. Bonnie Zimmerman, "Gwendolen Harleth and 'The Girl of the Period,'" in *George Eliot: Centenary Essays and an Unpublished Fragment,* ed. Anne Smith (Totowa, N.J.: Barnes and Noble, 1980), 196–217.

32. Charles Shattuck, *Mr. Macready Produces "As You Like It"* (Urbana: Beta Phi Mu, 1962), 55n.

33. Ian Adam, *"The Winter's Tale* and Its Displacements: The Hermione Episode in *Daniel Deronda," Newsletter of the Victorian Studies Association of Western Canada* 9 (Spring 1983): 10.

34. Thomas Campbell, *Life of Mrs. Siddons* (New York: Harper and Brothers, 1834), 124, quotes Siddons's description of Lady Macbeth as "fair, feminine, nay perhaps even fragile"; but she also described her as someone who "had probably from childhood commanded all around her with a high hand" (129), like Gwendolen. Gwendolen's pose as Hermione, "her arm resting on a pillar," is borrowed from the stance used by Siddons and other eighteenth-century actresses in this part, in which she was famous, according to Hugh Witemeyer, *George Eliot and the Visual Arts* (New Haven: Yale University Press, 1979), 93–94.

35. With cross-gender imagery like that in the sonnets, Mordecai has "something of the slowly dying mother's look when her one loved son visits her bedside" (462) and says to Daniel, "It has begun already—the marriage of our souls" (698).

36. And emphatically more than the Shakespearean characters who contributed to his image of the experience of illegitimacy—he is "the reverse of that type

painted for us in Faulconbridge and Edmund of Gloster" with their "coarse ambition for personal success" (437).

37. Bonnie Zimmerman, " 'The Mother's History' in George Eliot's Life, Literature, and Political Ideology," in *The Lost Tradition: Mothers and Daughters in Literature,* ed. Cathy N. Davidson and E. M. Broner (New York: Frederick Ungar, 1980), 92. It should be noted that these are Mordecai's images. On the relation between Judaism and sympathy here, see Donald Stone, *The Romantic Impulse in Victorian Fiction* (Cambridge: Harvard University Press, 1980), 243, and David Marshall, *The Figure of Theater* (New York: Columbia University Press, 1986), 219.

38. Though not as activist as Deronda's, this solidarity involved an interest in social change; Gillian Beer has recently shown her familiarity with the "writing and actions of the women's movement." See her *George Eliot* (Bloomington: Indiana University Press, 1986), 180. Beer also notes the active feminism of many of Eliot's close friends—Clementia Doughty, Bessie Rayner Parkes, Barbara Bodichon, and Edith Simcox (181)—and recalls that Eliot signed Bodichon's petition in support of the Married Women's Property Bill and distributed sheets for it (169).

39. Carolyn Heilbrun, *Reinventing Womanhood* (New York: Norton, 1979), esp. 151.

40. However, Daniel's plot becomes more "realistic" in such moments as his confrontation with his mother, where, as Marshall shows (215), Eliot explores the limits of sympathy.

41. Ellen Moers, *Literary Women* (Garden City: Anchor/Doubleday, 1977), esp. 71–80; Beer, 41–51, adds to the intertextuality with the writers Moers discusses as well.

42. See essays in this volume by Susan Stanford Friedman and Christine Froula.

PAULA BENNETT

"The Orient is in the West": Emily Dickinson's Reading of Antony and Cleopatra

Vails of Kamtchatka dim the Rose—
in my Puritan Garden

Emily Dickinson, 1881

While Emily Dickinson was unquestionably an omnivorous reader, the only work now held in the Dickinson collection at Harvard University which shows signs of habitual use is the poet's edition of *Shakspere.* Two volumes, those containing the tragedies, have broken spines and loose pages. *Othello* has a number of pencil markings. *Antony and Cleopatra,* the most well-read of all the plays, contains three markers: a string at Act 3.11, Antony's "let that be left / Which leaves itself" speech; another string at 4.13, Antony's death scene, and a triangular piece of dress cloth at 5.2, the beginning of Cleopatra's death scene. After the Bible, Shakespeare is also the author to whom Dickinson alludes the most in her writing, the tragedies again taking pride of place.[1]

In assessing the extent of Shakespeare's influence on Dickinson (or indeed the influence of any other writer on this most cryptic and original of poets), such bits of material "evidence" are crucial. Dickinson did not elaborate her thoughts on the art of writing in prose disquisitions. A phrase here or there is the most we have, and often these phrases—like her much-quoted description of Emerson's *Representative Men* (a "little Granite Book"[2])—can be misleading. The poet's apparent admiration notwithstanding, her own copy of *Representative Men* seems hardly to have been read. Distinctly unlike *Shakspere,* its condition is pristine.[3]

The influence of Shakespeare's dramas on Dickinson was deep and pervasive, a matter of identification as well as apprenticeship, in which Dickinson utilized the playwright's ambiguity to find mirrors for herself. But it is an influence that must be teased out of brief allusions and felt in the complicated patterns of imagery which encode Dickinson's thought. It is not there for the asking. This essay explores one such image pattern— Dickinson's "Oriental" imagery—and the group of allusions which relate it to Shakespeare. Although the Orientalism of this imagery undoubtedly owes something to nineteenth-century Orientalism generally, as I now hope to show, it was specifically in Shakespeare's "Egyptian" tragedy that Dickinson found the justification and validation for the vision of romantic love and poetic imagination that shaped her poetry and her life.

The full significance of Dickinson's devotion to Shakespeare, and especially to *Antony and Cleopatra,* can only be appreciated within the context of her period's far more ambivalent response. While nineteenth-century educators and scholars were lavish in their praise of Shakespeare's greatness as a poet-dramatist, they were deeply troubled by his moral ambiguity (as indeed many feminist—and new historicist—critics are today). In the schools Emily Dickinson attended, Amherst Academy and Mount Holyoke Female Seminary, students read Milton, Watts, Cowper, and Young, not Shakespeare. Edward Hitchcock, Amherst's leading educator, called the bard "a libertine in principle and practice"[4] and Emerson, similarly, faulted Shakespeare for his "Egyptian" lifestyle. "[I]t must . . . ," the Concord sage mourned in *Representative Men,* "go into the world's history, that the best poet led an obscure and profane life, using his genius for the public amusement."[5]

Not surprisingly, nineteenth-century critical assessments of *Antony and Cleopatra* exhibit a similar double vision. Critics follow Coleridge in praising the play's poetry but carefully distance themselves from the morals of its protagonists. Thus, for example, Charles Knight, the editor of Dickinson's *Shakspere,* heaps praise on the tragedy's "flood of noonday splendour" but describes Antony as an "infatuated lover" and "reckless short-sighted voluptuary."[6] Similarly, F. J. Furnivall believes that the play depicts Antony's "ruin, under the gorgeous colouring of the Eastern sky, the vicious splendour of the Egyptian queen."[7] Such oxymoronic assessments were duplicated again and again in the course of the century. Despite the period's own fascination with the exotic East (evident in Furnivall's choice of qualifiers), these assessments represent the nineteenth century's mainstream judgment of the play and its protagonists. Like the judgment on Shakespeare himself, it was an opinion compounded in equal parts of admiration and distaste.

Confronted by such attitudes in her late adolescence, in the person of a young tutor who wished to bowdlerize her text, Dickinson is said to have declared: " 'There's nothing wicked in Shakespeare, and if there is I don't want to know it.' "[8] As she matured, her unreserved bardolatry seems only to have deepened. After 1865, in particular, when she recovered from a serious bout with eye disease, Dickinson turned to Shakespeare regularly, peppering her letters with allusions to the plays. "After long disuse of her eyes," Thomas Wentworth Higginson claims she said of this period, "she read Shakespeare & thought why is any other book needed"(*L476*). According to Dickinson herself, in a letter to Joseph Lyman, *Antony and Cleopatra* was the play she read first:

> Shakespear was the first; Antony & Cleopatra where Enobarbus laments the amorous lapse of his master. Here is the ring of it.
>
> > "heart that in the scuffles of
> > great fights hath burst the
> > buck[l]e on his breast"
>
> then I thought why . . . clasp any hand but this. Give me ever to drink of this wine.[9]

She chose Shakespeare because he supported and nourished her most fully ("hand," "wine"); and of his plays, she chose *Antony and Cleopatra* because the Roman tragedy stirred her the most.

Without exception, Dickinson's allusions to *Antony and Cleopatra* are of a piece and remarkably consistent in emphasis. Indeed, a number are repetitions. Not surprisingly, given Dickinson's general habit of writing, these allusions are also exceedingly cryptic, sometimes no more than a word or two, designed to set off reverberations in the reader's mind. However, if we fill in the gaps, their general intent can be grasped, together with their relevance to Dickinson's art and life.[10] Once this relevance has been established, *Antony and Cleopatra*'s shaping effect on the imagery Dickinson employed, as well as the life she lived, will become clear.

About 1874, Dickinson wrote to Susan Gilbert, her sister-in-law and the one person whom, it may be fairly said, she loved passionately all her life,[11] " 'Egypt—thou knew'st'—" (*L533*). In her laconic fashion, the poet was alluding to Antony's anguished statement of faith: "Egypt, thou knew'st too well / My heart was to thy rudder tied by th' strings,/And thou shouldst tow me after" (3.11.56–58). Far more elusively, Dickinson refers to the same bond between herself and Sue two other times, once in 1852, when she wrote to Sue, "Loved One, thou knowest!" (*L203*),[12] and once, the year before her death, when she declared: "The tie between us is very fine, but a Hair never dissolves" (*L893*). Although Dickinson's relationship to her sister-in-law underwent periods of profound tension, Susan was the poet's "Cleopatra" to the end of her life.

Also in 1874, Dickinson informed Thomas Wentworth Higginson that " 'Field Lilies' are Cleopatra's 'Posies' " (*L518*). With his typical mix of caring and condescension, Higginson had commented to the poet respecting a water color of yellow and scarlet field lilies: "[t]hese are not your favorite colors . . . but perhaps we should learn to love & cultivate these ruddy hues of life" (*L*519–20). Since Susan's name means lily in Hebrew,[13] Dickinson may be retorting that such "ruddy hues" belonged more appropriately to her vivacious sister-in-law than they did to her. In any case, she is rejecting them for herself.

Contextualizing her refusal to publish, Dickinson reminded Higginson in 1877 of his own words on the subject (" 'Such being the Majesty of the Art you presume to practice, you can at least take time before dishonoring it' ")[14] and adds, "Enobarbus said 'Leave that which leaves itself.' " (*L*573) She had the attribution wrong. The lines are Antony's: "Let that be left/Which leaves itself" (3.11.19–20); but the equation she is drawing between publication and self-betrayal (of her artistic ideals, her other Cleopatra) seems clear.

In a far more obscure set of fragments from 1882, Dickinson told Judge Otis P. Lord, then seeking to marry her, that "the Propounder of Paradise [Christ] must indeed possess it—Antony's remark . . . to a friend, 'since Cleopatra died' is said to be the saddest ever lain in Language— That engulfing '*Since*'—." In the fragments, Dickinson seems to be contrasting Antony's plight with Christ's confident statement to the thief, " 'This Day thou shalt be with me in Paradise' " (*L*754); but her sympathies lie, obviously, with the Roman general who was deprived of the one paradise Dickinson believed mattered.

In 1883, she again casts herself in Antony's role, albeit this time sarcastically, when writing Susan:

> Will my great Sister accept the minutae of Devotion,
> with timidity that it is no more?
> Susan's Calls are like Antony's Supper—
> "And pays his Heart for what his Eyes eat, only—"
>
> (*L*791)

Dickinson was to use this final tag line twice more before she died: once to her nephew, Ned Dickinson, two years later, thanking him for bringing over a supper Susan had cooked for her: "What an Embassy— / What an Ambassador! / 'And pays his Heart for what his Eyes eat only!' / Excuse the bearded Pronoun—" (*L*894), and once in a late prose fragment, accompanying a gift of fruit (*L*920).

Without naming him, Dickinson also appears to allude to Antony in a letter to Mrs. J. Howard Sweetser in 1883 when she asks "one more beggary of Love" (*L*757). Her request is to be remembered in Mrs. Sweetser's dreams; but the reference is to Antony's famous assertion, "There's beggary in the love that can be reckoned" (1.1.15).

In prose fragment PF66, she prays even more obliquely, "Let me not thirst with this Hock at my Lip, nor beg, with Domains in my Pocket—" (*L922*), an allusion to Cleopatra's description of the imagined Antony after his death: "in his livery / Walked crowns and crownets: realms and islands were / As plates dropped from his pocket" (5.2.90–92). Embedded in what for Dickinson was a long prose statement on the *value* of the imagination, this last allusion has a significance that is inversely proportional to its one-word length. I will return to it later.

Finally, reminded once more of Cleopatra by the artistic use of red and yellow, Dickinson sent an ironic Shakespearean thankyou to Mabel Loomis Todd in 1885. Todd, involved with the poet's brother, Austin, had send Dickinson a yellow jug with red trumpet vines painted on it. Given nineteenth-century Amherst's conventional values (the Todd-Dickinson affair was eventually to become notorious),[15] the poet's note had a double edge: "Thanks for the Ethiopian Face. / The Orient is in the West. / 'You knew, Oh Egypt,' said the entangled Antony—" (*L870*). Whether consciously or not, it may have given Dickinson a certain amount of pleasure to see her brother "entangled" at last in a situation in some ways as frustrating as her own with Sue.

While a total reading of Shakespeare's play cannot be drawn from these few, scant references, a *pattern* of reading is discernible in them. This pattern fits, moreover, extraordinarily well with what we know of other aspects of Dickinson's life and thought and with the poetry that she wrote both on love and—equally important—on the power of the romantic or poetic imagination. (As we shall see, the two cannot, finally, be separated.) Briefly, by 1874, Dickinson identified with Antony, "the bearded pronoun." Like him, indeed, even more than him, she longed for a "Supper" (a vision of love) she could eat with her eyes only. And like him, she was prepared to pursue this vision, this paradise, even though pursuing it meant sacrificing everything here. To a lover—or artist—with Dickinson's dedication, anything less would have been self-betrayal (a "leaving" of the self).

Indeed, it is precisely because, from her point of view, it was unrealizable on earth that the object of Antony's "amorous lapse" is so attractive to her. "Emblem," Dickinson wrote to Higginson in 1883, "is immeasurable—that is why it is better than Fulfillment, which can be drained—" (*L773*). The undrainable "emblem" of human desire ("she makes hungry/ Where most she satisfies," Enobarbus says of Cleopatra [2.2.238–39]), Cleopatra becomes in these passages the touchstone by which the gifts of love are judged. Not just Susan, but fruits, flowers, suppers, and vases are surrogates for the unobtainable Egyptian Queen. The heart and soul of the poet are "entangled," even as was Antony's, and she is compelled to "follow after," forced as she says not once but thrice to eat "with [her] eyes only" a "Supper" she can never actually have. And perhaps because she cannot have it, she returns to the idea again and again, even in the most mundane circumstances, whenever gratitude must be expressed or the beggary of love counted, until finally the Roman general's sad but heroic plight becomes a figure for her own life: not just the long-standing frustration of her love for Susan but the entirety of her existence and in particular the unswervingness of her dedication to art.

Although, as we shall see, she associated her "Egyptian" longings with an Oriental self, there is no evidence in these quotations that Dickinson identified with Cleopatra to anything like the same extent. Rather, Cleopatra represents that which is loved: the life, the vision, that is sought. She is the red and yellow field lily, the "Ethiopian Face," the "Supper" to be eaten, the "Paradise" for which we yearn. Exotic and unobtainable, her desirability lies in her power to arouse in the poet/protagonist the passionate desires from which Dickinson creates her art. In these passages, Cleopatra is the "land" ("Egypt," the "Orient," the "East") that draws the imagination forth and stimulates the speaker (like Antony) to follow after. Loving her, whether in herself or in her many surrogates, the poet is able to grasp a new, sublime vision of the world ("The Orient . . . in the West" or, as Dickinson says much more flippantly elsewhere, "Asia" in Vermont).[16] And in loving her, Dickinson is transformed. Filled with visions she could not otherwise possess (Antony's "new heaven, new earth" [1.1.17]), like the Roman general, she rises above the "element" in which she lives. She carries "Domains [poems?] in [her] Pocket." She will never thirst.

Given her Eastern identification, Cleopatra is unquestionably part of the huge and complicated network of exotic "Oriental" imagery which, as Rebecca Patterson observes, permeates Dickinson's writing as a whole, filling it with symbols of "incalculable wealth and unattainable desire."[17] Drawn from material as diverse as *The Arabian Nights, The Song of Songs, Revelations, Lalla Rookh,* Byron's "Tales," and *Peter Parley's Method of Telling about Geography to Children,* and very much an outgrowth of nineteenth-century literary Orientalism generally,[18] this network not only covers but conflates Egypt and Ethiopia, roses and lilies, vineyards and deserts, leopards and palm trees, satin and gold, Golconda and Libya, and Ophir and (Dickinson being Dickinson) Peru. From these far-flung pieces, it constructs an alternate world within Dickinson's verse, a world of "gorgeous coloring" and vast poetic wealth, which Dickinson contrasts time and again to the colorlessness and rigidity of the bourgeois nineteenth-century culture in which she lived, a culture which frowned, as Emerson indicates, on "Egyptian" values.

But as Dickinson's allusions to Shakespeare's play make clear, it was Cleopatra who most fully embodied and justified this alternate world—together with its divers riches—in Dickinson's thought. For she is not only the "Orient," from Egypt to Asia, from the Caspian to the Nile. *Through her association with Shakespeare,* she is also, and far more importantly, the appropriate emblem of the poet-lover's quest. And the search for her is, finally, the search of the imagination for itself. In *PF*66, Dickinson writes, "We thank thee Oh Father for this gay (strange) guide . . . to Days unbound, and whose Search but surpasses the occupying (—ascertaining—certifying—ratifying—) estimation" (*L*922). For Dickinson, it was the "Search," not the occupation, that mattered, for it was the search that endowed her (the poet) with the (imaginative) vision for which she longed. In a typical Dickinsonian paradox, the Antony who could sublimate desire into "what his eyes eat only" was the figure who came closest to having the "Cleopatra" that both love and poetry were. It was this Antony, not the nineteenth-century's figure of dissolute but satisfied desire, in whom Dickinson "found" (or created) the all-important model for herself, the necessary mirror for her own situation.

Whether Dickinson's conception of Antony as the avatar of the transcendental poet/lover represents Shakespeare's "intention" in *Antony and Cleopatra* or whether (as is most probable) it represents Dickinson's own "reading" of a hero about whom Shakespeare was nothing if not ambivalent does not, in my opinion, finally matter. The point is that for Dickinson it was through identifying with Antony's "Oriental" longings that she was able to articulate where her true homeland ("Asia") lay. In this, his most woman-centered, playful, and exotic tragedy, Shakespeare had figured forth the country to which Emily Dickinson felt she belonged and for whose sake—like Shakespeare's displaced Roman general—she was prepared to sacrifice all. More successfully (and positively) than any poet of her own, considerably more cramped period, he had put words to what Dickinson saw as her desire. And it was to these "Memories—of Palm—" that she devoted her poetry and her emotional life:

> Civilization—spurns—the Leopard!
> Was the Leopard—bold?
> Deserts—never rebuked her Satin—
> Ethiop—her Gold—
> Tawny—her Customs—
> She was Conscious—
> Spotted—her Dun Gown—

> This was the Leopard's nature—Signor—
> Need—a keeper—frown?
>
> Pity—the Pard—that left her Asia—
> Memories—of Palm—
> Cannot be stifled—with Narcotic—
> Nor suppressed—with Balm—[19]

The "Civilization" to which Dickinson refers in this poem is the patriarchal, moralizing civilization which both she—and Shakespeare—identified with the West. Represented by Octavius in the play and by the Master in the poem, this civilization has no place (or use) for the sensual, the female, or the poetic—in Emerson's term, "Egyptian" qualities all. Together these qualities comprise the "Other," with which, as Edward Said observes, the Orient has traditionally been associated in Western literature. In the West, such qualities are seen as disruptive. They are identified with lust (the "Spotted" gown of "Dun" flesh) and with transgressive behavior ("boldness"). In the West, the submissive, mute, and victimized Octavia, whom Furnivall (taking Antony at his word) identifies as "the gem of women,"[20] is the ideal female type—not her antithesis: the spotted Egyptian Queen (Shakespeare describes Cleopatra as "tawny" and pinched "black" with the sun [1.1.6 and 1.5.28]).

As Dickinson represents her desires in this poem, they had nothing in common with the values embodied in the latter gem-like, Octavia type. The need for passion and poetry (for opulence and splendor) were part of her "nature," a nature discovered and revealed in the very act of loving (writing). She cannot suppress this nature, any more than she can suppress her art, without violating what is essential in herself: her need for "Satin" and "Gold." Nor could she turn her back on the world that love or poetry disclosed simply because it had no place in the society in which she lived. On the contrary. Incompatible though it was with the pragmatic and largely utilitarian soil of the nineteenth-century New England, it was precisely this world that Dickinson sought to cultivate in her verse. In the brief but remarkable "Soil of Flint," she declares:

> [On the Bleakness of my Lot
> Bloom I strove to raise—
> Late—My Garden of a Rock—
> Yielded Grape—and Maise—]
>
> Soil of Flint, if steady tilled—
> Will refund the Hand—
> Seed of Palm, by Lybian Sun
> Fructified in Sand—
>
> (#681)

In opposition to her time and place—to the "Bleakness," as she puns in the discarded first stanza of this poem, "of [her] Lot"—Dickinson was determined to fructify New England's obdurate cultural and emotional soil. Through the "coeval" powers of love and poetry (#1247), she would bring the "Orient" to the "West" and enrich her writing and her life with all the sensual and aesthetic values which her immediate culture lacked.

As with her attempts to raise frost-sensitive sweet sultans in her garden, Dickinson knew hers was a perverse decision. (In a letter to Martha Gilbert Smith, she called the rearing of the exotic flowers in her garden "a perversion of Hemispheres" [L670].[21]) But from her point of view, there was no choice. For it was only by gaining access to the imaginative realms which love disclosed that Dickinson could nourish her life and verse. In "Your Riches—taught me—Poverty" (dedicated to Susan), Dickinson makes clear that for her there was no separation between the beloved and the visionary world which the beloved represents. Like Antony, Dickinson addresses her Queen metonymically in terms of the "Dominions" she embodies. If Cleopatra is the Roman general's "Egypt," Susan, far more lavishly, becomes Dickinson's Buenos Ayre, India, Golconda, and Peru:

> Your Riches—taught me—Poverty.
> Myself—a Millionaire
> In little Wealths, as Girls could boast
> Till broad as Buenos Ayre—
>
> You drifted your Dominions—
> A Different Peru—
> And I esteemed All Poverty
> For Life's Estate with you—
>
> . . .
>
> I'm sure 'tis India—all Day—
> To those who look on You—
> Without a stint—without a blame
> Might I—but be the Jew—
>
> I'm sure it is Golconda—
> Beyond my power to deem—
> To have a smile for Mine—each Day,
> How better, than a Gem!

(#299)

"To be Susan is Imagination, / To have been Susan, a Dream—," Dickinson wrote in 1883, concluding: "What depths of Domingo in that torrid Spirit" (L791). Pointing to the fact that Dickinson refused to visit her brother's house, The Evergreens, for fifteen years, critics have tended to view such late statements as, at best, holdovers of the poet's early, sentimental, attachment to her sister-in-law. But it is not that simple. Whatever Susan may have been in the flesh, and however strained the relationship between the two women at times became, to Dickinson *the poet,* her sister-in-law and beloved remained what she had always been: the long-sought lane to Domingo, Ophir, and Peru, the symbolic object of an all-too-human desire. She dreamt of Susan one night in 1878 and sent her the following poem (with a flower) the next day:

> Sister of Ophir—
> Ah Peru—
> Subtle the Sum
> That purchase you—
>
> (*L*632)[22]

Whether in reality or imagination this was what loving Susan, indeed what loving anyone, meant to her.

In the crucially important PF66, Dickinson writes: "We have . . . two Saviors—an Earthly and a Heavenly—This one [the "imagination"] is the Heavenly, for the other . . . says of himself he was seen of the Twelve, and . . . this one had no Hours of Flesh." "Other Sails must slack," she added in the same fragment, "other steeds . . . *expire*—but this is it's own divine Relay—" (*L*922).

For Dickinson, the capacity of the romantic imagination to transcend reality enabled it to create a "heaven" (an "Eden," an "East") more divine than God's. And it was this "heaven" that nourished her verse. "With the exception of Shakespeare, you have told me of more knowledge than any one living—To say that sincerely is strange praise," Dickinson wrote to Susan in 1882 (*L*733). "Strange" though the praise is ("strange" here, as in PF66, probably means "rare"), the poet seems to have meant it.

It is also true, however, that the romantic and transcendent values that Dickinson celebrates in these quotations and with which she invested her love (whether for Susan or for others) measure more than her vision. As a number of the passages suggest, these values also measure her profound alienation from the culture in which she lived. However much they may have enriched her poetry, giving it the texture—and power—of a stiffly embroidered brocade, the riches Dickinson sought through love and imagination were far too intense, too all-consuming, to be acceptable in her society. Like her sweet sultans, which she also denominated "Shahs" and "Viziers" (*L*670, 724)—or, alternatively, like Antony in Rome—the rewards she sought through loving were out of place. Ultimately her pursuit of them led her into blasphemy. For they made her, as she told Helen Hunt Jackson emphatically in 1885, "a Pagan" (*L867*), who wished to find on earth (that is, through the instrumentality of human love) "the Happiness / That too competes with Heaven" (#1601).

As I have discussed elsewhere,[23] Dickinson was keenly aware of the precariousness of her situation. As early as 1854, her twenty-third year, in the well-known "go or stay" letter to Susan, she raised the question of blasphemy, defiantly insisting upon her idolatry even while allowing that God might well remove her loved ones from her because of it (*L305–6*). And it was of course from precisely such feelings of idolatrous passion that some of her most deeply felt and powerful expressions of despair come during the tumultuous period in which she poured forth in verse her unrequited love for the unknown "Master."

> I should have been too glad, I see—
> Too lifted—for the scant degree
> Of Life's penurious Round—
> My little Circuit would have shamed
> This new Circumference—have blamed—
> The homelier time behind.
>
> . . . .
>
> Earth would have been too much—I see—
> And Heaven—not enough for me—
> I should have had the Joy
> Without the Fear—to justify—
> The Palm—without the Calvary—
> So Savior—Crucify—
>
> Defeat whets Victory—they say—
> The Reefs in Old Gethsemane
> Endear the Shore beyond—
> 'Tis Beggars—Banquets best define—
> 'Tis Thirsting—vitalizes Wine—
> Faith bleats to understand—

(#313)

In wanting to have "the Joy/ Without the Fear," "The Palm—without the Calvary," Dickinson was violating the basic religious tenets of her culture. Despite the nineteenth century's romantic proclivities (proclivities vividly demonstrable in the period's enthusiasm for the "vicious splendour" of the "decadent" East), these tenets still stressed the utility, not the romance, of love, reserving "bliss" for paradise. In the conflation of imagery which this extraordinary poem represents, however, it was Antony's supper that Dickinson wished to have, complete with banquet and wine, here, not in the land beyond. Like her brother after her, who also seems to have taken his romantic "day-dreams" seriously, the poet longed to possess in this life the vision that, as Austin wrote Mabel in 1884, lay all too enticingly "beyond the gates": "While we breathe the heavenly air, and see the beauty beyond the gates, and are buoyed by an invisible power, and our highest hopes cannot but soon blossom into matchless realities, we move on a lower plane, in the world, but not of it, among men and women who do not understand us—cannot comprehend us—hold to the letter which killeth and not to the Spirit which giveth life—and we must, if we would not be followed and tormented, conform—in a measure—outwardly to the elements of the great throng."[24] Brother and sister were in some ways made of the same stuff and wanted a kind of love, a kind of passion, for which nineteenth-century bourgeois values made little room at best.

But Austin was at once more foolhardy than his sister and less brave. Much as he wanted paradise, he also wanted to be "in the world" if "not of it." Outwardly, at any rate, he was prepared to conform, placing his hopes in an illicit and "secretive" affair. Dickinson, on the other hand, seems to have decided fairly early that such strategies were useless. And so—albeit not without many complaints—she found another way out of the closed circle of nineteenth-century Christian eschatology and bourgeois Christian life. If she could not consummate the "heaven" of love in her flesh, then like her mentor, Shakespeare, she could possess it through her imagination, and a heaven that much richer, that much more vital, by virtue of the fact that it was not tied to the "dim real" (*L229*). For Dickinson, this heaven proved in the end enough. Love might be the motive force, the original power behind her poetry, but poetry became the "Lybian Sun" that brought the Palm to fruit and made the vision real. Poetry brought Egypt to Amherst and the Orient to the West. It allowed Emily Dickinson to partake fully and deeply of the banquet of life. "As it takes but a moment of imagination to place us anywhere, it would not seem worth while to stay where it is stale—" (*L922*), she began PF66. Nowhere is the role played by imagination in her life—and art—more clear. Poetry (the land of "Palm") *was* her Cleopatra. It gave her all the satisfaction—the transport, the ecstasy, the erotic splendor and abundance—the real world could not provide. Like the Egyptian Queen, it was an infinite variety neither convention nor habituation could "stale."

It is no wonder then that as she grew older Dickinson venerated Shakespeare, praying to him in much the same way that, one suspects, Erasmus prayed to "Saint" Socrates: " 'Stratford on Avon'—accept us all!"

(*L573*). If he was not God to her—and clearly he was not—he neverthe-less offered the possibility of an alternate "Savior," one who was "it's own divine Relay" (*L922*). Ultimately, I believe that it was Shakespeare, partic-ularly the Shakespeare of *Antony and Cleopatra,* who validated for Dickin-son her role as artist and lover of the beautiful and who confirmed her belief that she could indeed fructify New England's intransigent soil. "To have seen Stratford on Avon—and the Dresden Madonna," she wrote to the fortunate Higginson, then abroad, "must be almost Peace" (*L611*). The "Peace" Dickinson was referring to was the peace of salvation; but the salvation was not from God. Its origins were, ironically, as human as the Madonna herself.

As Richard Sewall has observed,[25] Dickinson's writing throughout her life is suffused with the work of the Renaissance playwright. In her rhythms and her diction, her abundant metaphor, and her sense of the he-roic, she turned to Shakespeare as she turned to the Bible consistently for enrichment. But of all his plays, it was *Antony and Cleopatra* to which she drew the closest and from which she drew the most. In creating an Egypt opulent with gold, love, beauty, and abounding with the forces of life—forces he depicted as distinctly female and distinctly pagan—Shakespeare (whatever his own opinions were) had named the country to which Emily Dickinson believed she belonged. And as her unique integration of *Antony and Cleopatra* into her own figurative system suggests, in doing so he pro-vided the Amherst poet with a vision that would nourish her imagination throughout her life. Though it was a vision she could "eat with [her] eyes only," it was a supper that did not fail.

NOTES

1. A list of Shakespearean allusions in Dickinson is available in Jack L. Capps, *Dickinson's Reading* (Cambridge: Harvard University Press, 1966), 182–85. Next to *Antony and Cleopatra,* whose importance Capps overlooks, *Othello* appears to be the play Dickinson responded to most intensely. See Rebecca Patterson, *The Riddle of Emily Dickinson* (Cambridge: Houghton Mifflin, 1951), 260–61, and Capps, 184–85. I am much indebted to Patterson for first making me appreciate the ways in which Dickinson integrated her identification with Shakespearean characters into her sense of self.

2. Dickinson to Mrs. Thomas Wentworth Higginson, Christmas 1876, in *The Letters of Emily Dickinson,* ed. Thomas H. Johnson and Theodora Ward, 3 vols. (Cambridge, Mass.: Belknap Press, 1958), 2:569. Subsequent references to this edition will be cited parenthetically in the text. In quoting from this edition of Dickinson's letters, I have followed the Johnson/Ward text verbatim, including the editors' use of parentheses to indicate the presence of variants in manuscripts left in rough draft.

3. While Dickinson scholars have probed the poet's relationship to Emerson in great detail, her relationship to Shakespeare—though often assumed—has been left all but entirely unexplored. Helen McNeil has called for a reevaluation of Shakespeare's influence on the Amherst poet. I concur. See *Emily Dickinson* (New York: Random House; London: Virago Press, 1986), 185n.7. McNeil's book contains a brief but excellent discussion of Dickinson's use of "Shakespearean" image clusters, 26–29.

4. Edward Hitchcock, quoted by Richard B. Sewall in *The Life of Emily Dickinson*, 2 vols. (New York: Farrar, Straus and Giroux, 1974), 2:353.

5. Ralph Waldo Emerson, *Representative Men: Seven Lectures by Ralph Waldo Emerson*, rev. ed. (Boston: James R. Osgood, 1878), 174, 175. This is Dickinson's edition.

6. *The Comedies, Histories, Tragedies, and Poems of William Shakspere with a Biography and Studies of his Works*, ed. Charles Knight, 8 vols. (Boston: Little Brown, 1853), 6:434; 8:420, 421.

7. F. J. Furnivall, quoted in *The Tragedy of Antony and Cleopatra*, ed. William J. Rolfe (New York: Harper and Brothers, 1881), 25.

8. Dickinson, quoted by Emily Fowler Ford in her memoir of Dickinson in *Letters of Emily Dickinson*, ed. Mabel Loomis Todd, new and enlarged ed. (New York and London: Harper, 1931), 128.

9. Richard B. Sewall, *The Lyman Letters: New Light on Emily Dickinson and Her Family* (Amherst: University of Massachusetts Press, 1965), 76. Dickinson is quoting from memory. The lines are actually spoken by Philo (1.1.6–8).

10. For a discussion of the difficulties involved in Dickinson's way of quoting, see Jay Leyda, *The Years and Hours of Emily Dickinson*, 2 vols. (New Haven: Yale University Press, 1960; rpt. New York: Archon, 1970), 1:xx. Because of these "gaps," my method of reading Dickinson will inevitably involve many of the same difficulties confronting the reader of *Antony and Cleopatra*—i.e., one's perspective determines one's interpretation, as Shakespeare's opening scene makes clear.

11. I treat Dickinson's relationship to Susan Gilbert at length in *My Life a Loaded Gun: Female Creativity and Feminist Poetics* (Boston: Beacon Press, 1986), 28–55.

12. I am indebted to Rebecca Patterson for this citation. As she observes, the consistency of Dickinson's symbolism makes the allusion likely. See *Emily Dickinson's Imagery*, ed. Margaret H. Freeman (Amherst: University of Massachusetts, 1979), 154–55.

13. Patterson, *Emily Dickinson's Imagery*, 153.

14. Dickinson is quoting from memory Higginson's essay "Letter to a Young Contributor" which appeared in the April 1862 issue of *The Atlantic Monthly*.

15. For the circumstances of the affair, see Polly Longsworth, *Austin and Mabel: The Amherst Affair and Love Letters of Austin Dickinson and Mabel Loomis Todd* (New York: Farrar, Straus and Giroux, 1984).

16. "Vinnie," Dickinson wrote Mrs. Holland in 1876, "thinks Vermont is in Asia" (*L561*); and five years later, she reports with equal delight of a young runaway who gave as his destination "'Vermont or Asia'" (*L687*). In both cases

"Asia" stands for the exotic and unknown, regions only the young, the foolish, or the poet could hope to find so close to home.

17. Patterson, *Dickinson's Imagery*, 143. I believe Patterson errs in trying to make a clear-cut division between African and Asian imagery in Dickinson's work. Like other Orientalists of her day, Dickinson tends to merge Middle-Eastern, North African, and Far Eastern geographical locations together (see Edward Said, *Orientalism* [New York: Vintage Books, 1979], 49–73). Africa, Arabia, Asia, Burmah, Cashmere, the Caspian, Ceylon, Egypt, Ethiopia, Golconda, India, Kamchatka, Lybia, Ophir, the Orient, Numidia, Persia, Smyrna, the Spice Isles, Tripoli, Tunis, and Zanzibar—all stand one or more times for the same geographical/imaginative area in her work.

18. Said, *Orientalism*, 41–42, 48; also see 42–44. Said's discussion of the sexual content of literary representations of the Orient is also pertinent; see 179–97. The Dickinson household library contained six books on Eastern matters (including the Koran and three on the "Turkish Question") which do not seem to have belonged to Dickinson herself. Perhaps the poet's own "Orientalism" was in part a playful parody of her father's more politically directed interests.

19. *The Poems of Emily Dickinson*, ed. Thomas H. Johnson, 3 vols. (Cambridge, Mass.: Belknap Press, 1958), 1:375. Subsequent references to the *Poems* will appear parenthetically in the text as the # symbol, followed by the Johnson number of the poem.

20. Rolfe, ed., *Antony and Cleopatra*, 26. The reference is to Antony's line, 3.13.108.

21. See also *L* 724, where she comments that the sultan is "an Eastern culture and does not like this soil."

22. This poem exists in three variants. See Johnson's commentary, *Poems*, 3:944. The fact that Dickinson reused lines does not necessarily implicate their sincerity. She reused material from the elegies she wrote on her nephew Gilbert's death—and no event devastated her more completely.

23. Bennett, *My Life*, 31–37, 58–60.

24. Longsworth, *Austin and Mabel*, 197–98. Austin also saw parts of himself in Antony but believed he was managing better than the Roman general had: "What a fool Abelard was! and Antony. Madly in love with Cleopatra—but with the opportunity before him marrying Octavia instead, for political policy" (233–34). Peter Gay has discussed the Todd-Dickinson affair and its implications for our understanding of bourgeois Victorian sexuality in *The Bourgeois Experience: Victoria to Freud*, 2 vols. (New York and Oxford: Oxford University Press, 1984), 1:71–108. The kind of romantic eroticism which both Emily and Austin Dickinson engaged in was by no means unique to them; but it did contradict prevailing moral codes in their culture, as the quotation I have cited makes clear.

25. Sewall, *Life*, 2:702–3.

CHRISTINE FROULA

Virginia Woolf
as Shakespeare's Sister: Chapters
in a Woman Writer's Autobiography

> ... depressed to feel I'm not a poet. Next time I shall be one.
> Virginia Woolf, *Diary*, 5:35,
> 24 November 1936

In her last, unfinished essay, "The Reader," Woolf wrote that all Shakespeare criticism is "autobiographical" because Shakespeare inexhaustibly mirrors his readers: "every critic finds his own features in Shakespeare. His variety is such that every one can find scattered here or there ... some one of his own attributes."[1] Woolf knew whereof she spoke: if Johnson, Bradley, and Coleridge invented autobiographical Shakespeares, she too projected her writer's self upon Shakespeare and Shakespeare upon her writer's self during forty years of sketching his image into her letters, novels, essays, and diaries. Figures of Shakespeare in Woolf's writings are often figures of Woolf: moments of oblique *self-portraiture* that catch important features of her artistic self-fashioning. Throughout her life Woolf drew upon Shakespeare's art to inspire and to measure her own, even as she pressed beyond the limits of his male-centered plots and characters.

While Woolf's reclaiming of Shakespeare for women writers in *A Room of One's Own* has been well explored, much remains to be said of the use she herself made of him in her art.[2] In this essay I trace Woolf's construction of an autobiographical Shakespeare in her fiction and in the feminist aesthetics of *A Room of One's Own;* and I analyze her self-reflexive use of this Shakespeare in the forging of her own artistic authority during the prodigiously creative years between 1925 and 1931, during which she wrote *To the Lighthouse*, a related short story titled "The Introduction," *Orlando, A Room of One's Own,* and *The Waves*. In all these works Shakespeare's appearances help to interpret the aesthetic philosophy that the works either theorize or body forth. As we shall see, though Woolf begins in anxiety about the daughter-artist's cultural dispossession, she ends by creating a Shakespeare to which she lays powerful claim on behalf of women writers—most immediately, herself. In practicing the aesthetic theory that she draws upon Shakespeare to formulate, she herself strives to "put on the body that [Judith Shakespeare] has so often laid down."[3]

The earliest document for Woolf's autobiographical Shakespeare that I know is a letter of November 5, 1901, which she wrote at the age of nineteen to her elder brother Thoby at Trinity College to confess a change of heart as to the merits of "a certain great English writer":

> I read Cymbeline just to see if there mightnt be more in the great William than I supposed. And I was quite upset! Really and truly I am now let in to [the] company of worshippers—though I still feel a little oppressed by his—greatness I suppose. I shall want a lecture when I see you; to clear up some points about the Plays. I mean about the characters. Why aren't they more human? Imogen and Posthumous and Cymbeline—I find them beyond me—Is this my feminine weakness in the upper region? But really they might have been cut out with a pair of scissors—as far as mere humanity goes—Of course they talk divinely. I have spotted the best lines in the play—almost in any play I should think—
>
> Imogen says—Think that you are upon a rock, and now throw me again! and Posthumous answers—Hang there like fruit, my Soul, till the tree die. [*Cymbeline* 5.5.262–65] Now if that doesn't send a shiver down your spine, even if you are in the middle of cold grouse and coffee—you are no true Shakespearian! Oh dear oh dear—just as I feel in the mood to talk about these things, you go and plant yourself in Cambridge.[4]

The young Virginia's ambivalent critique foreshadows Woolf's complex treatment of Shakespeare over the next four decades. Her image of herself as belatedly "let in" to a "company of worshippers" makes Shakespeare a sacred text encrypted in the hallowed halls to which her brother holds privileged access while she can enter only on sufferance. Already hers is an outsider's perspective: whereas Thoby, reading Shakespeare at Cambridge and taking part in "talk," duly inherits this rich literary treasure, Virginia, reading Shakespeare by herself and receiving wisdom at secondhand from Thoby, alternately doubts her own authority as a reader and doubts Shakespeare's authority. She is a reluctant worshipper, and her "upset" and "oppressed" admiration becomes inflected by gender as she moves from attributing her doubts to "feminine weakness" to judging his characters wanting in "mere humanity," no matter if they "talk divinely." She measures Shakespeare's characters against life and finds them not universal but either marked by an implicitly masculine imagination or "superhuman" (*L* 1:46).

But if Virginia resents being shut out from the education that passed the staff of cultural authority to young men like Thoby, she does not acquiesce in the cultural dispossession that fell to late-Victorian "daughters of educated men." She responds to Shakespeare not as her brother's docile pupil but as the writer—indeed, the woman writer—she is already becoming. If she is acutely self-conscious about her status as a woman reader, she is also irrepressibly confident in her judgment of "the best lines in the play," and she pits herself as aesthetic judge against her apparently more fortunate brother, as though "cold grouse and coffee" might dull his ear for poetry. In the Stephen family futures, Thoby was headed for the bar while Virginia, Sir Leslie predicted, would be a writer. The debate about "the great William" acts out a covert sibling rivalry in which Virginia adroitly moves from uninitiated scoffer to "oppressed" worshipper to exacting critic to "true Shakespearian": thrilling to Shakespeare's "best" lines, she paints herself his true inheritor. Even as she concedes with chagrin her earlier mistake in dismissing Shakespeare, her letter lays bold claim to him. And the Shakespeare she makes her own is already a complex figure: a great genius and poet, yet lacking in the "humanity" that she as a woman reader looks for; associated with male cultural privilege, yet not inseparable from it—on the contrary, admitting of appropriation by the daughter-writer, even from her position outside the line of succession.

Shakespeare reappears as an icon of a privileged male culture in an unfinished short story titled "The Introduction" that Woolf composed in 1925 as part of a sequence leading up to *To the Lighthouse*.[5] Its heroine, Lily Everit (like Woolf herself in 1925), has just written an "essay on the character of Dean Swift," which her professor has marked with "three red stars."[6] But when Lily enters Mrs. Dalloway's drawingroom, she feels her proud accomplishment pale under the eyes of that "famous place: the world" (37, 38). Introducing Lily to Bob Brinsley, a "young man just down from Oxford, who would have read everything and would talk about himself," Mrs. Dalloway introduces her also to the public world in which cultural authority belongs to men—throws her, Lily feels, "into the boiling depths" (38–39, 37). For Lily at once senses that the culture of which Woolf once more makes Shakespeare the representative belongs properly to this young man, not to her. With obsessive clarity she sees that Brinsley, the cultural son, stands in "direct descent from Shakespeare . . . In the direct line from Shakespeare . . . Churches and parliaments, flats, even the telegraph wires—all . . . made by men of toil, and this young man, she told herself, in direct descent from Shakespeare" (41–42).

Like Brinsley, Lily loves literature, or has thought she did. But, initiated at the hands of Mrs. Dalloway, she falls from innocent love of Shelley, Shakespeare, Swift into dawning awareness that her sex profoundly affects the way literature can belong to her. Suddenly conscious of her difference from Brinsley, she thinks "hers was not love compared with his" (41); and she feels not only her accomplishment but her very ambition shrivel in his presence, like the fly she imagines him destroying as he speaks: "she saw him—how else could she describe it—kill a fly. That was it. He tore the wings off a fly, standing with his foot on the fender, his head thrown back, talking insolently about himself, arrogantly. But she didn't mind how insolent and arrogant he was to her, if only he had not been brutal to flies" (42). Entering the estate of femininity, Lily is likened to a butterfly; and her identification with the flies highlights the incongruity of joining femininity with cultural authority (symbolized by such metaphoric wings as bear Stephen Dedalus aloft) in Mrs. Dalloway's drawingroom. Brinsley's brutality recalls both Gloucester's "wanton boys" and *Titus Andronicus* 3.2.52ff., in which the outrageously raped and mutilated Lavinia helplessly watches Marcus kill a fly and then debate whether the killing is "A deed of death done on the innocent," a "Poor harmless fly, / That, with his pretty buzzing melody/Came here to make us merry!" or revenge upon "a black ill-favoured fly" that represents their enemy.[7] Resonating with Lavinia's misery, Lily's distress makes felt her unvoiced fear that what Brinsley does to the fly, his culture does to women, to Lily herself. The fly's torn wings symbolize the woman's torn tongue, both casualties of "wanton boys."

Longing to be a part of the world, Lily struggles to confine herself within acceptable femininity, but she finds she cannot: she "thought of the towers and civilisation with horror, and the yoke that had fallen from the skies onto her neck crushed her, and she felt like a naked wretch who having sought shelter in some shady garden is turned out and made to understand (ah, but there was a kind of passion in it too) that there are no sanctuaries, or butterflies, and this civilisation, said Lily to herself . . . depends upon me" (43). Lily's expulsion from the garden marks a crisis in her understanding of what her culture is: not sacred ground, a body of thought revered by the fully *human* mind, but a political territory whose masculine colonization she must contest. Yet Brinsley is the villain in this piece, while Shakespeare, Shelley, and Swift represent the literature that she too wishes to "love." Though the culture she now sees as masculine "crushes" her and though she feels cast out of the mind's Edenic sanctuary, the revelation brings not only loss but power, responsibility: "this civilisation . . . depends on me." Lily stands on a threshold from which Woolf's ensuing work takes its departure—most obviously, *A Room of One's Own,* in which she reconstructs the broken line of succession between Shakespeare and women writers, thinks back through the literary foremothers so disturbingly absent from Lily's education, and questions the authority of the male canon.

In her new awareness that "civilisation" depends upon her as well as in her name, Lily Everit is a harbinger of Woolf's best-known autobiographical artist-figure, Lily Briscoe. Lily emerged as the heroine of *To the Lighthouse* only after Woolf had sketched and discarded an earlier version of her, "Miss Sophie Briscoe," a fifty-five-year-old spinster. Glad to have refused all offers of marriage and so "retained her right to view eccentricity from a distance," Sophie does not actually paint but has "spent much of her life sketching."[8] In March 1925 Woolf projected a story about "the girl who had written an essay on the character of Bolingbroke talking to the young man who destroys a fly as he speaks" and listed "The Introduction" as one of the stories she planned. "My idea is that these sketches will be a corridor leading from Mrs. Dalloway to a new book," she wrote. "What I expect to happen is that some two figures will detach themselves from the party & go off independently into another volume."[9] On July 20 Woolf recorded the completion of her essay on Swift and proposed to write a "little story" before beginning *To the Lighthouse* at Rodmell; this makes "The Introduction" almost certainly the "corridor" Woolf traveled on her way to the novel.[10] Lily Everit's discovery that Mr. Brinsley, not she, stands in "direct descent from Shakespeare" issues in Lily Briscoe's struggle to realize her vision against Mr. Tansley's bogey, "Women can't write, women can't paint." And Lily Briscoe's painting allegorizes Woolf's own struggle to move beyond the shadow of male antagonism into creative freedom—to put on the body Shakespeare's sister has so often laid down.

In the closing scene of "The Window," before Lily has succeeded in painting her picture, Shakespeare stands in for her unrealized aspiration through Mrs. Ramsay's reading of sonnet 98. After dinner is finished and the youngest children are abed, Mrs. Ramsay comes downstairs feeling obscurely that "she had come here to get something she wanted. First she wanted to sit down in a particular chair under a particular lamp. But she wanted something more, though she did not know, could not think what it was that she wanted."[11] With her husband reading Scott beside her, her own thoughts wandering, she continues to feel, "there is something I want—something I have come to get," until, murmuring the lines of poetry that her husband and Carmichael had repeated after dinner, she picks up a book from the table beside her and turns the pages—"not know[ing] at first what the words meant at all," "swinging herself, zigzagging this way and that from one line to another as from one branch to another, from one red and white flower to another" (*TL* 178–79). Reading in this sensuous way she alights on Shakespeare's poem:[12]

> She was climbing up those branches, this way and that, laying hands on one flower and then another.
> "Nor praise the deep vermilion in the rose," she read, and so reading she was ascending, she felt, on to the top, on to the summit. How satisfying! How restful! All the odds and ends of the day stuck to this mag-

net; her mind felt swept, felt clean. And then there it was, suddenly entire; she held it in her hands, beautiful and reasonable, clear and complete, the essence sucked out of life and held rounded here—the sonnet. (*TL* 181)

Shakespeare's sonnet answers Mrs. Ramsay's obscure desire, seeming to gather the day's ephemera into its order. She makes her way in it as in a garden of the mind, a symbolic refuge from time's destroying powers. But the true subject of this scene, I suggest, is not Mrs. Ramsay but the daughter-artist, Lily/Woolf. Woolf the writer, self-reflexively doubled in Lily the painter, is the unseen watcher of the mother reading by lamplight: the scene confirms and nourishes the daughter-artist through her covert alliance with the poet. Earlier, Mrs. Ramsay is figured as the symbolic origin for Lily's art as Lily, vainly desiring to become one with her "like waters poured into one jar," wonders what art might "by love or cunning" create that "intimacy . . . which is knowledge" (*TL* 79). Though Mrs. Ramsay little values Lily's painting, the way she loses herself among Shakespeare's "different flowers" affirms Lily's vision of art as a communion of minds—intimacy, knowledge. That Mrs. Ramsay's desire quenches itself in Shakespeare's poem nurtures Lily's hope that her art too might mediate this curiously impersonal yet real and valued "intimacy"— a success she tastes when William Bankes looks at her unfinished picture and "share[s] with her something profoundly intimate" (*TL* 83).[13]

Letting Shakespeare answer the mother's desire as Lily would have her art do, Woolf symbolically wrests Shakespeare away from the Brinsleys and Tansleys and bestows him upon Lily and herself. Foreshadowing *A Room of One's Own*, the Shakespeare of *To the Lighthouse* is not a threat to the woman artist; his art neither prohibits nor preempts hers. Rather, his reds and whites beckon her on toward her "bright violet and . . . staring white," down the dark "passage from conception to work." (*TL* 31, 32) As the differential between Shakespeare's accomplished genius and Lily's struggling talent is not at all an issue here, so Woolf could measure her own gifts against Shakespeare's with more equanimity than anxiety. In the summer of 1926, at work on *To the Lighthouse*, she wrote in her diary that "*Returning Health* / is shown by the power to make images: the suggestive power of every sight & word is enormously increased. Shakespeare must have had this to an extent which makes my normal state the state of a person blind, deaf, dumb, stone-stockish, & fish-blooded. And I have it compared with poor Mrs. Bartholomew almost to the extent that Sh[akespea]re has it compared with me" (*D* 3:104).

"[B]ooks continue each other," Woolf noted; so *Orlando, A Room of One's Own*, and *The Waves* continue the evolution of the woman artist beyond *To the Lighthouse* (*RO* 84). While still at work on that novel, Woolf glimpsed a new form that would lead to *The Waves:* "Why not invent a new kind of play—as for instance / Woman thinks: . . . / He does. / Organ Plays. / She writes. / They say: / She sings: / Night speaks: / They miss / . . . Away from facts: free; yet concentrated; prose yet poetry; a novel & a play" (*D* 3:128; 21 February 1927). A few weeks later, *Orlando* broke into her thoughts: "I feel the need of an escapade after these serious poetic experimental books. . . . I want to kick up my heels & be off" (*D* 3:131; 14 March 1927). Both books were in solution over that summer, but by October Woolf found herself launched upon *Orlando*. She published it a year later and delivered the lectures that became *A Room of One's Own* in November; after that, she gave her mind to *The Waves*. All three works invoke the benign, enabling Shakespeare summoned up in *To the Lighthouse*.

Orlando presents itself as a biographical fantasy on Vita Sackville-West, Woolf's friend from 1923 and sometime lover between 1925 and 1928.[14] Vita's son has described it as "the longest and most charming love-letter in literature."[15] But there is a good deal of Woolf in Orlando, too, particularly in his/her long and eventually successful career as poet. This fantastic transsexual poet-adventurer burst into being after Lily/Woolf's arduous struggle to break the shackles that the Brinsleys and Tansleys of male culture would impose upon her imagination. Indeed, *Orlando,* created with greater speed and ease than any of Woolf's other books, was "splashed over the canvas" as Lily's next painting might have been (*D* 3:164, 20 November 1927). Woolf's desire to "kick up [her] heels & be off" is a wish to kick off the gender constraints that impede the daughter-artist like so many Victorian petticoats, letting her imagination race free.

Orlando's estate is based on Knole in Kent, the ancestral home of the Sackville-Wests that kindled fantasies of Shakespeare in both Vita and Virginia. Granted by Elizabeth I to Thomas Sackville in 1566, Knole held "chairs that Shakespeare might have sat on" (*D* 2:306, 5 July 1924). Embarking on *Orlando*, Woolf reread Vita's *Knole and the Sackvilles,* in which Vita recalls her "wild dreams that some light might be thrown on the Shakespearean problem by a discovery of letters or documents at Knole. What more fascinating or chimerical a speculation for a literary-minded child breathing and absorbing the atmosphere of that house? I used to tell myself stories of finding Shakespeare's manuscripts up in the attics, perhaps hidden away under the flooring somewhere."[16] Apart from Vita herself, who cross-dressed as "Julian" during her affair with Violet Trefusis, it is Shakespeare's androgynous cross-dressing heroines who most obviously inspire Orlando—though Woolf goes Vita, Rosalind, and Viola one better by changing Orlando's sex *in medias res*.[17] Woolf's comic androgyne at once mirrors and reverses Shakespeare's Rosalind: where Shakespeare, a man, creates Rosalind, a woman, who becomes Ganymede, a man of sorts who yet resembles a woman, Woolf, a woman, appropriates Shakespeare's Orlando and recreates him as a man who becomes a woman who sometimes dresses as a man yet gives birth to a baby—remaining through it all his/her "many thousand" selves.[18] As Orlando is to Rosalind, Woolf is to Shakespeare: creating Orlando, she becomes Shakespeare's sister, a transsexual Shakespeare who adventures with her own literary authority through the fantasy of a writing self free from every kind of constraint: of economy, of gender, even of the normal human lifespan.

Shakespeare is the guiding spirit both of Orlando's imagination and of *Orlando*. Orlando's biography begins in Elizabethan England and ends at midnight, October 11/12, 1928—the book's publication day. From the beginning, Orlando—first man, then woman, but always a writer—is "haunted" by poetry. In youth he harbors "an ineffable hope . . . that he himself belonged to the sacred race rather than to the noble—was by birth a writer, rather than an aristocrat" (*O* 83); and through a centuries-long career s/he progresses from "Aethelbert: A Tragedy in Five Acts" and other derivative juvenilia, which he later burns, to the completion of his/her prizewinning poem "The Oak Tree." Throughout this progress, Shakespeare, poet *par excellence,* is Orlando's idol. Embodying the poetic power to which Orlando aspires, he early on makes a cameo appearance at Orlando's estate. On his way to receive the queen, Orlando glimpses him at the servants' table—"a rather fat, rather shabby man" in a dirty ruff, gazing, musing, and then quickly writing. "Orlando stopped dead. Was this a poet? Was he writing poetry? 'Tell me,' he wanted to say, 'everything in the whole world' . . . but how speak to a man who does not see you? who sees ogres, satyrs, perhaps the depths of the sea instead?" (*O* 21–22).

Orlando is temporarily distracted from his awe of Shakespeare by Nick Greene, through whom Woolf dramatizes an opposition between anonymity and "gloire," between poetry and literary gossip, between love of words and love of Fame. A pompous, self-serving academic critic, Greene honors only two kinds of writing: the ancients' and his own. The art of poetry, he tells Orlando, is "dead in England." Shakespeare "had written some scenes that were well enough; but he had taken them chiefly from Marlowe"; like all young writers, Shakespeare was "in the pay of the booksellers and poured out any trash that would sell" for which he was "already paying the penalty" (*O* 88–89). Greene derides Kit Marlowe's prediction: "'Stap my vitals, Bill' (this was to Shakespeare), 'there's a great wave coming and you're on the top of it'" (*O* 89); and he regales Orlando with gossip about how the poets he reveres quarrel with their wives, lie, intrigue, and scribble their poetry "on the backs of washing bills held to the heads of printer's devils at the street door. Thus Hamlet went to press; thus Lear; thus Othello. No wonder, as Greene said, that these plays show the faults they do" (*O* 91). Greene, by contrast, devotes himself to "La Gloire (he pronounced it Glawr, so that Orlando did not at first catch his meaning)" and prevails upon Orlando to pay him a quarterly pension (*O* 89).

Greene's influence wanes when he writes a derisive squib on Orlando's literary endeavors, "Greene's Visit to a Nobleman in the Country" (*O* 96), plunging Orlando into a crisis over his embarrassed poetics. "Why not simply say what one means and leave it?" he thinks. "So then he tried saying the grass is green and the sky is blue and so to propitiate the austere spirit of poetry. . . . Looking up, he saw that, on the contrary, the sky is like the veils which a thousand Madonnas have let fall from their hair; and the grass fleets and darkens like a flight of girls fleeing the embraces of hairy satyrs from enchanted woods. . . . And he despaired of being able to solve the problem of what poetry is and what truth is and fell into a deep dejection" (*O* 101–2). Although Orlando at first submits his chastened poetic efforts to an internalized Greene, he soon exorcises Greene's bogey along with his own desire for "Gloire": " 'I'll be blasted,' he said, 'if I ever . . . write another word to please Nick Greene or the Muse. . . . I'll write, from this day forward, to please myself' "; and he tears up an imaginary scroll "appointing himself . . . the first poet of his race, . . . conferring eternal immortality upon his soul[,] . . . a grave among laurels and the intangible banners of a people's reverence perpetually" (*O* 103–4).

Flinging off love of fame to embrace a "dark, ample and free" obscurity that "lets the mind take its way unimpeded," Orlando finds his way back to poetry and so to Shakespeare. Nature, the sacred, and the common life merge in his reconstructed poetics. He muses on "the value of obscurity and the delight of having no name, but being like a wave which returns to the deep body of the sea," and on "how obscurity rids the mind of the irk of envy and spite; how it sets running in the veins the free waters of generosity and magnanimity; and allows giving and taking without thanks offered or praise given; which must have been the way of all great poets . . . Shakespeare must have written like that, and the church builders built like that, anonymously, needing no thanking or naming" (*O* 104–5).

Orlando's anonymous Shakespeare—exemplifying his discovery that casting off the personal burden of grievances, anxieties, and wants allows the poet's imagination to flow into the greater common life—is the same sketched in "The Reader": "the person is consumed: S[hakespea]re never breaks the envelope. We dont want to know about him: Completely expressed."[19] Woolf sees the Elizabethan play as a collective art form, "written by one hand, but so moulded in transition that the author had no sense of property in it. It was in part the work of the audience . . . who made the playwright capable of his great strides, of vast audacities beyond the reach of the solitary writer" ("Anon" 395). *Orlando's* ice carnival scene embodies her theory of the play as communal voice, as Orlando and the Russian princess Sasha find themselves swept along in a vast London crowd—"apprentices; tailors; fishwives; horse dealers; cony catchers; starving scholars; maidservants . . . ; orange girls; ostlers; sober citizens; bawdy tapsters; . . . all the riff-raff of the London streets"—to encounter, by accident and for the first time, Shakespeare's theater (*O* 56). Othello's words seem Orlando's own: "now and again a single phrase would come to him over the ice which was as if torn from the depths of his heart. The frenzy of the Moor seemed to him his own frenzy, and when the Moor suffocated the woman in her bed it was Sasha he killed with his own hands" (*O* 56–57).

The power to transmute the common life into speech allies the anonymous poet with the sacred—a point given a comic cast as Orlando, now a woman and home from her travels, meditates in her chapel—not on "the usual God" but on "a faith of her own," poetry:

> With all the religious ardour in the world, she now reflected upon her sins and the imperfections that had crept into her spiritual state. The letter S, she reflected, is the serpent in the Poet's Eden. Do what she would there were still too many of these sinful reptiles in the first stanzas of "The Oak Tree." . . . The poet's then is the highest office of all, she continued. . . . A silly song of Shakespeare's has done more for the poor and the wicked than all the preachers and philanthropists in the world. . . . Thoughts are divine. Thus it is obvious that she was back in the confines of her own religion which time had only strengthened in her absence, and was rapidly acquiring the intolerance of belief. (*O* 172–74)

Orlando's god remains the anonymous poet—the Shakespeare lost in visions at the servants' table who writes "not for thanking or naming."

Orlando's Shakespeare circumvents anxiety by representing not the obstructing genius whose words leave nothing more to say but the passion to transmute *the present moment* into poetry. In "Anon," recalling *Orlando's Othello* scene, Woolf imagines how Shakespeare must have shocked his contemporaries: "To the Elizabethans the expressive power of words after their long inadequacy must have been overwhelming. . . . There at the Globe or at the Rose men and women whose only reading had been the Bible or some old chronicle came out into the light of the present moment [and] heard their aspirations, their profanities, their ribaldries spoken for them in poetry. . . . The preacher and the magistrate were always denouncing their emotion. That too must have given it intensity" ("Anon" 395–96). As Woolf's Shakespeare coined into words the living thought that would otherwise remain unspoken, unheard, unknown in his audience's lives, so Orlando and *Orlando* strive to bring their readers inarticulate and surprised into the as-yet-unspoken present moment. When Orlando meets up with Nick—now Sir Nicholas—Greene again in the twentieth century, he applauds her long poem "The Oak Tree," finished at last, and publishes it to critical acclaim, comparing her to Milton "save for his blindness" (*O* 324). Earlier, reading Greene and his friends has given her the "extremely uncomfortable feeling—one must never, never say what one thought. . . . one must always, always write like somebody else. (The tears formed themselves in her eyes)" (*O* 285). But if lesser writers burden her, the image of Shakespeare returns from four centuries earlier to light Orlando's way to the present moment: " 'He sat at Twitchett's table . . . with a dirty ruff on. . . . Was it old Mr. Baker come to measure the timber? Or was it Sh__p__re?' (for when we speak names we deeply reverence to ourselves we never speak them whole)" (*O* 313). Shakespeare inspires Orlando not to imitate "certain styles; certain forms" but to do for her own time what Shakespeare did for his ("The Reader" 412).

As Orlando/Woolf's autobiographical Shakespeare represents it, then, the difficulty of writing renews itself every day, not because other people have written but because time, the world, continue to unfold past every act of writing. Despite the success of "The Oak Tree," Orlando remains " 'Haunted! ever since I was a child. There flies the wild goose . . . out to sea. . . . I fling after it words like nets. . . . And sometimes there's an inch of silver—six words—in the bottom of the net. But never the great fish who lives in the coral groves' " (*O* 313). Shakespeare's legacy for Orlando is the passion to fling nets of words about the present moment—dramatized when she revisits her estate and sees "Rows of chairs with all their velvets faded . . . ranged against the wall holding their arms out . . . for Shakespeare it might be . . . who never came" (*O* 318). Orlando undoes the rope and sits down herself, the poet of her own time as Shakespeare was of his. Orlando and Woolf converge in the novel's last pages, in the deep dark pool of the poet's mind where "things"—the things of *Orlando*—"shape themselves . . . now Shakespeare, now a girl in Russian trousers, now a toy boat on the Serpentine" (*O* 327). And *Orlando*'s last words tear through the written page to deliver the reader to "the present moment": " 'It is the goose!' Orlando cried. 'The wild goose. . . .' And the twelfth stroke of midnight sounded; . . . Thursday, the eleventh of October, Nineteen Hundred and Twenty-eight" (*O* 329).

In *To the Lighthouse* and *Orlando* Woolf counters men's essentialist arguments against women's powers of symbolic creation. While Tansley notoriously proclaims, "Women can't paint, women can't write," Lily paints and Orlando writes, proving gender to be a "costume" of the creative mind, not a condition of its existence.[20] Lily's and Orlando's artistic triumphs freed Woolf to explore the ways historical contingency has limited women's literary production in *A Room of One's Own,* delivered as lectures to the women of Girton and Newnham a month after *Orlando*'s publication. In *Room,* Shakespeare is the ground against which Woolf figures the woman writer as she has been and as she might become. Woolf's creation of the fantastic Orlando as Shakespeare's androgynous yet ultimately female counterpart articulates the ideal of the woman writer that she brings to bear upon reality in *Room.* If Orlando is the utopian version of Shakespeare's female counterpart, Judith Shakespeare is a realist's Orlando, the woman writer plunged back into history—into a world appropriated by men, hostile to women culture-makers. Yet Woolf's project is not simply to take stock of the contingencies that have burdened women writers but insofar as possible to *realize* her vision of the woman writer's potential: first, by creating a fictional yet realistic counterexample of the woman novelist, in Mary Carmichael in *Room,* and, second, by herself striving to become one example of Shakespeare's sister, the woman poet, by writing *The Waves.*

Woolf's interest in the woman poet's fortunes explains her otherwise surprising critique of English women novelists. Her fictional biography of the imaginary Judith Shakespeare (a genre that owes much to *Orlando*) argues that, while a woman certainly *could* have written Shakespeare's plays, "it would have been extremely odd" had any done so: any Judith Shakespeare seeking her fortune in a man's world would have become entangled in circumstances that either block creativity altogether or impede the "incandescent" state of mind necessary to give form to vision (*RO* 48). Looking at what women wrote when they did write, Woolf measures English women novelists against Shakespeare and finds them wanting. Assuming poetry to be the "original" and "supreme" expressive medium, she asks why women have instead written mainly novels—perhaps, she speculates, because all their training was "in the observation of character, in the analysis of emotion" (*RO* 69–70). Only Austen and Emily Brontë, Woolf finds, "hold fast to the thing as they saw it"; the others—Charlotte Brontë, Eliot—lacking a female tradition and burdened by a male tradition ill-suited to their purposes—"stumbled and fell" (*RO* 77, 80).

This startling judgment emerges from Woolf's own immediate concerns as a woman novelist, deeply absorbed in developing a prose form to encompass a range of experience formerly reserved for poetry—specifically, *The Waves,* that "abstract mystical eyeless book" mentioned in a diary entry of about this time (3:203, 5 November 1928). In 1925, Woolf had sought another word than "novel" for her fictions, perhaps "elegy"

(*D* 3:34, 27 June 1925). Now she enlarges on the gender of genres, speculating that such "older" forms as epic and the poetic play were, like the "man's sentence," too "hardened and set" for the woman writer's purposes. "The novel alone was young enough to be soft in her hands," and even it—"this most pliable of all forms"—is not perfected yet (*RO* 80). What the woman novelist needs turns out to be, not surprisingly, the form that Woolf herself is in the process of creating. Autobiography and theory merge as Woolf tells her readers, "No doubt we shall find her knocking it into shape for herself when she has the free use of her limbs; and providing some new vehicle, not necessarily in verse, for the poetry in her. For it is the poetry that is still denied outlet" (*RO* 80).

With Shakespeare as her model, Woolf goes on to "ponder how a woman nowadays would write a poetic tragedy in five acts—would she use verse—would she not use prose rather?" (*RO* 80). In Orlando, Woolf had created an imaginary woman writer to whom she gave all that male culture denies her, including a tradition: writing and rewriting "The Oak Tree" over four centuries, Orlando is her own tradition. In *Room*, Woolf maps out an actual tradition of women writers, from Aphra Behn to the imaginary but plausible *Life's Adventure* by one Mary Carmichael, published "this very month of October." Taking it up to see what women are writing, and reading it as "the last volume in a very long series," Woolf finds that Carmichael has broken the sentence and the sequence in order to say something new (*RO* 83–84). Her novel cannot bear comparison as poetry with Shakespeare, but it writes into literature what Shakespeare and his tradition leave out:

> "Chloe liked Olivia," I read. And then it struck me how immense a change was there. Chloe liked Olivia perhaps for the first time in literature. Cleopatra did not like Octavia. And how completely *Antony and Cleopatra* would have been altered had she done so! As it is, I thought, . . . the whole thing is simplified, conventionalised, if one dared say it, absurdly. Cleopatra's only feeling about Octavia is one of jealousy. Is she taller than I am? How does she do her hair? The play, perhaps, required no more. But how interesting it would have been if the relationship between the two women had been more complicated. (*RO* 84, 86)

Here Shakespeare's Cleopatra and Octavia provide the matrix for Carmichael's Chloe and Olivia, emblem of all that the male tradition leaves out. Woolf's critique of *Antony and Cleopatra*'s "absurd" simplifications, omissions, and conventions recalls the young Virginia's complaint that Shakespeare's characters lack "mere humanity": her ironic "if one dared say it" does nothing to mute the mature Woolf's challenge to Shakespeare's universality and realism. Shakespeare dramatizes women, Woolf concludes, "almost without exception . . . in their relation to men. . . . And how small a part of woman's life is that; and how little can a man know even of that when he observes it through the black or rosy spectacles which sex puts upon his nose" (*RO* 86). Shakespeare's limited plots and characters, then, only confirm the value of Carmichael's:

> Suppose . . . that men were only represented in literature as the lovers of women, and were never the friends of men, soldiers, thinkers, dreamers; how few parts in the plays of Shakespeare could be alloted to them; how literature would suffer! We might perhaps have most of Othello; and a good deal of Antony; but no Caesar, no Brutus, no Hamlet, no Lear, no Jaques—literature would be incredibly impoverished, as indeed literature is impoverished beyond our counting by the doors that have been shut upon women . . . if Chloe likes Olivia and they share a laboratory, which of itself will make their friendship more varied and lasting because it will be less personal; if Mary Carmichael knows how to write, and I was beginning to enjoy some quality in her style; if she has a room to herself, . . . ; if she has five hundred a year of her own . . . then I think that something of great importance has happened. . . . she will light a torch in that vast chamber where nobody has yet been. (*RO* 87–88)

As Orlando makes good a certain blindness in Milton, Mary Carmichael makes good a certain blindness in Shakespeare, despite the fact that she is as yet "no more than a clever girl" (*RO* 96). For Carmichael has in common with Orlando and Shakespeare the unexplored country of her own present moment—"that vast chamber where nobody has yet been"— and a freedom to explore it which "women of far greater gift lacked even half a century ago" (*RO* 96). In Carmichael's day, Woolf insists, utopia can become reality: the woman writer need not, like Jane Eyre, "climb on to the roof and ruin her peace of mind longing for travel, experience and a knowledge of the world and character that were denied her." Like Orlando she can see things in themselves: "Fear and hatred were almost gone, or traces of them showed only in a slight exaggeration of the joy of freedom. . . . She had a sensibility that was very wide, eager and free. It responded to an almost imperceptible touch on it. It feasted like a plant newly stood in the air on every sight and sound that came its way. . . . It brought buried things to light and made one wonder what need there had been to bury them" (*RO* 96).

For Carmichael, as for Lily Briscoe and Orlando, Woolf forestalls the anxiety Shakespeare's genius might inspire by making him a benignly incomplete model as well as an exemplary one. His art manifests poetic power at its fullest and freest, but he still leaves half the cultural canvas blank for women's representations, potentially equally full and free, but different, because of women's different perspectives. If Woolf's androgynous Shakespeare could write like a man who has forgotten that he is a man, Mary can now write "like a woman who has forgotten that she is a woman" (*RO* 96). When, then, Woolf evokes a modern London in which "Nobody . . . was reading *Antony and Cleopatra,*" she invites women writers into the present moment, as she does when Orlando sits down in a chair that holds out empty arms for a Shakespeare long vanished (*RO* 99). The living poet gives voice to "a feeling that is actually being made and torn out of us at the moment" (*RO* 14); for that, Woolf found Shakespeare an inspiring model.

It is above all Woolf herself who drinks at the fountain of the Shakespeare she has created, for *Room,* like *Orlando,* is profoundly autobiographical. Woolf concludes *Room* by saying that Shakespeare's sister "lives in you and in me," and this "me" gives her book all its specificity: Woolf projects her own creative life into Mary Carmichael as she had into Lily Everit, Lily Briscoe, and Orlando, for herself as well as her audience of young women to think back—and so, forward—through (*RO* 117). When, late in *Room,* Woolf urges Mary Carmichael to press beyond the "naturalist-novel" to the "contemplative," she herself is thinking forward to *The Waves* (*RO* 92). When she writes that she wants to see Mary Carmichael "catch those unrecorded gestures, those unsaid or half-said words, which form themselves, no more palpably than the shadows of moths on the ceiling, when women are alone, unlit by the capricious and coloured light of the other sex" (*RO* 88), she describes her own next book (at this stage titled *The Moths*).[21] And when she tells Mary, "Above all, you must illumine your own soul with its profundities and shallows," Woolf foreshadows her own sense of *The Waves* as "autobiography"—not, obviously, in the ordinary sense, but rather as Shakespeare's plays are autobiography—with the self (or selves) "completely expressed," perfectly present and by the same token invisible (*RO* 93; *D* 3:229, 28 May 1929).

After visiting Stratford in 1934, Woolf remarked on Shakespeare's impersonality in terms that shed light both on the paradoxical conception of autobiography that underlies *The Waves* and on Shakespeare as its model:

> I cannot . . . describe the queer impression of sunny impersonality. Yes, everything seemed to say, this was Shakespeare's, had he sat and walked; but you wont find me not exactly in the flesh. He is serenely absent-present; both at once; radiating round one; yes; in the flowers, in the old hall, in the garden; but never to be pinned down. . . . all air & sun smiling serenely; & yet down there one foot from me lay the little bones that had spread over the world this vast illumination. . . . Now I think Shre was very happy in this, that there was no impediment of fame, but his genius flowed out of him, & is still there, in Stratford. (*D* 4:219–20, 9 May 1934)

This Shakespeare whose genius flows out unimpeded is the anonymous Shakespeare of *Orlando, Room,* and "Anon." In *Room,* Shakespeare's anonymity is bound up with the androgyny that Woolf attributes both to the poet and to Mary Carmichael. Her concept of androgyny has given rise to much vexed commentary, but the autobiographical context of *Room* and *The Waves* makes clear its uses for her immediate purposes. When Woolf praises Mary Carmichael for writing "as a woman, but as a woman who has forgotten that she is a woman," she is not advocating an asexual, a masculine, or a falsely universalizing mode of authority—in Elaine Showalter's terms a "flight" from femaleness.[22] On the contrary, she seeks literary *representations* of femaleness unhampered by the prohibitions and conventions of male culture: "that curious sexual quality which comes only when sex is unconscious of itself" that she praises in Carmichael's writing and that is her own goal in *The Waves* (*RO* 96). So Lily paints at the end of *To the Lighthouse:* like a woman who has forgotten that she is a woman, in contrast to the "alien and critical" state of the woman who, walking down Whitehall, finds herself not the "natural inheritor" of her civilization but an outsider.

Both Lily Briscoe and Woolf's "outsider" are women, and Woolf herself writes sometimes as Lily paints, sometimes as an outsider. The one mode does not, of course, exclude the other. Rather, Woolf's concept of androgyny expands the woman writer's range by laying claim to "things in themselves," by urging her not to submit her imagination entirely to the "alien emotions like fear and hatred" that masculine culture imposes (*RO* 101, 61). The Woolf who wrote *The Waves* also wrote *Three Guineas:* the two works illustrate the breadth and complexity of her ambitions for women writers and for herself. The goal Woolf sets Mary and herself is the farthest goal. She urges women writers *as women* toward poetry, toward things in themselves, toward freedom to partake of the common life and to create a tradition from it:

> if we live another century or so—I am talking of the common life which is the real life and not of the little separate lives which we live as individuals—. . . if we have the habit of freedom and the courage to write exactly what we think; if we escape a little from the common sitting-room and see human beings not always in their relation to each other but in relation to reality; and the sky, too, and the trees or whatever it may be in themselves; . . . if we face the fact . . . that we go alone and that our relation is to the world of reality and not only to the world of men and women, then . . . the dead poet who was Shakespeare's sister will put on the body which she has so often laid down. (*RO* 117–18)[23]

The Waves is a philosophically and formally radical experiment aimed at realizing Woolf's working ideal of androgyny—writing like a woman who has forgotten that she is a woman. Feeling her way toward the book, Woolf wrote, "One must get the sense that this is the beginning: this the middle; that the climax—when she opens the window & the moth comes in. . . . But who is she? I am very anxious that she should have no name. I dont want a Lavinia or a Penelope: I want 'She'" (*D* 3:229–30, 28 May 1929). This "She" recalls Woolf's pleasure in the unconscious sexual quality of Mary Carmichael's writing. No less clearly, Woolf's examples of what she *doesn't* want show her rejecting names burdened with histories of womanhood violated and constrained: Shakespeare's Lavinia, raped and mutilated, writing in sand of the outrages she has suffered at men's hands; Homer's Penelope, left behind in "Life's Adventure," waiting, weeping, weaving, and unweaving. Woolf had, of course, written of women's abuse at the hands of male culture by rape and by the marriage plot, and she would do so again.[24] But at this moment she is imagining what "the unity of the mind" might be like. She is conceiving a woman's voice speaking of "things in themselves," not of things as mediated by masculine culture.

In the early drafts of *The Waves,* this voice is explicitly unsexed: "the lonely mind, man or woman, young or aged, it does not matter"; yet "She" returns in the final text, almost invisible, "serenely absent-present," almost completely subsumed in the metaphor of authority on the novel's opening page: "as if the arm of a woman couched beneath the horizon had raised a lamp."[25] An anonymous, invisible "She" lights the world of *The Waves,* as the anonymous, invisible Shakespeare Woolf felt in Stratford had once "spread over the world this vast illumination." As Woolf's Shakespeare submerged his personal self in the great common life that teems in his plays, so Woolf could write of *The Waves:* "Autobiography it might be called"—registering the reality underlying this "inner life of a woman" (*D* 3:229, 28 May 1929). The "shadows of moths," the thoughts Woolf nets, belong to "people [set] against time and the sea," to "Childhood; but . . . not *my* childhood" (*D* 3:264, 5 November 1929; 3:236, 23 June 1929). In the wake of her anonymous Shakespeare, Woolf moves from the realist or "naturalist-novel" into a new poetic prose (as she urges Mary to do) and from literal to lyric autobiography. Against a chorus that she hopes Mary Carmichael does not hear, made up of bishops, deans, doctors, professors, patriarchs, and pedagogues who shout, "You can't do this and you shan't do that!," Woolf urges her: "Think only of the jump . . . as if I had put the whole of my money on her back; and she went over it like a bird" (*RO* 97). Woolf rode at that fence herself: finishing *The Waves,* she wrote that she "felt the pressure of the form—the splendour & the greatness—as—perhaps, I have never felt them. . . . I have taken my fence" (*D* 3:298, 28 March 1930).

The Waves is the flower of Woolf's autobiographical involvement with Shakespeare in its most intense phase. Yet her book did not at all resemble Shakespeare, she told John Lehmann, who had written an essay suggesting that it did: "if you print it, as I hope you will, leave out Shakespeare, because I don't think anyone in their senses can have mentioned him in that connection. (I almost put a capital H, and that is rather my feeling)" (*L* 5:422, 1 August 1935). Still, Shakespeare's poetry led Woolf toward her own: she set the height of her fence by him. In the midst of composing *The Waves* she wrote,

> I read Shakespeare *directly* I have finished writing, when my mind is agape & red & hot. Then it is astonishing. I never yet knew how amazing his stretch & speed & word coining power is, until I felt it utterly outpace & outrace my own, seeming to start equal & then I see him draw ahead & do things I could not in my wildest tumult & utmost press of mind imagine. Even the less known & worser plays are written at a speed that is quicker than anybody else's quickest; & the words drop so fast one can't pick them up. Look at this, Upon a gather'd lily almost wither'd (that is a pure accident: I happen to light on it.) Evidently the pliancy of his mind was so complete that he could furbish out any train of thought; &, relaxing lets fall a shower of such unregarded flowers. Why then should anyone else attempt to write. This is not "writing" at all. Indeed, I could say that Shre surpasses literature altogether, if I knew what I meant. (*D* 3:301, 13 April 1930)

Yet for all Woolf's awe of Shakespeare, his brilliance lighted the world for her, as it did for her characters Lily Everit, Orlando, and Mary Carmichael, rather than spelling her failure. If Shakespeare could at moments make her feel "why write?", he is also the muse of that "ecstatic book" *The Waves* (*D* 4:39, 15 August 1931). And if his dazzling speed and fecundity struck Woolf as somehow closer to nature than to writing, his anonymity made his nature a part of her own, a part of the world. Forty years after her daunting encounter with "the great William," Woolf dissolves his very name in the fluid, anonymous voice of the world, the "we" that she evokes in her "philosophy . . . that the whole world is a work of art; that we are parts of the work of art. *Hamlet* or a Beethoven quartet is the truth about this vast mass that we call the world. But there is no Shakespeare, there is no Beethoven; certainly and emphatically there is no God; we are the words; we are the music; we are the thing itself."[26]

NOTES

1. See " 'Anon' and 'The Reader': Virginia Woolf's Last Essays," ed. Brenda R. Silver, *Twentieth Century Literature* 25 (Fall/Winter 1979): 431; hereafter cited as "Anon" and "The Reader."

2. See Karen Lawrence, " 'Shikespower': Shakespeare's Legacy for Virginia Woolf and James Joyce," paper on Woolf's transformation of Shakespeare into an anonymous, androgynous model for the woman writer and of his "patriarchal signature" into a "collective consciousness and voice" delivered at an MLA session on "Virginia Woolf and James Joyce: Gender and Modernist Writing," Chicago, 1985.

3. Virginia Woolf, *A Room of One's Own* (New York: Harcourt, Brace and World, 1928), 118; hereafter cited as *RO*.

4. *The Letters of Virginia Woolf,* ed. Nigel Nicolson and Joanne Trautmann, 6 vols. (New York: Harcourt Brace Jovanovich, 1975–80), 1:45–46; hereafter cited as *L*.

5. "The Introduction," *Mrs. Dalloway's Party: A Short Story Sequence by Virginia Woolf,* ed. Stella McNichol (New York: Harcourt Brace Jovanovich, 1973), 37–43. Cf. *The Complete Shorter Fiction of Virginia Woolf,* ed. Susan Dick (New York: Harcourt Brace Jovanovich, 1985), 178–82, and 297n.

6. Woolf finished "Swift's *Journal to Stella*" (*The Second Common Reader* [New York: Harcourt Brace Jovanovich, 1960], 58–67) on July 20, 1925; it appeared in the *TLS* on September 24.

7. I thank Marianne Novy for bringing this point to my attention.

8. See *To the Lighthouse: The Original Holograph Draft,* transcr. and ed. Susan Dick (Toronto: University of Toronto Press, 1982), 29; for Lily's first appearance, see 31.

9. *To the Lighthouse: The Original Holograph Draft,* Appendix A, 44–46. The change from Bolingbroke in the notes to Swift in the actual story may be a chance reflection of Woolf's concurrent reading.

10. *The Diary of Virginia Woolf,* ed. Anne Olivier Bell assisted by Andrew McNeillie, 5 vols. (New York: Harcourt Brace Jovanovich, 1977–84), 3:36; hereafter cited as *D*.

11. Virginia Woolf, *To the Lighthouse* (New York: Harcourt Brace Jovanovich, 1955), 176; hereafter cited as *TL*.

12. See Jane Marcus's essay on gender and reading, which contrasts Mrs. Ramsay's rapturous loss of self in Shakespeare's sonnet with Mr. Ramsay's egocentric reading of Scott, in *Art and Anger* (Columbus: Ohio State University Press, 1988), 242–46.

13. For the thematic importance of sonnet 98, see Maria DiBattista, *Virginia Woolf's Major Novels: The Fables of Anon* (New Haven: Yale University Press, 1980), 91f., and Avrom Fleishman, *Virginia Woolf: A Critical Reading* (Baltimore: Johns Hopkins University Press, 1975), 127–29.

14. See Louise A. DeSalvo, "Lighting the Cave: The Relationship between Vita Sackville-West and Virginia Woolf," *Signs* 8 (1982): 195–214, for an account of their friendship and love affair.

15. Nigel Nicolson, *Portrait of a Marriage* (London: Weidenfeld and Nicolson, 1973), 201.

16. Vita Sackville-West, *Knole and the Sackvilles* (1922; Tonbridge, Kent: Ernest Benn, 1984), 57–58. Sackville-West offers some sketchy evidence of Shakespeare's connections with Knole.

17. Cf. DiBattista, *Major Novels,* 116f.

18. Virginia Woolf, *Orlando* (New York: Harcourt Brace Jovanovich, 1956), 309; hereafter cited as *O*.

19. "Notes for Reading at Random" in " 'Anon' and 'The Reader,' " 375. See also DiBattista, *Major Novels,* 134f., and Lawrence, " 'Shikespower.' " Where T. S. Eliot, in "Tradition and the Individual Talent," views impersonality as escape from neurotic confinement in the self, Woolf's anonymous artist breaks the self's boundaries to experience and imaginatively become other selves; in other words, s/he escapes the limits of a single, consistent, unitary self (*O* 309).

20. Sandra M. Gilbert, "Costumes of the Mind: Transvestism as Metaphor in Modern Literature," *Critical Inquiry* 7 (Winter 1980): 391–417, sees Orlando as "no more than a transvestite . . . not because sexually defining costumes are false and selves are true but because costumes *are* selves and thus easily, fluidly, interchangeable" (405). As I read it, *Orlando*'s idea is that gender is mere costume and selves myriad and interchangeable in the freedom of anonymity—as for Shakespeare, who, paradoxically, got all his selves "completely expressed." Because self and sex are independent categories, Orlando remains after the sex-change "in every other respect . . . precisely as he had been. The change of sex, though it altered their future, did nothing whatever to alter their identity" (*O* 138).

21. Similarly, when Woolf urges Carmichael to record the lives of ordinary women talking with "the swing of Shakespeare's words," she recommends her own project on "the Lives of the Obscure—which is to tell the whole story of England in one obscure life after another" (*D* 3:37, 20 July 1925).

22. See Elaine Showalter, "Virginia Woolf and the Flight into Androgyny," *A Literature of Their Own: British Women Novelists from Brontë to Lessing* (Princeton, N.J.: Princeton University Press, 1977), 263–97. See also Carolyn Heilbrun, *Toward a Recognition of Androgyny* (New York: Harper and Row, 1973) and *Women's Studies* 2, no. 2 (1974).

23. Woolf's concept of androgyny does not, as Showalter argues, simply deny obstructions that continue to impede women writers but urges women to reappropriate culture, to inhabit as large a freedom as possible despite male culture's Brinsleys and Tansleys, and to get beyond not "femaleness" but anger as *the only possible* position for women writers in patriarchal culture. In dismissing Woolf's androgyny as lifelessly "utopian," Showalter overlooks the dialectic between visionary and realist representation in Woolf's work (as in feminist theory and practice more generally) and the way this dialectic challenges canonical and social "reality" to incorporate possibilities that must otherwise remain *literally* utopian.

24. For example, in *The Voyage Out* (1915), "Professions for Women" (1931), *The Years* (1937), and *Between the Acts* (1941).

25. Virginia Woolf, *The Waves: The Two Holograph Drafts,* transcr. and ed. J. W. Graham (Buffalo: University of Toronto Press, 1976), 6; and *The Waves* (New York: Harcourt Brace, 1959), 7.

26. Virginia Woolf, *Moments of Being,* ed. Jeanne Schulkind, 2nd ed. (New York: Harcourt Brace Jovanovich, 1985), 72.

SUSAN STANFORD FRIEDMAN

Remembering Shakespeare Differently: *H.D.'s* By Avon River

H.D., the modernist poet who began writing in the epic mode in the midst of World War II, wrote an experimental work of considerable complexity about William Shakespeare. This avant-garde text, *By Avon River* (1949), stands thematically and formalistically between her better known epics, *Trilogy* (1944–46) and *Helen in Egypt* (1961).[1] It deserves to be better known, not only for its poetic achievement and what it reveals about H.D.'s development, but also for its fascinating revelation of the process by which a woman poet transforms the man many consider the greatest English writer of all times from a male threat into a male ally.

By Avon River is a text engaged in "remembering Shakespeare always, but remembering him differently," as H.D. writes of her tribute (31). Its re-vision of a male literary tradition gives us a reinterpreted Shakespeare whose greatness authenticates the female poet: her existence, her quest, her woman-centered vision. As Virginia Woolf knew so well in her creation of Shakespeare's sister, the recognition of Shakespeare's greatness has often been used to counter the feminist assertion of female genius. "Why have there been no great women artists?" the misogynists have asked generation after generation. "Why have you produced no Shakespeare?" Woolf's answer to the challenge women writers have faced pointed to the ideological and material conditions that have inhibited female genius from finding expression in language.[2] In contrast, H.D. answered by saying in *By Avon River,* "But if you only knew—he was really one of us." In transforming Shakespeare, H.D. self-consciously dissolved the androcentric challenge to her existence as a poet. Her recreation of Shakespeare is a symbolic reenactment of the woman writer's confrontation with the maleness of literary tradition. It represents not the Oedipal rivalry between fathers and sons posited by Harold Bloom, not the mutual seductions of fathers and daughters presented by Jane Gallop, not even the disguises and displacements decoded by Sandra Gilbert and Susan Gubar. Instead, *By Avon River* presents the dialectical process of cultural transformation that characterizes H.D.'s other dialogues with patriarchal religion, psychoanalysis, and art.[3]

First, to describe the text: *By Avon River* is a tribute to Shakespeare, the third text in the tribute genre H.D. wrote in the forties. Like *The Gift* (for her mother, written in 1941–43) and like "Writing on the Wall" (for Sigmund Freud, written in 1944 and later republished as *Tribute to Freud* in 1956), *By Avon River* uses the mechanism of a tribute to another as means for self-exploration.[4] The autobiographical project of the text is twofold, both artistic and religious. The subject is herself as woman writer seeking her place in a dominant male literary tradition and equally herself as a woman questor seeking faith in a dominant male religious tradition. For H.D., art and religion were inseparable dimensions of spiritual quest with a common source in a Delphic unconscious. H.D.'s autobiographical self-definition counterpoints two radically different voices in a bifurcated text integrated only in the imagination of the reader. *By Avon River* comes in two parts: "Good Frend" is a three-part meditative-narrative poem dated "Shakespeare Day," 23 April 1945, and dedicated to Winifred Bryher and Robert Herring. "The Guest" is a modernist essay on Elizabethan poetry with Shakespeare as its central figure, dated 19 September–1 November 1946 and dedicated to Bryher.[5] H.D. was particularly attached to *By Avon River*. To George Plank, she wrote, "I am almost 63 & have been writing for 40 years but *Avon* is the first book that really made me happy." Usually remarkably detached from her published volumes, often unable to locate copies for friends, H.D. liked to carry *By Avon River* in her purse or pocket for re-reading and memorizing during the period when the ideas for *Helen in Egypt* began to take shape. It was her self-created "talisman," empowering her to rewrite the story of Troy from Helen's perspective and thereby to rewrite the place of woman in culture.[6]

Why Shakespeare? H.D. read voraciously and widely. During the war and immediate post-war years, she delved into Dante, Henry James, Emily Dickinson, and Euripides, all of whom have an important presence in the backgrounds of *Helen in Egypt*. Why wasn't her one literary tribute to a classical Greek author, since her sensitivity to Greek literature was well known? Or since she was so concerned about her status as a woman writer, why didn't she look back through her literary mothers, as Woolf advised in *A Room of One's Own*, a book H.D. had read? The compelling reasons for her choice of Shakespeare are both biographical and literary, much more complex than a simple recognition of his greatness.

First, in the broadest sense, H.D.'s aesthetic followed the general prescriptions of T. S. Eliot's "Tradition and the Individual Talent," as did the poetics of so many modernists. As much as H.D. prized her "difference," as she repeatedly called her rebellion against social, sexual, and literary conventions, she wrote with the whole of Western religious and artistic culture permeating her very bones. While she subjected Western culture to a radical re-vision, she never abandoned it altogether. Rather, her inter-action with culture was profoundly dialectical, a process whereby she de-veloped usually understated aspects of a given mythos until she had transformed it into its opposite.[7] In particular, H.D. repeatedly personi-fied her confrontation as a woman with male culture in a series of dia-logues with men, of whom Freud was the most significant. Her analysis with Freud in 1933 and 1934 ended her writer's block and provided the experience which transformed her sense of artistic destiny and its related aesthetic. Since Freud's theories of female psychology were so potentially destructive to H.D.'s creativity, however, her interaction with both the man and his ideas reproduced this dialectical pattern of attraction, then subversion, and transformation.

Both before and after Freud, many men served this function, among them Ezra Pound (to whom she was engaged for a time), Richard Alding-ton (her husband from 1913 until 1938), and D. H. Lawrence. Each man in his own way posed a threat to H.D. as a woman in the world, as a woman writer. As Rachel Blau DuPlessis has demonstrated, H.D. wrote her confrontations with these men into her art, frequently recreating them as ideal lover-companions who did not challenge her autonomy as a woman or a writer.[8] Indeed, a dialogue of opposites moving toward syn-thesis provides the underlying structure of many poems and novels in her oeuvre. H.D.'s Shakespeare in *By Avon River* belongs in the context of these male figures. In selecting the man so often said to be the greatest English writer, H.D. signaled that her underlying subject was her place as a woman writer in a male literary tradition.

Shakespeare's reputation alone, however, is not enough to explain H.D.'s choice in *By Avon River.* Thematically, both Dante and Spenser are closer to the courtly love tradition H.D. celebrated in her tribute to Shakespeare. But Shakespeare acquired an overlay of personal meaning connected to the origins of her own modernism. To H.D., Shakespeare was inseparable from war, its devastating effects on her life, and her result-ant "war phobia."[9] Throughout both world wars, H.D. deliberately chose to stay in London, the scene of her first literary success as an imagist and the cultural center of her adopted homeland. She began *By Avon River* af-ter her friends insisted in April of 1945 that she must leave the rubbled city for a restorative visit to Stratford-on-Avon, which appeared un-touched by the war. She went in search of healing, temporarily finding it not only in her gift of flowers at Shakespeare's tomb, but also in writing the poem "Good Frend" that quickly followed.

H.D. experienced history as a palimpsest of superimposed events in which the public and the private intersected. Memories of the first world war were "literally blasted into consciousness" by the bombs of the sec-

ond, she wrote in her "Hirslanden Notebooks."[10] At Stratford, she gave
thanks for surviving the terrible fly bombs of the fall of 1944. The superimposed memory was her own survival of the bombings of London in the
Great War, the flu epidemic of 1919, and the birth of her daughter when
the doctors had given both mother and baby up for dead. H.D. named her
child Perdita, which means "the lost one who is found" and recalls the
long-lost Perdita of Shakespeare's romance, *The Winter's Tale*. In the play,
Hermione is brought back to life by the return of her long-lost daughter
Perdita. In Greek myth, Hermione, like H.D., is the daughter of Helen.
Destined by her mother Helen and her daughter Perdita, H.D. twice
chose the name Hermione for herself in her *romans à clef Asphodel* (1921–
22) and *HER* (1926–27).[11] H.D.'s intensely personal tie to Shakespeare
was born in the first world war and relived in the second.

H.D.'s situation at the end of World War I is instructive for the
meaning she gave Shakespeare at the end of World War II. Her marriage
to her poet-lover, Richard Aldington, had nearly dissolved by 1918. The
stillbirth of their first child in the spring of 1915 probably initiated the divisions, for Aldington did not understand H.D.'s grief, nor her fear of another pregnancy. Her physician had told her to avoid sex until after the
war, and to H.D.'s profound shock, Aldington turned to other women
with his strong desires born of life at the front. He was delighted, however, when H.D. went to Cornwall to live with music historian Cecil Gray
in the spring of 1918—delighted, that is, until she unexpectedly became
pregnant. Wavering about the child and their marriage, his letters
throughout her pregnancy variously urged her to abort, warned her about
the dangers of "that operation," promised to care for them both, or vio-
lently told her that he would offer no help.[12] In *Asphodel*, H.D. wrote
about her conscious, defiant decision to keep the pregnancy viable, to re-
capture in the second child what she had lost in the first. Rejected by Aldington and repudiating Gray as the father whom she did not want to
marry, she imaginatively recreated the embryo as the child of Apollo—the
god of light, of Delphi, of art, music, and healing.[13] Independent of both
Aldington and Gray, her pregnancy became a living symbol of her over-
lapping creative and procreative powers. But just before she was about to
deliver, she learned of her father's death (which she connected with news
of her brother's death in the war) and caught the deadly influenza, from
which she and the baby only miraculously recovered. A brief mental
breakdown followed Perdita's birth and Aldington's final, brutal rejection
in April, when he threatened her with "penal servitude" if she registered
the fatherless child with his name.[14]

H.D.'s physical and spiritual recovery took place in the context of her
love for Bryher. Herself a deeply troubled young woman, Bryher relied on

H.D. to sustain her desire to live and help her escape the confinements of her wealthy family. For both women, the baby provided a lifeline to the future. Perdita became a child with two mothers, a fact recognized legally in 1928 by Bryher's formal adoption of the child. Perdita's Shakespearean name resonates with the conditions of her birth. She was a child thrice lost and finally found: lost in the stillborn sibling, lost in the pressure to abort, lost in the near-death of traumatic birth; found in her mother's empowering decision to keep, found in the miraculous survival, found in the affirmation of life surrounded by death. Shakespeare was irrevocably entwined in this dynamic of interlocking spheres—public and private, male and female, death and birth, war and peace.

The weaving of personal and historical catastrophe resurfaced at the end of World War II, when Shakespeare again played a central role in H.D.'s symbolic death and rebirth. "Good Frend" and "The Guest," the two parts of *By Avon River,* frame H.D.'s collapse and recovery at the end of the war. The healing effects of H.D.'s visit to Stratford in April of 1945 and re-visit in August of 1945 led to the composition of "Good Frend." But a combination of events thereafter led to a six-month period of illness from April to September of 1946, the most serious breakdown she ever experienced and the one whose end coincided with the composition of "The Guest." Once again, the events are instructive, identifying the personal threads that run through *By Avon River.* As in 1919, the breakdown probably began with physical illness and progressed to mental illness through the betrayal of a soldier-figure to whom she was deeply attached. In February, 1946, H.D. had to cancel all plans to go to Bryn Mawr College, which had contracted for her to lecture on poetry for six months. Her work on Elizabethan poets had begun with their invitation in November of 1945 and continued in spite of her distress at the bombings of Hiroshima and Nagasaki. But she contracted "acute meningitis," on top of severe malnutrition and anemia, according to Bryher, who wrote to Pearson that "our poor Hilda nearly died."[15]

Also in February, Sir Hugh Dowding, who had been chief air marshal of the Royal Air Force during the Battle of Britain, rejected both her and the messages she believed she had received from his dead RAF pilots. Well-known for his spiritualist lectures, Dowding and H.D. shared séances, but he refused to accept the warning she had received about the coming atomic age and a third world war. His rejection, which paralleled on an esoteric plane Aldington's earlier betrayal, released the repressed feelings left over from World War I and led to what Bryher called "a complete breakdown."[16]

In *The Sword Went Out to Sea,* H.D. writes openly about the dimensions of her madness that related to broad historical issues of war and peace. In the spring of 1946, she hallucinated the arrival of the third world war, believing that Europe was mined with explosives and that bombs were still falling in her garden.[17] But private sources suggest that her madness also included a crisis of identity, one that was foreshadowed in "Good Frend" and resolved in "The Guest." The physician who was attempting to prevent H.D.'s disintegration reported to Bryher that H.D. was hearing voices, seeing bombs, fearing that when her spirit left her body it might not return. During bombing raids, H.D. had relied on this psychic trick to carry her through an attack. Further, she believed that her apartment was filled with "bad articles," presumably her own, which had to be locked up. Pearson wrote that during this period she ripped out all her specially designed signature bookplates, an act which he believed represented "a destruction of identity." Perdita's imminent departure for the States—the loss of the child who had been found—completed the picture of H.D.'s disintegration. On 16 May 1946 Bryher flew H.D. to Seehoff, Kusnacht, a Swiss sanitorium run by the analyst Dr. Brunner. There she rested, ate, walked in the garden, talked to the analysts, possibly underwent heavy drug and shock therapy, and finally recovered. By 16 October 1946 Bryher reported to Pearson that "suddenly with a bang our dear Hilda came to herself. Dr. Brunner said she was free last Monday to leave the sanitorium." This sudden recovery, which came months before Dr. Brunner had anticipated, coincided with her completion of her extensive study of Elizabethan poets and the composition of "The Guest."[18] As with Woolf, a period of intense creativity followed H.D.'s breakdown and recovery.

Framing her breakdown and recovery, H.D.'s meditations on Shakespeare in *By Avon River* explore the meaning of her illness and, phoenix-like, create herself anew from the ashes of the old. Conversely, biographical context illuminates the literary creation of a symbolic Shakespeare. As she wrote Pearson, "with AVON...I crossed literally my Rubicon."[19] The birth of Perdita, Shakespeare's namesake, in 1919 becomes the birth of *Avon*, Shakespeare's tribute, in 1949:

> The book has come, one copy. I could almost cry; it is the first BOOK I have had, I feel; that is odd, as I was happy with the Trilogy and the other earlier "slim volumes." Though our darling AVON is slim, it seems to contain really, the whole of me, not an intense cerebral ice-edge merely. . . . I am prouder than Elizabeth with young Charles!

H.D.'s re-vision of Shakespeare falls into two parts, mutually interrelated but separately explored in the two voices of *By Avon River*. "Good Frend" is a meditative narrative relying on the conventions of romance, much like *The Tempest* with which H.D.'s poem opens. "The Guest," in contrast, is a prose essay exploring the poet in the world, the man Shakespeare as he existed in historical context. While the modes are radically different, each moves the reader toward a vision of Shakespeare as an androgynous man and poet dedicated to the mystical Love at the center of esoteric tradition.

The narrative grounding of "Good Frend" is the contemporary poet's journey at the end of World War II on Shakespeare Day to place flowers on his grave in Stratford-on-Avon—"tribute," in both senses of the word, to his healing genius. "Awkwardly, tenderly," the poet says, "We stand with our flowers." "Shyly or in child-like / Delicate simplicity," the poet pays homage to the master (9). But her child-like shyness belies what is about to happen in the poem. "Good Frend's" epigram is Shakespeare's epitaph warning no man to move his gravestones:

> GOOD FREND FOR IESVS SAKE FOREBEARE,
> TO DIGG THE DVST ENCLOASED HEARE!
>   E   T
> BLESTE BE Y MAN Y SPARES THES STONES,
>   T
> AND CVRST BE HE Y MOVES MY BONES.

The poet's tribute defies Shakespeare's last command and curse as she proceeds symbolically to move his stones, to disturb his bones, to reveal the inner mysteries he encoded in his plays. Just as the poet in the *Trilogy* defied John's warning in *Revelation* by creating an alternative revelation of the Lady, the poet in *By Avon River* begins her quest by denying male authority, whether religious or artistic.[20]

Entitled "The Tempest," Part 1 of "Good Frend" begins with a pun linking the Elizabethan and modern worlds to initiate the poet's meditation on the play commonly thought to be Shakespeare's parting gesture to the London theater: "I came home driven by *The Tempest*." This echoes not only the storm which opens the play but also Shakespeare's return to Stratford after completing *The Tempest* and the poet's effort, driven by the storms of war, to seek peace in her homage to Shakespeare. Surprisingly, the center of her meditations on the play which supremely represented his romance plays and post-tragic vision is not Prospero, with his reconciling magic, not the freed spirit Ariel, not even the young lovers Ferdinand and Miranda. Instead, it is Claribel, the daughter of Alonso and sister of Ferdinand, who attracts the poet's attention. Just married to the King of Tunis and the indirect cause of her father's shipwreck, she exists only offstage. Encoding H.D.'s coming breakdown of identity, the poet's fascination is with Claribel's very invisibility. She listens for the sounds of Claribel's untold story which took place before the action of the play began:

> She is not there at all, but Claribel,
> Claribel, the birds shrill, Claribel,
> Claribel echoes from this rainbow-shell,
> I stooped just now to gather from the sand;
>
> (6)

H.D.'s choice of Claribel as the center of meditation emphasizes the process that is beginning as she stands in line waiting to place her flowers on the grave. The humble suppliant bringing tribute to the grave of genius is not content to invoke his vision; she must begin to create her own out of the shards of the tradition he represents. Shakespeare himself was a plunderer, she irreverently tells us: "He stole everything, / There isn't an original plot / In the whole lot of his plays." His "little success with the old Queen" came from "patching up / Other men's plots and filling in / With odds and ends he called his own" (8).[21] Imitating him, she borrows Claribel, the character he named but did not incarnate. Her story of Claribel becomes the key to her re-vision of Shakespeare and the self-exploration encased therein.

In "Rosemary," Part 2 of "Good Frend," the poet's defiance deepens. As her turn finally approaches, she regards Shakespeare's grave as an "altar" to which she has come to worship. But recalling the line in the epitaph,

> E   T
> BLEST BE Y MAN Y SPARES THES STONES,

she nonetheless plans to touch the gravestone's script:

> My fingers knew each syllable,
> I sensed the music in the stone,
> I knew a rhythm would pass on,
> And out of it, if I could stoop
> And run my bare palm over it
> And touch the letters and the words,
> Reading the whole as the blind read.
>
> (10)

As she stoops to touch the magic script, however, her act of defiance leads to an apocalyptic vision that speaks directly to the modern survivors of a devastating war. The stone vanishes "as if under / Azure and green of deepsea water." In its place, the poet sees how "the power / of Love transformed Death to a flower." Shakespeare's warning curse yields to a secret message and mystery visible only to the initiate:

There were no letters anywhere,
But on each bud, each leaf, each spray,
The words were written that beneath
The laurel, iris, rosemary,
Heartsease and every sort of lily,
Speak through all flowers eternally,

Blest be y̆ man—that one who knows
His heart glows in the growing rose.

(11)

As is already deeply reflected in *The Gift* and *Trilogy,* H.D. had been reading Moravian history, the esoteric Christian Kabbalah of Robert Ambelain, and the hermetic history of the Cathar heresy according to Denis de Rougemont's *Love in the Western World.*[22] Her vision of Shakespeare alive in the growing rose represents her epiphany that connects this literary giant to the esoteric mysticism which flared up brilliantly in the late Middle Ages and early Renaissance before the Inquisition drove it underground. The sweet herb rosemary becomes sign and symbol of Shakespeare's identification with heterodox religion. In esoteric tradition, rosemary is the flower of resurrection, the *Ros maris* or Rose of the Sea, used "To trim the bride, / To deck the shroud," magically present at the sacraments of marriage and death (12). "Rooted within the grave, / Spreading to heaven," rosemary embodies the mystery of life-in-death and death-in-life. With it, the poet celebrates her resurrection before death— that is, her survival and that of civilization itself during the war:

For strife

Is ended,
We ascended
From gloom and fear,
Not after death
But now and here.

(12)

The "rose of memory" returns the poet once again to Shakespeare and a catalogue of his female characters in Arden, Navarre, and Illyria. But having loved these powerful women well, she nonetheless chooses Claribel to represent Shakespeare. The invisible, voiceless Claribel becomes her persona, not Shakespeare's magnificently drawn strong women:

I had no voice
To chide the lark at dawn,

> Or argue with a Jew,
> Be merciful;
>
> I had no wit
> To banter with a clown,
> Or claim a kingdom
> Or denounce a throne;
>
> I had no hand
> To snatch a dagger,
> Or pluck wild-flowers,
> For a crown.
>
> I stand invisible on the water-stair,
>
> (16)

"Why," the poet wonders, "did I choose / The invisible, voiceless Claribel?" (14). The answer lies in H.D.'s impending crisis of identity. All the symptoms of her own invisibility are written into her reading of Shakespeare in the spring of 1945. The negative syntax in which she four times denies her connection to Shakespeare's powerful women is a highly characteristic stylistic pattern in her work. But in volumes like *Sea Garden* (1916) and *Heliodora* (1924), where it is common, the negative syntax is a sign of power, the poet's defiance of sweetness, sentiment, and things stereotypically feminine. In *By Avon River,* however, the denials are a sign of her weakness and the imminent breakdown of identity.[23]

It is Claribel's very voicelessness, her possession by her creator, that draws the woman poet to her. The silent Claribel exists in the play only as "an emblem, a mere marriage token," as the "King's fair daughter" who "marries Tunis" (14).[24] Claribel, not Rosalind or Portia, mirrors the poet's position—possession—in male culture. In relation to Claribel and her modern avatar H.D., Shakespeare is the epitome of male literary power. He wields the pen that gives existence to the text, the woman. Claribel's marriage parallels the "marriage" of the woman poet to Shakespeare, a bond both inspiring and threatening. Joined in their similar relationship to Shakespeare, the poet and Claribel have become one and the same:

> I only threw a shadow
> On his page,
> Yet I was his,
> He spoke my name;
>
> He hesitated,
> Raised his quill,
> Which paused,
> Waited a moment,

And then fell
Upon the unblotted line;
I was born,
Claribel.

(15)

"'Twas a sweet marriage," the poet says, and in her "one short line," "I live forever" (15). In one sense Claribel's immortality in Shakespeare's text and the poet's "marriage" to Shakespeare are "enough." But in another sense, "Rosemary" freezes in tableau the essential dilemma of the literary woman. In the "text" of patriarchal culture, woman has an identity, an existence—perhaps as man's muse, his beloved, his virgin, his whore; perhaps just as a "mere marriage token." But just as rosemary trims both marriage veil and shroud, this immortality is a kind of death. When the woman writer takes up the quill to mark the page with her own magic script, she must overcome her invisibility and speechlessness as man's creation to birth herself before she can birth her own text.[25]

In the underlying dialectical argument of "Good Frend," H.D. began "The Tempest" in worship of Shakespeare. "Rosemary" plunges deeper into the esoteric dimension of that reverence to recreate Shakespeare as a Renaissance embodiment of *Ros maris*. But within the mystery of the death-marriage cycle, the poet finds Claribel, the projection of her own silence within the male tradition that Shakespeare epitomizes. H.D.'s focus on Shakespeare and his nonexistent character reflects her ambivalence as a woman writer toward his very greatness. In conjuring Shakespeare out of his grave, she has created two Shakespeares—one, the symbol of the power that silences her own poetic voice, and the other, the embodiment of the vision she wants to capture in her own poetry.

"Claribel's Way to God," Part 3 of "Good Frend," attempts to resolve the contradiction established in "Rosemary." The speaker is no longer the poet, but Claribel herself. In the first person, she narrates the romance that she could never utter as only the marriage token whose unwilling but obedient marriage set up the action of *The Tempest*. Empowered by the woman poet, Claribel steps out of the pages of Shakespeare's text to reveal her identity as questor. The ten-section narrative written in a near-ballad mode heavily influenced by medieval romance tells the tale of Claribel's journey. As the queen of Tunis, she approaches a number of men and women to find the answers to her questions. The quest is both personal and religious. To some, she tells her "secret," that she is "nothing but a name," "who never had a word to say," as if by giving speech to her speechlessness she could break Shakespeare's power to silence her. But her quest is also religious, a search for the hidden mysteries of life and death.

First she meets a "poor Clare" who teaches her to make a rosary out of rosemary beads; then, a poor friar of St. Francis, who speaks mysteriously of his Lady; next, the pope himself who vaguely blesses, then dismisses her; then, the relics of St. Francis; then a Mother of the Clares, who teaches her herbal lore. Each reveals an approach to God, but none offers Claribel her own way to God until she meets a wounded *trouvère* under an archway in Venice. With rosemary, she heals his wounds. Her power leads him to call her "Mary" and tell her about the secret band of "trouvères." He is one of the troubadours described by de Rougemont, who argued that these lyric poets were secret members of the Cathars, an esoteric sect who worshipped the "ineffable Mystery" in the coded rituals of courtly love. The roles of Lover and Lady were a disguise adopted by both to hide from the Inquisition. But their love expressed through song also paralleled the centrality of Love in the mystical tradition. In this heretical sect, wrote de Rougemont, the woman in the form of the Lady served as symbol for the divine.[26] As Claribel's *trouvère* says, the Lady is "Holy Wisdom, / *Santa Sophia*, the SS of the *Sanctus Spiritus*." This is the secret the *trouvère* reveals to Claribel. In this religion of Love, her religious quest ends. As she kisses his brow, she is free to tell her own secret—her nothingness. But he calls her beautiful Spirit and breaks "the spell" of Shakespeare's power. Within the Cathar tradition, she has a real voice, a power recognized and worshipped. She is not simply the Virgin Mary, who is the Mother *of* God. Rather, she is the Mother *as* God, the divine in female form.

In the final section of "Claribel's Way to God," Claribel accomplishes her final quest—to relate her new identity and religious vision to art. Like the poet with whom she is once again identified (the "I" is both women), Claribel journeys to Avon in tribute to Shakespeare, her creator from whom she has just freed herself. Her final epiphany is also the poet's:

> And suddenly, I saw it fair,
> How Love is God, how Love is strong,
> When One is Three and Three are One,
> The Dream, the Dreamer and the Song.
>
> (25)

Claribel is no longer just Shakespeare's Dream. She is also the Dreamer, whose voice and visibility make possible a new aesthetic Trinity. The poet's original identification with the speechless woman has been transformed to an identification with artistic and religious power. No longer threatening, the poet's homage to the "Master" has set her free to give woman in Western culture the speech denied her—a task to which H.D.

was soon after to dedicate herself in *Helen in Egypt,* the next major poem she wrote and an epic in which the frozen, silent statue of her earlier "Helen" comes to life.

Claribel's quest starts up again in "The Guest," the second half of *By Avon River,* in the avatar of a new persona, in many ways Claribel's opposite. Not voiceless, the product of the male pen, the narrator in "The Guest" is a knowledgeable researcher with full scholarly trappings. An acknowledgment at the beginning establishes her debt to and departures from "the discoveries of modern scholarship"; the text itself is peppered with dates and quotations; and the conclusion is a chart with the names and dates of forty-nine Elizabethan poets. The poetic symbols of birth and death in "Good Frend" re-emerge in "The Guest" with the essay's major structuring device—each poet's birth and death dates.[27] The repetitive introductions of fact into the text—almost to the point of irony—contrast with the spirit of romance which pervades "Good Frend." Although the re-creative task of the text's two parts is essentially the same, the contrasting modes reflect the two sides of H.D's divided self: the transcendental self and the empirical self, always represented in her life by the duality of her Moravian-artistic mother and her scientist father. The form itself of *By Avon River* embodies the divisions between mother and father, art and mathematics, religion and science, that she spent her life attempting to transcend.[28] As such, these modes also frame the process of her descent into the madness of hallucination and her return to the world anchored in, though not limited to, empirical reality.

The shift in H.D.'s tone from romance to research was not only biographically motivated, however. It also reflects a change in the focus of her meditations on Shakespeare. While the romance explores Shakespeare's symbolic meaning, the scholarly essay sets out to establish his historical legacy for poets in the modern world. "Good Frend" portrays Shakespeare out-of-time against the backdrop of the eternal; "The Guest" presents him in-time, in the context of social, political, and literary history. H.D.'s historical Shakespeare represents as much a re-vision of the great man as her symbolic Shakespeare. Once again, her underlying purpose is to recreate Shakespeare in such a way that her identification with him as poet empowers her own voice instead of extinguishing it. Such a task is challenging, the scholar warns us in the beginning; for in the Elizabethan anthology of poets and dramatists from which she works, Queen Elizabeth is "the only woman listed among the more than one hundred Elizabethan lyrists." As if to emphasize her alienation from the maleness of literary tradition, she immediately thereafter quotes a lyric of Shakespeare and by context gives it a specifically feminist meaning:

Blow, blow thou winter wind,
Thou art not so unkind
As man's ingratitude;

(32–33)[29]

Resonating with the richly drawn and fictionalized lecturer of Woolf's *A Room of One's Own,* H.D.'s researcher relies on an associative, circular narrative structure. Sequence in "The Guest" is neither chronological nor conventionally logical. Recreation of the historical Shakespeare and "the living tradition" must rely on association, indirection, and imagination, which lead into the pathways of desire:

> We wander through a labyrinth. If we cut straight through, we destroy the shell-like curves and involutions. Where logic is, where reason dictates, we have walls, broad highways, bridges, causeways. But we are in a garden. (34)

H.D.'s re-vision of the scholar prefigures the process by which she transforms culture. Fact alone presents an image of the Elizabethan literary tradition as exclusively male. But imagination in conjunction with fact creates a "living tradition" in which woman as actor and empowering symbol is central. As the scholar warns, "it is better to follow one's own clues and have of each of these poets, a living and personal memory, rather than grow weary and confused with disputable facts about them" (43). Consequently, the scholar's recitation of facts yields repeatedly and irresistibly to imagination. In particular, she frames her essay with several imagined scenes from Shakespeare's life, created in tableaux so that she can explore the depths of meaning within the frozen moment. Echoing "Good Frend's" focus on *The Tempest,* she imagines Shakespeare returning home to Stratford after the performance of his farewell play in 1611:

> Of William Shakespeare, alone, can we visualize a chair drawn up before an open window, an apple-tree in blossom, a friend or two and children. There was Elizabeth and, with her, Judith. Hamnet, Judith's twin, is not forgotten. . . .
> A child tugged at the knotted edge of his grey shawl. Another child was laughing, but it wasn't Hamnet. He looked at her-his face. They were both his children, but Judith with her hair tucked over her ears, was no Juliet. Judith was Hamnet. Hamnet was Judith. (34, 36)

"Of Shakespeare, alone," the scholar says, we can imagine such a scene: the poet with his children, the poet maternal staring into the face of his daughter and seeing "her-his face." The scholar's decision to evoke Shakespeare in retirement with his children is as perverse from a conventional perspective as the poet's earlier fascination with a character who has no part.[30] The special bond between Prospero and his daughter Miranda is reborn in the father-daughter relationship in H.D.'s "history." Repeating what the scholar calls Shakespeare's disregard for "the unities of time and place"(91), the passage constructs an imaginary time-space that layers different points in Shakespeare's life into a single tableau that highlights the father-daughter relationship. In 1611, when Shakespeare left London for retirement in Stratford, his son Hamnet had been dead for some fifteen years, Judith was twenty-six years old, and his elder daughter Susanna had a child named Elizabeth who was about three years old. But in the passage, Judith is once again a child, with her twin Hamnet ambiguously there and not there. The glance between daughter and father condenses complex psychologies into genealogical symbolism. The old man, having broken the magic wand of his art in *The Tempest,* finds in the "her-his face" of Judith the mirror of his own soul. She is both androgynous herself and representative of his own "twin" nature through her twinship with Hamnet. It is important that the researcher imagines Shakespeare's *daughter,* rather than his son, to be the outward symbol of his essence. This bond with Judith, representing his own androgyny, frames the essay. Introduced near the beginning, it reappears in the closing sentence: "He had come home because he loved Judith" (96). The presence of woman within Shakespeare counters the absence of women in the Elizabethan anthology. Judith's power in turn foreshadows the development of a strong female literary tradition in later generations. In H.D.'s re-vision, Shakespeare has become the androgynous father-muse, whose gift bypasses the son to be passed on through the daughter.[31]

In the context of H.D.'s genealogical literary history, the extensive recitation of Shakespeare's fellow poets in the main body of "The Guest" takes on special meaning. H.D. catalogues the succession of lyric poets in order to establish a foil that characterizes Shakespeare largely through contrast. Shakespeare appears as the supreme voice of the Elizabethan Age, but more importantly, the scholar sets out to establish how *different* he was from everyone else. Echoing the imagery of androgyny in her family tableau, she notes that he was always known as "Gentle Shakespeare" (46). Impossible to imagine him as the fiery Christopher Marlowe who "died at the age of twenty-nine, stabbed in that mysterious tavern brawl," she says (32). Impossible also to see him as Sir Philip Sidney, the courtier who died "through reckless chivalry," or as Sir Walter Raleigh, the buccaneer who rotted in London Tower (33–34). Instead, he was the "gentle poet" who gave up London and quietly retired to Stratford to be with his daughter. His death likewise came gently from a chill caught at "a merry meeting" of poets in a local Stratford tavern, the scholar notes (68).

The scholar is not content to define Shakespeare's difference solely in terms of his genius or other idiosyncrasies. She turns instead to the social and political history of the late Middle Ages and early Renaissance to determine its impact on his art and vision. She finds in Europe's emergence from the cocoon of the autocratic medieval church dogma a period of political and symbolic chaos: "If there was doubt or indecision [in the Middle Ages], it could be countered by the logic of the church. There was no logic, no reason now. There was no safety.... Mary Tudor is the first queen of England, in her own right. How far the atrocities committed in her name were actually of her connivance or due to the power of Rome, will also remain a mystery. Now, terror took the place of sanctuary" (77, 79). As the scholar speaks of "the black wave of terror and depression" and "the black shadow of the charred city," we realize that H.D.'s description of the Elizabethan Age represents her vision of the modern world as well. The breakup of symbolic systems and the omnipresence of war characterized the twentieth century for H.D., as she had stated in the *Trilogy*:

> *we are powerless,*
>
> *dust and powder fill our lungs*
> *our bodies blunder*
>
> *through doors twisted on hinges,*
>
> . . . .
>
> *we know no rule*
> *of procedure,*
>
> *we are voyagers, discoverers*
> *of the not-known,*
>
> *the unrecorded;*
> *we have no map;*
>
> *possibly we will reach haven,*
> *heaven.*[32]

Trilogy's band of poet-questors seeking a new symbolic order amidst the ashes of a destroyed civilization parallels the Elizabethan poets, Shakespeare preeminent among them for H.D. Poets, the scholar tells us, were the natural "heretics" of the Elizabethan Age. Her description makes these bards the prototypes of the modernist poets:

The poet is always suspect. In spite of himself and all his good intentions, he comes to no good....

Two roads were open to these heretics or poets. There was the way of stark reality and there was escape from that reality. There was one door always open, but they looked fearful and diminished, straight through the portals of Death, and saw what was or was not there. It was no longer possible to accept dogma or even inspiration from another, as to the steps down to Hell or those leading up to Heaven. They must see for themselves and they did see. As the boundaries of the known world, so the boundaries of the unknown were extended. This was a spiritual necessity. (83)

The poet's answer to a culture of terror and disorder echoes Claribel's discovery. It is "the dream," the imagination which is "greater than reality" (84). Dante found his answer to this mad world in a dream, the scholar says. But it is Shakespeare more than all the others who epitomizes the poet's response to the chaos of history. Shakespeare's implicit modernism appears in his refusal to pronounce dogma. "The Deity is seldom mentioned by William Shakespeare," the scholar informs us. The "tirades or exhortations are in character, in costume, you might say. The dramatist himself remains discreetly non-committal. He is as abstract as Aeschylus, yet he speaks personally. He is diplomatic, yet he leaves us in no doubt as to how the scales of Justice will tilt" (76). Form follows content, and the scholar connects Shakespeare's "broken and shattered" unities of time and space with the broken, shattered era of which he was a part.

By making Shakespeare a proto-modernist shaped by and reshaping his historical context, H.D. remade the Elizabethan into a muse-figure relevant to her own poetic tasks. Moreover, the scholar's revisionist history takes on an esoteric dimension reminiscent of Claribel, as she pores through the historical documents to discover the hidden history encoded on the surfaces of time. Like Claribel, she finds the remnants of the Cathar heresy, another "living tradition" whose history shaped Shakespeare's art.[33] "Through Elizabethan poetry," she notes, "there is this obsession with the lost Virgin. The moon, a symbol of chastity, was associated with the Mother of God. Now Cynthia herself must be invoked, in the guise of Queen Elizabeth" (91). Relying upon de Rougemont, the scholar suggests that woman's presence as symbol in Elizabethan poetry is a vestige of the Church of Love spread throughout Provence by the troubadours and brought to England by Eleanor of Aquitaine, mother of Richard-the-Lion-Hearted: "the roots of that flower still flourished and sent out thorny branches" (84).[34] Driven underground by the Inquisition, the Church of Love countered the chaos of history with the vision of Love, symbolized by the Lady. Disguising its aesthetic and religious heresy in the metaphors of "earthly passion," the Church of Love spread the code of *cortezia* through the songs of the troubadours. De Rougemont also linked St. Francis and St. Teresa to this tradition, as well as the early Moravians from whom H.D. herself was descended.

Set in the context of historical fact, Claribel's exchange with the friar, the Mother, and the *trouvère* becomes even clearer. While Claribel's romance ends with her gift at Shakespeare's grave, the scholar accomplishes a parallel task by discussing a number of Shakespeare's plays in the context of the historical confrontations between the forces of state power and the forces of heretical Love incarnated by the poet's words. It does not matter to the scholar whether Shakespeare was conscious of the living tradition that found its way into his art: "What he taught, he taught unconsciously" (91). In the guise of the literary historian, H.D. remakes Shakespeare by presenting his poetry as the supreme Elizabethan expression of the troubadour tradition, an art dedicated to the power of mystical Love embodied in woman's form. This transformation is symbolized by another imaginative tableau. Near the end of "The Guest," the scholar recreates a transcendent moment in which Shakespeare hands flowers he gathered on the banks of the Avon to his mother, Mary Arden: "Then he was back in the kitchen and smelt wood-smoke and space, and the delicate fragranced flowers with the too-long green-white stems that he held toward Mary Arden" (87). The text which begins in homage to Shakespeare with the poet's gift of flowers at his grave ends in Shakespeare's homage to woman symbolized by the flowers he gives his mother.[35]

H.D.'s Shakespeare, the man and poet emerging from the two voices of *By Avon River,* is a series of doubles. He is both in-time and out-of-time, of history and beyond history, of the world and retired from it, Elizabethan and modern, male and female, the expression of his age and its prime heretic. It is the contradictions she perceived within Shakespeare that allowed H.D. to portray him as a transcendent figure whose challenge to the woman writer could be neutralized and then transformed into a source of power. H.D. almost always conceived of her muse as female, indeed as mother, but in *By Avon River* she created a Shakespeare whose role as father-muse validates her artistic destiny in the tempest of the modern world. Shakespeare could not play this part in her personal and poetic development until she had remade him in her own image, until *he* became the text brought to life by her pen.

NOTES

This essay is a shorter version of an article published in *Sagetrieb* 2 (Summer-Fall 1983): 45–70. I am indebted to Perdita Schaffner (H.D.'s daughter and executor) and Beinecke Rare Book and Manuscript Library at Yale University for their generous permission in letting me quote from the H.D. Papers.

1. H.D. [Hilda Doolittle, 1886–1961], *By Avon River* (New York: Macmillan, 1949). All quotations will be from this edition and cited in the text.

2. See Virginia Woolf, *A Room of One's Own* (1929; rpt. New York: Harcourt, Brace and World, 1957). H.D. never met Woolf, but according to her daughter, Perdita Schaffner, H.D. owned and read all of Woolf's books.

3. See Harold Bloom, *The Anxiety of Influence* (New York: Oxford University Press, 1973); Sandra M. Gilbert and Susan Gubar, *The Madwoman in the Attic: The Woman Writer and the Nineteenth-Century Literary Imagination* (New Haven: Yale University Press, 1979); Jane Gallop, *The Daughter's Seduction: Feminism and Psychoanalysis* (Ithaca: Cornell University Press, 1982).

4. H.D., *Tribute to Freud* (1956; rev. ed. Boston: David R. Godine, 1974). An abridged version of *The Gift* has been published by New Directions (1982).

5. Winifred Bryher (1894–1983) was H.D.'s intimate friend from 1918 to 1961; they lived together, separated by frequent travel, from 1919 to 1946. Robert Herring was editor of *Life and Letters Today* and a close friend of both women from the late twenties through the forties. The dedication reflects H.D.'s gratitude for Bryher's support and her shared interest in Elizabethan culture with Herring.

6. See H.D.'s letters to George Plank, July 2, 1949; Robert McAlmon, Nov. 29, 1950; and Norman Holmes Pearson, Sept. 21, 1950 at Beinecke Rare Book and Manuscript Library, Yale University.

7. See T. S. Eliot, *Selected Essays, 1917–1932* (New York: Harcourt, Brace, 1932), p. 3. For extended discussion of H.D.'s sense of her "difference" and her dialectical interaction with psychoanalytic and religious tradition, see my *Psyche Reborn: The Emergence of H.D.* (Bloomington: Indiana University Press, 1981).

8. Rachel Blau DuPlessis, "Romantic Thralldom in H.D.," *Contemporary Literature* 20 (Summer 1979): 178–203. See also my *Psyche Reborn* and Albert Gelpi, "Hilda in Egypt," *Southern Review* 18 (Spring 1982): 233–50.

9. H.D., *Tribute to Freud*, 93–94.

10. H.D., "Hirslanden Notebooks," 3:2. Written between 1957 and 1959, the manuscript is at Beinecke.

11. *HER* was published with the title *HERmione* by New Directions (1981). Still unpublished, *Asphodel* is at Beinecke. See H.D.'s letter to Bryher linking *The Winter's Tale* to her daughter's name (March 8, 1936).

12. See Aldington's letters to H.D. from the front in the summer and fall of 1918 at Beinecke. For extended discussion of the documentation for this biographical account, see the longer version of this essay (50–51).

13. *Asphodel* is a fictionalized autobiography of H.D.'s life from 1911 to 1919 and should not be used as an absolute source of biographical fact. Nonetheless, many aspects of the novel are corroborated by other memoirs and letters. H.D.'s letters to Bryher in the 1930s contain many references to Gray as the father of Perdita. See Perdita Schaffner's discussion of her father in "Unless a Bomb Falls . . . ," in H.D., *The Gift* (ix–xv).

14 See *Tribute to Freud* (40–41); Bryher, *Heart to Artemis: A Writer's Memoirs* (New York: Harcourt Brace Jovanovich, 1962), 186–89.; H.D.'s letters to Pound (Feb. 20, 1929?; Friday, Spring 1919?), Beinecke; *Asphodel* (2:167–76); H.D.'s divorce papers, Beinecke.

15. For an account of H.D.'s meningitis, see H.D.'s letter to Pearson, Sept. 26, 1946; Bryher's letters to Pearson, March 7, 1946, March 17, 1946, March 23, 1946, and June 8, 1946. These references to physical illness may be accurate, or they could also be a screen for H.D.'s more serious mental illness.

16. For Bryher's reports to Pearson about H.D.'s mental breakdown, see especially her letters of March 23, 1946, April 12, 1946, May 1, 1946, June 8, 1946, July 6, 1946, Sept. 22, 1946, and Oct. 16, 1946. For H.D.'s accounts of Dowding's significance, see her "Autobiographical Notes" (1949), Beinecke; her unpublished roman à clef, *The Sword Went Out to Sea (Synthesis of a Dream)* (1946–47), about their séances; her unpublished memoir, *Compassionate Friendship* (1955), 29, 72, 81; and "Hirslanden Notebooks," 1:17–29, 2:9–10, and vol. 3.

17. Begun immediately after the completion of *By Avon River, The Sword Went Out to Sea* suggests the anti-war perspective out of which *By Avon River* emerged. To Aldington, H.D. wrote that the novel's "Message" was that the "world was, perhaps is and possibly will be 'crashing to extinction,' if those in authority, no matter where and who, don't stop smashing up things with fly-bombs, V2 and the ubiquitous (possibly) so-called 'atom.' They could do something with the atom—better than smashing cherry-orchards" (June 6, 194?).

18. See at Beinecke the letter from Dr. Dennis Carroll to Bryher, April 30, 1946, and Pearson's notes for a biography of H.D. that he never wrote. See the longer version of this essay for more details on H.D.'s stay at Kusnacht, the issue of her commitment, and her pleas to be released (54).

19. H.D., letters to Pearson, June 24, 1950 and June 22, 1949.

20. H.D., *Trilogy* (New York: New Directions, 1973), 65. See *Psyche Reborn*, 220–21, 252–53, and Susan Gubar, "The Echoing Spell of H.D.'s *Trilogy*," *Contemporary Literature* 19 (1979): 196–218, for discussions of H.D.'s defiance of John's command and re-vision of *Revelation* imagery.

21. H.D.'s image of Shakespeare as a thief echoes the figure of Hermes Trismegistus in *Trilogy* (63) and foreshadows her portrait of Shakespeare as a proto-modernist in "The Guest." See *Psyche Reborn* for a discussion of how Hermes' theft and alchemy provide major metaphors for H.D.'s modernist aesthetic (207–28).

22. Denis de Rougemont, *Love in the Western World*, trans. Montgomery Belgion (New York: Pantheon, 1956). In a letter to Viola Jordan (July 30, 1941 or 1944), Beinecke, H.D. described this book, which she also read in two earlier editions (1939, 1940) as "MY BIBLE." See *Psyche Reborn* for extended discussion of hermetic tradition and the influence of de Rougemont's blend of psychoanalytic, mystic, and literary analysis.

23. This attraction to the voiceless Claribel represents a dramatic change from H.D.'s earlier interest in Shakespeare's women. She recalled in a letter to Herring, Jan. 11, 194?, that her earliest attraction was at age twelve or thirteen to Shakespeare's androgynous women: "My first 'Shakes' was pure panto: I did not know it then but enjoyed it in the best panto tradition. Thankful I am, that it was Rosalind in tights and not too fat and the earlier 'wear this for me' spoken from a terrace above card-board steps with petunia-like roses . . . it must matter so much to me that it came early, 12–13 1st! . . . To come back to Panto-. . . . The Sh. first play was the first play for which one had the TEXT. One could go home and do it all over again . . . with one father's 'cane' from downstairs for the staff SHE carried and in ones own PANTS! Boy-girl-panto-." See also *HER*, in which Hermione wavers between identification with "Hermione from the *Winter's Tale* (who later

froze into a statue)" and "Rosalind with sleek, deer-limbs and a green forester's cap with one upright darting hawk quill" (66).

24. Claribel is discussed in *The Tempest* in Act 2. 1. 110–26, 205–14, 249–65 and Act 5. 1. 116. "Good Frend" not only quotes from several of the passages about Claribel but also weaves the story of Shakespeare's probable source (the pamphlets on the wreck of the *Sea-Adventure*) into her poem. H.D.'s copy of *The Tempest*, edited by M. R. Ridley (London: J. M. Dent, 1943), is thoroughly marked.

25. See Susan Gubar's discussion of the woman as "text" in patriarchy in " 'The Blank Page' and the Issues of Female Creativity," *Critical Inquiry* 8 (Winter 1981): 243–64, and with Gilbert in *Madwoman in the Attic*, 1–30.

26. See de Rougemont, *Love in the Western World*, 78–138. In identifying with de Rougemont's theory of troubadour poetry, H.D. probably regarded her Catharian troubadour as her answer to Pound's different recreation of the Provençal troubadour.

27. These dates probably had an inner, esoteric fascination for H.D., who had used numerology since the late twenties. But H.D. wrote Pearson that she was "very proud" of her research and thought it quite "scholarly" (Sept. 21, 1947). This "factual" mode may have played some part in her recovery. Pearson may have suggested that H.D. put the scholarly and poetic voices together in *By Avon River*, for she wrote to him "that the idea of the poem and prose in AVON was yours, too" (Dec. 23, 1949).

28. See especially *HER, Tribute to Freud, Trilogy, Helen in Egypt*, and *Hermetic Definition* (New York: New Directions, 1972). The title "Good Frend" links the text to Freud and the "family romance." H.D. wrote Herring about "our own 'Good Frend' ": "And doesn't that Frend ('for Iesus sake forbeare') look like *Freud. Freud* as an opener of closed doors, penetrating and re-vitalizing—and how Freud helps with the father-mother-brother-sister-son-daughter-boy-out of the Shakespeare 'family romance' " (July 24, 194?).

29. H.D.'s feminist context changes the generic "man" to its male-specific meaning. See Shakespeare, *As You Like It*, 2.7.174 ff.: also reprinted in the collection H.D. may have used for her study of Elizabethan lyrics, Norman Alt's *Elizabethan Lyrics from the Original Texts* (New York: W. Sloane, 1925). H.D.'s partial library at Yale also includes the well-marked *Shakespeare as Poet*, ed. A. R. Entwistle (London: Thomas Nelson, n.d.); some fifteen additional Shakespeare volumes, all edited by M. R. Ridley for the New Temple Shakespeare Series, including a carefully marked copy of the sonnets; John Dover Wilson, *Life in Shakespeare's England* (London: Penguin, 1944); and several of G. Wilson Knight's books on Shakespeare, which she greatly admired. H.D. also liked Edith Sitwell's *Fanfare*, about which she wrote Pearson: "Fortunately, I did some rough notes on Elizabethan poets [in 1947], before I read her *Fanfare*, otherwise I would be afraid to touch the period."

30. See for example Sylvan Barnet, "Prefatory Remarks" for *The Tempest* (New York: Signet, 1964): "that Shakespeare was born is excellent; that he married and had children is pleasant; but that we know nothing about his departure

from Stratford to London, or about the beginning of his theatrical career, is lamentable and must be admitted. We should gladly sacrifice details about his children's baptism for details of his earliest days on the stage" (viii).

31. For an analysis of androgyny in Shakespeare's work, see Robert Kimbrough, "Androgyny Seen through Shakespeare's Disguise," *Shakespeare Quarterly* 33 (Spring 1982): 17–33, and "Androgyny Old and New," *Western Humanities Review* 35 (1981): 197–215. H.D. had long been interested in the concept of androgyny, which she connected to her attempt to transcend the duality of art and science represented by her mother and father; her own bisexuality; and the concept of an androgynous Divine One in esoteric tradition (see *Psyche Reborn*, 121–54, 273–96). In particular, Shakespeare's androgyny in *By Avon River* leads directly into the exploration of psychic division and wholeness in *Helen in Egypt*.

32. H.D., *Trilogy*, 58–59. The parallels H.D. drew between the Elizabethan and modern worlds may well have been inspired by Knight's *The Olive and the Sword*. Written at the height of World War II, this survey of Shakespeare's plays is explicitly an anti-Nazi book celebrating British national character. In her later memoir of the war years, *The Days of Mars* (New York: Harcourt Brace Jovanovich, 1972), Bryher repeated this theme, stating that the Elizabethan Age was a "moment," "nearest to our own battle" (163). Like Woolf, however, H.D. had little sympathy for national chauvinism.

33. De Rougemont notes that Shakespeare's connection to "the secret traditions of the troubadours" was speculative (20), but he argues that *Romeo and Juliet* reflects vestiges of the Cathar tradition (200–202). He also included Milton in the Cathar tradition, but like Woolf fearing "Milton's bogey," H.D.'s scholar leaves him out and apologizes lamely for the omission (68–69).

34. See de Rougemont, *Love in the Western World*, 130 ff. for the role played by Eleanor of Aquitaine.

35. This movement parallels the shift in *Trilogy*, in which in the first volume the poet worships the Christos-figure (the Divine in male form) and in the last volume, Kaspar brings the jar of myrrh to Mary at the birth of her child. It is not the child he worships, but the mother, the Divine in female form.

GAYLE GREENE

Margaret Laurence's Diviners *and* Shakespeare's Tempest: *The Uses of the Past*

This is the use of memory:
For liberation—

T. S. Eliot, "Little Gidding,"
Four Quartets

Margaret Laurence is usually regarded as a "regional" writer concerned with Canadian history and myth. It is true that her writing gives
voice to what she has called Canada's "cultural being," "roots," and
"myths";[1] and *The Diviners*, the last novel of the five-volume Manawaka
series which occupied a decade (1964–74) of her career, associates personal quest with the search for Canadian past.[2] But in *The Diviners* Laurence writes against wider and older traditions, reworking epic quest and
Shakespearean romance in a re-vision of a central myth of our culture, that
of the "fortunate fall," redefining "paradise" as a process, the "doing of
the thing,"[3] rather than something tangibly and finally won.[4]

Both *The Tempest* and *The Diviners* are final works which are concerned with redeeming the sins of the past and transmitting what is of
value to the future. *The Tempest* is also Shakespeare's version of the "fortunate fall": Prospero, whose name means "I make to prosper," re-creates a
world, restores what is lost, restores the creatures of this world to themselves. Yet this play, with its one bland and conventional female character,
seems an odd and unlikely model for the development of a strong female
protagonist.[5] The epic quest, which concerns a young man's search for his
father as part of his search for himself, seems similarly inapplicable: for, as
Mary Ann Ferguson suggests, since women "must assume their husband's
name" as well as their husband's home, an "identification with the father
can only interfere with development."[6] But Laurence shows Morag engaged in a quest for the father and maturing from an identification with
"Prospero's Child" (the name of a novel Morag writes) into the powers of
Prospero himself.

The Diviners also has affinities with feminist quest novels published in the early seventies. Within 1972 and 1974 were published Erica Jong's *Fear of Flying,* Gail Godwin's *Odd Woman,* Margaret Drabble's *Realms of Gold,* Margaret Atwood's *Surfacing,* Lisa Alther's *Kinflicks,* Dorothy Bryant's *Ella Price's Journal*—and *The Diviners.* These novels follow a pattern, even a formula: woman seeks "freedom" from conventional roles, looks to her past for answers about the present, speculates about the cultural and literary tradition that has formed her, and seeks a plot different from the marriage or death that are her customary ends.[7] This quest had been explored and developed in the preceding decade by Doris Lessing: in *The Golden Notebook* (1962), Anna Wulf seeks new forms in her fiction and in her life; and in *The Children of Violence* (1952–69), Martha "Quest" seeks "something new" against "the nightmare repetition" of the past—a nightmare which is represented by Martha's mother, Mrs. Quest.[8] Indeed, bad mothers are everywhere in this fiction, symbol of the past the protagonist is trying to avoid.[9]

Morag Gunn, protagonist of *The Diviners,* is a writer who—like the protagonists of Lessing's *The Golden Notebook,* Drabble's *The Waterfall,* Jong's *Fear of Flying,* and Atwood's *Lady Oracle*—uses her fiction to make her way in the world and to make sense of the world: as Morag says, "If I hadn't been a writer I'd have been a first class mess" (4). Like these protagonists, Morag is also a reader, though what she reads is not nineteenth-century fiction centering on love and marriage, but Shakespeare, Milton, and Donne (178, 191). Whereas the protagonists of Drabble, Jong, and Godwin develop their expectations of life from novels by Austen, Eliot, and the Brontës,[10] Morag reads—and Laurence writes against—works which center on male figures, concern male experience, and are at the heart of a male-defined and male-dominated canon.

Unlike other protagonists of feminist fiction, Morag is not shown in relation to a mother; she is shown in relation to a stepfather and to a daughter. Christie, the town "scavenger," is a splendid mentor who teaches her qualities unbecoming to a lady—a disrespect of respectability gained from his long acquaintance of the town's "muck"; more than a little of his rage, that side of herself she will come to recognize as "the black Celt"; and a scepticism concerning the value of any authority—" 'you don't want to believe everything them books say' " (83). He also teaches her never to "say sorry" (209) or to make herself a "doormat" (107). Morag disowns Christie and spends years trying to be "normal" (as she says, 81) before finally coming to recognize him as "my father to me" (396) and to know her "home" as "Christie's . . . country. Where I was born" (391). In the second part of the novel, we see her as an adult and parent engaged in making a home for herself and her daughter, a home on a farm purchased from her earnings as a writer, to which she takes "title." The novel concludes with Morag ready to "set down her title," ready to write the novel we have just read; and the links between "title" as "claim," deed to property, and "authorship"—an "author" is one who "gives existence to something, a begetter, *father*... or founder"—suggest that making a home is part of gaining authority.[11] Morag attains an authority which is customarily male and which authorizes her to author, to originate a new order—to make "something new".[12]

Christie is Morag's mentor in other important ways, in that it is he who gives her a past and teaches her the power of the creative imagination. Since her parents died when she was a child, Morag's past is a blank, and according to the book of *Clans and Tartans* which Christie consults, Clan Gunn is "undetermined" (48). But Christie gives Morag a heritage with his stories of Piper Gunn (a "great tall man" who has "the strength of conviction") and "his woman Morag" and their conquest and settling of a new land. Part legend, part history, but mainly spun "wholecloth" "out of his head—invented" (367), these are tales of action and adventure of the sort more customarily associated with boys than with girls; and unlike the romantic fictions that shape the consciousness of other female protagonists, they do not teach Morag to expect that her "end" will be a man. Identifying with male action and potential, Morag has more freedom than heroines customarily have; for, as Carolyn Heilbrun suggests, women may gain by "look[ing] at the male protagonists who have until now stood as models for human action and say[ing]: that action includes me."[13]

Christie's stories provide Morag with the inspiration for her first literary creations; and her adaptations are significant, for what minimal gender differentiation Christie introduces, Morag (at age nine) obliterates, appropriating his hero's powers for her heroine. Christie describes Piper as having "the strength of conviction" and "Piper's woman" Morag as having "fine long black hair," but Morag's first story gives Morag "*the power and the second sight and the good eye and the strength of conviction*" and makes her unafraid "of anything" (51–52). Christie gives Morag "the warmth of a home and the determination of quietness," but Morag has her Morag make, not a home, but a chariot which is a means of transport for Piper, herself, and their girl child throughout the new country (85). Even in her earliest literary efforts, Morag, like Laurence, adapts male models in a way that empowers her female protagonist.

The structure of the novel—in which time present alternates with time past until, in the final section, the past catches up with and becomes the present—suggests the interdependence of past and present and foregrounds Morag's efforts to transmit something of value to the future. The sections which take place in the past concern (young) Morag's relationship with a father and those which take place in the present concern (older) Morag's relationship with her daughter, Pique. The alternation of past action with present action shows the influence of past upon present, demonstrating that the past has made Morag and Pique what they are; but the structure also shows the present acting upon the past, as Morag's remembering and narrating the past alters her sense of it and thereby *changes* the present, enabling her to make terms with herself and her daughter—to let go of her guilt about the way she has raised her and to let go of her, sending her on her way with the best wisdom she has gleaned from her own past. The test of what Morag achieves will be in what she passes on to Pique, "the inheritor" (452).

Morag's efforts to "reconnect . . . time lost and time continuing" and transmit "inheritable wisdom" to the future make *The Diviners* exemplary of what Peter Brooks sees as the fundamental motive of narrative: the recovery of the past, transformation of the present, and transmission of inheritable wisdom to the future.[14] The past is replayed to a more successful outcome, repeated in order for there to be an escape from repetition, in order for there to be change or progress. In fact, Laurence discusses her writing in terms that suggest a focus like that described by Brooks, as an "attempt to come to terms with the past" "partly in order to be freed from it"; she refers to "the explorations inherent in the writing itself" as a way "of changing" the patterns of the past.[15] Morag contemplates problems related to reconstructing the past. She tries to remember "what really happened" and to understand the powers of language ("*I used to think words could do anything. Magic. Sorcery. Even miracle. But no, only occasionally*" [51]); she ponders the meaning of photographs and the "memorybank movies" in her head. She faces problems of memory and knowledge: "*I am remembering myself composing this interpretation*" (8); "*I don't even know how much of that memory really happened and how much of it I embroidered later on*" (17–18).

Like *The Golden Notebook*, *The Diviners* is a "self-begetting novel" which ends with the protagonist ready to write the novel we have just read.[16] Ends work back to beginnings as Morag realizes that though "You Can't Go Home Again . . . You have to go home again, in some way or other" (302); final scene returns to first scene, with Morag contemplating the river which "flows both ways" (3)—a symbol that similarly suggests that the way forward is the way back, through an understanding and recovery of the past. This "apparently impossible contradiction" (3) is one of several central paradoxical truths, wisdom exemplified, like so much of what is important in the novel, by Christie.

In both *The Tempest* and *The Diviners*, art is the means by which the past is redeemed and art is compared to magic; and in both works, the future is represented by a daughter. But Laurence's revisions empower the female, replacing a patriarchal with a matriarchal line. Whereas in *The Tempest* Prospero's daughter, Miranda, is merely "chaste, silent, and obedient," a receptacle for the future, in *The Diviners,* Pique is an artist in her own right: power passes from father (or stepfather) to daughter and thence to daughter—through a female line and to a female "inheritor."

Laurence grafts *Tempest* allusions onto a pattern of loss and recovery which is her version of the fortunate fall and suggests, in her reworkings, a sense, like Shakespeare's and Milton's, that redemption involves the loss of fragile innocence and a re-creation from painful experience and that this process requires faith. (And that Laurence no more values a "cloistered virtue" than Milton does is clear from her portrayal of the innocents of this novel, the childish Prin [205, 250] and Bridie [373].) But Morag's powers are considerably more attenuated than Prospero's, which makes faith more difficult for her, since her purposes are not sanctioned by God or a providential plan.

Morag lives through a series of losses and recoveries, losing paradise and regaining it, then losing it again to rebuild it on firmer ground. With her parents' death when she is six, she is expelled from an edenic childhood—"the metallic clink of the farm gate being shut. Closed" (17)— which she re-creates imaginatively as a "garden of the mind" (227). Life with Christie initiates her prematurely into adult experience, and though she later sees this initiation as "both fortunate and unfortunate" (257), she is, as a child, overwhelmed by it. As soon as she is old enough, she leaves Christie and Manawaka for the big city, to make "a proper marriage," imagining (like Lessing's Martha Quest) that this will free her from her past. The man she marries, Brooke Skelton, is antithetical to Christie not only in that he is respectable but also in that his idealization of innocence is antithetical to Christie's acceptance of "muck." Brooke's desire that she be an innocent coincides with Morag's desire to lose her past: and though she knows that she has always "known things"—about Eva's aborting herself, about the aborted child buried in the dump and the burnt shack in the valley—she imagines that she can conceal "what she was really like"; "I feel I don't have a past, as if it was a blank" (194–98). She pretends to be a virgin and resolves never to show him the Black Celt (227). But as she outgrows Brooke's ideal of her, her darkness and past reassert themselves as an irresistible impulse to speak Christie's language— "the loony oratory, salt-beefed with oaths, the stringy lean oaths with some protein in them, the Protean oaths upon which she was reared" (255–56).

As her English professor, Brooke represents the authority of the cultural and literary tradition Morag reveres, but as she herself becomes a writer, her authority comes into conflict with his and destroys the marriage. But her writing also becomes the means of regaining the self she has suppressed to be with Brooke, the means of "regaining paradise"—and the publisher's representative who arrives at the Vancouver boarding house where she takes refuge after leaving Brooke is described as "an angel of the Lord . . . come to explain how paradise can be regained" (297). Her writing is also a means of exploring the questions of innocence and experience that she confronts in her life. Morag's first novel, *Spear of Innocence,* which portrays innocence as damaging (225), is a repudiation of Brooke's ideal of her; and her second novel, *Prospero's Child,* similarly repudiates the person she was in the marriage, the child-wife in awe of male authority. Morag describes this novel, in a letter to a friend, as having "certain parallels with *The Tempest,*" which she fears may be "presumptuous" but is "the form the thing seems to demand"; "It is called *Prospero's Child,* she being the young woman who marries His Excellency, the Governor of some island in some ocean very far south, and who virtually worships him and then who has to go to the opposite extreme and reject nearly everything about him, at least for a time, in order to become her own person" (330).

Morag allies herself definitively with her past and her "darkness" when she flees Brooke and becomes pregnant by Jules, a "half-breed" who, like herself, grew up on the margins of Manawaka society and who represents—as Sherrill Grace suggests—not only "her immediate Manawaka past, but the historical Indian and French roots of Canada."[17] Bearing his child, a daughter who has the dark skin of the Metis, Morag burns her bridges back to the respectable world. Her departure from the "doll's house" occurs in the middle rather than at the end of her story, with the rest of the novel a "writing beyond" this ending. In presenting her protagonist a choice between two men, Laurence evokes what Jean E. Kennard terms the "two-suitor convention," according to which the growth of a woman is marked by her choice of the right suitor over the wrong suitor, the right suitor embodying the goals the protagonist aspires to. In the contemporary version of this, "the husband has become the 'wrong' suitor, the representative of patriarchal restrictions; the lover represents freedom."[18] But Laurence evokes this convention only to subvert it, for Jules does not provide a resolution or even a resting place. Having outgrown the role of child-wife Morag must become an adult herself: "if she is to have a home, she must create it" (291). The association of the home she makes, the farm at McConnell's Landing, with "some kind of garden" (406) suggests that the creation of home is the means of regaining paradise; though since "the state of original grace ended a long time ago" (196), this paradise is a mere approximation—or "shadow"—of Eden (*Shadow of Eden* is the title of one of Morag's novels). And that this home is near a small town like the one she fled and represents a return to a place which is "different, but . . . the same" (354) suggests that regaining paradise requires coming to terms with the past. The home Morag makes for herself and her daughter is "different" from her edenic childhood and the false haven of her marriage: it is a new order wrested from adult experience and pain.

Accepting her past and experience, Morag comes to understand what Christie has always known. Part of what Christie knows is suggested by his name: he is, as his name and frequent oaths suggest, a "Christly" character who, like Shakespeare's fools, gets his license to speak truth from his position as outsider who has nothing to lose; and, like them, he expresses his sense of complexity in paradoxes and riddles.[19]

Christie plays the fool deliberately and defiantly when he comes up against representatives of respectable society, shocking them by offering a buffoonery that caricatures the behavior they expect of him. Underlying his mockery is a knowledge of the townspeople gained from long experience of their garbage, a knowledge they suspect and fear. Christie expresses his fool-wisdom in logically impossible, self-contradictory statements—"You have to work hard at it . . . to be such a bloody flop as I stand before you. . . . Although that's not the truth of it, neither. It's all true and not true." And his paradox expresses "the truth" of the situation, that he is and is not a "flop": he is, according to the standards of the world, but is not according to the standards that matter—an insight he buttresses by reference to Shakespeare: "*Oh what a piece of work is man. Who said that? Some brain. . . .* Oh what a piece of work is man oh what a bloody awful piece of work is man enough to scare the pants off you when you come to think of it the opposite is also true" (88). The association of paradox with Shakespeare is appropriate, since it is the mode not only of Shakespeare's fools but of Shakespeare himself, whose genius has been described by more than one critic as "complementarity," "ambivalence," a capacity to see both sides of a question.[20]

Similarly, when Christie reassures Morag that it was all right for her to leave him and Manawaka ("it's a bloody good thing you've got away from this dump"), and she asks, "Do you really think that, Christie?" he answers with a paradox: " 'I do . . . And also I don't. That's the way it goes.' " Again his illogic suggests a truth—that Morag's leaving Manawaka has been both good and bad: good in that she has escaped what is bad about the town, bad in that she has left something of value behind. Christie continues, offering his one bit of prophecy: " 'It'll all go along with you, too. That goes without saying.' 'You mean—everything will go along with me?' 'No less than that, ever,' Christie says" (207). As is characteristic of prophets and jesters, his utterance is ambiguous: does the "it" which will "go along" with her mean good luck, or Manawaka, or both? In fact "it" comes to mean both, in that Morag's taking Manawaka "along with her" will be her means to good fortune. Later in the novel, Morag herself has picked up his habit of paradox, when, arranging for Christie's funeral, she expresses her sense that Niall Cameron "did and didn't, both" want to go on living and develops this insight with a reference to Shakespeare: "to be or not to be—that sure as death is the question. The two-way battle in the minefield. The mindfield of the mind" (399).[21]

Christie's Piper Gunn tales similarly express a sense of the complexity of things—not that the tales are complex in themselves but that Christie's free-wheeling adaptations fabricate a past which becomes as "real" to Morag as any "true story": "the myths are my reality" (390), as she says. Christie gives Morag a personal past with his tales of her father Colin's heroism in the Battle of Bourlon and he creates a heritage for her with the Piper Gunn tales. Culling from such disparate sources as James Macpherson's Ossianic Poems and *The 60th Canadian Field Artillery Battery Book,* he conjures spirits "who probably never lived in so-called real life but who live forever" (418), conjuring when "the spirits are in him" and "when the spirit moves him" (47–48), truly "inspired." But his scepticism about what "them books say" (83) extends even to those authorities he most trusts: he says of the description of the Battle of Bourlon in *The Field Artillery Book,* "it was like the book says, but it wasn't like that, also" (90). (This scepticism of official versions is a quality he shares with Jules, also an outsider: when confronted with what the history books say about Riel, Jules knows that "the books lie" [147] and that Dieppe "wasn't the way the papers told it" [164].) What Prin reveals, when she surfaces for a rare moment of lucidity to tell the truth of the Battle of Bourlon—that it was Christie who rescued Colin and not Colin who rescued Christie—comments on the "truth" of his tales generally; but Morag later comes to realize that "it doesn't matter a damn" whether they happened or not (350).

From believing Christie's tales, Morag comes to disbelieve them and then to "believe in them again, in a different way" (367)—a movement which replicates other patterns of loss and recovery, difference and sameness, in the novel. Though young Morag once sought the certainties her daughter now seeks, Morag has, as we meet her in the present episodes, a sense of complexity like Christie's. To Pique's questions about "the truth" of Christie's stories and Jules's songs, whether they "really happened," Morag says, in language like Christie's—

"Some did and some didn't, I guess. It doesn't matter a damn. Don't you see?"

"No," Pique said, "I don't see. I want to know what really happened."

Morag laughed. Unkindly, perhaps.

"You do, eh? Well, so do I. But there's no one version. There just isn't." (350)

She has come to accept the uncertain status of Christie's tales—stories "real and . . . imagined" (249) about "those who have never been and yet would always be" (244)—and this sense of complexity informs her attitudes generally ("things remained mysterious" [4], "ambiguity is everywhere" [402]) and makes her humble about judging: *"Whatever is happening to Pique is not what I think is happening, whatever that may be. What happened to me wasn't what anyone else thought was happening, and maybe not even what I thought was happening at the time"* (60). Morag understands that the past, present, and the self in its "many versions" (396) are comprised of tales we tell ourselves and one another, constructs of the fictionalizing imagination, and that these fictions are constantly being revised. Even the past undergoes revision—*"A popular misconception is that we can't change the past—everyone is constantly changing their own past, recalling it, revising it"*—and this process makes all knowledge provisional: *"What really happened? A meaningless question"* (60). These realizations are related to her profession as writer: "a daft profession. Wordsmith. Liar, more likely. Weaving fabrications. Yet, with typical ambiguity, convinced that fiction was more true than fact. Or that fact was in fact fiction" (25); "What is a true story? Is there any such thing?" (144). That the tales lead back not to "real things" but to other tales suggests a post-modern sense of referentiality, a sense of the fiction of truth and the truth of fiction, and a conception of the self as comprised of self-fabricated fictions.

In the letter which describes her novel *Prospero's Child,* Morag speculates about Prospero's need of "grace," wondering if he will be able to keep his "strength" after he dismisses his spirits: "I've always wondered if Prospero really would be able to give up his magical advantages once and for all as he intends to do at the end of *The Tempest.* That incredibly moving statement, 'What strength I have's mine own, Which is most faint—' If only he can hang onto that knowledge, that would be true strength. And the recognition that his real enemy is despair within, and that he stands in need of grace, like everyone else" (330). Her suggestion that his "enemy" is "despair" indicates her sense that this is her "enemy" also—which explains why, in her earliest stories, Morag gave her character Morag "the strength of conviction."

But the faith required to regain paradise is more difficult for Morag than for Prospero because it is unsanctioned by belief in God or an after-

life. The world Morag inherits does not resemble a paradise or even inspire confidence in the future: she has a sense, rather, of "doom all
around" (27), of the present as "nightmare" (106) and the future as
"apocalypse" (4). As she says in one of her imaginary exchanges with
Catherine Parr Traill, the pioneer woman she conjures and argues with,
"the evidence of your eyes showed you Jerusalem the Golden," "the evidence of my eyes, however, does little to reassure me" (171). Though
some critics have read the novel as "profoundly religious," Laurence's af-
firmations are made in the *absence* of God, and she sees "grace" as a process, a creation and re-creation, a patterning rather than a transcendental
pattern.[22]

Morag's resolutions are worked out in terms that recall *The Tempest*.
She wonders if the home she has made is an "island": *"I've made an island.
Are islands real? . . . Islands are unreal. No place is far enough away. Islands ex-
ist only in the head. And yet I stay. All this . . . may be a fantasy. But I can bear
to live here until I die, and I couldn't elsewhere"* (356). These speculations
are answered by her vision of the "Great Blue Heron," which, in the "soar-
ing and measured certainty of its flight" (357), symbolizes the equanimity
she aspires to. This vision leads to the important realization "that here and
now was not, after all, an island. Her quest for islands had ended some
time ago, and her need to make pilgrimages had led her back here" (356–
57). Morag's "quest for islands" has ended, both in the sense that she has
dispelled the illusion that the "British Isles"—England or Scotland—are
home and she now knows that home is Canada and in the sense that she
has ceased to "insulate" herself, to make herself an island—a metaphor
which recalls Donne's. Morag's "here and now" is "not an island" (357)
because it represents a connection with a human community and with the
past so that, unlike Prospero, she does not have to leave this place to return
to society. The last section of the novel is the first section to conclude with
Morag *not* moving on to a new place, though her daughter Pique does
move on.

That Morag has attained a measure of faith is indicated by her dismissal of her "spirit," Catharine Parr Traill, a superwoman who raised
nine children, tilled the fields, *and* wrote books, and whom Morag has
conjured to make herself feel inadequate.[23] She has learned, as she says, to
"stop feeling guilty that I'll never be as hard-working or knowledgable or
all-round terrific as you were. . . . So farewell, sweet saint—henceforth, I
summon you not" (406). Having dismissed her spirit, Morag's powers
are—like Prospero's—"her own." But Morag's powers have always been
"her own" in a way that Prospero's are not. Whereas Prospero's purposes
are in harmony with providence, there is no suggestion that Morag's are.
Whereas Prospero redeems the creatures of his world, Morag can only re-

create the stories of those she writes about, making her characters live symbolically but not actually. Though Prospero can request applause as a sign of his power, Morag has no way of knowing whether she has pleased, no idea how her books are received or understood. Yet she has attained sufficient self-assurance to risk confronting the most desolate of possibilities, that her work has been for nothing: "At least Royland knew he had been a true diviner. There were the wells, proof positive. . . . Morag's magic tricks were of a different order. She would never know whether they actually worked or not, or to what extent. That wasn't given to her to know. In a sense, it did not matter. The necessary doing of the thing—that mattered" (452). She must resign herself to the more ephemeral and uncertain consolation of process, "the necessary doing of the thing," knowing that what has been created will need to be re-created. In this sense that what matters is process, Laurence more resembles Virginia Woolf than Shakespeare, and Woolf is the one woman writer referred to in this novel—"a woman, if she is to write, Virginia Woolf once said . . . must have a room of her own" (293–94).[24]

Morag contemplates the possibility that her skills as diviner may be as mysteriously taken from her as Royland's were, and even wonders "was this, finally and at last, what Morag had always sensed she had to learn from the old man?"—that "the gift, or portion of grace, or whatever it was, was finally withdrawn, to be given to someone else." This is, as he tells her, "not a matter for mourning," for divining is "not something that everybody can do, but . . . quite a few people can learn to do it" (451–52). Morag can resign herself to the loss of her gift because she knows that it will pass to somebody else—as it actually does pass from Christie to Morag to Pique. Laurence's vision of the artist stresses not the development of individual talent or the imposition of self on experience but a letting go of self and a wise resignation to processes beyond one's control, a sense of continuity and community, of the involvement of self with all. Realizing that she cannot control or even understand the processes that shape people and events, Morag learns to let go, not only of her "gift" and her books, but of the people in her life—and not only of the men (Brooke, Jules, Dan McRaith) but of her daughter. She has learned—like Prospero—to let them go "free," in a gesture which parallels the movement of narrative toward release. (Laurence describes her own writing in similar terms: "Perhaps this is all one can do with one's characters—try to set them free as much as possible, or rather, to accept the simple fact of their freedom."[25])

The novel began with Morag unable to accept Pique's setting out on her own; it ends with her reconciled to her departure: "Who could ever enter anything with a guarantee? Let her go. This time, it had to be possible and was" (440). She has come to understand her part in her daughter's life, to accept "the hurts" she has "unwittingly inflicted upon Pique," and to accept Pique's forgiveness as well: "Morag had agonized over these often enough, almost as though, if she imagined them sufficiently, they would prove to have been unreal after all. But they were not unreal. Yet Pique was not assigning any blame—that was not what it was all about" (441). Pique does not "assign blame" because she understands that the processes by which people become what they are reach back to an unknowable past. This understanding is central to the novel, and, like many others, it starts with Christie: " 'Nobody can't help nothing . . . so best shut up about it' " (209). Morag expresses a similar awareness with regard to Jules's sister Piquette (158) and Fan Brady (310), and Royland says of the aunt who raised him, "it wasn't really her fault, either. You don't know how it is for other people, or how far back it all goes" (241). As in *The Tempest,* the sins of the elders are forgiven by the young.

Pique sets out at the end with the strengths it has taken Morag a lifetime to acquire. She leaves true to herself over a relationship, "on some kind of search" (237) which is "different [from] . . . but the same" as Morag's (422): it is "the same" in that she too seeks a father and home and certainties such as young Morag once sought, but it is "different" in that she seeks the past rather than fleeing it. Pique is headed for her uncle's farm, the place of her father's people, to help make a new community and a better future.

As she leaves, she already possesses much of the past, and she takes her legacy with her in the form of art. The songs she has composed combine the Scottish legend and history of Christie's tales (via Morag's stories of Christie) with the Metis legend and history of Lazarus's stories (via Jules's songs). Thus personal past intersects with cultural heritage and Pique is "the inheritor" of her mother's and father's traditions and of old and new worlds. Pique also has something of the paradoxical wisdom of her forbears, knowing that "it will and it won't" go well for her (440), and Morag suspects that she "almost" has "the gift of second sight" (439). Whereas the men in the novel—Jules, Brooke, Dan—declare their determination *not* to be like their fathers (141, 219, 354), Pique does not have to repudiate Morag. In a way that is unusual in contemporary women's fiction, this mother leaves her daughter something of value. Morag's legacy is not a "nightmare repetition" but "a place to stand," in the words of the epigraph.

Morag's description of her terms with life—"I've worked out my major dilemmas as much as I'm likely to in this life"—suggests the provisional nature of all resolutions; and her qualification corroborates this sense of life as process: "Now that I read that over, I wonder if it's true.

The calm plateau still seems pretty faroff to me. I'm still fighting the same bloody battles as always, inside the skull. Maybe all there is on that calm plateau is a tombstone" (289). Morag's "Rites of Passage" (the title of the long fourth chapter) is a process extending over an entire lifetime rather than a single initiation from adolescence into adulthood (as Morley points out [*Laurence* 125]): change is accomplished not by dramatic ends and new beginnings but by a slow process through each stage.

Laurence's view of experience as a process subject to continual revision makes any ending provisional. Endings are problematized in this novel by Morag's speculations: young Morag criticized the endings of her stories for being "implausible" (180), "rubbish" (189); but the first short story she ever showed anyone was praised for not "opting for an easy ending"—by which her reader meant she didn't marry its protagonist off (122,124). Laurence's novel may be similarly described, for Morag does not "opt for an easy ending." Though *The Diviners* makes gestures toward conventional closure, ending with a death (Jules's) and departure (Pique's), Morag's end is not "easy" or conventional: unmarried, a "maverick," living in an isolated place by a river, known by the town as the local crazy woman, her situation requires strengths not customarily associated with women.

Having disowned Christie, Morag then tries to recover him, comes to understand him on deeper and deeper levels, and ends in a place very like Manawaka but having established a different relation to it: she returns to her beginning to know it for the first time. But this circular return does not suggest Lessing's "nightmare repetition," for Laurence sees the past as nourishing, feeding, and renewing the present and future. The circular movement of the novel suggests a fruitful intertwining of ends and beginnings, a sense of life like that symbolized by the Ouroboros, the serpent swallowing its tail, figure for "the continuity of life" and "continual return, within a cyclic pattern."[26]

The image Laurence uses to suggest the interdependence of past, present, and future is that of the river that flows both ways, and the novel concludes with the paradoxical injunction, *"Look ahead into the past, and back into the future"* (453). This backward and forward movement implies that past influences present, but it also suggests that the present influences the past, that we *can* change the past; and indeed within the present episodes of the novel, Morag does change the past. By imaginatively reconstructing it, conjuring it with memory and language, she wrests what is valuable from it and transforms bondage to freedom, bequeathing a more hopeful legacy to the future.

Laurence's "use of memory," then, is "for liberation." So also does she enlist the literary tradition in the interests of liberation. On the simplest level, she gives her female protagonist the male part, allowing her to act as epic hero who founds a new order and assumes the powers of Prospero—artist, magician, and Shakespeare's figure for himself. Actor, writer, and director of her "plot," Morag attains an authority and authorship which enables her to transmit something of value to the future. But Laurence reworks the idea of the artist and paradise regained to a contemporary feminist perspective: the power of the artist is redefined as a resignation to the limits of power, a relinquishing of characteristically "masculine" attributes of rationality and control, and an attainment of a difficult humility that comes from involvement with others. This reworking of epic quest is as bold and original as Milton's adaptation of classical epic to Christian values, Wordsworth's adaptation of Milton's *Paradise Lost* to his autobiographical *Prelude,* or Joyce's adaptation of *The Odyssey* to his epic of modern life, *Ulysses.* Laurence's adaptation of Shakespeare both demystifies and revitalizes, is both homage and critique, in a complex appropriation which suggests a way that feminists can continue a relationship with Shakespeare that does not require us to disown ourselves.[27] Unfortunately, the parallels with *The Tempest* also suggest the sense of finality Laurence expressed elsewhere—a foreboding that turned out to be all too true, since this was her last novel.[28]

NOTES

1. Clara Thomas describes Laurence as "predominantly engaged in writing out of the experience of Canadians and in their accustomed speech patterns" ("The Chariot of Ossian: Myth and Manitoba in *The Diviners,*" *Journal of Canadian Studies* 13, no. 3 [Fall 1978]: 55–63, quote, 62. Laurence describes herself as trying to convey a "strong sense of place and of our own culture . . . to give Canadians a . . . sense of who they are, where they came from, and where they may be going . . . by forging our myths and giving voice to our history, to our legends, to our cultural being" (Bernice Lever, "Literature and Canadian Culture: An Interview with Margaret Laurence," in *Critical Views on Canadian Writers: Margaret Laurence,* ed. William New [Toronto: McGraw-Hill Ryerson Limited, 1977]: 27).

2. The Manawaka series, so-called because it is set in the fictional town of Manawaka (a version of Laurence's native Neepawa), is the work on which Laurence's literary reputation rests. It includes *The Stone Angel* (1964); *A Jest of God* (1966), on which the film *Rachel, Rachel* was based; *The Fire-Dwellers* (1969); *A Bird in the House* (1972), a book of short stories; and *The Diviners* (1974).

3. Margaret Laurence, *The Diviners* (Toronto: Bantam, 1974), 452.

4. Stephanie A. Demetrakopoulos, "Laurence's Fiction: A Revisioning of Feminine Archetypes," *Canadian Literature* 93 (Summer 1982): 42–57, describes the novel as "reiterat[ing] the idea of the Fortunate Fall that a redemptive growth and wholeness come from engaging in struggling and taking risks" (52–53).

5. *The Tempest* is arguably the most sexist and racist of all Shakespeare's plays. See Lorie Jerrell Leininger, "The Miranda Trap: Sexism and Racism in

Shakespeare's *Tempest*, in *The Woman's Part: Feminist Criticism of Shakespeare*, ed. Carolyn Ruth Swift Lenz, Gayle Greene, and Carol Thomas Neely (Urbana: University of Illinois Press, 1980), 285–94; and Gayle Greene, "Women on Trial in Shakespeare and Webster," in *The Elizabethan Woman*, special issue of *Topic* 36 (1982): 10–11.

6. Mary Anne Ferguson, "The Female Novel of Development and the Myth of Psyche," in *The Voyage In: Fictions of Female Development*, ed. Elizabeth Abel, Marianne Hirsch, and Elizabeth Langland (Hanover, N.H.: University Press of New England, 1983), 228.

7. Feminist novelists and critics have expressed dissatisfaction with traditional endings. See Nancy K. Miller, *The Heroine's Text: Readings in the French and English Novel, 1722–1782* (New York: Columbia University Press, 1980), xi, and "Emphasis Added: Plots and Plausibilities in Women's Fiction," *PMLA* 96, no. 1 (Jan. 1981): 36–48; Annis Pratt, *Archetypal Patterns in Women's Fiction* (Bloomington: Indiana University Press, 1981), 36; Rachel Blau DuPlessis, *Writing beyond the Ending: Narrative Strategies of Twentieth-Century Women Writers* (Bloomington: Indiana University Press, 1985), 1–19; Lee Edwards, *Psyche as Hero: Female Heroism and Fictional Form* (Middletown, Conn.: Wesleyan University Press, 1984), 27.

8. Martha Quest, overwhelmed by her sense of "the nightmare *repetition*," is wearied that "*it had all been done and said already*" (*A Proper Marriage*, 77, 95, 34) and thinks "it was time to move onto something new" (Martha Quest, 8–9). The term "something new" recurs in Lessing's *Golden Notebook* (New York: Bantam, 1973), 61, 353, 472–73, 479 (referred to as GN), and in *Martha Quest* (53, 141, 216), *Landlocked* (117) (all references to these books in the *Children of Violence* series are to the New American Library editions and are referred to as MQ, PM).

9. Bad mothers appear in Sylvia Plath's *Bell Jar* (1963); Margaret Drabble's *Jerusalem the Golden* (1967), *The Waterfall* (1969), *Realms of Gold* (1974), *The Middle Ground* (1980); Margaret Atwood's *Lady Oracle* (1978) and *Bodily Harm* (1982); Laurence's *Jest of God;* Lessing's *The Grass is Singing* (1950) and *The Memoirs of a Survivor* (1975).

10. Jane Gray of Drabble's *Waterfall* is "haunted" by "fictitious heroines" ([New York: Fawcett Popular Library, 1969], 161–62); Isadore Wing of Jong's *Fear of Flying* (New York: New American Library, 1973) asks "where were the women who were *really* free?": "What a group! Severe, suicidal, strange . . . Where could we turn for guidance?" (101); Godwin's Jane Clifford "ransacks novels for answers to life" (30); Lessing's Martha Quest has been "formed by literature" (MQ 166, PM 61), by "novels from earlier times" (MQ 7).

11. Edward W. Said, *Beginnings: Intention and Method* (New York: Basic Books, 1975), 83. Sandra M. Gilbert and Susan Gubar, *The Madwoman in the Attic: The Woman Writer and the Nineteenth-Century Literary Imagination* (New Haven: Yale University Press, 1979), cite Said (4) in their discussion of the woman writer's challenge to male authority "in a culture whose fundamental definitions of literary authority are . . . both overtly and covertly patriarchal" (45–46).

12. That "Morag" is Gaelic for Sarah points to her role in the founding of a new order and to the position of *The Diviners* as the culmination of the Manawaka

cycle. Morag/Sarah fulfills the promise left unfulfilled by Hagar, protagonist of *The Stone Angel,* first of the Manawaka novels. The biblical Hagar bore a son to Abraham, but it was Sarah's child who became the basis of the new dynasty. Laurence's Hagar is, like her biblical precedent, a "bondswoman" in the sense that she is bound to destructive conventions. She, too, flees to the wilderness and is in an important sense left wandering there; and her legacy to her sons is destructive. But Morag finds a way out of the wilderness to "freedom" and bears a daughter who becomes "the inheritor." See Joan Coldwell, "Hagar as Meg Merrilies, the Homeless Gipsy," in *The Work of Margaret Laurence,* ed. John R. Sorfleet, special issue of the *Journal of Canadian Fiction* 27 (1980):92–100, 99.

13. Carolyn Heilbrun, *Reinventing Womanhood* (New York: Norton, 1979), 124.

14. Peter Brooks, *Reading for the Plot: Design and Intention in Narrative* (New York: Random House, 1985), 63, 235, 285.

15. Laurence, "A Place to Stand On," in *Heart of a Stranger* (Toronto: McClelland and Stewart Bantam, 1984), 5, 2, 1.

16. The "self-begetting novel" is an "account usually first person, of the development of a character to a point at which he is able to take up and compose the novel we have just finished reading" (S. Kellman, "The Fiction of Self-Begetting," *MLN* 91 [Dec. 1976]: 1243). Jean E. Kennard describes the feminist version of this as "woman's search for her own story, which ends in its creation" ("Convention Coverage; or, How to Read Your Own Life," *New Literary History* 13, no. 1 [Autumn 1981]: 84).

17. Sherrill Grace, "A Portrait of the Artist as Laurence Hero," *Journal of Canadian Studies* 13, no. 3 (Fall 1978): 64–71, 69.

18. Jean E. Kennard describes the "two-suitor convention" in *Victims of Convention* (Hamden, Conn.: Archon Books, 1978), 10–11, 14, and discusses its contemporary version in "Convention Coverage," 79.

19. Michel Fabre calls Christie "a clown, jester, a sacred idiot" and "an incarnation of Christ" ("Words and the World: *The Diviners* as an Exploration of the Book of Life," *Canadian Literature* 93 [Summer 1982]: 60–78, 62.) David Blewett refers to him as "one of the greatest fools in modern literature, but for that reason a channel and an image of divine grace" ("The Unity of the Manawaka Cycle," *Journal of Canadian Studies* 13, no. 3 [Fall 1978]: 31–39, 32), and sees Morag's education as an emulation of his wisdom: "Morag gives up 'everything' in order to possess the only thing that really matters: but in this way, by becoming a fool, she finally learns Christie's lesson" (36). Patricia Morley describes Christie as a "clown, fool, hero, and religious prophet" like "the fool figures" in Russian novelists, "a mystic, whose simplicity and honesty is interpreted by conventional society as stupidity, even madness"; she suggests that "his name, little Christ, underlines Laurence's intention. The loving simpleton, or foolish sage, points to the limitations of reason and to a super-rational vision" (*Margaret Laurence,* Twayne's World Author Series [Boston: G. K. Hall, 1981], 126–27). None of these critics notes the Shakespearean resonances, however.

20. "Complementarity" is the term Norman Rabkin uses to describe the coexistence of opposing viewpoints in Shakespeare's plays (*Shakespeare and the Com-*

mon Understanding [New York: Free Press, 1967], 22). "Ambivalence" is A. P. Rossiter's term: "two opposed value judgments are subsumed, and both are valid. . . . The whole is only fully experienced when both opposites are held and included in a 'two-eyed' view; and all 'one-eyed' simplifications are not only falsifications; they amount to a denial of some part of the mystery of things" ("Ambivalence: The Dialectic of the Histories," in *Discussions of Shakespeare's Histories,* ed. R. J. Dorius [Boston: Heath, 1964], 128).

21. Some of Morag's most important realizations are paradoxical: her awareness of the "apparently impossible contradiction" of the river which "flowed both ways" (3), her realization that "You Can't Go Home Again. . . . You have to go home again" (302); her recognition, when she sees Jules again after many years, that he is "both older, and younger" (429). She expresses understanding of the paradoxical intertwining of sameness and difference in her sense that "it's different" for Pique, but . . . the same, too" (422), that the farm Dan makes will be "different, but . . . the same" (354) as his father's, that things are both "better" and "worse" now than they were in the past (95). She also sees that her notion of Gaelic accents in Christie's language is "perhaps" sentimental, and "perhaps not" (371), that the fiction Pique makes of Jules will be both "more and less true than himself" (449), and that Pique is "*harbinger of my death, continuer of life*" (290).

22. Clara Thomas reads the novel as "the story of a profoundly religious pilgrimage, the affirmation of faith and the finding of grace" (*The Manawaka World of Margaret Laurence* [Toronto: McClelland and Stewart, 1975], 131), and claims that the Miltonic parallels point to Laurence's belief in "a Miltonic Eternal Providence" (170–71). Fabre also suggests that Laurence uses divining to mean the ability "to read the meaning inscribed in the world, in nature, and in events by the hidden hand of God . . . to discern a design or a 'pattern'" (63–64). Melanie Mortlock, "The Religion of Heritage: *The Diviners* as a Thematic Conclusion to the Manawaka Series" (Sorfleet, *The Work of Margaret Laurence,* 132–42), describes Laurence's "modern philosophical religion" as a "mythological religion, based on the concept of heritage" (139); her terms come closer to my sense of Laurence's faith in community and the continuity of generations. Eleanor Johnston, "The Quest of *The Diviners,*" *Mosaic* 11, no. 3 (Spring 1978), quotes Laurence as saying, "I don't have a traditional religion, but I believe that there's a mystery at the core of life" (108).

23. For Laurence's use of Catherine Parr Traill, see Thomas, "The Chariot of Ossian," 58.

24. It is Christie who is Morag's mentor in this way as others, in giving her a room of her own. When Morag first arrives at the Logans and sees her room, she feels "you could be safe in a place like that if it was really yours" (30); she later realizes that it is "really hers, it has always been hers" (51).

25. Margaret Laurence, "Gadgetry or Growing: Form and Voice in the Novel," in Sorfleet, *The Work of Margaret Laurence,* 54–62, 57.

26. J. E. Cirlot, *A Dictionary of Symbols* (New York: Philosophical Library, 1962), 235. See also Thomas, *The Manawaka World of Margaret Laurence,* 168.

27. She avoids being either "obedient daughter" or "rebellious daughter," two stances the feminist critic takes toward Shakespeare which Marianne Novy

describes as unsatisfactory ("Demythologizing Shakespeare," *Women's Studies: An Interdisciplinary Journal*, special issue ed. Gayle Greene and Carolyn Ruth Swift, 9, no. 1 [1981], 25).

28. Johnston quotes Laurence as saying, "I don't think I'll ever write another novel. It's not because I don't want to. I just have this knowledge, it's sort of a Celtic second sight." ("Quest of *The Diviners*," 116–17). See also Margaret Atwood, "Face to Face," *Maclean's*, May 1974, 46.

PETER ERICKSON

Adrienne Rich's
Re-Vision of Shakespeare

. . . not to pass on a tradition but to break its hold over us.
                    Adrienne Rich, "When We Dead
                    Awaken: Writing as Re-Vision"

I begin with two interrelated questions. The first concerns Rich's focus on her father: how does her presentation of the father-daughter relationship change, and what is the significance of these changes for her
work as a whole? Second, what is the place of Shakespeare in Rich's development? The two questions converge, for example, in the poem "After
Dark," with its explicit allusion to *King Lear*: what are the long-term re-
percussions of the parallel evoked here between Cordelia and Lear and
Rich and her father?

In outline, the father-daughter motif in Rich's work can be viewed in
three distinct phases. The early work, consisting of the first four volumes
of poetry and culminating in "After Dark" in *Necessities of Life,* portrays a
troubled fusion with her father. Drastic separation from the father, dramatized as the precondition for establishing an independent self, occurs in
the great middle phase conducted both in prose—sharply etched versions
of the father appear in "When We Dead Awaken: Writing as Re-Vision"
(first published in 1971) and in *Of Woman Born* (begun in 1972)—and in
poetry from *Leaflets* to *A Wild Patience Has Taken Me This Far.* A third
phase is suggested by the essay "Split at the Root" (1982) and the poem
Sources (separately published in 1983), which witness the surprising and
moving reemergence of the father.

After considering each of these three phases in turn, I then concentrate on the issue of how we are to characterize Rich's recent attention to
her father. This point of interpretation, I shall argue, is crucial to the
question of how the term "re-vision" from her essay "When We Dead
Awaken: Writing as Re-Vision" applies to Rich's relation to Shakespeare.
It is also crucial to the ancillary question of what Rich's work means for
Shakespeareans. My paper is an essay on reading Adrienne Rich with ref-

erence to Shakespeare, but equally, as I hope my conclusion will make clear, it is an essay on reading Shakespeare with reference to Adrienne Rich.

When Rich echoes *The Tempest* in "After Dark," in *Necessities of Life,* the emotional focus is on the daughter's ongoing attachment to her dying father: "Alive now, root to crown, I'd give / —oh,—something—not to know / our struggles now are ended."[1] This line presents in microcosm the problem of revision, for though Rich's substitution of "struggles" for "revels" acknowledges the conflict with her father, the overall pull is toward denial of separation and hence the Shakespearean motif of an idealized father-daughter relationship prevails. The same stifled revision is writ large in Rich's appeal to *King Lear* as a vehicle for articulating her grief. Rich changes the preposition in Lear's line to Cordelia—"Now let's away from prison"—as though to reverse the direction of the deathward move that encompasses the loyal daughter. But the minor modification is no proof against the play's overwhelming image of the daughter's submission to her father's needs, a submission figured by the vividly rendered fantasy of reunion with the father in symbiotic death: "and you embalmed beside me." Despite its token revisionist gestures, the poem reaffirms and perpetuates the authority of *King Lear's* father-daughter dynamic, in which the daughter's love constitutes self-sacrifice. Adapting Lear's language, Rich as daughter accepts her prescribed part: "I'll sit with you there and tease you / for wisdom, if you like. . . . " The compliant, self-sacrificial impulse of taking as received wisdom the paternal inheritance which she needs critically to assess is compounded by the absence of forgiveness on the father's part, the forgiveness proffered by Lear to secure Cordelia's submission.

The hollowness of the reconciliation enacted is suggested by the juxtaposition of "After Dark" with Rich's later reflection on her father's lack of reciprocation: "I wanted him to cherish and approve of me, not as he had when I was a child, but as the woman I was, who had her own mind and had made her own choices. This, I finally realized, was not to be; Arnold demanded absolute submission to his will" ("Split at the Root," 116). Two figures prevent Rich from an earlier articulation of this perspective and thus betray her into granting this submission in "After Dark": her father and Shakespeare, the representative of the literary heritage she had received through her father; both inhibit more than they assist exploration of the identity Rich prematurely claims for herself in "After Dark."

In *Leaflets*—Rich's fifth volume of poetry, which marks the opening of a second phase in her work—Rich directs an explosive attack against the constraints of the given cultural tradition: "I was trying to drive a tradition up against the wall"; "I can't live at the hems of that tradition—/ will I last to try the beginning of the next?" The attempt to construct a new tradition specifically involves the need to imagine points of view other than those sanctioned by Shakespeare: "Someone has always been desperate, now it's our turn—/ we who were free to weep for Othello and laugh at Caliban." But it is in part her own desperate and failed attempt to stay within the bounds of identification with Cordelia that drives this shift in perspective, this refusal to abide by Shakespearean-shaped expectations.

Two mourning poems in *The Will to Change* suggest in a transitional way what it might mean to recast the tradition. "The Stelae," written after her father's death in 1968, politely observes decorum, but its composure exudes a strength and self-confidence missing from "After Dark" five years earlier. The poet gently alters the terms of his bequest by imagining that she could inherit something he did not intend to give: "It's the stelae on the walls I want . . . / You offer other objects." Because they are not books written in the father's language but stone slabs "incised with signs / you have never deciphered," the stelae are beyond his control and hence hold out the possibility of a new start.

The other poem, referring to her decision to end her marriage, is necessarily more stark in its insistence on a revised tradition.[2] The use of Donne's title, "A Valediction Forbidding Mourning," and the rejection of the content of his poem mark in a simple but effective way the promise of an alternate tradition. Not only does Rich's poem bear witness to an irreversible separation from her husband in contrast to the temporary separation of the lovers confident of reunion in Donne's; its challenge is more fundamental because Rich also, giving a sharp twist to the idea of "forbidding mourning," deliberately chooses not to mourn. "To do something very common, in my own way" she asserts in the final line, as though determined to act according to the voice in "Snapshots of a Daughter-in-Law" that urged *"Save yourself; others you cannot save."* This commitment to self signals a rejection not just of the circumstances of Donne's poem but of its very assumptions about male-female relationship. Wilbur Sanders, commenting on the term "home" in Donne's poem, emphasizes its "domestic" quality.[3] Beyond the ending of one particular relationship, Rich's poem records the dissolution of this whole domestic mode.

The retrospective poem "From a Survivor" in *Diving into the Wreck*, where one meaning of the wreck whose damage she has to explore is the destruction of her marriage, confirms Rich's independent stance. The loss is recorded—"you are wastefully dead / who might have made the leap / we talked, too late, of making"—but the death is defined as a waste in which she has no further investment. The emphasis falls instead on her own survival, her future growth. The direction of that growth is implied by the opening two poems which form a contrasting pair. "Trying to Talk with a Man" has behind it the force of a long series of poems concerning Rich's struggle with her father and her husband and hence serves as a summation of this whole line of development. In "When We Dead Awaken," Rich's newly awakened consciousness turns to the possibility of female bonds as the central relationship:

> even you, fellow-creature, sister,
> sitting across from me, dark with love,
> working like me to pick apart
> working with me to remake
> this trailing knitted thing, this cloth of darkness,
> this woman's garment, trying to save the skein.

The transfer of loyalties to women inaugurates Rich's vast project of re-writing the family romance, recovering the mother, and establishing a lesbian identity. As the image of dismantling ("pick apart") and reconstructing ("remake") suggests, the notion of rewriting the literary tradition is at the heart of Rich's effort. As Rich puts it in a subsequent prose counterpart to this lyrical evocation: "For the lesbian poet it means rejecting the entire convention of love-poetry and undertaking to create a new tradition. She is forced by the conditions under which she loves, and the conditions in which all women attempt to survive, to ask questions that did not occur to a Donne or a Yeats" (*On Lies, Secrets, and Silence,* 252).

The importance of Rich's version of "A Valediction Forbidding Mourning" is that it begins to demonstrate what it could mean, as Rich puts it in "When We Dead Awaken: Writing as Re-Vision," "to do without authorities." In the prose work to which Rich now devotes a major portion of her energy, Rich's father and Shakespeare appear as inter-twined familial and literary authorities with whom she can do without. Rich's personal survival of the demise of her marriage gives her a strength—an inner authority—from which she can generalize: "Re-vision—the act of looking back, of seeing with fresh eyes, of entering an old text from a new critical direction—is for women more than a chapter in cultural history: it is an act of survival." In her 1971 essay "When We Dead Awaken: Writing as Re-Vision," Rich indicates her survival of the intense bond with her father as her first teacher and audience: "The ob-verse side of this, of course, was that I tried for a long time to please him, or rather, not to displease him." In the same essay she also puts Shake-speare behind her, noting his limitations as a resource: "We know more than Jane Austen or Shakespeare knew: more than Jane Austen because our lives are more complex, more than Shakespeare because we know more about the lives of women."

Similarly, in *Of Woman Born,* Rich specifies both her father and Shakespeare as obstacles she has had to overcome to achieve the different perspective from which to break the hold of the old tradition and to start a new. Rich's title strikes the "not" from Macduff's claim to be not of woman born (*Macbeth,* 5.8.15–16). The assertion that Rich relies on Shakespeare's warrant for doing so is not convincing, for Rich's study of motherhood and gender relations has a depth that makes it substantively different from any critical perspective we may attribute to Shakespeare. Rich makes clear that her quest is not continuous with Shakespeare's: "The loss of the daughter to the mother, the mother to the daughter, is the essential female tragedy. We acknowledge Lear (father-daughter split), Hamlet (son and mother) . . . as great embodiments of the human tragedy; but there is no presently enduring recognition of mother-daughter passion and rapture" (*Of Woman Born,* 237). When Rich goes on immediately to celebrate the Demeter-Persephone relationship embodied in the Eleusinian mysteries, Shakespeareans may want to claim that Rich has unwittingly neglected her debt and adherence to the old tradition. But the Hermione-Perdita reunion at the close of *The Winter's Tale* does not speak to the reconfiguration that Rich addresses here. It is not simply that Rich reinstates the mother-daughter connection to serve as the basis for lesbian sexuality—a development not present in Shakespeare. It is also that *The Winter's Tale* restores to Leontes his central position as paternal authority, while, for Rich, an essential element in the definition of the "self-chosen woman" is that she is "the woman who refuses to obey, who has said 'no' to the fathers" (*On Lies, Secrets, and Silence,* 202). *The Winter's Tale* does not say "no" to the fathers but concentrates on reforming patriarchy and assimilating women with a boundless capacity to forgive into the revised image of benign patriarchy.

By contrast, Rich presents father-centered and mother-centered worlds as counterpointed sets of values, as two different psychological and political systems between which one must choose. The drive to seek the mother requires the withdrawal of allegiance to the father, a change announced in "Re-forming the Crystal" from *Poems Selected and New, 1950–1974:*

> If I remind you of my father's favorite daughter,
> look again. The woman
> I needed to call my mother
> was silenced before I was born.

When the reformulation of the family is completed in "Sibling Mysteries" in *The Dream of a Common Language* and Rich, through the bond with her sister, reimagines the connection to her mother, the father is displaced: "then one whole night / our father upstairs dying / we burned our childhood, reams of paper. . . . " Gone is the Cordelia- and Miranda-like solicitousness and suffusion in "After Dark."

The feminist vision which Rich articulates in *Of Woman Born* and which receives poetic fulfillment in *The Dream of a Common Language* is further consolidated in the next volume, *A Wild Patience Has Taken Me This Far.* The father occasionally appears, but only on the periphery. The emotional charge is still there, readily surfacing when new occasions "turn up the jet of my anger," but the father-daughter episode appears to function largely as a baseline, as testimony to a process that she has completed and resolved:

> my Jewish father writing me
> letters of seventeen pages
> finely inscribed harangues
>
> "For Ethel Rosenberg"
>
> Yet smoldering to the end with frustrate life
> ideas nobody listened to, least of all my father
>
> "Grandmothers 1"
>
> All through World War Two the forbidden word
> *Jewish* was barely uttered in your son's house
>
> "Grandmothers 2"
>
> and absolute loyalty was never in my line
> once having left it in my father's house
>
> "Rift"

The sudden reemergence of the father as a central figure in Rich's recent work—"Split at the Root" (1982) and *Sources* (1983)—represents a striking and unforeseen development. Rich's statement in "Resisting Amnesia: History and Personal Life" (1983), however, offers a compelling reason for the continued interest in her father:

> The desire to be twice-born is, I believe, in part a longing to escape the burdens, complications, and contradictions of continuity. . . . Too much of ourselves must be deleted when we erase our personal histories and abruptly dissociate ourselves from who we have been. We become less dimensional than we really are.
>
> . . . We may know no other way to separate from parents, sisters, brothers, lovers, husbands except awkwardly and violently, so great are the pain and anger. But to deny that the connection ever existed, to pretend that we have moved on a direct, single-minded track—that is to subtract from ourselves the fullness of what we are. . . .

One can locate the poetic work behind this prose summation in the juxtaposition of "Toward the Solstice" in *The Dream of a Common Language* with "Integrity" in the next volume, *A Wild Patience Has Taken Me This Far.* The first poem formulates both the desire to be free of the family preoccupations that haunt her ("I can feel utterly ghosted in this house") and the inability to find a definitive, concluding gesture that would give the desired "release." The poet seeks "to ease the hold of the past / upon the rest of my life / and ease my hold on the past" by means of a "separation"

> between myself and the long-gone
> tenants of this house,
> between myself and my childhood,
> and the childhood of my children. . . .

But the pressure for closure ends in an impasse: "and my hand still suspended / as if above a letter / I long and dread to close." The mood of suspension and irresolution stems from the frustration of this longing:

> A decade of cutting away
> dead flesh, cauterizing
> old scars ripped open over and over
> and still it is not enough

"Integrity" reverses the action of "cutting away" and "cauterizing" in favor of an inclusiveness that affirmatively recasts the image of fragmentary selves—"I am trying to hold in one steady glance / all the parts of my life"—in "Toward the Solstice." "Release" is now redefined as release into wholeness: "*Nothing but myself?* . . . *My selves.* / After so long, this answer."

> Anger and tenderness: my selves.
> And now I can believe they breathe in me
> as angels, not polarities.
> Anger and tenderness: the spider's genius
> To spin and weave in the same action
> from her own body, anywhere—
> even from a broken web.

This resolution makes possible the emotional timbre of Rich's new approach to her father in *Sources,* where she readmits the hold of the past and acknowledges the family home as a permanent feature of her psychic landscape.

The immediate cause for the turn to her father as a source is Rich's new focus on her divided religious heritage ("neither Gentile nor Jew" she had put it twenty years earlier) and, in particular, her concern to come to terms with the Jewish identity that she has only by thinking back through her father, despite his attempts to erase his Jewish origins. Here, too, the intertwined influences of her father and Shakespeare have to be disentangled. In "Split at the Root," Rich comments on her childhood role as Portia, a part in which she was coached by her father: "he tells me to convey, with my voice, more scorn and contempt with the word 'Jew'... " Portia's resounding defeat of the patriarchal figure Shylock validates female power but also legitimizes anti-Semitism as its vehicle. "Like every other Shakespearean heroine," Rich concludes, "she proved a treacherous model."

Rich's recovery of her Jewish identity leads in *Sources* to a more modulated and sympathetic view of her father: "I saw the power and arrogance of the male as your true watermark; I did not see beneath it the suffering of the Jew. . . . " Yet the poignant attention to her father is not a reversion to the suffusion in sympathy dictated by the Cordelia-like pose in "After Dark." Rich goes on, "It is only now, under a powerful, womanly lens, that I can decipher your suffering and deny no part of my own"; there is no retraction of her criticism of her father and no denial or softening of the requirements of her identity. When Rich ends the poem by repeating the words "powerful" and "womanly," these terms draw strength from their earlier use in the specific context of the relationship with her father. The long history of her struggle in that relationship is thus affirmed in full rather than moderated: only by maintaining this struggle could Rich preserve her "powerful, womanly lens."

This account of three stages in Rich's poetic development to date establishes a context from which I can consider the larger implications of *Sources* for the direction of Rich's work as a whole and for the spirit of her revision of Shakespeare. It is possible to view *Sources* as the long-delayed realization of the "generosity" Helen Vendler called for after *Diving into the Wreck* in 1973,[4] thereby aligning *Sources* with the Shakespearean precedent of the final turn to the late romances. Though I am moved by the new tenderness in Rich's regard for her father and husband, I think it is inaccurate to read *Sources* simply as a poem of reconciliation.

What would be lost in a line of interpretation based on Vendler's equation of "generosity" with "self-forgetfulness" is Rich's ongoing commitment to "the eye of the outsider" (*Blood, Bread, and Poetry*, 3). Rich's critique of the father-daughter relationship continues to serve as the personal reference point for her general analysis of the dangers of a tokenism that "acts to blur her outsider's eye, which could be her real source of power and vision. Losing her outsider's vision, she loses the insight which both binds her to other women and affirms her in herself" (6). In my reading of *Sources,* the outsider's eye remains strongly present, the political perspective strongly in force.

Ultimately, interpretation involves the status of politics in Rich's work. Rich defeats the easy formula that equates the political with the reductive because her political explorations are enormously complicated. Her views are not static but changing, and they are becoming more complex rather than less; for Rich, revision applies not only to the received literary tradition but also to her own politics: "What writing and politics have most in common, perhaps, is that both are creative processes requiring many false starts and strange go-rounds, many hard choices" (*Blood, Bread, and Poetry,* xi).

In their excellent essay, "Toward a Materialist-Feminist Criticism," Judith Newton and Deborah Rosenfelt criticize Rich's recourse to the notion of an "ahistorical patriarchy."[5] But the criticism is out of date. Having ruefully admitted in the Introduction to the 1986 edition of *Of Woman Born* that she used "the concept of patriarchy as a backstop in which all the foul balls of history end up" (xxiii), Rich now speaks of multiple versions of patriarchy in specific contexts: "patriarchy has no pure and simple existence" (*Blood, Bread, and Poetry,* xii). The earlier emphasis on female experience as a continuum gives way to a sharper, more complex account of differences among women. A footnote in the new edition of *Of Woman Born* marks the shift: "There has been a feminist temptation to replace a 'primary contradiction' of class with a 'primary contradiction' of sex. A majority of the women in the world, however, experience their lives as the intersection of class, sex and race" (112). This enlarged international perspective, fostered by the sharpened awareness of her national "location" that Rich's experience in Nicaragua brings, receives increasing attention. The essays from 1983 on in *Blood, Bread, and Poetry* probe Rich's concern that Virginia Woolf's statement—"as a woman I have no country . . . . As a woman my country is the whole world" (162, 183, 211)—can be used as a shortcut to "false transcendence" (183). Rich's reconsideration of Marxist analysis leads to a view of global economy that is consistent with Gayatri Spivak's insistence on the international division of labor as antidote to a universalizing tendency in Western feminism.[6]

The specific focus of this essay on the father-daughter relationship can now be placed in its larger context as one element in the process of exploring the whole range of multiple selves, along with the multi-cultural social conflicts they reveal: "The woman who seeks the experiential grounding of identity politics realizes that as Jew, white, woman, lesbian, middle-class, she herself has a complex identity. Further, that her very citizenship, which gives her both grief and privilege, is part of her identity: her U.S. passport, in this world, is part of her body, and she lives under a very specific patriarchy" (*Blood, Bread, and Poetry,* xii). The reassessment of differences among women makes Rich newly attuned to her own array of differences, including the Jewish identity that revives the connection with her father and enables the new view of him. The changed father-daughter dynamic in *Sources* cannot be separated from this overall project, nor can it be portrayed as a purely psychological development within a self-enclosed individual relationship.

The relevance of the larger vision for *Sources* is enacted in "Split at the Root," the essay that specifically focuses on her father, in which the three concluding paragraphs movingly evoke the motif of multiple selves in its entirety. This action is political and not merely personal because it involves "enlarging the range of accountability": "There is no purity and, in our lifetimes, no end to this process."

In conclusion, I return to the question of Rich's relation to Shakespeare, of Shakespeare's relation to Rich, as these relations are negotiated in the transition from "After Dark" to *Sources*. Women's forgiveness is so central to the articulation of what we find moving in *King Lear* and *The Winter's Tale* that it can become fixed in our minds as an inviolable element of father-daughter relations. The prospect of the father's redemption in *Sources* is bound to arouse all our Shakespearean expectations with an intensity that will not tolerate disappointment. Yet the weight of the tradition cannot override the differences that detailed analysis reveals. The assimilation of Rich to Shakespeare is blocked. *Sources* does not recapitulate the Lear-Cordelia paradigm. Rather Rich breaks its hold, and her departure justifies in a positive way the anxious bravado of her earlier protest that "The old masters, the old sources, / haven't a clue what we're about" ("In the Evening," *Leaflets*).

The study of Rich is relevant for Shakespeareans because our knowledge of the new tradition embodied in her poetry provides a new frame of reference that changes our relation to Shakespeare. Rich's opening up of new possibilities—new feelings and values—makes us realize in a concrete, experiential way that Shakespeare does not encompass everything, is not universal. Her exploration of the father-daughter motif exemplifies how our perceptions of Shakespeare are altered. Coming from Rich, we see *King Lear* with fresh eyes, with a new awareness of what Shakespeare can and cannot do. *King Lear* is dramatized primarily from Lear's point of view; consequently, as Janet Adelman remarks, the play loses touch with Cordelia's inwardness.[7] Whether or not Shakespeare is seen as critical of Lear, Shakespeare cannot give us Cordelia's point of view.

Cordelia's story cannot adequately be told in Shakespearean terms. Rich rewrites Cordelia's "silence" by taking the daughter's point of view, thus making Shakespeare's limits understood and actively felt as limitations. This perspective prevents our slipping into total identification with Lear; compassion for Lear is qualified, partially withdrawn. Our new awareness of alternate modes for conceiving the father-daughter relationship may be temporarily bracketed for the sake of historical investigation, but this awareness can never be eradicated, left completely out of account. Shakespeare can no longer be treated as an absolute, unframed standard as though his art were fully adequate to the range of thought and feeling possible for us in the present.

It is easy to caricature Rich's remark that we know more than Shakespeare by treating it as a myopic self-congratulatory claim to be more liberated than Shakespeare. The only reasonable alternative then seems to resume a posture of humility and to reaffirm Shakespeare's supreme artistic greatness. Such reverence, however, can become an avoidance mechanism by which issues of historical difference are circumvented. Feminist critics can acknowledge the lasting power of Shakespeare's verbal and dramatic brilliance without acceding to the pretense that his values are permanent or above criticism. Shakespeare's artistic greatness is not in question, only his use as the ultimate, inviolable arbiter of experience. His work provides not a body of timeless, inexhaustible or unmodifiable knowledge but rather an historical baseline that helps us to measure our difference.

My understanding of feminist practice includes reorganizing our sense of the literary canon so as to validate elements of contemporary literature, to temper some of the claims made for Shakespeare, and to create space to move back and forth between these two discontinuous worlds. The negotiations that a critic conducts between past and present should involve full recognition of each and not require diminished awareness of the present or arbitrary constraints on our contemporary imagination. Attentiveness to the present is not a solution, a salvation or an escape: the present contains its own intractable difficulties. It is an evasion to act as though Shakespeare's work provided a cultural field so capacious that it adequately addresses the lives that we are living now, to see our lives for the purposes of historical investigation as mere distortions rather than the positive resources they are. Full-strength feminist criticism of Shakespeare can be made to appear negative when it is cut off from its larger context, its contribution to the feminist revaluation of the tradition as a whole. The constructive spirit of the project of re-vision can emerge fully only if we reject narrow period specialization as the exclusive definition of what comprises the professionally legitimate and acknowledge responsibility to the entire range of cultural heritage, including the present.

Not all revisions are the same in degree and scope. We should not expect women writers from diverse historical contexts to be fundamentally the same; there is no one single model of revision applicable to all situations. Rich's revision of Shakespeare, for example, differs markedly from Virginia Woolf's. In "When We Dead Awaken: Writing as Re-Vision," Rich's critical perspective extends not only to Shakespeare but also to Woolf, and in particular to Woolf's problematic accommodation with literary tradition: "I think we need to go through that anger, and we will betray our own reality, if we try, as Virginia Woolf was trying, for an objectivity, a detachment, that would make us sound more like . . . Shakespeare." Rich's poem "A Primary Ground" in *Diving into the Wreck* adds the anger absent from *To the Lighthouse,* while her subsequent rejection of androgyny breaks with a principal means by which Woolf connects with Shakespeare. I bring out these differences because I think they are major and because an overemphasis on continuity blurs distinctions that should be sharply etched if we are to experience the full force of Rich's particular version of revision.

In my view, Rich's work has a special role within the general effort to reformulate the literary tradition because of her historical positioning. The sharpness and depth of her move outside Shakespearean precedent seem to me to be distinctively new and to be possible only because of particular political and cultural developments, including contemporary feminism, in her—and our—historical moment.

NOTES

1. Citations of Rich's poetry are to the following: *Necessities of Life: Poems 1962–1965* (New York: W. W. Norton, 1966); *Leaflets: Poems 1965–1968* (Norton, 1969); *The Will to Change: Poems 1968–1970* (Norton, 1971); *Diving into the Wreck: Poems 1971–1972* (Norton, 1973); *Poems Selected and New, 1950–1974* (Norton, 1975); *The Dream of a Common Language: Poems 1974–1977* (Norton, 1978); *A Wild Patience Has Taken Me This Far: Poems 1978–1981* (Norton, 1981); *Sources* (Woodside, Calif.: Heyeck Press, 1983). Prose extracts are drawn from *On Lies, Secrets, and Silence: Selected Prose 1966–1978* (Norton, 1979); *Blood, Bread, and Poetry: Selected Prose 1979–1985* (Norton, 1986); *Of Woman Born: Motherhood as Experience and Institution,* 10th anniversary ed. (Norton, 1986).

2. The *New York Times* reports the suicide of Rich's husband in an obituary notice on October 20, 1970, and "A Valediction Forbidding Mourning" is dated 1970, but whether the poem refers only to the breakup of their marriage or is more specifically a response to the suicide is not certain. Wendy Martin gives the sequence of events as follows: "In 1970, she left her marriage; later the same year, Alfred Conrad, her husband, committed suicide" (*An American Triptych* [Chapel Hill: University of North Carolina Press, 1984], 187).

3. Wilbur Sanders, *John Donne's Poetry* (Cambridge: Cambridge University Press, 1971), 86.

4. Vendler hopes for "a new generosity" in Rich's work in the final line of her review of *Diving into the Wreck*, in *Part of Nature, Part of Us: Modern American Poets* (Cambridge: Harvard University Press, 1980), 262. For a discussion of Rich's latest volume, *Time's Power: Poems 1985–1988*, in terms related to the argument of the present essay, see my review in *Hurricane Alice: A Feminist Quarterly* 6, no. 4 (Fall 1989/ Winter 1990).

5. Judith Newton and Deborah Rosenfelt, "Toward a Materialist-Feminist Criticism," in *Feminist Criticism and Social Change: Sex, Class, and Race in Literature and Criticism*, ed. Newton and Rosenfelt (New York: Methuen, 1985), xxxii n.9. By contrast, see Catharine Stimpson, "Adrienne Rich and Lesbian/Feminist Poetry," *Parnassus* 12, no. 2/13, no. 1 (1985): 249–68.

6. For Spivak's work, see "Feminism and Critical Theory," in *For Alma Mater: Theory and Practice in Feminist Scholarship*, ed. Paula A. Treichler, Cheris Kramarae, Beth Stafford (Urbana: University of Illinois Press, 1985), 119–42, and "Imperialism and Sexual Difference," *Oxford Literary Review* 8 (1986): 225–38.

7. Janet Adelman, "'This Is and Is Not Cressid': The Characterization of Cressida," in *The (M)other Tongue: Essays in Feminist Psychoanalytic Interpretation*, ed. Shirley Nelson Garner, Claire Kahane, Madelon Sprengnether (Ithaca: Cornell University Press, 1985), 140–41.

JOAN HUTTON LANDIS

"Another Penelope": Margaret Hutton Reading William Shakespeare

> You would be another Penelope; yet they say all the yarn she spun in Ulysses' absence did but fill Ithaca full of moths. Come; I would your cambric were sensible as your finger, that you might leave pricking it for pity. Come, you shall go with us.
>
> *Coriolanus* 1.3.79–83

On Tuesday evening, April 3, 1984, the phone rang. It was my mother. "Are you going to make it?" My dissertation on Shakespeare was due the following day. My mother and I talked weekly, usually on Sunday mornings, but she hadn't been able to wait; she had to know. I told her she had spoiled my little drama of annunciation. We talked a long while that night as if the following Sunday were far away. I reminded her that it would be my birthday on the 22nd and she assured me she was knitting something: "the best yet." On Saturday, April 7, my uncle phoned to tell me that my mother had died, suddenly, that morning, probably of a stroke. At least, I thought later, driving to her house in Connecticut, searching for any small consolation, she knew I'd got the thing done. It had pleased her that she'd have yet another link to the author that I'd met so late in my life and that, as a consequence, she'd met even later in hers.

Before I try to describe the ways in which a woman between the ages of seventy-eight and eighty-two reacted to what seemed a virtual first reading of Shakespeare, about half the canon, I want to give a brief biography. Margaret Agnes Foster was born in Newark, New Jersey, on August 14, 1902. She was the second child of seven. The family moved to Morristown, where her father, Harry, bought and ran a hardware store in the attempt to recoup several "fortunes" made and lost as an inventor. Her mother, Harriet Smith Edwards, was the daughter of two doctors; Emma Ward Edwards was the first woman to practice in Newark. Harriet had graduated from Smith College and Margaret expected to go there too. Three of her brothers attended Williams; a fourth went to Cornell. While

Margaret scored higher on her English College Board than anyone in the country, she failed chemistry. Instead of encouraging her to prepare for the exam again, her parents sent her off to a finishing school in Bethlehem, Pennsylvania. Later, she went to secretarial school in New York, worked for the Girl Scouts, taught Sunday school and ran the family household as her mother became progressively immobilized by rheumatoid arthritis.

At twenty-eight she married Lewis T. Hutton. She was to discover that, although he was handsome and clever, he had never graduated from high school, having run away from every school and military academy to which he was sent. I was born in April 1930. They divorced, finally, in 1942 and she went to work as a secretary. In 1946, Mother sold our house. We moved to Connecticut to live with her brother Lincoln, whose wife had long been in a mental hospital. She was to help care for his two children. After several years he remarried, and she moved to New Haven to work in the dress shop of an acquaintance and then to become the secretary to the head of the Sterling Library at Yale. Finally, she moved back to Falls Village to be close to her two brothers and a beloved sister-in-law. She took a series of secretarial jobs, ending up at the Hotchkiss School. Her biggest adventures were a trip to England with my husband and me and two of our sons in 1963 and a three month visit to us in Beirut, Lebanon, in 1965. She retired then and lived in a small house that belonged to an aunt. She remained, always, close to me and her three grandsons but refused to travel or make visits to us, withdrawing into her small radius of village and familiar house and garden, a few friends and relatives, her books, her painting, knitting and crewel work, her birds.

The first time I realized that my mother was reading Shakespeare was, I think, in 1980. She recited Portia's speech on mercy while we were having a drink in her living room. I had heard her do it before; she had memorized it and the "seven ages of man" speech from *As You Like It* at high school. She had gone back to the *Merchant* in an effort to resupply a context for that great setpiece. It had thrilled her to find it both new and familiar at once and sent her on to *Twelfth Night* and *As You Like It*. I was astonished. My seventy-eight year old mother, inveterate reader of mysteries, biographies, and glamorized English history, doer of at least three crossword puzzles daily, solo player of Scrabble, was at last reading something worthy of her own fine but undervalued intellect. Never, since my Bennington days, had we talked seriously about literature; she rejected or was simply silent about my favorite novels.

What these plays meant to her and how she understood them I was to learn later. She explained, tentatively, that it was the heroines of these plays that had "befriended" her. She noted that all three, Portia, Viola, and Rosalind, had resorted to disguises, reminding her of her own adolescent fantasies of dressing up in someone else's clothes, of becoming someone other, a man, and so putting on freedom. She had been conscious of lacking that, at home or anywhere. Of course, those heroines had had to protect themselves on journeys and in strange places from those dangers to which women have always been subject. But they donned a special power with their disguises: paradoxically, the power to become themselves. That entailed, for her, being listened to by men, by one's elders, being attended to without that curious climate of condescension occasioned solely by one's gender. Shakespeare saw the superiority and maturity of young women and the necessity of disguise in order to say or do the "real thing" or, perhaps, to signal that they were learning to be themselves through playing at being someone else.

"It's as if he not only knew what it was like to *be* a woman, but that *he* wanted to be one. And he could, vicariously. Or perhaps he was showing us that it wasn't until men could *feel* as women that they could grow up? Orlando likens himself to a doe; Adam becomes his fawn. He *mothers!* At any rate, Shakespeare had a woman's mind inside his man's mind."

I remarked that that was true and maybe she had just defined the great artist of any sex.

"I used to want to dress up as a man and go off and act the way men ought to but didn't know how. Or to have that freedom of going where *I* wanted, not taking nurses home and Brownie to her house and Dick to school. . . ."

"That's why you always gave me such freedom?" She had given me so much, always, I could still hear that sound the other mothers made, their "cluck" of disapproval.

She outlined the kind of scope that Shakespeare's women achieved in their specific incognitos and went on to wonder if his men used role-playing and clothing in similar ways. Orlando had, but only through donning a simile. What, for example, did I think of Hal and his playing at being his own father? Was that the same? I had such strong feelings on that score, I told her, that I wanted to postpone that discussion until she'd read all the *Henry*s. As if to disprove her own intuitions that women "play" and fantasize and imagine in ways not so natural to boys and men and that Shakespeare dramatized this in specific ways, she brought up the name of Vincentio. *Measure for Measure* was, to date, her favorite play.

"He puts on a disguise, the failed duke, and that enables him to do for his subjects, and himself, what Rosalind helped to do for Orlando."

She was indignant when I said that many critics would disagree, deeming the duke inferior, the play problematic, the end botched or ironic, with its "orgy of clemencies" and its forced pairings. She saw the play as a continuation of Shakespeare's obsession with disguising and role-playing in its best sense, but in a peculiar sense.

There was something eerie in her remarks; they were so close to my own ideas about the play. She thought it was perfectly clear that each one of the characters was marred by being shut up in the cell of a viewpoint too narrow. This included the duke. But, as he busied himself with his schemes and his little charities, as Isabella went from the cell of her convent to the courtroom to Angelo's house to the prison to the grange to the public space at the end, as others went on voyages of equal variety so that they all literally changed places, education was undertaken. Nor was the ending a problem. The duke, who had been forced to look at his own portrait in the hyperbolic slanders of Lucio, just as Isabella had been forced to consider her possible self in the picture of Julietta painted by Lucio, had fallen in love with Isabella—as Angelo had—but was now ready to marry, to provide heirs, to cure his sick society. It all hinged, didn't it, on the bed trick?

"Are you suggesting that the bed trick is good?"

Margaret reminded me, at that moment, of Portia as Bellario; but rather than pleading for Shylock, she was arguing for Vincentio. In total earnest. She found that the bed trick was good. Look at Isabella, that icy nun who overvalued her maidenhead. She had concurred in the substitution suggested by the duke and fulfilled by Mariana and so had been deflowered herself, if at one remove. That is, when one person takes the place of another, both persons "experience" the action. It was tricky; Shakespeare did confuse reality and imagination there, but that was just it, just what educated *us*, the readers. We were like Isabella, weren't we? Pure yet violated.

"It's like playing dress ups, which goes back to my point about disguise. Once you put on a costume and become someone else, you are two people in one. You've moved out of your own narrow space. Isabella is a virgin in Act 5, still, but through her assent in the substitution of Mariana for herself she has not only been merciful, or conniving, but has had to imagine what took place in that locked garden. She has been violated by the knowing of physical realities and is really connected to Kate Keepdown and Mistress Overdone."

"Only connect." I quoted that Forster imperative at her, feeling two amazements at once: that Margaret was doing so in such a sophisticated way (by which I hope I meant that her instinctive ability to see well and her intelligence were mated) and that her vision of the play was, uncannily, like mine.

"What's the example Isabella uses as the best argument for putting oneself in another's place?"

"Christ!" she said, in a tone that told me not to examine her, but answered me. "That's the underlying vision, that only when we can put ourselves in the place of another will anything good occur. It's what Portia calls for in my mercy speech. That's what I mean about disguise," she insisted, repeating herself as though I hadn't yet gotten her point; "that's the theatrical way of saying it—that you take on another person's identity in order to change for the better. Theater as church," she laughed, delighted at her own ability to abstract in just this way, passionate under her laughter about the truth as she saw Shakespeare dispensing it. We talked during that exchange about the fact that men were playing women who played men who played women. Rosalind's chosen alias was "Ganymede," a mythic catamite. She loved that, co-opting it as an illustration of her own meanings. "And it's not just the actors or the playwright who get into the act, it's all of us."

Some months later, on a quick trip through Falls Village, she closed our ritual game of Scrabble with the announcement that she had been reading *Henry IV. 1 & 2.* and *Henry V.* The answer to the question about men being able to wear costumes and play parts effectively seemed clear enough there. They do. But they can't.

"Oh?"

"Well, look!" Her tone was already angry. "Hal plays at being his father just like he plays at being one of the Boar's Head crew. He boasts that he will be able to drink with any man of his country once he's king, that he'll command all the lads of Eastcheap."

"And you don't take this as preparation for understanding the commonfolk, for becoming that 'mirror of all Christian kings'?"

"No! First of all, Hal has a hidden script, which we learn in his soliloquy—the cold rational male at work. Do you see, at 2.4, where Hal is talking to Poins and he says that he can call a leash of drawers by their christen names, as Tom, Dick and Francis? Not Harry, Francis. That's because he already dreams of calling France his. And look at the way he treats poor Francis. He makes him a promise he never intends to keep and tricks him out of that thousand pounds with words. That is just the way he fools himself that France belongs to him, isn't it? With Ely and Canterbury's sententious words? And what does he tell Poins he can do? 'Drink with any tinker in his own language, during my life.' And, 'they call drinking deep dyeing scarlet.' Of course, because when he's king they will be sent to France to get it for him and they will die and their blood will be scarlet. Francis, the drawer, gave Hal sugar, as if to try to sweeten him up, but Hal just gives it to Ned as if it were a joke and shows him how the 'under-skinkers' of his kingdom will be betrayed. And so, when Henry goes to France and puts on the cloak of Erpingham, to disguise himself from the soldiers . . ."

"And you don't find this exonerating? Or, in the light of our hymns to changing costume in the comedies, a thing Henry does to inform himself? Transform himself? To mother his men?"

"No. Hal never transforms himself. Look at him with the common soldiers! They ask the only sensible questions of the war and what does the king do? Gives them things that *sound* like reasons."

"I've always had a theory that Williams is really William S.," I admitted. She loved that.

"Of course he is. And shares Shakespeare's understanding of war as total madness. War is a version of male lust. Hal never grows up but works out ways to aggrandize himself by owning more and more property. Geography as ego. And," she added, "he's a rapist too."

"Your reproof is something too round," I quoted, looking at the line in her book (*Henry V* 4.1.192).

"Connect the speech that Henry makes before Harfleur with the wooing of Kate and you'll see; it's *in* the language. Kate suspects it; she knows she's a pawn in his game, a piece of property already. She's his female Francis. When she is compared to a flower-de-luce she *is* Harfleur. When she says 'I know not dat,' [5.2.205] she is echoing Williams, who doesn't know if the war is just or the quarrel honorable. And" (Margaret was sounding now like the queen of the same name in *Henry VI!*) "Harry admits that the maid that 'stood in the way for my wish shall show me the way to my will!' [313–14] A man's will is what this play is about."

She continued to make cogent accusations as she paced around her room, smoking, gesticulating. "If the play ends with a wedding in view, it really ends with the Wars of the Roses in view; all his pillaging and murdering is for nothing. Which refers back to the fact that he let his old friends, Bardolph and Nym, die for the stealing of a 'pax.' He is the one who stole the peace; they are merely his smaller shadows. He sacrifices them!"

"Henry V was called 'an amiable monster' by some critic. You would delete the 'amiable'?" She would. Returning to Harry Monmouth, as she called him, she reflected that his geographical name echoed the fact that he had a prodigious appetite for more and more, like Alexander of Macedon. But he was only just worse than other English kings, Richard II or III, because of that cloak.

"Cloak?" I knew I was about to learn something new.

"He puts on a disguise that really stands for him. Mr. Cloak. What I mean is that he can't connect, see into his own motives. Any more than his audience probably can. But look"—heating up again—"at the advice his father gives him when he's dying, and it's scarlet advice—unify your men, make war. And just as everyone is thrilled to think Hal has at last buried his wildness and grown up, true wildness comes out; he moves from East-cheap and highjinks to a new kind of rapacity: more cloaking."

I reflected that Harry's cloak was an early version of that arras in Elsinore: a prop which spoke of the difficulty of seeing into reality itself. She told me that she felt sure, reading this play over, that Shakespeare shared all of her own prejudices against war, politicians, men's way of running the world, the male ego that needed and needed until nothing was too cruel or ignoble for its feeding. Hal's rejection of Falstaff was murderous, if not literally: it was tantamount to the killing of a father and the shutting out of the comic perspective. Only with that saving grace banished could a man give the command, "Then every soldier kill his prisoners!" (*Henry V* 4.6.37). That, she said, was "a little touch of Harry in the night."

"Your father's name was Harry," I suggested.

"My father," she said carefully, "was an embarrassment to us all. But he wasn't a monster. I never thought so."

"That's a shame, because it would make such a splendid response, to displace the hostility against the father onto the character with the same name." Shakespeare loved such misplacings, as she had seen herself. We went on to think out the various crafty doublings of the play: Fluellen with the king; Alexander the Pig with the king; the British with the French until the French were withdrawn, and then, in their quickness to fight, with one another; Hotspur and Hal; all four Harrys. Margaret anointed them "Harriers." She came back to *Henry V* again and again, as if she wanted reassurance that Shakespeare had meant us to see through the rhetoric to the killer and rapist. I had thought so since my first readings but had never found a man who shared my view entirely. My male students often did, but only after strenuous debate. Most assessors wanted ambiguity. We tried to figure out why our readings should coincide, as they had in *Measure for Measure,* for although I had learned most of my real values at her knee, we did disagree about public figures and ideas, sometimes radically. She had every personal reason to distrust men, but she had never operated in that way; it was only particular men she had blamed. Perhaps, she thought aloud, her fury at Henry V was contingent on her Anglophilia. No, it was rather because he stood for a kind of male blindness and ruthlessness that was at the heart of what was wrong with the world, not only her beloved "nook-shotten isle."

"But surely any woman would see that the wooing scene is a horror? A sham?" she insisted.

My students did, but usually they needed some demonstration, wanting to read it as a comic ending, a new beginning, a humanization of Henry.

"Which it isn't, clearly! It's in the little details, added up, that Shakespeare builds his case. These shine out at the careful looker but are cloaked over by the language that sounds so rich and right, that seems to speak of his caring for his subjects but which is really caring for himself! 'Cry "God for Harry! England! and Saint George!"' (*Henry V* 3.1.34)

"Margaret, you are 'dyed scarlet' yourself."

She laughed and admitted that Harry was bad for her blood pressure.

Like all astute students of Shakespeare, Margaret collected instances of what she called "the bright and the dark in one." That doubleness is, of course, a cliché in critical response, but, not knowing that she was often reinventing the wheel, she was elated at the patterning they made. We had, I think, been talking about my father and the reasons for her accepting him—her desire to escape from home, to have children, to be a wife, and so an insider. His appearance had not been the reality. She had been utterly disillusioned as early as her wedding night but out of this terrible coupling had come her only child and all the things she now valued. She said of him that he was a nettle and flower in one. This kind of Janus was everywhere in the plays and she proposed to call them "the Lew Huttons" in his wretched honor. We traded instances, making a game of it: the witches' dictum in *Macbeth* that "Fair is foul and foul is fair"; the moment in which Tamora's son is sacrificed for the supposed good of the Romans which is simultaneously the cause of Lavinia's rape; the medicinal/poisonous herbs of Friar Lawrence in *Romeo and Juliet*. Returning to her favorite *Measure for Measure,* she invoked the whorehouse. It was, she said, a place like all the others in the city but an even more fallen establishment—a source of disease, a house for which the duke was responsible in his overdone laxity. But wasn't it there that warmth, humor, life flourished? Even the room with the fire in it, that room "good for winter" (2.1.124), had a name, "The Bunch of Grapes." That suggested fruitfulness of a sort. It had, as she put it, the "most *vie* in Vienna," at the same time that it was a stew, where "stewed prunes" were desirable. We agreed that her "Bunch of Grapes" (and its dark double, the locked garden "with a vineyard backed" [4.1.28]) was the prize "Lewhutton" of them all.

It was *Much Ado About Nothing* that she found, long after her first trip into the comedies, and deemed her favorite. Beatrice was the ultimate heroine, the one she would most like to have been. What power to use language! Her wit was to be valued above rubies. Her standing up for Hero against all odds: that was integrity which filled Margaret with admiration. The cry "Kill Claudio!" was just. Except for the rarest, men were Claudios. My mother had never thought of herself as a feminist; she would have disclaimed the term. But, it seemed to me now, she was finally expressing a view of men filled with bitterness and disdain, an avenue for the building angers of old age, and that she was, via Beatrice, finding a voice that was essentially new to her at eighty. It was as if Shakespeare had led her to see the injustices of the patriarchal society in which she had grown up and which she had, with unusual equanimity, accepted for so long.

"Claudio did none of his own wooing! He sent Don Pedro in his place." Women knew it when they were being courted like this, out of lust and avarice, but usually they hadn't the backbone to protest. Henry's Kate was an extreme version of this. They fooled themselves in the face of every signal. (Had I known then, I would have told her about the Quarto text which listed Innogen, wife of Leonato, as a character. Editors had since erased her from the stage as she had, evidently, nothing to say. But present, she would speak eloquently enough for the fate of women in the Renaissance: seen but not heard, present but unattended.[1]) Cassandra-like, Margaret congratulated herself on having seen, early in the play, that Claudio would learn nothing but the expedient move, would get his money as well as Hero, who deserved what she got: "She was as mealy-mouthed as young Margaret Foster," she said. Claudio's yearly (*yearly*, mind you) atonement at the grave had meant nothing, taught him nothing, even *in potentia*. He would again leave Hero at the first rattle of a sword. And all the jokes about horns showed us that men feared the loss of their possessions and the subsequent ridicule precisely because they did not know the women they had arranged to acquire. Except for Benedick. Even though it took a trick to open his eyes. . . . Margaret stopped in her tirade and laughed. Didn't she make a good Paulina? I told her she did but that it interested me to see her fury at the use of so many substitutes—not only Don Pedro for Claudio but Margaret for Hero, etc.—in *Much Ado,* when she had been singling that device out for praise in *Measure for Measure.* She paused only long enough to light one of her cigarettes.

"The remedy of one play can be the disease of another," she said. "It's just another 'Lewhutton.'" I told her that she was undoubtedly brilliant and that she had also named such a paradoxical area for her late, unbeloved husband as a way to show him some mercy, to exonerate him. It was, I thought afterwards, her playing with words, her crossword puzzles, her extended bouts of talking to herself, that made her capable of such reading, particularly such lexically acute play as the recognition that

Shakespeare had substituted the name Francis for the customary Harry of "Tom, Dick and Harry" in *Henry IV, Part 1,* seeing that, in a way, Francis was a forerunner of geographical France, and all the reasons for his doing so. I would be jealous of that hit forever!

"Does your reference to Paulina mean you've been reading *The Winter's Tale* again?"

"No. I don't like the romances."

I assured her she would. As we talked of other things, I watched her knitting. I remembered a green dress which she'd knitted for me as a child, with wooden buttons down the front that spelled my name. There was something blissful about a mother knitting. I asked her if she thought her prowess as a knitter was, in part, behind her ability to tie the various strands of the plays together so beautifully. I speculated that Shakespeare's mother was a knitter and sewer. For proof, there was Virgilia, in *Coriolanus,* mending away in a pathetic, if eloquent, womanly gesture, opposing the unravelling action of the war. She hadn't read *Coriolanus,* but she cited Philomel as the myth that lay behind *Titus.* She'd be a weaving mother? We thought of Marina, Shakespeare's artist who could "sing, weave, sew and dance" (*Pericles* 4.6.174) of Bottom in *A Midsummer Night's Dream,* if not exactly a mother, a *metteur-en-scene.* We thought of Penelope as the model for all weavers: all creating women. We suppressed Mme. De-Farge—Margaret said she was "full of the dickens." I submitted Nelly Dean, the knitting, sewing narrator of *Wuthering Heights.*

"And of course, there's Mrs. Ramsay in *To the Lighthouse.*" Mother thought she had read it long ago but had no substantial memory of it. I sent her a copy shortly afterwards. She thanked me by phone, saying she'd get around to it but was currently enjoying a life of Lady Ottoline Morrell and two detective novels.

It was in July 1983, on a stopover on the way to our house in Vermont, that she told me how she had gone back to *The Winter's Tale* and was finding it hard going. What did I think was behind Shakespeare's fixation with daughters, with restoring family members to one another after such horrendous rendings apart? She wondered if the actual life was implicated in the obsessions of the plays. I admitted that, like Polonius, Shakespeare did seem to harp on daughters. She objected to the fact that he worked too hard at achieving unity, unity at all costs, and that romance endings seemed to her a regression rather than a progression. It was as if Shakespeare were trying to cheer himself up in old age or return to the womb itself. It occurred to me that the uniting of husbands and wives, fathers and daughters, mothers and daughters, was a closure so infinitely desirable that she rejected it. She singled out the Leontes/Hermione reconciliation as being too radical for her. *That* act of forgiveness could not be made. I suggested that Shakespeare provided that great gap of time so that such healing *could* take place, that the forgiveness should be so hard because, if the world is ever to change, to move toward that harmony scored somewhere toward the center of his dramatic world, we have to be capable of making such accommodations. Maybe we name these plays romances because our imaginations can't accept such vast magnanimity as realism; we have to pretend that it could happen only in the pastoral world of the story or staged drama. I was puzzled, I admitted, by her "recalcitrance"; hadn't she brought me up on fairy stories and, more to the point, hadn't she practiced such forgivenesses all her life?

"Don't romanticize your mother," she advised wryly. Changing the tack, I wondered what she made of Leontes' jealousy: was it too, too unreal?

"Two's company, three's a crowd," she replied, shutting me up with a maxim as she used to do when vexed. But then, after a while, she relented, thinking out ways to explain that sudden turn. She thought that Leontes really did love both Polixenes and Hermione but that the first love was formed in childhood, a bond so strong it was equal to a sexual relationship, or, more likely, had been. When Leontes took that love and put it into an adult scene and added his wife to it, the time frames, the elements wouldn't mesh. He couldn't have borne such a betrayal and so, rather than repressing the idea, his imagination gave it to him as reality, with no reference to the actual nature of his wife. Shakespeare plays with such triangulations everywhere, doesn't he? The tragic number is three. I remember wanting to ask why she could accept all that forgiving at the end of *Measure for Measure* as opposed to those elegiac last plays that I loved and that moved me to tears on every reading, but I never did.

I called Mother on her birthday, August 14. It was then that she asked me whether Virginia Woolf knew Shakespeare. I didn't know. But I pointed out that Woolf starred Shakespeare's supposed sister, Judith, in *A Room of One's Own* as an example of the fate of the gifted woman in the Renaissance. Why?

She laughed. She'd been reading *To the Lighthouse;* she needed knitting up herself after all those goddamned carpenters had been banging away in her house for months and it seemed to her, probably it was just a mirage, that Woolf wove some Shakespeare into her novel in odd ways.

We did, again, stop overnight on our way to Pennsylvania. Mother and I had what was to be our last long talk. Her questions and suspicions were tentative and random. She laughed about her comparative lit., as she called it, but described how she was reading two works at once which struck her, incrementally, as mirror images of one another. Both *The Win-*

ter's Tale and *To the Lighthouse* dealt with families, had long gaps of time between beginning and end, concerned mothers and daughters, death and rebirth. One could probably find that structure in many works, and I offered her *Pericles* and *Wuthering Heights* as examples. What had struck her in particular were the names and flowers. Mrs. Ramsay names her girls Rose and Cam(elia?); her surrogate daughter is Minta; her dear friend and antagonist is Lily. Mrs. R. is a gardener as well as a knitter and tries to create, constantly, a green world of beauty and fertility, to mend the greenhouse considered too extravagant by her husband. And, she underlined, the flowers were so special. She discoursed on the "red hot pokers" of male aggression which get into the garden but wanted, really, to show me the mythic dimensions that connected it to *The Winter's Tale*.[2] She pointed out Mr. Bankes's vision of Mrs. Ramsay's face seen in meadows of asphodel and Lily Briscoe's seeing her stepping across fields of hyacinths and lilies and disappearing, a kind of Proserpina going into the underworld. Mrs. Ramsay was a Ceres-Proserpina figure in one—a Hermione-Perdita, a Perdita-Flora. And, I should remember that Minta Doyle was afraid of bulls, her only fear, as if she were expressing some racial memory of rape by a male god—Jupiter—or by the animal nature of men. Cam, too, was frightened of a boar's head. Margaret was fascinated by this symbolism, for she felt that it was the way Woolf chose to represent fear of the loss of the innocent self, of the imminent intrusion of the male into the female space—a fear all women know at some level but one that bore the traces of Woolf's reading of Shakespeare. I remember that I doubted that, lecturing her a bit stiffly on the dangers of "influence" that wasn't specific enough. Shakespeare had always used sources, of course, and he built plays on myths, both explicit ones and implicit, too, as I would be arguing that *Othello* was linked to the myth of Nessus, as told by Ovid, translated by Golding. Well, she would just read me some lines from the play, spoken by Florizel to Perdita:

> The gods themselves,
> Humbling their deities to love, have taken
> The shapes of beasts upon them. Jupiter
> Became a bull, and bellowed; the green Neptune
> A ram, and bleated; and the fire-robed god,
> Golden Apollo, a poor humble swain,
> As I seem now. Their transformations
> Were never for a piece of beauty rarer,
> Nor in a way so chaste, since my desires
> Run not before mine honor, nor my lusts
> Burn hotter than my faith.
>
> (*The Winter's Tale* 4.4.25–35)

That could be the genesis of the name *Ram*say and the conception of those bulls. Then she read me the names of all the flowers and herbs mentioned by Perdita: hot lavender, mints, savory, marjoram, the marigold.

"It's farfetched to say that Minta Doyle was born in that line or that the golden aura given off so often is a reflection of 'the fire-robed god,' but now listen to these lines:

> O Proserpina,
> For the flowers now that, frighted, thou let'st fall
> From Dis' wagon; daffodils
> That come before the swallow dares, and take
> The winds of March with beauty; violets dim,
> But sweeter than the lids of Juno's eyes
> Or Cytherea's breath; pale primroses,
> That die unmarried, ere they can behold
> Bright Phoebus in his strength—a malady
> Most incident to maids; bold oxlips and
> The crown imperial; lilies of all kinds,
> The flower-de-luce being one.

(4.4.116–26)

I asked her if she had a copy of *Paradise Lost*. She hadn't. I heard in my head Richard Wilbur reading to us Milton's lines:

> Not that fair field
> Of Enna, where Proserpine gathering flowers
> Herself a fairer Flow'r by gloomy Dis
> Was gathered, which cost Ceres all that pain
> To seek her through the world . . .

(Book 4.268–72)

and wondered if Milton had got them from father Shakespeare or from Ovid. Woolf may have been stealing those flowers directly from Milton's "bogey," acknowledging or exorcising the literary father as forcefully as she seemed to be her actual father: those male gods. Margaret had tracked down the sonnet Mrs. Ramsay was reading—Shakespeare #98—and read that aloud, showing me the references to winter, to roses, to the seasonal, cyclical rhythms on which Woolf's book depended. Mr. Ramsay had taken his wife, as Dis had Proserpina, to a kind of seaworld, or underworld, in which she tried to keep those flowers growing, or present, to name her children for them, to plant carnations, those flowers so purely Perdita's, especially when they mixed with cabbages—as they did in the novels— but in which memory and circumstance as well as green Neptune, a ram, continually oppressed her: that winter side to her summer side, the pull down against the pull up. One part of her, Margaret speculated, really wanted to die, to get away from the household and its heaviness, its unremitting call on her sense of duty, her knitting for everyone. Everyone wants, in that book, to unify. It was, she said, as if everyone craved those romance endings or some version of those. Or to die. Mrs. Ramsay had reminded Margaret so much of her own mother. As if she were one more character that emerged from a text, we both saw Harriet Foster, my grandmother, materialize to be compared to Mrs. Ramsay. I remembered her as beautiful, regal, a mother of seven, poet and gardener memorialized in Phil's jumpy 1931 film as she cut and pruned her roses. She was not married to Mr. Ramsay, but to Harry Foster, a Victorian tradesman, failed inventor, hunchback, whose physical deformity was never mentioned at home but who embarrassed his children into a silence not broken until they were past middle age. I had always wondered how my grandmother had borne it—him; what odd sense of pity or idealistic girlhood hope had generated her assent to marry him. Mother herself didn't know. She had always thought of her mother as Florence Nightingale continually rescuing or nursing this small, conventional, scrupulously manicured man with one hump on his back, another on his chest. Margaret had thought that her mother's crippling arthritis might have been a sign of just how much she had borne. But, we agreed in a moment of guilty amendment, perhaps she had loved him for some self that we couldn't see. He must have read and reread Shakespeare himself for he had, always, the appropriate tag of quotation to fit any occasion. What could he have seen there, she wondered, and had he shared it with Harriet?[3]

We had moved back into our familiar territory: our family, hers, parents, the past. Ceremoniously, we thanked Woolf for creating Mrs. Ramsay out of whatever literary waystations, memories, and cross-pollination had served her and become, quite literally, a doorway into our own. Margaret remarked how reading had always been a bond for us, not only as images and plots to share but the physical closeness that began as a child sitting on her mother's lap.

"Lily wanted to become James and sit in Mrs. Ramsay's lap," she thought, "just as Virginia Woolf wanted to be returned to Julia Stephen's. To go back—that is a strong pull, isn't it?"

As we sat there, late at night, Shakespeare and Woolf opened on her coffee table, flowers in all her bowls, crewelwork pillows everywhere, and a half-knitted sweater for one of my sons spilling out of her knitting bag, I felt suddenly tyrannized by memory and literature and family, by so much love for my mother and the pathos it served up when there was such overwhelming conjunction: such collapse between the literal and the literary. Perhaps this feeling was implicated in Margaret's recalcitrant rejection of the romance ending—because she, too, felt it to be an artist's way of enacting that desire to sit again in a mother's lap, or represent an old woman's belated hold on dead mothers, or, I thought, an aging playwright's unincestuous embracing of the subject of daughters.

In recalling these few years and the ways in which my mother responded to Shakespeare, I see that most of her readings were entirely characteristic of her. The psychological insights into situation and character had always been natural to her, as had the intelligence aided by a memory capable of total recall. She had read the plays at so belated an age because she was, in a way, keeping her only daughter company. What Joyce, James, Melville, or even Emily Dickinson could not do, Shakespeare had; after some thirty years of separation on literary ground, we had met again. Not only had she found a language that enchanted her as no other ever had, but she learned to trust and take sustained pleasure and pride in her own mind. One astonishing aspect of her response seemed to me to be the ways in which she made the plays personal without sentimentality. And, more surprising, while her own world was dwindling in scope and marked by the growing angers of old age, perceived betrayals, and physical deterioration, she read the plays as freshly, or more freshly, than she might have as a young woman. She identified with admired characters and with a Shakespeare she intuited to be *there*. Why it was that we read so similarly we couldn't decide, nor can I now. My "liberty" and her "restraint," to use words from *Measure for Measure,* our difference in generation, education, and general good fortune seemed, finally, unimportant. With the exception of the romances and a few small details, we saw as one—"rightly," as Margaret insisted. She was certain that Shakespeare endowed his heroines and most of his women with a strength and depth superior to that of his men because he was saying that the patriarchal world he knew was tragic to the exact extent that it had banished the Falstaffian or the feminine from its precincts. That insight gave her the sense that she was re-envisioning her life. Shakespeare had "authorized" her to see that. Most remarkable to me—and to her—was her ability to knit together the various plays she had read, to juxtapose them, to make analogies between them in ways that surpassed what is usually termed scholarship. She never read literary criticism; her interpretations were her transaction with the text. Her wisdom, that perspective that I had counted on like a Rock of Gibraltar all my life, was, after all, the poetic gift of making the right comparisons and analogies; of seeing things "feelingly"; of sewing, like Virgilia, in the face of continual undoings.

To bring a sense of closure to this elegy for my mother, I need to go back to an early discussion we were having about Shakespeare. I had reproached her for giving in to some view I held about his life, a life that fascinated her as much as his art. I remarked that what was topsy-turvy was "that you're the daughter and I'm the mother, or so you seem to feel."

"No," she responded, "we're both the daughters. Shakespeare is the mother."

NOTES

1. I learned the story, or history, of Innogen from Professor Joseph Kramer of Bryn Mawr College during a lecture on *Much Ado About Nothing* which he gave to my class at the Curtis Institute of Music in Oct. 1987.

2. I discovered Maria DiBattista's brilliant essay *"To the Lighthouse:* Virginia Woolf's *Winter's Tale,"* in *Virginia Woolf: Revaluation and Continuity,* ed. Ralph Freedman (Berkeley: University of California Press, 1980), 161–88, while teaching the novel for the first time in a course on women's writing at Curtis. It would have confirmed all of Margaret's insights, and then some!

3. As I began this paper I wrote to my aunt, Bunny Foster, my mother's beloved sister-in-law, to ask her if Margaret had ever told her about reading Shakespeare. On January 10 I received her letter of response which included the following:

> Your question is intriguing. Phil and I have talked about it since your letter came. Did you know that his father, your grandfather, read Shakespeare over and over? He would read the newspaper in the evening and then take out Shakespeare to study till late, drinking that awful black tea that sat on the stove all day. I don't think Mag ever talked to me about it, but I'm sure she had read most of the plays many times. In the long winters up here, she would go through the bookcases and reread shelves. You must have the Delphian Society volumes, probably up in your Vt. barn. Phil remembers Mag taking her mother to the meetings on Tuesday nights. Dear old Delphian; that's how I busted into the family circle. When you were about six (you never had a babysitter before that!) I stayed with you while Mag went to meetings such as Delphian. It took a lot of persuasion to convince her that you would survive if I took "care" of you. Of course, Phil found his way into the picture then, so we persuaded her to go places.

NATALIE B. STRONG & CAROLYN R. SWIFT

Toward a Feminist Renaissance:
Woman-Centering Shakespeare's Tragedies

Feminist critics have suggested that Shakespeare's comedies, with their affirmation of wit and flexibility, validate women's strengths while the tragedies emphasize male struggles that ultimately victimize women. Loyal, funny, and beautiful Beatrice, bold and courtly Rosalind, brilliant and brave Portia celebrate female energy. But Desdemona's death, like Ophelia's suicide, shatters our dream of a self-determined, joyous, and healthy life. Even in the comedies, feminist critics note the limited roles of women characters who gain only one reward: marriage.[1] Women's Studies has received one benefit from the view that Shakespeare's plays limit women: more and more feminist critics of Shakespeare have turned their professional attention to women writers. Yet, we recognize that we do not want to deprive ourselves of the pleasure of teaching the playwright who, with good reason, is esteemed the greatest in English. Furthermore, we would then be leaving a powerful academic field to colleagues who, even with the best of intentions, may not satisfy the needs of female students any more than earlier professors did.[2]

As I (Carolyn R. Swift, the coauthor who is a professional teacher) look back on my life, it is clear that I have benefited from studying Shakespeare. Cynically, I observe that I am a tenured full professor while my peers who studied women writers are too often teaching part-time. But more than that, my ability to feel deeply is continually awakened and intensified by reading and discussing with my students all works, whether by women or men, in which the possibilities of the human spirit are probed profoundly. As I approach sixty, I recognize that Shakespeare has continued to enlarge my experience and enrich my point of view because Lear and Cordelia, Macbeth and Lady Macbeth, and Hamlet and Ophelia have all become parts of me. This cross-gender identification extends my world view as it increases my understanding of the characters. Yet, I still wonder if Shakespeare's plays may alienate a woman reader from her own gender since he shows some aspects of humanity only in men.[3] In his plays virtuous men like Albany and Edgar can conquer the enemy and live, but the excellent and powerful Cordelia dies after her brief victory in war. A patriarch like Lear arouses critical sympathy, but critics seem to detest the matriarch Volumnia. If Shakespeare limits women in ways that we dislike, does he then harmfully reinforce gender stereotypes just as our contemporary society does?

In spite of this constantly present question, the journals of students at Rhode Island College have offered me strong evidence that studying Shakespeare from a feminist perspective aids women students to respond fully to the plays as well as to understand the ways a patriarchal society has affected their lives. When they are encouraged to reach into their feelings and into their own lives as they read, my students become perceptive critics as they also gain the confidence that may free them both personally and intellectually. My goal is that they become more than the receivers of knowledge that women have in the past been encouraged to be. I hope that in their journals they begin to accept themselves as sources of knowledge and as the critics and creators of tradition.[4]

Since I am a feminist critic, my course in Shakespeare's tragedies, English 346 at Rhode Island College, asks students to observe the role of women in the plays as they are observing also Shakespeare's development of the tragic hero. To aid students to become critics, I believe that a feminist teacher must first aid them to experience their emotions as they read. As C. L. Barber recorded in his notes, "perhaps in all tragedy, certainly in some, we experience the almost unnameable qualm and dread that comes from opening the gates . . . gates which, once opened in our individual minds, make us tremble, regardless of the fate of the fictive protagonists, because *we ourselves* might go through, might go down into the whirlpool. . . . the fullest life is grounded in this terror."[5] I believe that all insightful criticism derives first from such personal responses to literary work. Academic custom binds scholars to a pose of "objectivity" that I believe reinforces hierarchy through complex, almost secret, forms of discourse. The more I examine my own critical processes, even my past historic/religious criticism seems to have been rooted in the same quest for identity that now motivates my feminist research. Writing a journal records my own approach to the abyss that Barber described; the journal has also helped me to stay in touch with the parts of the work that engender the passion that communicates. Communicating that passion is not, however, always easy. As I introduce my students to journal writing, I often disclose my fears about the differences among us. I hope that my vulnerability encourages my students to listen to me as a co-adventurer more than as an authority.

Early in the fall of 1987, I read to my class: "Two days after my fifty-ninth birthday, I struggle to write in this journal. I know what I want to say; the problem is saying it. Evidently at fifty-nine, I am still masked. I struggle with the fact that I call for honesty in my students while I fear disclosing myself since my values differ so much from theirs.... How much do students want to hear about a teacher's struggles anyway?

"I feel strongly that we respond to literature from our own needs. Shakespeare raises to a cosmic level our own daily, interior lives. If I talk about how alienated I felt in my middle-class childhood home, with two parents working and finally with a mother who went out of her mind, I might seem self-centered and self-pitying. But when we see in *Lear* a king's daughter exiled and the kingdom collapse from her father's self-centeredness and madness, we have great art. In fact, Lear's story is also my family's."

Natalie B. Strong, the student coauthor of this essay, was raised in a Portuguese-American family in which the father is a dominating force. We chose for her a pseudonym that would protect her privacy and at the same time project our hopes for both authors of this work. Like other collaborators, "we found that the line distinguishing academic from personal discussion faded," just as it had in our individual readings of Shakespeare. Although we are student and teacher, we found, like other collaborators, that our views meshed as we met almost weekly to read and revise drafts.[6] Natalie edited my drafts and refined my judgments on what had occurred for her. We both developed new ideas as we talked. The substance of this paper is based upon a dialogue between teacher and student in class, in journals, and as writers.

Natalie's perceptions confirmed me as feminist critic/teacher. Even though Natalie experienced tension from the difference in authority between us, she used it to increase her self-confidence and self-understanding. After the course ended, I asked her to describe her experience. She wrote,

> When I wrote in my Shakespeare journal, 'Lyn Swift teacher was present as recipient of my work, maybe as recipient of me personally as embodied in the journal. As I wrote, I was not *conscious* of her but rather of her method of teaching Shakespeare. I responded with feelings that a student does not necessarily divulge to a professor.
>
> The day the journal was due, I walked the length of my house, wringing my hands, tears streaming down my face, thinking "what have I done?" At that moment I was conscious that I would be handing my journal to 'Lyn Swift, a real person. How would she look at me? Am I overstepping the boundaries of teacher/student relations? Am I asking her for help? Should I rewrite the journal? I even left myself time to do that. Anyway, I dried my eyes and handed in my journal, on time.
>
> The writing of the journal has given me the confidence in other classes, no matter what the professor's teaching methods are, to state

what I really think and how I feel (although often masked in the formal student/teacher guise of objectivity). The journals I wrote taught me that my opinions and feelings count against both literary giants and teachers.

Intellectually and emotionally, we have influenced each other greatly. Natalie's role as student does not alter the fact that her comments in class and her journal have made me as much a student of hers as she has been mine. We are genuinely coauthors of this essay; yet in composing the final drafts of this paper, we used the benevolent but dominant first-person pronoun "I" with the more compliant "Natalie" because they seem to reflect accurately the power differential between us. This approach also expresses our own "deeply personal engagement" (Barber and Wheeler xxi) with Shakespeare, with our own critical processes, and with each other as feminists, as students, and as teachers. The reality is that I have more control over Natalie's life than she has over mine, yet we learned from each other as we allowed Shakespeare to enter our lives. As Shakespeare shows us, prerogatives shape us; the question is how sanctions are used, how free each person is to become herself. We can divide the kingdom with our children, but are we doing it only to aggrandize ourselves while we keep them in bondage, or are we also trying to free them even from ourselves?

Natalie's journal, written in 1987 to fulfill requirements for my upper-level course in Shakespeare's tragedies, is unique among the student journals that I receive in that it projects a complete drama. I suspect that its excellence derives from her having already kept a journal for a long time and from her having already begun to think and write about women's issues in an earlier class I taught on women's literature. Certainly, having earlier shared our journals with each other, Natalie and I had developed mutual trust. Yet it was studying Shakespeare's tragedies with their cast of female victims that provoked Natalie's realization of her own victimization; the women authors we read had created more hopeful images for women. Toward the end of the semester studying Shakespeare, Natalie summarized her new experience: "I think I've been . . . shaken up. . . . Execution and persecution seem to be the name of the game for this semester." Then in pain, she plaintively asked, "Why did Cordelia die? I need Cordelia to live . . .?" Natalie's journal is a courageous record of growing awareness of her role as victim and of the need for change. It documents the way at least one woman student benefited from studying Shakespeare's tragedies from a feminist perspective.

My students hand in journals three times during the semester, but throughout the semester (sometimes daily), I read my ongoing journals aloud in order to share my own current critical processes. Play by play the students and I react to our own experience as teacher and students with individual narratives of the ways the plays affect us as individuals. As I read *Richard III*, I wrote, "I hear the mothers and daughters crying, those vicious yet exploited queens who weep on stage as their fate is tied without their choice to Richards and Edwards and Georges. . . . I think of my own mother's anger, her attempts to gain recognition and understanding. Yet it was I who finally broke out, determined to govern my own fate and to achieve my own goals."

Natalie's journal began more objectively than mine. She sought rational causes for female acquiescence. She wrote, "They have nothing in their name." She saw that the women view their progeny as pawns in a long historic vendetta, and she commented that they are either "incredibly stupid and naive" or else "trying to survive in any way they know. . . ." She noted that these women, powerless against the men, victimize each other as well as their children and never break out of their passivity except verbally; even then, Anne curses herself when she curses Richard, his wife, "and any children they may have. Queen Margaret too believes that children are cursed at birth; she says to Richard, 'thou that wast seal'd in thy nativity' " (1.3.228). Later, when I studied Natalie's own personal drama as reflected in her journal, I saw that her attention had focused not only upon the victimization of women but upon their inability to protect children.

Natalie's journal entries on *Richard III* were analytic, but her journal became volcanic as she studied *Titus Andronicus*. When she examined her own process of moving from abstract analysis to a more excited response to *Titus,* she wrote: "I guess I couldn't see or believe it because it was so close to home. I couldn't really bring *Richard III* down to my level but I sure as hell could bring *Titus* down and I didn't want to because it would make me admit things that I didn't want to. I didn't want to see that my household almost mirrored Titus's and I identified with Lavinia and really didn't hate Tamora (well, only when she told her sons they could do what they wanted with [Lavinia]."

My own journal entry about *Titus,* which I read to the class, had continued reflecting my emotional responses. "*Titus Andronicus*—what turmoil! What chaos! Reading *Titus* is like experiencing a nightmare. Even the peaceful woods and fecund gardens become traps for the innocent and unwary. The play feels like unleashed, uncontrolled anxiety as I read it, perhaps because my day began with four hours spent attempting to balance my accounts. I approached the play already an anxious and fearful child in a world that I can not fully master, and as Quintus and Martius fall into the pit, I feel that I am also in a deep hole." After reading the class my journal entry about my own anxiety, I stressed the play's emphasis on the sacrifice of children, both male and female, to their fathers' goals. I expressed my own current awareness that I as a parent had too often seen my children only as extensions of myself. Natalie's response declared in vivid purple ink, "I went over the notes I took on *Titus Andronicus* and this is what I found—all I could see was Lavinia—maybe I identified with Lavinia and was blind to everyone else. I just couldn't get past the violence . . . women are treated as spoils of war; . . . people use one another to get ahead." But as Natalie centered on the play's violence, she began accusing herself rather than addressing the male brutality which Shakespeare dramatizes: "I think maybe it's me who has at times been extremely violent and now won't be violent at all—unless of course I really had to defend myself. Then I am sure I could just about kill someone. That's frightening."

Because I am interested as a critic in what creates our reactions to tragedy's violence, I asked Natalie to try to explore her reactions. Did the play enable women to get in touch with their own fury or with their fears of other people's savagery? In answer, Natalie began thinking about her reactions to violent films; she attempted to remain distant. "I don't watch or go to see violent films (that's a lie—I've seen *Rambo*—my father has all of them)." She then discussed an argument with a friend about terrorism against Americans in Iran. When the friend said that President Reagan freed the hostages, Natalie reacted, "It was probably just a publicity stunt on the day of his inauguration. . . . Do you actually believe he freed them?" Later, when I reread Natalie's journals, I realized that Natalie's turning point in her drama of self-discovery began when she confronted her own "lie" and then saw herself, her father, and the president as involved in varying degrees of masking truth. Unmasking required Natalie to turn from blaming her anger to facing the amount of violence that others brought into her life.

> Titus Andronicus is so upsetting because it's so believable. It's not only about physical violence but it's about violence within the family.
> Tamora—feeling the control taken away from her begging for the
>   life of her son having her request brutally denied
> Lavinia—utter helplessness w/o hands and tongue—defenseless

Natalie sympathized with both the brutal Tamora and the innocent Lavinia, rather than merely with Lavinia, because she recognized her own anger as well as her own victimization.

She continued in a volatile stream-of-consciousness to examine the way family emphasis on "honor" forces women to internalize shame; she described the family dynamic in *Titus* as "typical."

> About a year ago Elise and I made plans to go to see "Out of Africa," and as I was about to leave my father said no you cannot go—because you haven't finished your room—I was more than half way finished cleaning it. I begged him to let me go—nothing I said would sway him. I could

feel the violence come from him. I knew he was going to hit me. I degraded myself by begging—I hated him so much—I think maybe I still do—I couldn't communicate this to Elise. She was already at the cinema—When I finally got ahold of her she understood—did or does that mean that others have gone through the same thing? Even now it's hard for me to remember because I can feel the violence still in my father and the hatred rise in my throat and I calm myself down and try to put it out of my mind. Embarrassment also comes into this—I am embarrassed that I backed down but I'd been hit before and I don't like it. And embarrassed that I live like this—that my father's like this—but that part's not my embarrassment—maybe we haven't evolved at all from that sense of family honor where if you don't follow the rules then you've somehow shamed your family.

Not only did Natalie see her family's honor as demanding her own silence and creating her own shame, she also recognized that she feared for herself.

And yes, I could be 'lopped off'—he (my father) doesn't speak to his mother and wasn't talking to his father when he died and he's cut off all communication w/his brothers and sisters. And we (my immediate family) comply w/his wishes because if we don't—off comes a finger—my father believes in slow painful death. I think I am afraid that if I don't do his bidding then he won't speak to me anymore and I won't be part of my family—and I'd leave because I wouldn't want my being around to make anyone else's life miserable. It's strange because I like my father but I really don't. He really does try to be a good father but he doesn't know how and we have so much against him that we're not able or willing to help him.

Natalie's discussion then returned to considering the play in an abstract outline that could apply to both families—her own and Titus's. The violence in the play, she said, helped her to recall what she felt in the same situation: helpless, unsupported by a mother-figure in the face of male anger, and isolated by a union of parents with their son as opposed to their daughter. Her recollection of her own feelings also clarified her understanding of the roles that Shakespeare gives women and children in *Titus Andronicus*:

—[Tamora is] a mother who, . . . pushed to her limits, will resort to going after her jailer w/o regard for anyone but her own revenge. (I can hear my own mother saying, "I can fight him my own way now" and she uses my brother as a tool—if you don't take my son back (he's been thrown out a couple of times) then I don't come back—her not mentioning her 2 daughters as we sit in the parlour watching the 2 of them barter over the son. Strange but [we] weren't part of the negotiations—whatever they decided they just assumed we'd go along.

By looking at her own life honestly, Natalie was able to understand Tamora's anger. She saw female victimization in the play as beginning with male bonding that encourages even a mother, Tamora, to turn against young women as she seeks her own power. Natalie experienced Shakespeare's characters by reaching into herself.

In concluding the *Titus* section of her journal, Natalie examined the reasons *Titus* had caused her own emotional turmoil. She discovered that she did not want to admit that her home did not protect her. She also recognized that she did not want to face her desire to escape or her own fear that escaping would force her to test her own power.

> I think *Titus Andronicus* hurt me because it said some of the things I'd like to tell—that, no, everything isn't okay and I don't have that great of a home life and I am afraid I'll be lopped off. But I want to be but don't. I don't see the savage violence in *Titus* as [an answer] but my retreating to my room—my world of music and books [is not] the answer either. It's like I've been waiting all my life to leave but I have some goals and financially I'd be able to achieve some of them living at home. It's as if I cannot get away from this family thing—and if I failed on my own then I may be forced to come home and once I leave I don't think I'd ever come back. And it would ruin me if I did.

Natalie's willingness to explore deeply her reactions to *Titus* increased my understanding of the play. I saw for the first time irony in Lavinia's abduction. Lavinia got away when she was abducted, but not far enough. Because Lavinia has no choice but to allow men to determine her fate, she becomes dangerously entangled in their struggle for power. As Natalie asserted, return to family ruined Lavinia; she was lopped off. Natalie's story confirmed my view that the action in *Titus* is far more universal than early criticism of the play admitted.

Given the terrible implications of *Titus*'s universality, I felt frightened. I had discovered that Shakespeare told a story that resembled my student's life and that predicted a terrifying ending unless the student protects herself. I knew I was not a social worker nor a therapist, but I also knew that Natalie's journal might be a cry for help; I could not ignore her. I belong to that generation of feminist teachers who hope that feminist education will alter lives and ultimately change the world in which we all live; I would be irresponsible if I ran from the emotions my classes arouse. Therefore, when Natalie recounted being sent to her room, I wrote in the margin, "You are too old to be treated this way." When she wrote that she feared being hit, I wrote, "I'm horrified that you must endure this!" And when she wrote metaphorically about the possibility of "slow painful death," I wrote, "Please come see me about this." On the last page of the journal, I wrote, "Thank you for sharing your life with me. I'm sorry *Titus* is so alive and well still."

When Natalie came to my office, I expressed concern for her safety. Although Natalie felt that she was capable of handling the situation, I urged her to see a college counselor regularly for help in coping. Because many people still place a stigma upon those who seek counseling, I acknowledged that I often use therapists as facilitators of personal change. Later, Natalie told me that she had followed my advice.

When the class turned to *Romeo and Juliet,* Natalie's journal showed that she understood the source of its power: "I think *Romeo and Juliet* is still popular because the play is about a moment . . . that everyone has experienced—that's why it only takes two hours of traffic on stage—it's a moment that doesn't last." Natalie recorded her own resilience when she wondered why Juliet did not use any excuse to join Romeo. Like other students, she sought a new ending to *Romeo and Juliet.*

At the same time she once more looked at the hard facts of her own life. "I guess I can understand why Juliet just didn't leave her family to join Romeo in exile (it would have been ideal but how realistic is it?). When all you've known is what you've got, why should you leave to something that's unknown. You stay because you always hope that it will turn out all right. Hamlet had the same fear in his 'to be or not to be' speech. You always think you can . . . change the people around you." As a critic of Shakespeare, I observed Natalie's new insight that the hope of changing others may shape tragic endings. In addition, I felt confirmed in my view that insight into plays derives from our own experiences and potentialities. Certainly, Natalie was developing an ability to interpret Shakespeare's characters through seeing her own experiences in new terms.

Much of Natalie's remarkable journal concerns a struggle between future self-empowerment and acquiescence to other people's power. In reading *Richard II* at the beginning of the semester, she had fantasized that she would have made better use of power than Richard did: "If I were king, it [the quarrel between Bolingbroke and Mowbray] would have been settled right away." However, in reading *Julius Caesar,* Natalie expressed fear of her own use of power if she had Antony's gifts. She thought he is corrupted by the people's belief in him: "I'm not sure I'd trust someone who may have the power to make someone fruitful just by touching them. . . . If I knew I had the power [to end world hunger] I'd go ahead and do so but then hide in a cave somewhere so that no one could find me—people shouldn't have power like that—it corrupts and you begin to become selfish and tyrannical." Antony's blatant use of demagoguery had forced Natalie to acknowledge her fear of her own power at the same time that she understood more about the play. Other people's attributions, as much as Antony's belief in his own power, may in fact have caused his misuse of it in the last acts of the play. This critical perception was also vital to Natalie's own drama because it suggested that her own acquiescence may increase violence at home just as Brutus's increased Antony's.

When we read *Hamlet*, Natalie expressed fear of a future divine punishment. She noted in her journal that even in *Hamlet* unborn children are cursed as they were in *Richard III:* "Hamlet curses the children Ophelia will have. . . . Even Anne Bradstreet in her 'Morals' writings says that no matter how we raise our children or how good or bad parents are, God has control—he decides at birth what your destiny shall be." But Natalie proceeded to separate herself from Calvinism by commenting on a later American myth: "maybe that's why we like success stories of Abe Lincoln—someone breaks the pattern."

I read Natalie's *Hamlet* entry as recognizing individual responsibility to bring about change. In studying her journal, I thought that Natalie's ideas moved from an English reformation drama to an American Puritan poet to an American myth because Natalie was internalizing her reactions to Shakespeare and changing. If we recognize that people rationalize when they place the responsibility for their action on society or a commanding deity, surely then we can determine to do otherwise; we can take responsibility here, now, and elsewhere at the same time that we gain support from those who both love and respect us.

Natalie's drama of self-definition and self-determination continued in her discussion of *Othello.* I had pointed out that Desdemona's acquiescence in Act 5 stuns some viewers because of her earlier self-assertion. I asked the students to try to understand what might cause an assertive woman to become passive in a society that despises "disobedient" women. Natalie thought that the coexistence of love and fear causes Desdemona to internalize Othello's hatred. She wrote that as Desdemona blames herself she becomes paralyzed; Desdemona questions "what she's done to make Othello react with violence. She accepts blame [as she sings], 'Let nobody blame him, his scorn I approve' " (4.3.52). Natalie recognized that Desdemona's passivity finally makes her more vulnerable:

> The minute she becomes weak and lets her fate be taken from her own hands, he goes in for the kill. It must be horrifying to know someone is going to kill you and there is absolutely nothing you can do about it. Especially if it's someone you love. . . . Can you imagine someone waking you from your bed saying—have you said your prayers tonight because you're going to die? I'm not really sure if Desdemona believes it—she knows he's going to kill her, but you still cannot comprehend that your life will be over.

As our own drama continued in writing this paper, Natalie said to me, "It was like watching my own death if I stay at home." However, unlike Desdemona, Natalie became critical of Othello and questioned his love; she noted that Othello seems primarily to grieve his own loss, that he threw away his special possession, his "pearl," rather than that he ended Desdemona's life.

The death of Cordelia in *King Lear* catalyzed Natalie's desperation and her own desire to live vitally; "I need a daughter to live. I need a daughter to be okay and live and die of old age and be somewhat happy." I responded emphatically, "Yes." I had told the class that I first read *King Lear* when I was sixteen and was not able to reread it until I was forty. I had thought that the play had made me feel guilty about never understanding my father. Now I believe that when I was younger I recognized unconsciously the play's stress on the absence of Lear's love. Even audiences may prefer to blame the weak. I read from my journal, "In King Lear's sorrow, I surely experienced my own guilt at never appreciating my father enough. In Goneril's anger and Cordelia's exile, I also now see his ignoring me. Although I still react more as a daughter when I read *Lear* than as a parent, my children have questioned how much I understood their needs, and sometimes I echo Lear, 'In such a night/To shut me out?' " (3.4.17–18).

Natalie noted that society's creation of gender roles affects our reactions to the play: Goneril and Regan appear to be even "more loathsome" than Edmund because most people expect women to be more virtuous than men. In class I had asked whether Goneril and Regan had possibly modeled themselves on their father. Natalie continued exploring this question: "Maybe Regan and Goneril need 'something' from the 'nothing' he's given them emotionally as a father." Supporting this possibility, Natalie pointed to Lear's acknowledging Cordelia to be his favorite. "If you believe that a parent loves another sibling more than [he loves] you . . . you probably wouldn't (after a while) be able to see the love that a parent has for you; instead you would see only what you are not getting." Alienation from their father might then cause Regan to imitate Goneril's speech about love in the first scene "because they're stuck together against Lear/Cordelia. (I can see . . . my sister and I, bonding when my mother and brother left my father—we felt we'd been deserted—maybe G/R feel the same way,—they stick together and then go against one another because they know no other way." Within this drama of alienation, parent and child can feed on each other's need for love. "Like Goneril and Regan, we communicate by material things. If my father keeps my car in good working order, then I know he loves me. If I continue to sneak him fudge and talk about what we are going to put in our spring garden, then he knows I love him." When Natalie examined the young people in the play, she saw them as defying old beliefs about parent/child relations in "Nature's" scheme.

I too emphasized the children's independence. I read from my journal that Edgar restores his father's will to live only by lying about his father's fall from the cliffs. By defeating his father's chosen goal, Edgar affirms life. I began to think that Shakespeare had created a new Joan of Arc in Cordelia. She comes to England with her armies to save her nation as well as her father. In her lonely heroism, she epitomizes the "fools" of the play who love Lear unconditionally and follow him in spite of his folly. Although we may regret that the seventeenth-century author still needed to assign this female, heroic "poor fool" to die, we can note that in *King Lear* Shakespeare was once more able to envisage a female military hero.

Macbeth too stresses female strength. Natalie may have found a ritual for encouraging her own use of power when she decided to memorize the witches' speech. She noted Lady Macbeth's poise in contrast to Macbeth's unease at the banquet. As she mused upon Macbeth's imagination in a journal entry called "Macbeth sees daggers," Natalie thought about the way her imagination uses emotion. While she used to write about "the night life in our garden, more recently in my writings for journals I noticed my father ties the plants to sticks to make sure that they grow straight." She noted that she had chosen a constructive use of her hostility: "I guess my writing was my dagger."

The final play on the syllabus, *Anthony and Cleopatra,* is about human beings who change. For Natalie and me, the play reflects the changes that we each have experienced. I read to the class from my journal: "Because I have also felt the pull of past loyalties even as I have made new ones, I understand Antony's struggle with the voices of Rome that lure him from his present satisfaction in Egypt. As Antony in Rome ignores the claims of Egyptian passion and bargains for Roman respect, I have noticed that my ex-husband and I still fall into the roles of wife and husband as we tell each other to avoid too much salt. 'Yes, dear,' I respond when in Rome, while in Egypt I invite my new partners to jitterbug. As Cleopatra exchanged clothes with Antony and refused to have some squeaking Cleopatra 'boy' her, I too refuse roles that society assigns as suitable to respectable mothers and middle-aged academics. As a teacher and critic, I have turned from barren and limited New Critical textual analysis to a feminist criticism that allows me to draw from personal emotion as well as from reason. Like Antony, I have rejected in my personal and in my professional life a powerful majority culture that is alien to my current values."

Natalie responded in her journal that we use the Roman to protect our more vulnerable Egyptian selves. She commented that the play is a battle over ways of life, and she saw in Antony's choice of Cleopatra over Roman values a "continuation of *Othello*. As Othello chooses war over love or chooses to believe a friend of battle rather than his wife, Antony is somewhat uneasy believing Cleopatra . . . ," but he chooses her over his past soldier's life. In the struggle between Rome and Egypt and between Roman values and Egyptian values, Rome is " 'the stronger' but not 'the victor' " because all the Egyptians take their own lives, thus finally defying Rome. At the same time, Natalie asked, "What good is a dead martyr?" When Natalie rejected my validation of Cleopatra's choice of death on her own terms, I hoped she was reflecting her own choice of a constructive life. Our grief at the end of *Antony and Cleopatra* arises from perceiving that lovers can not win in a world dominated by Romans. Even so, the protagonists manifest the dignity of making choices from a passionate sense of self rather than from the need to survive minimally or from a desire for the empty respect of people whose lives we reject. Antony and Cleopatra choose risk on their own terms; what could be a better play for feminists to study?

We two women reading Shakespeare, a teacher in her late fifties and a student in her mid-twenties, found ourselves mirrored in the struggles of Shakespeare's English kings, the Danish prince, the Scottish and Egyptian queens that populate Shakespeare's stage. As Natalie and I discussed this essay, I began teaching my next class in the histories and comedies. Aware of Natalie's new claim to personal power and of my own continued struggle to empower myself, I read to them: "Shakespeare is my brother without a doubt because he lets me know how long we have been waiting to be heard. And in his plays, women are part of the process. While power finally rests in the play's male characters, the women are clearly making choices and helping to create the moral climate, whether they are victims or active villains as in *Richard III* and *Macbeth,* or heroes and active rescuers as in the comedies. Yet in my personal life, in my public life, in my professional career, I have in fact more power than they. As we teach and as we write, my students and I shape the tradition. None of us need accept the past as determining our current roles. We must pay tribute to our own talents as well as to the past; indeed, perhaps more to our own talents than to any person who does not help us to be our best selves."

As we wrote this paper, Natalie defined the relationships of characters within the plays in terms that also define the strength that feminist teachers of Shakespeare can offer students. "When you've always fought against power, and you finally have a victory, then what do you do with it? Where are your role models and guidelines in seeking to use power? The victims in the plays have no support from each other—like Hamlet—you wander about and try to make your own way. You can leave like Edgar or you destroy yourself like Hamlet. But Cleopatra has Iras and Charmian and sometimes Antony and she can choose her own ending."

Feminist teachers and students transform authority to female uses by creating a feminist renaissance. In Shakespeare, we find a startling depiction of our victimization, which may become the first step to empowering ourselves in this world. As Natalie's journal proves, Shakespeare still expresses our own past tragic losses in ways that strike our hearts. The next step for women might possibly be development of our own creativity in the benevolent patriarchal world of the reformed Leontes. Finally, however, the only way feminists can help Cordelia to live fully is to imagine "points of view other than those sanctioned by Shakespeare."[7] Like Peter Erickson, I believe that we can define our own female experience only by ultimately moving beyond Shakespeare's vision, becoming "self-chosen" women who refuse to be circumscribed by victimization or by benevolent male parameters.

NOTES

All quotations from Shakespeare are from *The Riverside Shakespeare* (Boston: Houghton Mifflin, 1974). We derived our title from Adrienne Rich's essay, "Toward a Woman-Centered University," in *Women and the Power to Change,* ed. Florence Howe (New York: McGraw-Hill, 1975), 15–16. We owe a special debt to Paula Bennett, who suggested this essay, and to Mariagnese K. Cattaneo, Judith K. Gardiner, and Marianne Novy, whose comments helped us to articulate its critical and pedagogical assumptions. In addition, we wish to thank Peg Kimball, Edith Kur, Laura McMurry, Shirley Sartori, Diana Siegal, and Jane Blood Strete for their patient and repeated readings, editorial suggestions, and encouragement. This paper was partially funded by the Faculty Research Fund of Rhode Island College.

1. Critics who have taken these points of view are Peter Erickson, *Patriarchal Structures in Shakespeare's Drama* (Berkeley: University of California Press, 1985); Carol Thomas Neely, *Broken Nuptials in Shakespeare's Plays* (New Haven: Yale University Press, 1985); Marilyn L. Williamson, *The Patriarchy of Shakespeare's Comedies* (Detroit: Wayne State University Press, 1986).

2. For a discussion of whether feminists should teach Shakespeare, see Lynda E. Boose, "The Family in Shakespeare Studies; or, Studies in the Family of Shakespeare; or, The Politics of Politics," *Renaissance Quarterly* 40 (1987): 723–24.

3. See Judith Fetterley, *The Resisting Reader* (Bloomington: Indiana University Press, 1978). An editor friend commented in the margin on this paragraph: "This is why I was so male-identified in my early years—I was rejecting the martyred, submissive female role I saw! It took me *many* years to change."

4. Mary Field Belenky, Blythe McVicker Clinchy, Nancy Rule Goldberger, Jill Mattuck Tarule, *Women's Ways of Knowing* (New York: Basic Books, 1986), 36–40.

5. C. L. Barber and Richard P. Wheeler, *The Whole Journey: Shakespeare's Power of Development* (Berkeley: University of California Press, 1986), xxi.

6. Elizabeth Abel, Marianne Hirsch, and Elizabeth Langland, ' "They Shared a Laboratory Together,': Feminist Collaboration in the Academy," in *Women in Academe,* ed. Resa Dudovitz, special issue of *Women's Studies International Forum* 6 (1983): 167. See also the Preface to Belenky et al., *Women's Ways of Knowing.*

7. Peter Erickson, "Adrienne Rich's Re-vision of Shakespeare," in this volume. Erickson's quotation from Adrienne Rich is from *On Lies, Secrets, and Silences: Selected Prose 1966–1978* (New York: W. W. Norton, 1979), 202.

MADELON SPRENGNETHER
Reading as Lady Macbeth

Recently, I have been reviewing my writing about Shakespeare: published and unpublished articles, in addition to notes and work in progress. In looking at this material, I can see the steady emergence of a reading of Shakespeare that critiques the concept of heroic individualism underlying the New Critical understanding of tragedy at the same time that it struggles to articulate another model of selfhood—one that draws for its definition on the process of reading itself.[1] I want to explore the interaction between these two concerns in this essay. In doing so, I shall also be looking at the issue of gender identification in reading and how this relates to my use of and discontent with psychoanalytic theory. In particular, I want to explore the figure of the "bad" mother and how she affects the process of empathy and interpretation. To illustrate these rather intricately interrelated matters, I will begin by reproducing the text of an autobiographical essay I wrote for presentation in a seminar on the psychology of theatrical experience at the International Shakespeare Association meeting in Stratford-on-Avon in 1981.

I have long thought that literary criticism is a form of autobiography, a rich, complex, mutable, and even unstable interweaving of texts and lives.[2] My own critical voice, stabilized to the extent that it can be on paper, distanced and "othered" in the way that one's own voice is "othered" in the process of psychoanalysis, reveals to me some of the ways in which a text speaks to me, moves me, reverberates in me, and alters my structures of perception. It acts not only as an articulation but also as a staging of relationship, both an unsettling and a reenacting of self in response to an implied other, to the text as other. While I recognize important differences between reading and watching or hearing, I want to consider some of the ways in which I have reacted recently to my teaching of Shakespeare's tragedies as a basis for some speculations about the power of literary and theatrical experience. I want to begin, however, by telling a story.

Not long ago I attended a play called *The Story of a Mother* by Martha Boesing, performed by At the Foot of the Mountain, a feminist theater group. There were several moments in the play designed literally to involve the audience. In the beginning, for instance, we were asked (if we wished) to say aloud our first names with those of our mothers, linked by the phrase "daughter of." I said: "Madelon, daughter of Roberta," feeling a little peculiar, in part because this was something I had never in my life said out loud. While most of the play enacted varieties of mother/daughter conflicts, there were other pauses in the action in which the audience was invited to make direct statements to our real or imagined mothers. I startled myself, at one point, by saying inwardly, "I don't want you to die." Clearly something in the play was touching me and in ways that surprised and even troubled me. And then I cried.

I remembered years ago in Vermont going to see a film called *Pather Panchali*—one in a trilogy directed by the Indian filmmaker Satyajit Ray. The story concerns a poor family struggling to survive on very little means. The father, in the hope of finding work, goes to the city, leaving his wife and two children. During his absence, the oldest child, a girl, falls ill and dies from a fever, while the mother, unable to provide the protein-rich food prescribed by the local doctor, watches helplessly. We do not see her mourn. When her husband returns, moreover, she cannot speak, and it is only when he asks for their daughter to give her the present he has brought that she breaks down and weeps, though the audience hears music, not her cries. At this point, I began to cry, and once I started, I couldn't stop. Embarassed by the intensity of my reaction, I hurried out of the theater when the film was over, only to find that I cried even harder when I got home. I was twenty-six years old; pregnant; having just started my first teaching job, anxious about the future (we were in the middle of the Vietnam War); and largely unconscious of my own history. The violence of my reaction was something I could only note; it was not something I could comprehend.

I can now see ways in which I felt like both the mother and the daughter in this film, but I am telling these stories here primarily to indicate some of the registers of feeling that may be activated by theatrical experience. Both the film and the play touched some need in me to grieve, as do most of Shakespeare's tragedies. The extent to which my reactions to *The Story of a Mother* and *Pather Panchali* involve my associations and identifications with women characters also seems important to me and more difficult for me to discuss when it comes to Shakespeare, where I find my reactions more painful and divided.[3] Not to mention them, however, would falsify for me the subject of response, and I want to explore in this essay both the positive and the negative poles of my relationship to

Shakespeare's plays. To do this, I must introduce the issue of gender response, drawing on some of my teaching notes, as a point of departure.

I have formed the habit in recent years (much as people talk to themselves as they grow older) of talking to myself on paper as preparation for my class lectures. While much of this communication remains private, some of it enters the classroom in muted form. For the purposes of this essay I am going to quote some passages verbatim, hoping that the more personal references will demonstrate the interweaving of self and text that I mentioned earlier as a process that is less isolationist than interactive and illuminating.

There are several strands of irritation in my jottings of the last few years. I will begin with an observation provoked by my witnessing the film version of *King Lear*, directed by Kosintsev.

> There are no good heterosexual relationships. The sexual plot revolves around Edmund and Goneril and Regan. In the Kosintsev film, this series of relationships is portrayed as perverse—Regan french-kissing her dead husband, Goneril thriving on rejection. She seems aroused by Edmund's brutality. Albany, on the other hand, is passive, but verbally abusive of Goneril. He sees her as monstrous for betraying her father. Is this a version of the suspicion that attends Desdemona's elopement? "If she deceived her father, she will deceive her husband." The father in each of these instances, is portrayed as having almost the rights of a husband. Is this a version of the man turning to his daughter for love because she can't challenge his power as successfully as an older woman?

Having said this, I began to enlarge the scope of my annoyance.

> Does the play as a whole in some sense portray a psyche? In other words, Goneril (and Regan) and Cordelia are two faces of the same woman. One is the nurturing mother, the other is the rejecting mother. What is missing here is the sexual woman. Or rather the rejecting mother is seen as the sexual woman.[4] For a woman to be sexual by definition is for her to be a betrayer. When it comes to actual sexual relations, the man dominates by becoming violent. Lear gets out of the violence trip by not having sexual relations with anyone. But his language towards his daughters is the language of violence. He curses Goneril's womb, and later sees all women as sexually corrupt. His rhetoric is equivalent to an attack. It is using words as daggers. See Hamlet and Benedick.

I tried out the notion that the play represents women in terms of male fantasy structures.

> The play seems on the whole to be dealing with male sexual problems. The women characters then correspond to the man's fantasies, or the fantasies generated by this kind of sexual dilemma. How is a woman to re-

spond to this? If she responds to the man's dilemma through empathy, what is she doing to her sense of self? It seems like an assent. The difficulty in terms of a woman's responses is that to feel with the man who has a distorted notion of women seems like agreeing with or complying with this vision. In a sense isn't this like the dilemma of the therapist, who must be able to empathize without losing his/her own awareness? A woman's awareness is thus double and ambivalent.

One sign of this ambivalence appears in a statement I came to at one point about vulnerability, the one area in which I felt that I could empathize.

> Maybe one should characterize the heroes of the tragedies as men unable to love. Othello is so blinded by jealousy that he can't appreciate Desdemona for what she is. Macbeth has no real conception of nurturing or caring, or rather suppresses it as quickly as possible. Hamlet confuses his mother with Ophelia and is so obsessed with betrayal that he can't function with women. The most obvious failures of these men is in the area of love and intimacy with women. They are self-absorbed, narcissistic. Where are the viewer's sympathies? Where are mine? I stand outside these men in part because I tend to identify more with the women whom they abuse than with them. They annoy me. I want them to shape up. It is in the area of vulnerability that I like them; I am willing to make excuses on these grounds.

I worried over these issues for a long time, returning to them again and again, attempting to understand a rising tide of feeling which I finally identified as anger. The structure of *Othello* allowed me to locate this feeling and to begin to explore my own involvement in it. While some of the passages I will quote about *Othello* overlap with those concerning *Lear*, they lead into the more complex and disturbing interactions I discovered in my reading of *Macbeth*.

> If I look at Othello from the position of Desdemona, I see a man who behaves outrageously, and it makes me angry. Angry that female sexuality is so distorted, that the very assumptions on which Othello's jealousy is based denies women autonomy, so that even if Desdemona is innocent she is deprived of the right to dispose of her body in the way that she chooses. It is assumed that if she were guilty of adultery that Othello's crime would be justified.

At least some part of my anger seemed to derive from the portrayal of an act of overt violence and my need to distance myself from it.

> The story is primarily about Othello and the bulk of the dramatic time is given to him. What are we to do if we don't find the portrayal of Othello sympathetic? To what extent does the language distance us emotionally from him, creating a kind of hypnotic effect? I tend to watch him, to

analyse him, to create my own emotional distance from him in order not to be vulnerable, to be in the position of Desdemona, to be murdered, the victim. Is interpretation a way of establishing distance or closeness— or a way of establishing closeness with safety?

Finally, having articulated so many responses based on my assumption of a gender position, my alliance with the female characters in the play, I asked myself one cross-gender question: "To what extent does Shakespeare identify with Desdemona, Emilia, Bianca? Where is the energy in this play? And what does it serve him to create these characters?"

I might as well have asked myself about my cross-gender involvements with the tragic heroes whose behavior towards women I found so distressing. In a series of notes I began to explore this issue—the degree to which my anger was theirs and theirs mine. I was concerned during this time with my periodic fascination with violent narrative.

> I was talking yesterday in the women's group about reading *In Cold Blood*. I was saying that I thought that it revealed some violence in my fantasies and that my attraction to the book reflected at some level what was going on inside me. I am feeling that it somehow has to do with my talking this fall more fully in therapy about my stepfather's death, with my renewed sense of pain about what happened to my family.[5] Shirley said that the murder of the Clutter family and the Tate murder is about the destruction of a family. Three years ago I was obsessed with violence and was reading narratives having to do with murder, specifically with people who kill members of their own families. I seem to be going over the same ground somehow now.

I began to consider the significance of family plots, family stories.

> Why are families so powerful? Is it because that is the context in which we learn how to be, in which we learn to speak, in which we come to understand the world? When it is taken away from us we feel deprived of our sense of orientation, of our ground. Being close to my family puts me in touch both with my deepest fantasies about comfort and warmth and with my deepest fears about loss. To have a family makes me feel both safe and frightened. In a culture where there is no unified understanding of the world, in which there are no commonly assented-to myths, families become all the more significant as providing the first context for personal myth, which is necessary for survival.

Not surprisingly, I was reading the tragedies during this time as stories of family catastrophe.

> Macbeth kills a "father" of the country, father of a child whom he fears, and the wife and children of a man he fears. His wife dies as a consequence, and then he dies. Lear sets in motion the gears that involve the

death of his entire family, of his daughters and himself and one of their husbands. Othello kills his only kin, his wife. Are these primarily heterosexual tensions, as I have argued, or are they other? What is it about families that calls for this kind of destruction? Hamlet is asked to kill his uncle and his family dies as a consequence.

If the comedies represent one kind of family myth, moving, as they do inevitably towards marriage, then the tragedies, I thought, may be concerned with the dissolution of this comic form. "If Shakespeare is writing about the destruction of families in the tragedies, why is this so, and why does he violate the conclusions of the comedies in order to do this? There seems something deliberate here, a kind of vengeance against the happy endings of the comedies." These thoughts about family violence and the destruction of the comic myth of union gradually came to focus on *Macbeth*.

Sometime last spring my musings about bad or catastrophic families found a disturbing counterpart in an actual event that intensified my questions and reactions to *Macbeth*. A little girl named Kathy Hodo, a fifth-grade schoolmate of my daughter, was murdered by her stepfather, who also raped and murdered her older sister, killed her brother, attempted to kill her mother (who escaped), and ended by commiting suicide. Kathy was eleven years old, and she and my daughter were friends. They had recently exchanged birthday party invitations. We were both profoundly upset by this story—a story that touched fears in both of us about failures of protection.

> What I felt in talking with Jess in the car going to Martina's house was that she was threatened by the idea that the mother would leave the house, abandoning her children to a murderer. She began by saying that she would not do that, that she would stay and try to calm him down. She began taking the role of the mother and reconstructing the situation in a more protective way, saying that she would stop arguing with him and wait until he was calmer, then phone the police and tell them not to turn on their sirens when they came or knock hard on the door, so as not to alarm him. She was imagining herself in the role of protector in place of the mother who was deficient. I wanted to reassure her that I would take care of her, that she is safe with me. Her immediate fear was that I or someone else might "go crazy" and that she would have no warning, no way to defend herself.

We both wanted to avoid the position of the victim.

> The image of Kathy Hodo lying behind the laundry machine, shot seven times because she tried to get up, is particularly devastating to me. I think that what this story touches in me is not so much fears of parental

violence, as fear of being allowed to die, of being not cared for, which may go back to my sense of being alone and frightened when my father died.

We were both haunted, I think, by the specter of an unprotective mother, my own haunting being doubled by my sense of responsibility as a mother myself. I was also reading at this time *The White Album* by Joan Didion, another woman preoccupied with mothers and, not incidentally, with bad families.

> The image of the ruined greenhouse stands both for the theme of para-dise lost, the protective family lost or betrayed, for the nostalgia for the past and preoccupation with history in her work and for the sense of the disruptiveness of the present, the absence of ordering narrative or plots that can cope with the surreal quality of modern life. She does not revel in this surreal quality, but rather tends to associate it with stories of fam-ilies gone awry, with the story of the parents who abandon their child on the highway for instance, the woman who burns her husband in his Volkswagen while he is sleeping. These are stories in part of people who trivialize themselves by not having a moral sense, and by not taking responsibility, but they are also stories of the failure of families, of the parent/child relationship, which is symptomatic in her novels of deep trouble.

My reading of *The White Album* provided another series of connections: the Manson family—Roman Polanski—*Macbeth*. By circling with fascina-tion and horror around these stories I was coming closer to the source of my own anger and my involvement with the figure of the bad mother.

My teaching of *Macbeth* this spring coincided with my watching a televised production of Zola's rather gruesome story of a woman and her lover who conspire to kill her husband: *Therese Raquin*. The conjunction of these two stories of murder and its self-destructive consequences dis-turbed me deeply, though I could not at first locate the source of my un-easiness, the tender spot in my psyche. The problem first appeared in the form of the witches.

> This play is bothersome to me in part because of the way in which women are portrayed. The witches are malevolent. There is nothing like this anywhere else in Shakespeare's plays. Why? There is some sense in which Macbeth's dilemmas have to do with women. The witches ally themselves with Lady Macbeth in being betrayers of men, and of anyone in the condition of innocence or vulnerability. How many references are there in this play to mothers who fail to protect their children? To what extent does this play revolve around the notion of a destructive mother, one who kills her children? In a sense the deep fantasy of the play is child

murder, isn't it, as it reveals itself late in the play. The horror of this is revealed in the killing of Lady Macduff and her children.

This speculation allowed me to think more closely about anger, my own and that of the play.

Where is the anger in this play? Is the anger that is denied an anger directed against women for failing to protect, to nurture, to guard innocence and weakness? Against this fear the concept of manhood as invulnerability is erected, or the concept of manhood as based on violence. To wield the sword oneself is to escape the blood of a woman.[6] None of this works, of course.

Finally I brought this home.

Is my anger with my mother stated in the following form: I feel that she didn't protect me enough? Is this what Shakespeare's heroes are seeking and not finding? What they want is protection and women seem not to offer that.

Being angry permitted me to see ways in which I saw myself in the main characters.

Macbeth bothers me because I identify with both Macbeth and Lady Macbeth. They are my negative fantasy of myself. I am afraid of being them. Is it the power of my anger that makes me feel afraid or evil, bad, someone to be punished? Anger, guilt, self-punishment. Is this the progression?

I had arrived at some understanding of a part of myself that horrifies me, not by distancing myself from Macbeth but by identifying with him. My formulation of the tragic process at this point reads as follows: "Is tragedy about anger in some way, about anger so deep that it eventuates in images of families destroyed in violent ways?" In coming to this idea, I had, despite my empathetic alliance with the female characters against the heroes, to be able to make some kind of cross-gender identification. The area in which I was able to do this was the area in which men and women share a significant relationship with a woman—with a mother. Having come to this awareness, I could see better the nature of my ambivalence toward the tragic hero. To the extent that I focus on the arena of sexual conflict, the heroes' obsessions with cuckoldry, for instance, I find my empathy broken or impeded and form my alliances with the women. To the extent that I see the hero, not in the position of adult, but in the position of child, I can find aspects of myself revealed in him.

The perception of the hero in the position of child, finally, was keyed to my attempts to understand another crucial aspect of his experience, that which concerns his awareness of vulnerability and dependence. I tended to understand the rage unleashed in the tragedies as generated by the fear of unprotection, specifically the fear of being abandoned by a woman, and the resulting space opened up in the hero, one in which he explores his feeling or vulnerable self.

> In Shakespeare the fundamental process is one of breakdown of artificial images of the self, or facades of selfhood, which in the tragedies reveals a chaos within, an inner reality that is so unknown, so unsuspected that it either threatens or produces madness. The system of relations by which the tragic hero has made his way fails him and for a while he cannot reorganize them, cannot see an alternative, another order or relation. This threatening inner world he associates with women, with weakness or vulnerability towards powerful women. The world of relatedness, of emotional recognition, makes him vulnerable. To remain in control, the tragic hero must remain emotionally removed, isolated. The part of himself of which he is afraid he considers feminine.

I have quoted at such length from this essay because it illustrates what I mean by saying that literary criticism participates in autobiography. Implicit in this essay, moreover, is a view of Shakespearean tragedy that I have expressed more pointedly in my published essays, all of which focus on the hero's violence toward women as a defense against vulnerability, specifically against the "femininity" he feels within. But this essay raises further questions (beyond the scope of my inquiry at the time) that touch on the mutually reinforcing ways that literature and psychoanalysis encode gender. For me, these questions coalesce around the figure of the mother.

In my exploration of cross-gender identification I find myself in sympathy with the hero's rage against the condition of unprotection and, in that sense, childlike. Like the tragic hero I feel, momentarily, at least, betrayed by a woman on whom I have wanted to rely for my sense of safety and well-being in the world. Pre-Oedipal psychoanalytic theory supports this kind of infantile identification at the same time that it idealizes the figure of the mother as an unambivalent source of gratification.[7] Such an idealization supports a split image of the mother: when she is good (devoted to the needs of her infant), she is very very good, but when she is bad, she is pathological. It becomes tempting, from this standpoint, in responding to Shakespeare's tragedies, to adopt the hero's stance of heroic suffering, to concur with his view that he is "more sinned against than sinning," and to conclude that he does not deserve his fate. To the extent that psychoanalytic theory relies on a vision of mother-infant symbiosis, or a timeless moment of maternal plenitude, which arouses expectations of women that are impossible of fulfillment, it is complicit with such a view. Because I believe, with Juliet Mitchell and others, that psychoanalysis reproduces in itself the essential features of the culture that it analyzes, I am not surprised to discover in Shakespeare's plays the good mother/bad mother split that plagues Freudian and post-Freudian theory.[8] Such a consideration sets a limit, of course, to the usefulness of (pre-Oedipal) psychoanalytic theory as a method of interpretation. Feminist analysis can take us further, I believe, toward an understanding of the status of the tragic hero as well as that of the pre-Oedipal mother.

In rereading my essay for the Stratford conference, I am most intrigued by my attempt to probe my identification with Lady Macbeth. How many readers, I wonder, would admit to such an alliance? Doesn't she, after all, embody our worst cultural fantasies? And yet Macbeth himself carries out the murderous intent she so fearlessly and cold-bloodedly articulates. He becomes what she imagines and thus participates in her mentality, including her psychic disintegration. If the gender expectations of our culture lead us to dissociate ourselves from her and to take the side of Macbeth (however unattractive that alternative), perhaps this has something to do with Shakespeare's own ambivalence concerning gender, one that leads him to withdraw from the most radical aspects of his portrayal of the tragic process.

I see the tragic hero's anxiety concerning intimacy as that which fuels his rage against women. To be "feminine," or to be dependent on a woman, threatens him with a loss of autonomous selfhood. And yet the hero often appears to seek this very condition—that is to say, to pursue or to desire his own destruction. Shakespeare himself, I believe, is interested in deconstructing the hero's mythic and monolithic construction of self; the tragic process involves a radical undoing of the hero's "perfect soul" (*Othello* 1.2.30) as manifest in his conviction of the rightness and wholeness of his identity. What interests me here is that such a deconstruction, for Shakespeare, is what constitutes tragedy itself. In other words, the hero's loss of a unified identity is catastrophic—to himself as well as to those who frame a context for his self-knowledge. I take this as an angry resolution, one that satisfies the hero's divided impulses toward women and toward the condition of femininity in general.

Shakespeare's critique of heroic individualism is finally inseparable from his ambivalent representations of femininity. To the extent that the hero's loss of autonomous selfhood causes him to fall into femininity or actually subjects him to a woman, it also appears as a loss of manhood. Moreover, if this process may be conceived or imaged as a form of sexual consummation ("But I will be a bridegroom in my death, and run into't/ As to a lover's bed." *A&C* 4.14.99–101), it can also appear as a violent fragmentation ("Cut me to pieces, Volsces, men and lads, / Stain all your edges on me." *Coriolanus* 5.6.110–11). This double view of the hero's fate—to be fused with the object of his desire as well as to be torn apart or mutilated—means that for Shakespeare the deconstructed self has something of the appeal of the death instinct that Freud understands as the desire to return to an inorganic state.[9] The hero defines himself, in part, through his resistance to this siren call.

Shakespeare's tragic hero resists women to the same degree that he resists the femininity he feels within, thus projecting onto women the condition of otherness that informs the awareness of non-self-identity he can achieve only at the cost of his life. This process, in turn, makes it difficult for us to empathize with characters like Goneril and Regan or Lady Macbeth, who seem to body forth our culture's deepest fantasies about "bad" mothers, its angriest representations of the woman who fails to provide total gratification. Yet for the reader to identify against Lady Macbeth, against the witches, is to reproduce the dilemma of Shakespeare's tragic heroes—to rage against the woman without who represents the woman within. Shakespeare, of course, is not unusual in asking us to align our sympathies with a hero who stages his inner conflict through his relations with an elusive or enigmatic woman. For the female reader, however, such an alignment may be particularly painful, causing her, for instance, to identify against the mother and hence to take sides against her sex.

I believe that there is another way to look at this problem, one that acknowledges the inner lack that structures the self and desire at the same time that it avoids the agonized position of Shakespeare's tragic heroes who make war on this awareness.[10] Shakespeare's critique of heroic individualism, however powerful in itself, does not go far enough. Like Freud's analysis of the death instinct, it leaves intact the concept of maternal plenitude that provokes the split image of the good/bad mother. Only if we imagine that there was once an all-gratifying mother, whose subjectivity is subsumed in that of her infant, can we conceive of her subsequent revelation of indifference or autonomy as a betrayal.[11] The "bad" mother, as we have culturally constructed her, is the ungratifying mother, the one who has designs and desires of her own, whose subjectivity is neither transparently self-evident nor simply coterminous with that of her child. But if we can begin to conceive of the mother as separate, or other, from the beginning, we may be able to construct a different set of fables by which to comprehend the drama of infant development as well as the enigma of selfhood it enfolds.

In Shakespeare's tragedies, a woman who lies or who is suspected of lying arouses fantasies of sexual betrayal, which in turn project the hero into a state of inner chaos. It is as though he cannot bear the thought of a woman's (mother's) infidelity. I believe that the figure of mother as liar is at issue here and furthermore that this figure transposed into the "bad" mother haunts patriarchal culture in the guise of the outcast, the witch. But she is also (in the context of *Macbeth)* an oracle, one who speaks the truth in riddles because it cannot be expressed otherwise. I propose that we give up the good mother/bad mother dichotomy that informs psychoanalytic theory and adopt instead the model of mother as uncanny other, or in Shakespeare's terms, as liar, as witch.

There is in fact a model for such a construction in Shakespearean tragedy—in his portrayal of Cleopatra, who is simultaneously mother, lover, liar, witch, and whore. The issue of her fidelity, in particular, is never resolved, so that she remains at some level unknowable. For a moment, it seems, Shakespeare was able to sustain a less than agonized view of femininity as that which renders oneself a stranger to oneself. Deconstructing the myth of maternal plenitude, which presumes a unified and idealized subjectivity, introduces the possibility of a selfhood that acknowledges the presence of the liar within. Psychoanalytic theory would do well, I believe, to follow such an example.

This brings me back to the subject of reading, and in particular to the form of the essay I wrote in 1981. Some models of reader response seem to be based on a version of heroic individualism—positing either an authoritative reader or an authoritative text.[12] To the extent that I can theorize about my own practice, I would say that there is in both reader and text an element of otherness that renders the process of their mutual interaction both unpredictable and unstable. In 1981 I expressed this in part as follows:

> What writes itself as a poem (or novel, or play, etc.) is also writing itself as the unspoken poem, as the wake or linguistic drift of language. No matter what we say we cannot achieve a condition of language in which there is no wake, or resonance, or echo, or trace. And it is the trace that calls to us, that impels us, that speaks to us, moves and haunts us and yet that we cannot ever make wholly conscious, wholly articulate or known. Anymore than we can be wholly known to ourselves. This more than anything else accounts for the fact that analysis is interminable. We never fully recover the aspect of ourselves that is resonant to consciousness. Every story that we tell will create its own specter, its own private ghost.

Reading, I believe, asks us to hazard our sense of individuality and autonomy by acknowledging the duplicitous voice of the text at the same time that we risk an encounter with the inarticulate in ourselves. The activity of literary criticism, for me, creates a narrative out of this process, one that is by its very nature mutable and finally unfaithful to the truth it seeks to define. It lies like the text, like the self. In this sense it is also au-

tobiography, a form of self-creation that is intertextual, allusive, even pla-
giarized, subsisting through the voice and the words of the other. In such
a construction there is no clear line of demarcation between reader and
text, any more than there is a form of selfhood that is not implicated in the
constellation of relations that we know as family, as culture. Reading, at
its most challenging, calls into question the identity that I think I know,
the one that is familiar. It haunts me, it inhabits me, like the voice of Lady
Macbeth.

NOTES

1. The following essays all deal with Shakespeare's deconstruction of heroic
individualism: "'I Wooed Thee with My Sword': Shakespeare's Tragic Para-
digms," in *Representing Shakespeare: New Psychoanalytic Essays,* ed. Murray
Schwartz and Coppélia Kahn (Baltimore: Johns Hopkins University Press, 1980),
170–87; "'And When I Love Thee Not': Women and the Psychic Integrity of the
Tragic Hero," *Hebrew University Studies in Literature* (Spring 1980), 44–65; "'All
That Is Spoke Is Marred': Language and Consciousness in *Othello,*" *Women's Studies: An Interdisciplinary Journal,* Feminist Criticism of Shakespeare, vol. 2, ed.
Gayle Greene and Carolyn Ruth Swift, 9 (1982): 157–76; "Annihilating Intimacy
in *Coriolanus,*" in *Women in the Middle Ages and the Renaissance,* ed. Mary Beth
Rose (Syracuse: Syracuse University Press, 1985), 37–49. The first three of these
essays were published under the name Madelon S. Gohlke. For recent non-
psychoanalytic critiques of heroic individualism in Shakespeare see Catherine Belsey, *The Subject of Tragedy: Identity and Difference in Renaissance Drama* (London:
Methuen, 1985), and Jonathan Dollimore, *Radical Tragedy: Religion, Ideology and
Power in the Drama of Shakespeare and His Contemporaries* (Chicago: University of
Chicago Press, 1984).

2. I have stated this position more explicitly and somewhat more theoreti-
cally in "Re-reading *The Secret Garden,*" *College English* 41 (April 1980): 894–
902, and in "Ghost Writing: A Meditation on Literary Criticism as Narrative," in
The Psychoanalytic Study of Literature, ed. Maurice Charney and Joseph Reppen
(New York: Analytic Press, 1985), 37–49. The first essay appeared under the
name Madelon S. Gohlke.

3. The issue of women readers' gender identifications in reading has been
much discussed among feminists. For a careful psychoanalytic treatment of this
subject see Judith Kegan Gardiner, "Psychoanalytic Criticism and the Female
Reader," *Literature and Psychology* 26 (Fall 1976): 100–107. For an illuminating
discussion of the divided responses of a woman reader of Shakespeare see Linda
Bamber, "The Woman Reader in *King Lear,*" *The Signet Classic Edition of King
Lear,* ed. Russell Fraser (New York: New American Library, 1987), 291–300.

4. Most of the personal notes I am quoting here date from the late seventies.
Since then feminist criticism of Shakespeare has dealt rather extensively with some
of the issues I was puzzling around privately. For a particularly fine reading of the

way that Lear regards his daughters as mothers see Coppélia Kahn, "The Absent Mother in *King Lear,*" *Rewriting the Renaissance: The Discourses of Sexual Difference in Early Modern Europe,* ed. Margaret Ferguson, Maureen Quilligan, and Nancy Vickers (Chicago: University of Chicago Press, 1986), 33–49.

5. When I speak of violence here, I do not mean literal physical violence, but rather the sense of inner psychic assault that I felt as a result of my father's accidental death by drowning when I was nine years old and my stepfather's sudden death from a heart attack when I was eighteen.

6. Janet Adelman examines the intimate workings of this fantasy structure in "Born of Woman: Fantasies of Maternal Power in *Macbeth,*" in *Cannibals, Witches and Divorce: Estranging the Renaissance,* ed. Marjorie Garber (Baltimore: Johns Hopkins University Press, 1987), 90–121.

7. For a lucid critique of the failure of psychoanalysis to imagine the mother's subjectivity see Susan Rubin Suleiman, "Writing and Motherhood," in *The (M)other Tongue: Essays in Feminist Psychoanalytic Interpretation,* ed. Shirley Nelson Garner, Claire Kahane, and Madelon Sprengnether (Ithaca: Cornell University Press, 1985), 352–77. I have also written about Freud's idealization of the pre-Oedipal mother-son relationship and its consequences for psychoanalytic feminism in "(M)other Eve: Some Revisions of the Fall in Fiction by Contemporary Women Writers," in *Feminism and Psychoanalysis,* ed. Richard Feldstein and Judith Roof (Ithaca: Cornell University Press, 1989), 298–322.

8. Both Juliet Mitchell, reading psychoanalysis from a Lacanian perspective, and Nancy Chodorow, who reads through object relations theory, regard psychoanalysis as a product of patriarchy as well as a means of analyzing it. See *Psychoanalysis and Feminism* (New York: Pantheon Books, 1974) and *The Reproduction of Mothering* (Berkeley: University of California Press, 1978).

9. For Freud, the death instinct seems to be identified with the return to the mother, a condition that is both profoundly desired and feared. Whereas cultural development, in his view, depends on renunciation of the mother, every organism desires its own undoing in the form of death, the cessation of striving and the return to a state of undifferentiation and quiescence. Freud's exposition of the fort/da game of his grandson Ernst makes clear his association between this regressive urge and the desire for fusion with the mother. See *Beyond the Pleasure Principle, The Standard Edition of the Complete Psychological Works of Sigmund Freud,* trans. and ed. James Strachey, 24 vols. (London: Hogarth Press and the Institute of Psycho-Analysis, 1986), 18: 3–64.

10. For a particularly illuminating discussion of the Lacanian view of the ego as structured around lack see Jacqueline Rose's Introduction II to *Feminine Sexuality: Jacques Lacan and the école freudienne,* ed. Juliet Mitchell and Jacqueline Rose (New York: W. W. Norton and Pantheon, 1985), 27–57.

11. I deal with this issue more extensively in "(M)other Eve: Some Revisions of the Fall in Fiction by Women Writers." See also Jane Gallop, "Reading the Mother Tongue: Psychoanalytical Feminist Criticism," *Critical Inquiry* 13 (Winter 1987): 314–29, and Martha Noel Evans, *Masks of Tradition: Women and the Politics of Writing in Twentieth-Century France* (Ithaca: Cornell University Press, 1987), 220–28.

12. Patrocinio Schweickart describes this problem as follows: "[M]ainstream reader-response theory is preoccupied with two closely related questions: (1) Does the text manipulate the reader, or does the reader manipulate the text to produce the meaning that suits her own interests?" Schweickart proposes a dialectical, rather than a dualistic, process of reading in order to facilitate feminist interpretation. Jonathan Culler offers a nonauthoritative view of reading derived from deconstructive theory. I am indebted to both positions. See "Toward a Feminist Theory of Reading," in *Gender and Reading: Essays on Readers, Texts, and Contexts,* ed. Elizabeth A. Flynn and Patricinio Schweickart (Baltimore: Johns Hopkins University Press, 1986), 31–62, and "Reading as a Woman," in *On Deconstruction: Theory and Criticism after Structuralism* (Ithaca: Cornell University Press, 1982), 43–64.

CAROL THOMAS NEELY
Epilogue: Remembering Shakespeare, Revising Ourselves

These essays, documenting about three hundred years of women's responses to Shakespeare, are remarkable for their convergence, and this will be the focus of my discussion. By this focus, I subordinate their particularity and the differences among them—differences of historical period, class, genre, nationality. What strikes me first is the extent to which these women's responses to Shakespeare galvanize their critique of patriarchal society's subordination of women and energize their capacity to fight this subordination. The women responding appropriate Shakespeare the artist as a "double" (H.D.), an "ally," a "mirror image" (Woolf), a "mother" (Hutton) by revising his characters, plots, endings. The strategies of this appropriation seem to me to incorporate elements of what, ten years ago, I identified as three modes in which contemporary feminist critics approach Shakespeare: compensatory, justificatory, and transformational.[1] Taken together, these women's responses to Shakespeare and the essays articulating them incorporate all of the modes in various combinations and, in their rewritings of Shakespeare, give substance to the third mode, the transformational.

In order to examine the process whereby these women construct Shakespeare, I will look at three kinds of response which parallel my three modes of feminist criticism, and go on to characterize the revisionary genre of feminist elegiac romance which is often generated by women writers out of their responses. Then I will ask why these female readers/ writers are able to command their precursor with so little anxiety, exploring what conditions make identification, empowerment, and revision possible and what obstacles and resistance to this appropriation present themselves. Finally, I will suggest some connections between the women writers' responses to Shakespeare and certain aspects of contemporary theory.

The first response, comparable to the mode of contemporary feminist criticism I designate "compensatory" (although it is here a less oppositional process than this designation suggests) is to identify with and rewrite aspects of the Shakespeare text which enable women's assertiveness, agency, resourcefulness. It is characterized by identification with the language of the text and with some female characters, by the foregrounding of female friendships. At the onset it is Shakespeare's language, apart from character or plot, which turns women on—which leads Dickinson to read Shakespeare "first" when she can see again ("Give me ever to drink of this wine"), which changes Woolf's mind about the playwright ("I have spotted the very best lines in the play"), which catalyzes Margaret Hutton to find "Lewhuttons" and generate her own. This text I find, after initial resistance, similarly endows my students with a sense of their own capacities—as it has my own children whose favorite putdown (when younger), borrowed from Falstaff, was "you bull's pizzle" (*1HIV* 2.4.47). The impact of Shakespeare's language, although inspiring awe and a sense of being "a little oppressed," as Woolf puts it, quickly becomes energizing for many of the writers.

Awe at the language is accompanied by an intense sense of connection with women characters who have the ability to speak wittily, act successfully, generate their own plots, their own endings—especially Rosalind, Beatrice, Helena, and above all Cleopatra. These characters are important to women readers, not just for their assertiveness, disguise, wit, passion, but for the female friendships which, central to their representations, are felt to have been disregarded by male critics. But the women's identifications are selective, discriminating, unsentimental; Cleopatra is criticized by Woolf for her patriarchally generated response to Octavia as rival, used by Natalie Strong as a role model by virtue of her friendship with Charmian and Iras, appropriated by Dickinson as symbolic of an object of desire and poetry. These characters, others, and indeed Shakespeare himself can be appropriated subversively to authorize and validate virtues perceived as womanly and crucial: flexibility, compassion, realism, autonomy for self and others. Identification is never with character in isolation, but with character as part of a larger symbolic exchange which includes language, plot, genre. These women, rather than struggling with Shakespeare, work with him.

The second way in which they use him is equally clear-sighted and unsentimental, equally energizing, but more detached. Identification with Shakespeare of the preceding sort does not lead to merger with him but to the balance of sympathy and judgment which Jameson advocates as the appropriate critical stance and which the rest of the women display. As in the second mode of contemporary feminist criticism, which I term justificatory, Shakespeare becomes a vehicle whereby the oppressiveness of patriarchal structures and the constrictions suffered by women are exposed and, sometimes, corrected through revision. Few of the sins of the fathers embodied in the plays go unnoted: pomposity is parodied in Woolf, crippling fantasies of women in the plays articulated by Madelon Sprengnether, the demands of a Lear denied by Rich, the brutality of the patriarchal family painfully and profoundly registered through *Titus Andronicus* for Strong. In these sophisticated responses, the analysis of oppressive patriarchy inevitably moves beyond particular characters, beyond Shakespeare himself, to result in analysis of his culture and the writer's, with Shakespeare's plays enabling the critique.

In order to defend Shakespeare for their own appropriation, many women readers direct their anger not primarily against Shakespeare as an author or as a man but against his characters or against the male culture which has appropriated and misread him on behalf of its own values. This strategy is most striking in Jameson's dialogue preface, in Eliot's and Woolf's comments in letters, and in the exposés of patriarchal misreadings commonplace in contemporary feminist essays (my own excoriation of all previous critics of *Othello* as Iago-like or Othello-like in the first feminist essay I wrote is a characteristic example[2]). Shakespeare is appropriated—and protected—in other ways too. Mary Lamb's adaptations of the stories often exaggerate both male power and women's resourcefulness and find accommodations between them. Other writers draw on Shakespearean characters to represent reformed male heroism: Laurence, in *The Diviners,* reimagines Prospero as her mother/tale teller, Morag; Eliot uses some aspects of Hamlet to create her sensitive hero, Daniel Deronda, and Charlotte Brontë's parallels with Coriolanus in *Shirley* emphasize the reform of her protagonist, Robert Moore. The strategies of exposing patriarchy, attacking critics who accept it, and revising it allow the woman writer to acknowledge and express anger while protecting Shakespeare from it. The anger serves to overcome the woman's sense of inadequacy, clearing space for her confident appropriation of Shakespeare. Christy Desmet, describing how for Jameson, "deference makes possible difference" (42), identifies a process important to many of these writers.

For these women responders, alternations between anger and empowerment, between critique of patriarchal culture and the creation of alternatives to it, lead to the creation of the mode I termed transformational and which, in these essays, is revisionary. The essays reveal that, like H.D., many women writers remember Shakespeare differently. Writing against the constructions of patriarchy and in alliance with Shakespeare they transform his scripts into their own. The essay writers, analyzing the revisions, extend and affirm them. The effect of these essays is to transform the concepts of reading and teaching, to provide revisionary readings of Shakespeare's texts *and* of the texts and the authority of women writers, to rewrite literary history and theory, and to transform the model of poetic succession and of criticism from that of Oedipal competition and heroic individualism to that of cooperation and community.

Women respond to or rewrite all of the Shakespearean genres: sonnets (H.D. and Woolf), histories (Jameson, Hutton), and tragedies (Brontë, Eliot, Strong, Sprengnether), as well as comedy, problem comedy, and romance (Lamb, Barnes, Laurence). They respond in all forms of writing—diaries, letters, essays, novels, poems, plays—and the nature of their responses and the strategy of the rewritings do not seem to me to differ significantly, whatever their form. The genre which seems most hospitable to revision is romance, especially if *As You Like It, All's Well That Ends Well,* and *Antony and Cleopatra* are viewed as borderline romances with many similarities to *Pericles, Cymbeline, The Winter's Tale,* and *The Tempest.* Romance is a genre which is domestic, but expansive—a genre which typically combines plots of ambition with plots of desire.[3] Women writers' revisions of the romance form create a new genre which might be called feminine(st) elegiac romance, represented by Barnes's *The Forest Princess,* Woolf's *Night and Day* and *To the Lighthouse,* H.D.'s *By Avon River,* Laurence's *The Diviners,* and Rich's *Sources,* and by the essays of Joan Hutton Landis and Carolyn Swift.[4]

Shakespeare's romances and feminist elegiac romance are similar in their mourning for difference, loss, rupture, death, and their working through these to painful reconciliation, to a blend of renunciation and exhilaration. Their focus is on generation and generations and especially on the appropriation of the past—familial, literary, historical—in the service of renewal. Both versions include journeys away and home again—from father (Rich), mother (Lily in *Lighthouse),* race (Pocahontas in *Forest Princess),* country (Morag in *Diviners),* from literary predecessors. Both versions include transformations of patriarchal authority which are a condition of recovery and renewal. In feminist revisions of romance, mothers, dead in Shakespeare's romances, are at the center, whereas fathers are decentered; their authority is blunted or challenged, their relics recaptured, their tales retold. Daughters achieve autonomy, and renewal is symbolized by concerns outside the family or by the creation of new, less oppressive "family" structures which center not on marriage but on a range of women's relationships: mothers and daughters, friends, lovers.

In all of these revisions of romance, the past is confronted to transform the present and Shakespeare is appropriated directly and indirectly on behalf of women's power. This is clearest in the representations of two visits to Shakespeare's grave. One is by the narrator of H.D.'s *By Avon River,* who is renewed by her visit at the start of the work, which ends with a fantasy of Shakespeare's return to Stratford in old age. The other is by Mrs. Hilbery, the mother of the protagonist, Katherine, in Woolf's

Night and Day, which, written in 1919, anticipates her appropriation of Shakespeare in the later novels which Christine Froula discusses.[5] It anticipates as well Woolf's own visit to Shakespeare's grave, reported in her diary in 1934: " . . . and what I had not reckoned with was the worn simple slab, turned the wrong way, Kind friend for Jesus' sake forbear—again he seemed to be all air and sun smiling serenely; and yet down there one foot from me lay the little bones that had spread over the world this vast illumination."[6] When Katherine (explicitly identified with Rosalind) is about to effect a "revolution" by breaking off her conventional engagement and choosing instead an unconventional and anti-romantic marriage with the rival suitor, Ralph Denham, her mother returns from her visit to Shakespeare's grave, fortified by an armful of flowers and a subversive theory that Anne Hathaway wrote the sonnets, which is "an implied menace to the heart of civilization itself" (427–28). This indirect affirmation of Katherine's "revolution" effortlessly thwarts the will of her husband, who had hoped to "civilize" Katherine into a sensible marriage by reading Sir Walter Scott with her. Woolf similarly associates Shakespeare with women's graceful subversion of male tyranny in *To the Lighthouse* where, as Mr. Ramsay reads Walter Scott, Mrs. Ramsay, gaining sustenance from her reading of Shakespeare's sonnet 98, "Yet seemed it winter still, and you away, / As with your shadow I with these did play," satisfies Mr. Ramsay's demand for love without sacrificing her integrity: "For she had triumphed again."[7] H. D., identifying her narrator in *By Avon River* with Shakespeare her double and the doubleness of his text, has her bring flowers to his grave on Shakespeare Day, April 23, 1945, and later quotes another part of the same poem, the only Shakespeare sonnet quoted extensively among all of the quotations of Renaissance lyrics lacing the "essay" which concludes that work: "From you have I been absent in the spring, / When proud-pied April, dressed in all his trim—... Nor did I wonder at the lily's white / Nor praise the deep vermilion in the rose, / They were but sweet, but figures of delight, / Drawn after you, you pattern of all those."[8]

More explorations are needed to discover whether women's responses to other canonical male authors display the same patterns and result in the same kinds of self-affirming revisions as do their responses to Shakespeare.[9] These essays suggest at least three reasons why Shakespeare may be especially susceptible to women's appropriation. First is the richness, the density, the power, and the polysemousness of Shakespeare's language. This text proves to be remarkably detachable from its context in play and in culture and from its author. We see the impact of this language in the passionate responses by many women readers to tiny fragments of text, derived from the most unexpected contexts and used on their own behalves; I think of Dickinson's passion for the "ring of" "heart that i' the scuffles of great fights hath burst the buckle on his breast," Woolf's "shiver down the spine" at "Hang there like fruit, my Soul, till the tree die," Laurence's Christie's "what a bloody piece of work is man." Shakespeare is an exemplary representative of Madelon Sprengnether's "duplicitous" text;[10] hence it is one in which the woman reader can find, or out of which she can construct, the most varied and shifting and unexpectedly new selves.

The second thing that frees women readers for liberating responses to Shakespeare is the objectivity and detachment characteristic of the dramatic genre, the fact that drama, more than other genres, is separated from its author, free of narrative mediation, exists in widely varying reproductions through performance, and perhaps engenders especially intense forms of identification. Like their thick language, their infinite reproducibility in performance or criticism helps make these dramatic texts more malleable than other male sentences or male forms and hence available for revision.[11]

The third thing that enables women's responses to and appropriations of Shakespeare is his personal anonymity combined with the powerful myths which he generates both as a person and as an Foucaultian author-function. Because so little is known about Shakespeare's life, he can be imagined as androgynous by Woolf, reinvented as a garbage collector by Laurence, as a shabby man at the servants' table (*Orlando*), as heterosexual, homosexual, or bisexual, as embodying or privileging female virtues. It is quite astonishing how often our writers identify directly with the person of Shakespeare, not just with his language, his characters, or with his plays, and how much similarity there is among the Shakespeare imagined by H.D. as her double, a visionary seer who, at the end of his life, "had come home because he loved Judith (96)," Woolf's androgynous Shakespeare who becomes identified with both the author and Mrs. Ramsay, and the Shakespeare recreated by Laurence in *Diviners* as Morag; all of these female authors, as Margaret Hutton best puts it, reinscribe Shakespeare as a mother to validate their own perceived strengths.

Although neither the historical period of the woman reader nor the genre read or written in necessarily hinder response, the essays reveal several instances of impediments to or anxiety about response and appropriation. The aspect of Shakespeare which is most difficult to incorporate or revise is his limited representation of female sexuality which excludes much of the range of female desire. The plays most often either associate female virtue with chastity or represent female sexuality defensively or negatively through jokes about it, attacks on it by misogynistic male heroes, or the vicious expression of it in, for example, Goneril and Regan.

Even Helena in *All's Well,* whose speech and plot are openly passionate and erotic, describes *her* response to the bed trick by denouncing the deceitfulness and blindness of male lust (4.4.21–26), and Cleopatra's passionate expressions of desire are countered by the numerous attacks on her sexuality in the play. In this area, there is, as might be expected, discernible historical development in the responses but no fully successful revision. The earlier writers accept cultural prescriptions for female chastity; Lamb and Jameson, both Helena's advocates, preserve their identification with her by silencing the bed trick, ignoring it in their discussions. Agnes Mure Mackenzie, in her 1924 openly feminist book, *The Women in Shakespeare's Plays,* acknowledges the bed trick but criticizes Helena for it and for her participation in the dialogue on virginity.[12] At about the same time, Virginia Woolf notes her own failure, because of cultural constrictions, at "telling the truth about my own experiences as a body" and claims that other women writers have not yet been able to do so either.[13] Her creation of an androgynous Shakespeare as the representative artist is one response, perhaps, to this sense of failure. Her novels tend to represent sexuality in highly sublimated forms as does H.D.'s appropriation of Shakespeare to represent a quest for ideal love in *By Avon River.* Even Laurence's Morag, like Prospero, concludes her book in isolation and self-chosen chastity.

Shakespearean fathers are another element of the plays demanding resistance and creating tension in some of the women's relations to Shakespeare. In Woolf's novels, the fathers, Mr. Hilbery and Mr. Ramsay, attempt to thwart their daughters' and wives' autonomy and must be resisted or subverted. Laurence's Morag, unlike Shakespeare's Prospero, does not attempt to control her daughter's future. Natalie Strong describes the violence emanating from Titus Andronicus and his "lopping off" his daughters and sons as "typical" and frightening. Adrienne Rich accomplishes in her poetic career a long journey away from her father—from his powerful will, his expectations for her, the books which represent his hold over her and thwart her self-discovery. Her anger at him, her refusal to forgive him, to be Cordelia, free her to assert the primacy of the mother-daughter relationship in *Of Woman Born,* to explore a woman-centered community, and to forge a lesbian identity. By means of this project, she is able to return to her father and her origins and reclaim some connections with him on her own terms. Rich's journey away from and back to her father, like the rest of the responses discussed, changes our perspective on Shakespeare, serving to decenter and demystify him while making him available for appropriation. These essays taken together certainly serve, as Peter Erickson's work on Rich demonstrates, to historicize

Shakespeare and to provide material for historicizing patriarchy and delineating a history of resistance to it.

These women's responses, these essays, in fact show me some limitations, some gaps, and some new possibilities not only in Shakespeare but in contemporary critical theory, which they make use of selectively, eclectically, and in the same spirit of revisionary appropriation with which they use Shakespeare. The women writers carry on an extended mediation between assertive female characters and the patriarchal oppressions in the plays, between the male author and his female readers, between male critics and themselves, between Shakespeare's texts and their own desires, between Shakespeare's culture and their own. Equally these essays, some self-consciously, some entirely unself-consciously, negotiate among the numerous theories competing for dominance in the academy, challenging both their claims of exclusiveness and purity and some of their underlying assumptions. All of these essays suggest that close textual reading and gender-specific identification with characters are important steps toward women reader/writers' identity formation, self-authorization, and revisions. These identifications, whether cross-gender or same-gender, are not necessarily oppressive or demoralizing, a number of papers and responses suggest. Nor are they absolute or unthinking. There is also always awareness of the gender of the author, the character, and the reader and of the difference which separates them. But there are few indications of the women writers experiencing crippling anxiety of influence. Where the predecessor, Shakespeare, is inadequate, the woman writer revises, extends, or departs from him.

Along with these more conventional methodologies there is—on the part of both women writers and essay writers—continuous historicizing of the sort that, for example, historicist critics regularly call for. The writers of these essays often situate themselves explicitly and poignantly in regard to familial, critical, and cultural influences in their present and their past and interrogate these. They situate the writers they discuss precisely in *their* family, culture, critical tradition, and historical period. The women writers are, in their turn, urgently aware of their situation in their time and of their historical and gender differences from Shakespeare. They write against their culture's conventional appropriations of Shakespeare as they write against their culture's conventional scripts for women. They register as well Shakespeare's own cultural formation and his perceived opposition to it. Although they participate in certain ways in the kind of ideological critique characteristic of cultural materialists, these women writers and these essays qualify claims that Shakespeare's plays everywhere authorize the unified power of the state, the dominant ideology, and that our culture's use of him everywhere authorizes the hegemonic power of a universalized male liberal human subject. These papers demonstrate that Shakespeare can be appropriated in behalf of other subjects and other sorts of power.

One last thing I especially like about these moving essays is the way in which they intersect with and illuminate my own history of reading/revising Shakespeare—which began with a paper on *Othello* and *The Winter's Tale* in my college Shakespeare class thirty years ago and continued with a dissertation on *The Winter's Tale* and the genre of pastoral romance. Fifteen years ago, an angry essay on *Othello* made me a feminist critic; a subsequent benign reading of *The Winter's Tale* found in it the possibility of growth and reconciliation that many of these women writers find or generate out of romance. These essays enable me to see how each of these revisions were ways of trying to reappropriate Shakespeare, the critical (or New Critical) tradition I inherited, and my own past and present.

They also put in perspective the responses to Shakespeare of my older daughter, Sophia, a sophomore at Dartmouth College (in 1988), a committed athlete, a feminist, a student seeking her own voice and her own place in a college characterized by the oppressive weight of male tradition and by much vigorous opposition to it. She found the two Shakespeare courses she took with Lynda Boose, a feminist critic and teacher, as engaging and eye-opening for their insight into gender roles as her other courses in, for example, American women's history, French women writers, or the psychology of gender. Like many of the women writers in these essays she responded with interest, enthusiasm, and wariness to comedy heroines. She wrote one paper on the blurring of gender boundaries and movement toward restoring sex role stereotypes in *Twelfth Night* and another arguing that although Kate, in *The Taming of the Shrew,* and Beatrice, in *Much Ado About Nothing,* "conform, in the end, to patriarchal society's norms by marrying, they have not been defeated; on the contrary, they have achieved the happiness associated with marriage and mutual desire and respect while retaining their independence and some of their original shrewish spirit, which has been tamed but not lost. That the husbands allow this retention helps show that they too have been 'tamed,' or at least have undergone some type of transformation, by the end of the plays." This is an accommodating reading, one which the many women precursors who have read Shakespeare before her provide precedent for, one which like their revisions creates the possibility of progress and difference without irremediable separation and loss. Her reading also serves to symbolize for me the powerful sense of ongoing community created by the essays in this collection and their affirmation that, by reading back through our mothers we are also reading forward through our daughters,[14] an insight articulated by Laurence's motif in *The Diviners: "Look ahead into the past and back into the future, until the silence"* (453).

NOTES

1. Carol Thomas Neely, "Feminist Modes of Shakespearean Criticism: Compensatory, Justificatory, and Transformational," *Women's Studies* 9, no. 1 (1981): 3–15, expanded as "Feminist Criticism in Motion," in *For Alma Mater: Theory and Practice in Feminist Scholarship,* ed. Paula A. Treichler, Cheris Kramerae, and Beth Stafford. (Urbana: University of Illinois Press, 1985): 69–90.

2. Neely, "Women and Men in *Othello:* 'What Should Such a Fool/Do with So Good a Woman?'" *Shakespeare Studies* 10 (1978), rpt. rev. in *The Woman's Part: Feminist Criticism of Shakespeare,* ed. Carolyn Lenz, Gayle Greene, and Carol Thomas Neely (Urbana: University of Illinois Press, 1980), and, with further revisions, in my *Broken Nuptials in Shakespeare's Plays* (New Haven: Yale University Press, 1985).

3. Elements noted by Nancy K. Miller in "Emphasis Added: Plots and Plausibilities in Women's Fiction," in *The New Feminist Criticism: Essays on Women, Literature, Theory,* ed. Elaine Showalter (New York: Pantheon, 1985), 339–360.

4. Other women writers use this form from Mary Wroth's *Urania* (1621) and Fanny Burney's *Evelina* (1778) to many contemporary novels including Margaret Drabble's *The Realms of Gold,* Margaret Atwood's *Lady Oracle,* Gail Godwin's *A Mother and Two Daughters,* Alice Walker's *The Color Purple,* and, perhaps, Toni Morrison's *Beloved.*

5. Virginia Woolf, *Night and Day* (New York: Harcourt Brace Jovanovich, 1948).

6. Virginia Woolf, *Writer's Diary,* ed. Leonard Woolf (London: Harcourt Brace Jovanovich, 1954), May 9, 1934, 209.

7. Virginia Woolf, *To the Lighthouse* (New York: Harcourt Brace Jovanovich, 1927), 182. George Eliot, in the *Leader* essay Novy discusses, similarly contrasts Scott with Shakespeare, criticizing the novelist for representing women's unnatural "propriety" and praising the dramatist for portraying their unconventional "frankness."

8. H. D., *By Avon River* (New York: Macmillan, 1949), 36.

9. In a longer version of her essay, Gayle Greene suggests that Margaret Laurence rewrites Joyce in much the same way she rewrites Shakespeare. Christine Froula's "When Eve Reads Milton: Undoing the Canonical Economy," *Critical Inquiry* 10 (1985):321–47, reinscribes the repressed mother and reads Milton through Dinesen's "Blank Page." An anthology of feminist essays on Milton, *Milton and the Idea of Woman,* edited by Julia Walker (Urbana: University of Illinois Press, 1988), provides a basis for comparing contemporary feminist critics' responses to these two authors.

10. Citations to 110, 124, 171, 238, in this volume.

11. Virginia Woolf, *A Room of One's Own* (New York: Harcourt Brace, 1957), Chapter 4, discusses the intractability of male forms. Only one of the

women discussed in this collection is a dramatist. It is possible that anxiety of influence might be stronger and appropriation more difficult in Shakespeare's own genre. It is also true that the material conditions of drama, the money and resources required to get plays produced, have long made it especially intractable for women writers. But there are a number of early plays by women which (like the contemporary one discussed by Novy in the Introduction) may be viewed as alternatives to or revisions of Shakespeare. Elizabeth Cary's *Tragedy of Mariam* (1613) uses the misogynist discourse common in Shakespeare's tragedies in such a way as to italicize it and generate sympathy for her female protagonist. Cf. Margaret Ferguson's discussion of the play in "A Room Not Their Own: Renaissance Women as Readers and Writers," in *The Comparative Perspective on Literature: Approaches to Theory and Practice,* ed. Clayton Koelb and Susan Noakes (Ithaca: Cornell University Press, 1988), 106 n.32. Carolyn Swift reads Mary Wroth's play *Love's Victorie* (c. 1621) as, like *Urania,* a revisionary feminist romance in "Feminine Self-Definition in Lady Mary Wroth's *Love's Victorie,*" (*ELR* 19, no. 2 [Spring 1989]). Aphra Behn's *The Rover* has the effect of revising Shakespearean comedy in its aggressive protagonist, Hellena, who uses her multiple disguises in more empowering ways than Shakespeare's heroines do to escape confinement in nunnery or marriage, to satisfy her desire for the appealingly promiscuous rover (allusively?) named Willemore, and to maneuver him to agree to a unconventional marriage with her, one based on reciprocal sexual attraction, wit, and inconstancy.

12. Agnes Mure Mackenzie, *The Women in Shakespeare's Plays* (London: Heinemann, 1924), 49–51, 38.

13. Virginia Woolf, "Professions for Women," in *Women and Writing,* ed. Michele Barrett (New York: Harcourt Brace Jovanovich, 1979), 62.

14. As Jane Marcus suggests in the moving dedication to her edited collection *New Feminist Essays on Virginia Woolf* (Lincoln: University of Nebraska Press, 1981), "For Lisa, a daughter to think forward through."

Contributors

MARGARET J. ARNOLD is an associate professor of English at the University of Kansas. She has edited three plays for *Renaissance Latin Drama in England,* 2nd series, has written on transformations of Greek tragedy in Shakespeare and Milton, and is currently working on *Samson Agonistes.* She regularly teaches courses in Women's Studies.

PAULA BENNETT is senior lecturer in English at University College, Northeastern University. She is the author of *My Life a Loaded Gun: Female Creativity and Feminist Poetics* (Beacon, 1986). Her study of Dickinson's poetry, *Emily Dickinson,* will appear in the spring of 1990 from Harvester Press.

CHRISTY DESMET is an assistant professor of English at the University of Georgia. She has written several articles on Shakespeare and his early critics and is completing a book on the rhetoric of Shakespearean character.

PETER ERICKSON is author of *Patriarchal Structures in Shakespeare's Drama* (California, 1985) and co-editor of *Shakespeare's "Rough Magic": Renaissance Essays in Honor of C. L. Barber* (Delaware, 1985). He contributed "The Order of the Garter, the Cult of Elizabeth, and Class/Gender Tension in *The Merry Wives of Windsor*" to *Shakespeare Reproduced: The Text in History and Ideology* (Methuen, 1987), and has also published essays on June Jordan, Toni Morrison, and Alice Walker.

SUSAN STANFORD FRIEDMAN is professor of English and Women's Studies at the University of Wisconsin-Madison. She is the author of *Psyche Reborn: The Emergence of H.D.* and co-author of *A Woman's Guide to Therapy.* She has written articles on women's poetry, autobiography, narrative theory, gender and genre, the childbirth metaphor, feminism and psychoanalysis, feminist pedagogy, and women's education. *Penelope's Web: H.D.'s Fictions and the Engendering of Modernism* is forthcoming.

CHRISTINE FROULA teaches English and Comparative Literature and theory at Northwestern University and writes about women and the Western literary tradition, modern literature, and feminist and contemporary theory. Her book on gender and literary authority in Joyce and Woolf will be published by Columbia University Press.

GAYLE GREENE has published articles on Shakespeare, contemporary women writers, and on feminist literary theory. A professor at Scripps College (Claremont, California), she co-edited *The Woman's Part: Feminist Criticism of*

Shakespeare (Illinois, 1980) and *Making a Difference: Feminist Literary Criticism* (Methuen, 1985). She is currently working on a book, "Re-Visions: Contemporary Women Writers and the Tradition."

JOAN HUTTON LANDIS teaches Shakespeare, Joyce, American literature and Women's Studies at the Curtis Institute of Music, where she is currently chairman of the academic faculty. Her poetry has appeared in various small magazines; her criticism and interviews in *Transatlantic Review, Midway, Salmagundi, Hamlet Studies,* and *Modern Language Studies.*

MARY LOEFFELHOLZ is assistant professor of English at Northeastern University. She is the author of articles on Milton and Shakespeare, Emily Dickinson, and other nineteenth-century American women writers and is completing a book on Emily Dickinson and romanticism.

CAROL THOMAS NEELY is professor of English at the University of Illinois and the 1989–90 president of the Shakespeare Association of America. She co-edited *The Woman's Part: Feminist Criticism of Shakespeare (Illinois, 1980)* and has written *Broken Nuptials in Shakespeare's Plays* (Yale, 1985) as well as articles on Shakespeare, sonnet sequences, and feminist criticism.

MARIANNE NOVY is associate professor of English and Women's Studies at the University of Pittsburgh. She has published *Love's Argument: Gender Relations in Shakespeare* (North Carolina, 1984), is currently writing on nineteenth-century women's responses to Shakespeare, and is editing a companion volume to this anthology.

MADELON SPRENGNETHER is professor of English at the University of Minnesota. She has co-edited *The (M)other Tongue: Essays in Feminist Psychoanalytic Interpretation* (Cornell, 1985) and has written *The Spectral Mother: Freud, Feminism, and Psychoanalysis* (Cornell, 1990), as well as poetry, personal essays, and articles on Shakespeare, Lyly, Spenser, Nashe, and Freud. Her earlier publications appeared under the name of Madelon S. Gohlke.

NATALIE B. STRONG is a pseudonym for a belligerently reverent and tired student at Rhode Island College whose solaces are her kittens and the wind.

CAROLYN RUTH SWIFT is co-editor of *The Woman's Part: Feminist Criticism of Shakespeare* (Illinois, 1980). She is currently writing about sixteenth- and seventeenth-century English women writers.

SUSAN J. WOLFSON is associate professor of English at Rutgers University, New Brunswick. She has published widely in the field of English romanticism. The essay in this volume is part of a book project about the language of gender in the Romantic Age.

Index

Aaron, Jane, 40
Actors, 5, 6, 14, 200
Adelman, Janet, 192, 240
African-American, 11, 100
Albany (*Lear*), 212, 229
Aldington, Richard, 145, 146
All's Well That Ends Well, 23, 29–33, 92, 245, 248
Alther, Lisa, 166
American Indians, history of, 59, 60, 62, 64, 70, 75; in Canada, 170, 176
Androgyny, 5, 129–30, 138, 142, 164n31, 194, 198. *See also* Shakespeare, William, images of: androgynous
Angelou, Maya, 15
Anne (*Richard III*), 216
Anti-Jacobin, 22, 37
Antonio (*Tempest*), 63, 65
Antony: *Antony and Cleopatra,* 9, 108–19, 122, 136, 223–25; *Julius Caesar,* 220–21
Antony and Cleopatra, 108–22, 135, 137, 223–25, 236, 245
Ariel (*Tempest*), 149, 174
Arnold, Margaret, 4, 9
As You Like It, 1, 9–10, 74, 90–91, 95–99, 104–5, 197, 245
At the Foot of the Mountain (theater group), 229
Atwood, Margaret, 166
Auerbach, Nina, 7, 41, 90, 104, 105, 106
Austen, Jane, 103, 134, 166, 186
Australia, 10

Bamber, Linda, 106, 239
Baptista (*Shrew*), 24–25
Barber, C. L., 213; and Richard Wheeler, 13, 215
Barnes, Charlotte: *Forest Princess,* 9, 58–75, 245; *Octavia Bragaldi,* 58, 73

Barnet, Sylvan, 39, 163–64n30
Bean, John, 25, 38
Beatrice (*Much Ado*), 6, 8, 11, 91, 203–4, 212, 243, 250
Beer, Gillian, 104, 107
Behn, Aphra, 3, 135, 252
Belsey, Catherine, 37, 239
Benedick (*Much Ado*), 204, 229
Bennet, Elizabeth (*Pride and Prejudice*), 8
Bennett, Paula, 3, 9
Bertram (*All's Well*), 30–33
Bianca: *Shrew,* 25–26; *Othello,* 231
Blackwood, John (publisher), 92
Blake, William, 36
Blau-Duplessis, Rachel, 145
Blewett, David, 180
Blom, Margaret, 78
Bloom, Harold, 5, 143
Bodichon, Barbara, 107
Boesing, Martha (*The Story of a Mother*), 228
Bonaparte, Napoleon, 76, 87–88
Boose, Lynda, 250
Bottom (*Midsummer Night's Dream*), 205
Boy actors, in women's parts, 6, 200
Bradley, A. C., 123
Bradstreet, Anne, 221
Brontë, Branwell, 76
Brontë, Charlotte, 103, 104, 105, 134, 166; *Shirley,* 4, 9, 10, 76–88, 244, 245; *Jane Eyre,* 77, 84, 88, 136; *Villette,* 84, 88
Brontë, Emily, 134, 166; *Wuthering Heights,* 205, 207
Brooks, Peter, 168
Bryant, Dorothy, 166
Bryher, Winifred, 144, 146–48, 161
Burt, John, 38
By Avon River (H. D.), 143–64, 245, 248

Caliban (*Tempest*), 19, 29, 36, 63–65, 68, 70, 87, 100, 185
Calvinism, 221
Campbell, O. J., 39
Campbell, Thomas, 56, 106
Canada, history of, 165, 166, 169, 170, 172, 176, 177, 178
Carter, Angela, 9–10
Cary, Elizabeth (*Mariam*), 252
Cathar heresy, 151, 154, 159, 163
Cather, Willa, 5, 13
Cavendish, Margaret, 3, 6
Celia (*As You Like It*), 90, 92, 97
Ceres-Proserpina myth, 207–8. *See also* Demeter-Persephone myth
Charles I (king of England), 68–69
Charmian (*Antony and Cleopatra*), 225, 243
Chenier, André, 84
Chodorow, Nancy, 5, 13, 240
Christie (*Diviners*), 166–77, 180–81, 247
Cixous, Hélène, 13
Claribel (*Tempest* and *By Avon River*), 8, 149–55, 159, 162–63n23
Clarke, Mary Cowden, 7, 36
Class, 15, 77–78, 82, 191
Claudio (*Much Ado*), 204
Cleopatra, 6, 8, 41, 108–16, 119, 122, 135, 223–25, 238, 239, 243, 248
Cohn, Ruby, 1
Coleridge, Samuel T., 4–5, 7, 30, 42, 48, 49, 52, 53, 54, 56, 57, 109, 123
Colonialism, 59. *See also* American Indians, history of; Canada, history of
Comedies, Shakespearean, 23, 99, 103, 232, 245
Connor, E. S., 58
Constance (*King John*), 7, 43–46, 48, 49, 55
Cooke, John Estes (*My Lady Pocahontas*), 72
Cordelia (*Lear*), 8, 10, 183–85, 187–88, 190, 192–93, 212–15, 222–23, 225, 229, 248
Coriolanus, 76–87, 244
Coriolanus, 4, 9, 76–87, 205, 237, 244
Cott, Nancy, 74
Cymbeline, 73, 124, 245
Cymbeline, 124, 245

Dallas Shakespeare Club, 11
Dante, 144, 145
Dash, Irene, 37

Dedalus, Stephen (*Portrait of the Artist as a Young Man*), 126
Defarge, Mme. (*Tale of Two Cities*), 205
Demeter-Persephone myth, 187. *See also* Ceres-Proserpina myth
DeSalvo, Louise, 141
Desmet, Christy, 7, 244
DiBattista, Maria, 141, 211
Dickens, Charles, 94, 205
Dickinson, Austin, 112, 119, 122
Dickinson, Emily, 3, 9, 108–22, 144, 210, 243, 247
Didion, Joan (*White Album*), 233
The Diviners, 9, 165–82, 244, 247, 251
Dollimore, Jonathan, 239
Donne, John, 166, 174, 185, 186
Doolittle, Hilda (H.D.), 3, 5, 8, 104, 143–64; *By Avon River*, 143–64, 244, 245, 246, 247, 248; *Helen in Egypt*, 143, 144, 155; *Trilogy*, 143, 151, 158, 164; *Tribute to Freud*, 144, 145; *Asphodel*, 146, 161; *HER*, 146, 162; *Sword Went Out to Sea*, 147, 162
Dowden, Edward, 38
Dowding, Sir Hugh, 147, 162
Drabble, Margaret, 166, 179
Dusinberre, Juliet, 16

Edgar (*Lear*), 212, 223, 224
Eliot, George, 4, 9, 89–107, 134, 166, 244, 245, 251; *Daniel Deronda*, 9, 89–90, 94–103, 105–7, 244, 245; *Scenes of Clerical Life*, 92, 102, 105; "Natural History of German Life," 94; *Mill on the Floss*, 95; *Middlemarch*, 95; "A College Breakfast-Party," 96, 99; "Notes on *The Spanish Gypsy*," 102
Eliot, T. S., 142, 144
Elizabeth I, 129, 155, 159
Elliott, M. Leigh, 31
Emerson, Ralph Waldo, 108–9, 114, 115
Emilia (*Othello*), 49, 231
Enobarbus (*Antony and Cleopatra*), 111, 112
Erickson, Peter, 8, 11, 225, 248
Erikson, Erik, 94
Ethnicity: Portuguese, 11, 214; Anglo-American, 11, 70; Jewish, 11, 102, 189–92; "Switzer," 65, 68. *See also* African-American; American Indians, history of; Canada, history of; Scotland, history of
Evans, G. B., 1

Fabre, Michel, 180
Faderman, Lillian, 91
Falstaff, 202, 210, 243
Father-daughter relationships, 24–25, 60, 156–57, 166–68, 183–93, 229, 248
Faucit, Helen, 98
Ferdinand (*Tempest*), 62–69, 74
Ferguson, Mary Ann, 165
Fetterley, Judith, 9, 18, 89
Fleishman, Avrom, 141
Fools, Shakespearean, 171, 223
Mrs. Ford (*Merry Wives*), 6
Forest Princess (Barnes), 9, 58–75, 245
Forster, E. M., 199
Foucault, Michel, 247
Francis (*Henry IV*), 63–64
Freud, Sigmund, 144–45, 163, 236–37, 240
Friedman, Susan S., 5
Froula, Christine, 5, 11, 15, 251
Fuller, Margaret, 71
Furnivall, F. J., 109, 115

Gallop, Jane, 143
Gardiner, Judith K., 239
Garrick, David, 24, 25, 26
Gaskell, Elizabeth, 87, 105
Gay, Peter, 122
Gilbert, Sandra, 142; and Susan Gubar, 2, 5, 37, 46, 89–90, 143, 179
Gilbert, Susan, 110, 111, 112, 113, 116, 117, 121
Girardin, Saint-Marc, 91, 92, 98
Godwin, Gail, 166, 179n10
Godwin, Mary Jane, and William Godwin, 22, 34
Goethe, Johann W. von, 94, 95
Goneril (*Lear*), 2, 222, 229, 237, 247
Gray, Neil, 146, 161
Grebanier, Bernard, 95, 106
Green, Rayna, 75
Greene, Gayle, 9, 11, 251
Greene, Robert, 6
Griffith, Elizabeth, 7

Hacker, Marilyn, 9
Hamlet, 5, 17, 35–36, 52, 90, 95–96, 99–101, 103, 136, 187, 212, 220, 221, 224–25, 229, 230, 232
Hamlet, 90, 95, 99–100, 131, 140, 221
Harris, Frank, 38–39

Hathaway, Anne, 246
Hazlitt, William, 4–5, 7, 27, 31, 32, 42, 44, 49, 50–52, 55, 56, 91, 93
Heilbrun, Carolyn, 103, 142, 167
Helena (*All's Well*), 7, 8, 11, 30–33, 39, 92, 243, 248
Helstone, Caroline, 4, 76–87
Henry IV, 67, 198, 200, 202, 243
Henry V (earlier, Hal), 198, 200–203
Henry V, 201–3
Henry VI, 201
Henry VIII, 87n1
Hermione (*Winter's Tale*), 97, 98, 106, 146, 162–63, 187, 205–7
Hero (*Much Ado*), 204
Herring, Robert, 144, 161
Higginson, Thomas, 110, 111, 121
Hitchcock, Edward, 109
Hodo, Kathy, 232
Hulme, Peter, 73
Hutcheon, Linda, 15
Hutton, Margaret Foster, 8, 196–211, 243, 247

Iago (*Othello*), 17, 48–49, 244
Imogen (*Cymbeline*), 7, 47, 124
Innogen (*Henry V*), 204
Iras (*Antony and Cleopatra*), 225, 243
Isabella (*Measure for Measure*), 7, 28, 38, 39, 51–54, 56, 199

Jackson, Russell, 91, 105
Jameson, Anna, 7, 31, 41–57, 243, 244, 248
Jameson, Robert, 45
Joan of Arc, 223
Johnson, Samuel, 32, 38, 51, 123
Jong, Erica, 166, 179n10
Jonson, Ben, 3, 5, 13
Joyce, James, 126, 178, 210, 251
Judaism, 102, 107; Zionism, 100. *See also* Ethnicity: Jewish
Juliet, 47, 48, 91, 92, 102, 220
Julius Caesar, 87, 220

Kahn, Coppélia, 17, 25, 240
Kate (*Shrew*), 7, 24–27, 37, 38, 250
Katherine of France (*Henry V*), 201, 204
Keats, John, 93
Kellman, Stephen, 180
Kemble, Fanny, 47, 55, 56

Kennard, Jean, 170, 180
Kenny, Thomas, 38
King Lear, 19, 36, 53, 131, 183–84, 187,
    192–93, 214, 222–23, 229–30
Kipling, Rudyard, 5
Klein, Joan L., 56
Knight, Charles, 109
Knight, G. W., 38, 163
Knoepflmacher, U. C., 89, 93, 96
Kosintsev, Grigori, 229

Lamb, Charles, 16, 19, 21, 22, 37, 82
Lamb, Mary, 7, 10, 16, 18–40, 82, 244, 248
Landis, Joan Hutton, 8, 245
Laurence, Margaret (*The Diviners*), 9, 11,
    165–82, 244, 247, 251
Lawrence, Karen, 141
Lennox, Charlotte, 12, 52
Leontes (*Winter's Tale*), 187, 205–6, 225
Lesbian identity, 186, 248. *See also* Women,
    love/friendship between
Lessing, Doris, 168
Leverenz, David, 94
Levin, Harry, 55
Levine, Lawrence, 15
Lewes, G. H., 92, 105
Lincoln, Abraham, 221
Linton, Eliza Lynn, 98
Lipking, Lawrence, 93
Locke, John, 31
Loeffelholz, Mary, 9, 11
Love's Labour's Lost, 11
Luddites, 77
Luther, Martin, 77
Lyssa, Alison, 10

Macbeth, 51, 212, 233, 234, 236
Macbeth, 19, 36, 87, 203, 223, 224, 230,
    232, 238; Lady Macbeth, 2, 5, 7, 8, 9,
    49–51, 56, 106, 212, 223, 233–34,
    236, 237; Lady Macduff, 234
Mackenzie, Agnes Mure, 248
McLuskie, Kathleen, 17–18, 35, 56
McNeil, Helen, 121
Macpherson, James, 172
Macready, William, 87
Manson family, 233
Marcus, Jane, 141, 252
Margaret (queen): *Henry VI,* 201; *Richard
    III,* 216

Marina (*Pericles*), 205
Marlowe, Christopher, 5, 130, 157
Marshall, David, 107
Martin, Wendy, 194
Measure for Measure, 23, 28, 39, 53, 56,
    198–200, 203, 206, 210
Merchant of Venice, 33, 190, 197
Milton, John, 2, 5, 83, 89–90, 109, 133,
    136, 164, 166, 169, 178, 181, 208, 251
Miranda (*Tempest*), 9, 19, 28, 29, 36, 41, 52,
    60–71, 74, 149, 156, 165, 169–70, 188
Misogyny, 7, 17–18, 143, 237, 238, 247
Mitchell, Juliet, 236, 240
Moers, Ellen, 103
Montagu, Elizabeth, 3–4, 6
Moore, Robert, 4, 76–88, 244
Morag (*Diviners*), 11, 165–82, 244, 247, 248
Morley, Patricia, 180
Mortlock, Melanie, 181
Mothers: empowered, 83, 154, 169, 245,
    247; and daughters, 108, 146–47, 156–
    57, 168–69, 186–87, 196–211, 221,
    245, 248, 250–51; "bad," 166, 179,
    227, 233, 235, 236, 238
Much Ado About Nothing, 203–4, 250

Nationality, 59, 67, 69–70, 102, 165, 174
Neely, Carol Thomas, 8, 11, 33, 37, 38,
    39, 49
New Criticism, 223, 227, 250
Newton, Judith Lowder, and Rosenfelt,
    Deborah, 191
Novy, Marianne, 17, 37, 181–82

O'Brien, Sharon, 5, 13
Octavia (*Antony and Cleopatra*), 135, 243
Ophelia (*Hamlet*), 8, 14, 41, 95, 100, 105,
    212, 221, 230
Orientalism, 108–9, 113, 114, 118, 122
Orlando (*As You Like It*), 74, 91, 97, 98,
    130, 198
Othello, 48, 49, 91, 98, 102, 132, 136,
    185,·221, 224, 230, 232, 244
Othello, 19, 49, 87, 108, 120, 131, 132,
    221–22, 230–31, 236, 244, 250
Ovid, 207

Nan Page (*Merry Wives*), 6
Mrs. Page (*Merry Wives*), 6
Parody, 10, 15

Patterson, Rebecca, 113, 120, 121, 122
Paulina (*Winter's Tale*), 205
Pearson, Norman, 163
Penelope (*Odyssey*), 139, 196, 205
Perdita (*Winter's Tale*), 146, 147, 148, 187, 207–8
Pericles, 207
Petruchio (*Shrew*), 24–27, 38
Philomel, 205
Pocahontas, 9, 58–75, 245
Polanski, Roman, 233
Polonius (*Hamlet*), 99–100, 205
Poovey, Mary, 13, 35, 89
Portia (*Merchant of Venice*), 10, 31, 52, 91, 197, 199–200, 212
Pound, Ezra, 145, 163
Prospero (*Tempest*), 9, 19, 28, 29, 36, 61–63, 66–70, 149, 156, 165, 169–70, 173–75, 178, 244, 248

Mrs. Quickly (*Henry IV, Henry V*), 6

Rabkin, Norman, 180–81
Race, 59, 70, 191. *See also* Ethnicity; African-American; American Indians, history of
Raleigh, Walter, 5, 67, 69, 74, 157
Rambo, 217
Ray, Satyajit (*Pather Panchali*), 228
Reagan, Ronald, 217
Regan (*Lear*), 2, 222, 229, 237, 247
Rich, Adrienne, 1, 8, 10, 11, 183–95, 244, 245, 248
Richard II, 220
Richard III, 87, 216, 221, 224
Richardson, Dorothy, 8
Richardson, William, 48
Riehl, Joseph, 37
Roberts, Jean, 34
Romance, 61–67, 70, 148, 155, 187, 205–10, 245, 250
Romeo, 91, 102, 220
Romeo and Juliet, 19, 105, 164, 203, 220
Rosalind (*As You Like It*), 1, 8, 9, 10, 74, 90–92, 95–99, 103, 129–30, 162–63, 198, 212, 243
Rose, Jacqueline, 240
Rossiter, A. P., 181
Rougemont, Denis de, 151, 154, 159, 162n22, 164n33

Rousseau, Jean-Jacques, 37

Sackville-West, Vita, 129
Said, Edward, 115, 122
Sand, George, 103
Sanders, Wilbur, 185
Schweickart, Patrocinio, 8, 12, 241
Scotland, history of, 176
Scott, Walter, 91, 127, 141, 246, 251
Segel, Elizabeth, 24
Shakespeare, Hamnet, 156–57
Shakespeare, Judith (daughter), 156–57, 247
Shakespeare, Judith (sister), 134, 143, 206
Shakespeare, Mary Arden, 160
Shakespeare, William, images of: male perspective limiting, 2, 8, 9, 10, 124, 135–37, 192–93, 212–13, 229, 237, 247; universal, 2; outsider, 2–4; Nature, not Art, 2–3, 53, 140; poetic imagination, poetic power, 3, 119–20, 130, 136, 140, 159; sympathy, wide-ranging characterization, 4–7, 42, 89, 93, 94, 103; actor, 5–6; androgyny, identifying with women, 5, 6, 7, 136–37, 138, 141, 142, 149, 157–60, 164, 198, 242, 247, 248; ideological property, 10, 58; icon, 10, 11, 84; high moral character, 48; romantic, 59; morally dubious, 6, 72, 109, 130, 150, 162; plays moving in performance, 92–93, 247; mirror, 108, 123; sacred, 2, 10, 11, 84, 124, 125, 132, 150; language, 124, 193, 243, 246–47; male privilege, power, 125–27, 141, 143, 149, 152, 166; ally of women, 128–29, 143, 242; anonymous, 131, 138, 139, 140, 141, 142, 247; communal voice, 131–32, 139, 141; poetry as contemporary, 132–33, 137; Cathar mystic, 151, 158–60, 164; mother, 156, 211, 242, 247; proto-modernist, 158–59; ambivalence, 171, 180–81; representing literary tradition, 184–87; heterosexual, homosexual, or bisexual, 247
Shaw, George Bernard, 27, 31
Showalter, Elaine, 13, 14, 56, 105, 138, 142
Siddons, Sarah, 43, 44, 49, 56, 57, 95, 99, 106
Sidney, Philip, 157

Sitwell, Edith, 163
Skura, Meredith, 13
Sly, Christopher (*Shrew*), 24
Sonnets, Shakespearean, 9, 100, 245; sonnet 98, 127–28, 208, 246
Spivak, Gayatri, 191
Sprengnether, Madelon, 8–9, 244, 247
Stoddart, Sarah, 33–34
Stone, Donald, 77, 88, 107
Stowe, Harriet Beecher, 103–4
Stratford-on-Avon, 120, 145, 147, 156–57; Shakespeare's grave, 137, 149–50, 160, 245–46
Strong, Natalie B., 8, 11, 243, 244, 248
Suleiman, Susan, 240
Swift, Carolyn R., 8, 245, 252
Sycorax (*Tempest*), 29

Taming of the Shrew, 7, 23–27, 37, 38, 250
Tamora (*Titus*), 216–19
Tearsheet, Doll (*Henry IV*), 6
Tempest, 9, 28, 29, 58–72, 74, 148, 149, 156, 165, 168–70, 173–79, 184, 245
Terry, Ellen, 7
Third-World women, 11
Thomas, Clara, 54, 181
Timon of Athens, 19
Titus Andronicus, 126, 203, 205, 216–19, 244, 248
Todd, Mabel Loomis, 112
Tompkins, Jane, 72
Townsend Warner, Sylvia, 3–4
Tragedies, Shakespearean, 103, 212–25, 227–41, 245
Traill, Catherine Parr, 174
Twelfth Night, 87, 197, 250
Two Gentlemen of Verona, 92

Vendler, Helen, 194, 195
Vickers, Brian, 1
Vietnam War, 228
Vincentio (*Measure for Measure*), 28, 38, 39, 198–99
Viola (*Twelfth Night*), 91, 129, 198
Virgilia (*Coriolanus*), 82, 205, 210
Volumnia (*Coriolanus*), 82, 213

Warburton, William, 7
Wellington, duke of, 76–77, 87–88
Welter, Barbara, 74
Wheeler, Richard, 39
Williams (*Henry V*), 201
Winter's Tale, 97, 98, 106, 146–48, 187, 192, 205, 206–8, 246, 250
Witches (*Macbeth*), 203, 223, 233
Witemeyer, Hugh, 106
Wolfson, Susan, 7
Wollstonecraft, Mary, 16, 17, 35, 36
Women, love/friendship between, 9, 10, 33, 34, 82–83, 90–92, 110, 116–17, 118, 128, 129, 135, 141, 146–47, 161, 186–87, 207–9, 214–15, 225, 243, 245, 248. *See. also* Mothers: and daughters
Women, in Shakespeare's plays: stereotypes, 2, 8, 124; active, 7–8, 11, 23, 30–33, 44, 48, 91–92, 151–52, 197–98, 210, 212, 224, 243, 250; remaining in patriarchy, 8, 17, 48, 82, 135–36, 152, 169, 184, 187–88, 190, 192–94, 212–25, 243–44, 248, 250; disguised as boys, 10, 23, 37, 90, 129, 162, 198, 200. *See also* Shakespeare, William, images of: androgyny; identifying with women; male perspective limiting
Woolf, Virginia, 3, 5, 104, 123–42, 148, 160, 164, 175, 194, 242, 243, 246, 247, 248; *Room of One's Own*, 8, 123, 126, 128, 129, 134–40, 144, 156, 175, 194, 206, 243, 248; *To the Lighthouse*, 123, 127–28, 129, 133, 134, 136–38, 141, 205, 206–9, 211, 245, 246, 247, 248; *Waves*, 123, 128, 129, 134, 137–40; "The Introduction," 123, 125–27, 140; *Orlando*, 123, 128, 129–38, 142, 247; "The Reader," 131, 133; "Anon," 131–32, 138; *Three Guineas*, 138; *Night and Day*, 245–46
Wordsworth, William, 5, 93, 178
World War I, 145–47
World War II, 145–47, 164
Wroth, Mary, 252–11

Zimmerman, Bonnie, 97, 107
Zola, Emile (*Therese Raquin*), 233